Inside Today's Home

RAY FAULKNER STANFORD UNIVERSITY

in collaboration with S A R A H F A U L K N E R

Inside

Today's Home

HENRY HOLT AND COMPANY · NEW YORK

Copyright, 1954, by Henry Holt and Company, Inc.

Printed in the United States of America

Library of Congress Catalog Card Number: 54-6601

PREFACE

A LIVABLE HOME is fundamental to satisfying home life. How can it be achieved? It must be planned, furnished, landscaped, and maintained. This book is written to help you achieve a home suited to you, today.

Among the first questions to be asked and answered are these: How do you and your family want to live? What activities give you greatest satisfaction? What forms, colors, and materials give you most pleasure? How much will your dream cost in money, time, and energy? Obviously, no ready-made answer will satisfy all persons. We have, therefore, attempted to stimulate you in the analysis of your own needs, to show varied solutions for each aspect of the problem, to introduce basic principles, and to provide the information needed to achieve the best environment for satisfying home life.

Getting this environment involves home planning, furnishing, and landscaping—three closely related aspects of one problem. And solving this problem is a matter of planning from "inside out," not merely from inside the house to the exterior and the yard, but from inside *you* to *your* home as a whole. In planning living rooms, for example, we begin with an analysis of the group activities for which the room is intended, and we proceed to consideration of the size, shape, and character of the space needed for these activities and the necessary furnishings. But we cannot stop with the living room as an isolated unit. How does it relate to the other areas in the home, to the sun and the wind, to the outlook and the outdoor living space? Because piecemeal planning is seldom successful we have emphasized the interrelatedness of many factors. Window-planning is another example: windows give light, outlooks, and usually ventilation, and they also bring heat, cold, and potential loss of privacy; their location and size affect the character of the interior space, indicate possible furniture arrangements, and determine much of the exterior design. Further, they have a relatively high original cost, are breakable, must be cleaned, and often need to be curtained. Window planning is not to be taken lightly.

Economy, original costs, and the equally important but often neglected continuing costs are given special emphasis because homes are not completely satisfying if they cost too much in any way. We can only hint here at the variety of possible economies discussed in the book, for they range from curtain fibers that do not rot when exposed to the sun to house plans that save steps.

Contemporary needs and contemporary ways of meeting them are also emphasized, far less as a matter of a "modern style" than as modes of analyzing and solving our problems directly. Not long ago modern houses and furnishings were regarded by many persons as another fad which would soon pass out of existence, but the past two decades have proved otherwise. It is abundantly clear, at least to the younger generation, that we cannot live in the middle of the 20th century and pretend that we are still in the 17th or 18th centuries. We cannot turn our backs on the pleasures afforded by large windows, outdoor-living spaces, and furniture designed for today's living any more than we can ignore automobiles, radios, television—and electrical kitchen and laundry equipment. We have hundreds of new products, many of them made of materials unknown twenty years ago, to make life easier or pleasanter.

Does this mean that we turn our backs on history and throw out our cherished antiques? Certainly not! History has much to teach us and many antiques are beautiful and inspiriting today. No longer, though, can we honestly plan, furnish, and landscape homes as if they were miniature museums.

Trends change as does the life from which they grow. In this century the modern movement has had three phases. The "modernistic" phase, which came in the twenties, was for the most part a rather clumsy attempt to get away from aping the past. Bulbous chairs and sofas, sky-scraper bookcases, a few precariously slender tables and chairs, and textiles and wallpapers with nervous, aggressive designs were among the first efforts. "Machine modern" came in the thirties and still persists.

It is a serious attempt to take full advantage of machine production and to simplify homes and furnishings. Many of the products are beautiful in a pure, precise way, but many are too cold and mechanistic to promise good home life. "Naturalism" is perhaps the best word to describe the leading trends today. It begins with our own natures and extends to a sympathetic understanding and modification of the nature that surrounds us. Wood for houses and furniture has come back into its own, textures with nature-like colors and textures are favored for their lasting beauty and ease of maintenance, houses and gardens are integrated with their surroundings. It is a period in which rigid prescriptions are avoided and in which well-founded individualism flourishes. It is today's way of living—and it is a very happy solution.

So many persons have contributed to this book, knowingly or not, that it is impossible to mention them all. Probably first, though, should be mentioned the many students who, through questions and comments, have shaped much of our thinking. The drawings by Mr. Matt Kahn and Mr. Victor Thompson are indispensable in illustrating some sections of the book, and the editorial suggestions of Miss Helen Prentice clarified much of the writing. Mrs. Gail Van Zyl, Mrs. William Yoder, Mrs. King Hathaway, and Mrs. Claude Brinegar not only typed the manuscript but made many helpful suggestions. Lastly, our four boys continuously reminded us that planning and keeping a home for family living is more than a matter of "decorative effects."

R. F.

S. F.

Stanford, California

February, 1954

CONTENTS

PART 5.   The Whole House

PART ONE

Our Activities,
Space, and Equipment

CHAPTER 1

Getting Started

INTERIOR DESIGN is the organizing of space and equipment for pleasant living. What makes a piece of furniture, a room, a whole house "good" for and contribute to pleasant living? A chair, for example, is "good" if it has the following qualities:

- First, it gives you comfortable support, thereby fulfilling well its primary requirement of *use*.
- Second, it is worth what it costs you in terms of the original price plus the time, energy, and money required to keep it clean and in good repair; in short, it is *economical*.
- Third, it gives you pleasure when you look at it or touch it; *beauty* is another word for this.
- Fourth, it is suited to you and your family so that it "belongs" in your home; then it gains *individuality*.

What makes a living room "good"? Providing appropriate space and equipment for your family's group activities; giving maximum yield for your output; giving those who use it a pleasurable feeling; and making your family feel that this is really their room. Such analyses lead us to say that home planning and furnishing has four goals: *use, economy, beauty* and *individuality*.

Use is a central concept in planning and furnishing today's homes. We want homes and furniture that serve their purposes, that "work"

3

PHOTOGRAPH BY GILBERT ASK

1-1 The Port Royal Parlor (1762), originally in Frankford, Philadelphia, and now in the Henry Francis du Pont Winterthur Museum, is a superb example of American 18th-century interior design. Philadelphia Chippendale furniture, Oriental rugs, French silk draperies and upholstery, and English cut-glass chandeliers and wall lights are combined in a formal room to produce a gracious, hospitable elegance.

effectively—good space purposefully planned for family activities, chairs that are comfortable, storage that is convenient and accessible, lighting, heating, and plumbing that do what we want them to. Overemphasis on the useful can, of course, lead to a laboratory-like coldness, a factory-like efficiency, but such excesses in no way diminish the primary importance of having our homes function well.

The use of any object should indicate its form. Chairs are shaped to support the human body in a sitting position, and the height, depth, breadth, and angle of seat and back are determined by human dimensions and habits. In all cases, the designer's and the purchaser's first, but by no means his last, consideration should be a chair shaped for good sitting. Further, it ought to look like a comfortable chair; its form should *express* as well as fulfill its function. Rooms, too, should be planned in terms of the human activities they are to shelter and encourage, and this type of planning demands a careful analysis of what people do and under what conditions each activity is most satisfactory. All too often this basic analysis of function is slighted, and that is why we find living rooms on the wrong side of the house with doors and windows interfering with usable furniture arrangement; or kitchens inconveniently shaped for kitchen activities, far from the garage, and exposed to the mercilessly hot afternoon sun. Good planning always rests on a solid foundation of consideration of use. Thus, use will be emphasized throughout this book, especially in the following three chapters.

Start thinking about use now by comparing the many kinds of chairs in the rooms illustrated in this chapter. Those in the Port Royal Parlor provide for comfortable but definitely upright, formal sitting, while those in Figs. 1-4, 5 are for more relaxed lounging. Then look at the rooms as a whole and think about the kind of living they suggest.

Economy is used here to mean the management of your human, material, and monetary resources, all of which are part and parcel of one package. All of our resources have their limits and for most of us these limits are lower than we would like them to be. Such being the case, it is wise to have a plan that will bring the greatest returns for the outlay. The first step toward economy has been described above—paying attention to use; the second step is to look carefully at our resources.

Human resources consist of our abilities, our time, and our energy. Every person has a complex of abilities peculiarly his own, and his productivity is determined in large part by opportunity to do what he does best. A woman who has a special knack for cooking thrives, as does her family, if she has a good, large kitchen; but this kitchen might be wasted on one who found preparing meals a bore. It is sound economy as well as the most effective way to promote individuality to give a good cook a good kitchen, a good mechanic shop space, a musician suitable space and equipment for making music. Doing the things we do best and most

1-2   A living room near Washington, D. C., planned and furnished for contemporary living. It is simple and forthright, informal and easy to maintain, and has a feeling of spaciousness even though it is not large. Other views of this house are shown in Figures 19-9 and 19-10. Keyes, Smith, Satterlee, and Lethbridge, architects.

enjoy can actually increase our resources of time and energy, and sometimes contribute to our finances as well. Using fully our best abilities
is sound economy; but this can be accomplished only if our homes, quite
as much as our places of work, are planned with this in mind.

Offhand, the time at our disposal seems to be rigidly governed by the
clock and the calendar because there are always and only twenty-four
hours in a day, seven days in a week. The big question is: how do you
want to spend them? What use of your time gives you the most immediate and intense, or the most lasting satisfactions; what contributes most
to your family life? Automatic furnaces, clothes and dish washers, and
vacuum cleaners give the family more time (and energy) for other purposes. More fundamental than the purchase of such equipment, though,
is planning every part of the home for maximum efficiency. If you are
building, buying, or renting space for living, check carefully the size,
shape, and location of rooms in terms of their use, durability of the materials, and finishes used for walls and floors. If you are furnishing a
home, think of the time someone will have to spend to keep each thing
in good condition. Keep asking yourself how much time you want to
spend on your home and how you want to spend that time.

Material resources include all the possessions that you have bought or
been given. In the beginning these are few in number, but they accumu-
late rapidly. Even when there are only a few it is surprising how easy
it is to forget some of them and to rush unthinkingly to buy a new object
when something already yours would do as well. Possibly it needs a little
work, a little adaptation, but that costs far less than a replacement. It
may be that it is not the "latest thing," but does that really matter? The
tendency toward being "galloping consumers" who can hardly wait to
cast off the old and buy the new is mighty costly. Make a list of what
you own, study it thoughtfully to see how each object can be used, and
your material resources are likely to be a revelation. Make the best use
of what you now have.

Economy, of course, refers to money too. Few families can have everything they want; few continue to enjoy what they cannot afford. A system of spending is well worth the slight amount of time it takes to plan
and follow. Each purchase should contribute to your total plan, should
be worth what you pay for it, and should not cost more than you can
comfortably afford. Remember, too, that cost is both original and continuing, and that the first cost must be balanced with the total maintenance and upkeep cost over the expected life of the object. Unfortu-

nately, those things that are beautiful, durable, and easy to maintain almost always have a high price tag. For example, wool or leather upholstery for a davenport costs considerably more than cotton, but cotton material is not easy to keep clean and may soon become shabby and have to be replaced. Over the years cotton may be a poor investment; on the other hand, it may be all that one can pay for when the need arises. This example illustrates clearly the close relationship of time, energy, and money.

Compare the rooms in this chapter in terms of economy—original cost together with the time and money necessary for adequate maintenance. The differences are probably even greater than your estimate. Which is the most expensive, the least expensive?

Beauty is that quality which pleases the senses and lifts the spirit. Is beauty easy to understand, simple to achieve in the home? The only answer is that academic irritant, yes and no. The ingredients can be listed as concisely as the ingredients of a cake; for beauty, not a cake, they are the raw materials of our visual and tactile world—form, line, light, color, texture, and space (often referred to as the *plastic elements*). As with the ingredients of a cake, there is no one way to put these together; but unlike a cake, there are no quick-and-easy recipes, rules, regulations, or laws to tell you exactly what to do. There are, however, some guiding aims and principles discussed in Chapter 5. Among the most useful of these are selecting and organizing the plastic elements so that they accomplish the following:

- Express and fulfill their *functions* (a chair should both look and be comfortable).
- Are *unified* by an all-pervading, basic spirit (developing a room around one dominant idea, be it economical informality or dignified elegance, is a major step toward beauty).
- Are enriched and *varied* for interest (a patterned textile gains richness through varied sizes and shapes).
- Give a satisfying feeling of *balance* (out-of-balance furniture arrangements induce an unpleasant sense of disequilibrium).
- *Emphasize* the parts in proportion to their importance (furniture is usually more important than floor coverings and should, accordingly, be more dominant).
- Give a sense of *rhythmic* continuity (the decoration on a dinner plate should lead the eyes easily from one part to another).

1-3 Individuality marks this old house furnished with antique and contemporary pieces. No time or money was wasted on attempting to "modernize" the structure but the selection and arrangement of furnishings and enrichment is ingenious and sensitive. Strong, unexpected contrasts produce a vital effect. James Lamantia, architect.

In addition, sensitively selected and used *materials* contribute to beauty (as well as to use, economy, and individuality). Each material, like each individual person, has its own special potentialities and limitations. The nature of materials will be discussed in Chapters 8, 9, and 10.

Individuality, the quality that differentiates your home from those of your friends and makes you and them feel as though it is really yours, is important. No one wants his home to have the generalized, impersonal quality of a hotel lobby or bedroom which necessarily aims to hit the common denominator of the tastes of the hotel's clientele. Usually, however, if a home is the natural outgrowth of the interests and preferences of the family, individuality will develop as naturally as do the personalities of those who live in it. Individuality, we repeat, should be an *out-*

growth, not a quality superimposed from outside: and it grows strongest out of fundamentals, not accessories. The quest for individuality is often overdramatized so that the result is a shallow, self-conscious desire to be different—often in a different way every few years—and it may lead to nothing more than a house full of impersonal "decorator's touches." Far better that most of us just be ourselves, making the most of our strengths and minimizing our weaknesses, and let our homes shape themselves easily and naturally to make our lives good.

Use, beauty, economy, and *individuality* are as closely interrelated as the warp and woof of a textile. None of them can be completely disassociated from the others and retain its full significance. On the other hand, we cannot consider all of them simultaneously. For example, in selecting a chair you might well focus first on the comfort it gives the sitter; then consider its durability, ease of upkeep, and life expectancy; then look critically at its form, color, and texture; and finally look at it in relation to your habits, preferences, and the room in which it will stand. This will probably raise difficulties because genuinely comfortable chairs may be homely, beautiful chairs may soil easily, durable chairs may be expensive, and the chair that "does" everything you want for you and your room is probably not manufactured. That leads you to the challenge of balancing one factor against the others so that your choice will be sound, not whimsical, and your satisfaction long-term.

APPROACHING THE PROBLEM

The six following steps will help you get started on planning or furnishing a home.

1. *Inventory your present possessions; then list what you expect to have in the future.*

Listing in an orderly way all that you now own is an easy but important first step which has many values for anyone planning to build, remodel, buy, rent, furnish, or re-furnish a home. It will tell you much about your personality and your resources.

Equipment for eating is a good example. Looking critically at your dishes, glassware, silver, and table linens tells you what sort of table you can set and that in turn determines the kind of meals you can serve. It may make you realize that some of it is not used and that you do not have some things you need. You may, for instance, be awakened to the hitherto dimly noticed fact that you are now unable to have successful informal buffet suppers because you do not have suitable trays, plates, and tumblers, while your accumulation of glass stemware is seldom used but represents a sizable investment in money and storage space.

It may be time to make some changes now. Certainly it is time to begin planning if you expect to move or build your own home.

If you do not have a household yet, even if you do not expect to have one for some years, start thinking about what you really want, because planning for the future is essential. Unpredictable as it may be, the future is coming. Intelligent prediction is good preparation. In making preparations, be guided primarily by your own best judgment, using such lists as "What Every Bride Should Have" only as a check. It is fun to dream, but sensible planning is realistic. Perhaps some of the things you think you want are extremely remote possibilities. Distinguishing between what you want and what you really expect to have will save time and future disappointment.

Dishes, glass, silver, and linens are, of course, only a small fraction of home furnishings. Furniture, lamps, rugs, and draperies are the major items, and then comes the miscellany that relates to your interests—books and magazines, musical instruments, sports equipment, paintings, and accessories. Making a carefully detailed inventory, perhaps at three- or five-year intervals, will alert you to what and how much you have, where it is used and how it is stored, how often you use or enjoy each object, and how large an investment your possessions represent. It may make you ask about some things, "Why do I have them?" Possessions help to make life more comfortable and pleasant. Use them and cherish them but do not allow them to force you and your family into ways of living not congenial to your real selves. They belong to you, not you to them, although it is often difficult to draw a line between the two types of ownership.

So far we have mentioned only positive factors: what you have and what you want. But it is illuminating to list the major items you neither have nor want. Maybe you do not want television, a piano, an aquarium, or a sewing machine. Putting that down in black and white protects you from merely forgetting all about them, starts you rethinking the problem, and may remind you of things you will want when your situation changes.

2. *Make a list of what you do and what you want or expect to do.*

This should be easy after you have listed your possessions, because activities and possessions go hand in hand. Some activities such as thinking or conversation take no specialized equipment other than comfortable seats, appropriate illumination, protection from disconcerting noise, and a generally pleasant environment. Other activities take specialized equipment and may require separate space in which to carry them out. For example, one cannot play a piano unless he has one, and a piano not only costs money but takes space, and when used may be distracting to others. Or suppose that you have a serious interest in weaving, an interest which cannot be satisfied in one corner of the living room or bedroom. Think over carefully the activities that now give you greatest satisfaction. Consider how well you are set up to carry them out and then think again of the future. The person interested in woodworking or gardening may have to give up that interest—only temporarily, let us hope—if he does not have adequate facilities at present, but if his interest is serious, plans for the future should be made.

Here again, make a *"do not and do not want to do"* list. If you do *not* like to eat outdoors or if you do *not* enjoy formal dinners, make a note of it; if you think bridge or other card games a waste of time, take a minute to record the fact. Then you will be more certain that you have not inadvertently forgotten to consider a type of activity.

By the time you have listed your possessions and activities you should have a good idea of what you are now and with your prediction some notion of what you will be and will need in the future. All of this helps in making your personality and character, your drives and interests, your likes and dislikes more specific; and as these become more precisely understood, the basis for planning is enormously strengthened.

3. *Decide on the general character you would like your home to have.*

After you have followed through on steps one and two, you will have gone a long way toward giving specific shape and character to your house. This is not the time to decide on specifics, but it is the time to consider generalities. Call this the "basic idea," the "theme," or the "character." It is up to you now to begin thinking about a way of expressing and providing for your possessions and activities which, if adhered to, will almost automatically give your home individuality.

Contrast the general characters of the living spaces illustrated in this chapter. Each one not only expresses but leads to a way of living. They

1-4 Knotty pine, used brick, plaster painted a dark color on one wall and white on the ceiling, and a textured rug make one part of the room securely enclosed.

1-5 A window wall and furniture small in size and scale open one side of the room to the terrace.

Two views of the same room demonstrate that comforting enclosure and integration with the outdoors can be combined. L. Morgan Yost, architect.

represent several degrees of formality, many kinds of stimulation, and marked diversity in simplicity or complexity. In some of them you would undoubtedly feel at home, in others you would not, but maybe none of them is exactly right for you. Look at the illustrations in the remainder of this book to see if you find one more nearly suited to you. When you find the one that seems best, figure out why you like it.

Beware of such pitfalls as these:

- Choosing a "theme" because you have been told that it is fashionable, the latest trend, or what a person like you ought to have this year. Manufacturers, magazine publishers, and even decorators often conspire each year to make you dissatisfied with what you have to increase their business. This practice has little or nothing to do with *you.*

- Trying to copy what your friends have done. Wait a year or so, see how it holds up for them, and think constantly of how it relates to you.

- Deciding on a theme and then forcing all of your own and your family's life to conform to it. To be sure, you want all parts of your home to be related to one another, but remember that different activities suggest different environments—children's play is not the same as quiet reading and attempts to force a common character on space for these diverse behaviors helps neither.

- Hurrying to get your theme decided before you have a good understanding of all the factors that can make your life pleasant. Do not, for example, get your heart set on a household exuding the gracious elegance of the 18th century until you know just what this entails. Make a tentative decision soon, but keep checking it as you go on reading this book and living your own life.

- Exaggerating the importance of this factor. You are not designing a setting for a play in which everything is sacrificed to pointing up the dramatic theme. You are simply planning an environment for the convenience and pleasure of your family and friends.

4. *Learn the ways and means of getting what you want.*

Learning the ways and means that will help you get the home you want can be invigorating. You can start by simply looking, listening, and touching. Then ask questions and make comparisons. This will develop a vocabulary, a fund of ideas, and some guiding principles.

Your sources of inspiration and enlightenment are legion: stores, museums, and motion pictures; books, magazines, and newspapers; your own home, the homes of your friends, and exhibition houses; and finally the many persons, not all professionals, who have faced and solved such problems.

A good start is to investigate one aspect of the total problem with some thoroughness. It matters not a bit with which one you start, but it is more fun to begin with something in which you have a special interest. Seating equipment provides a good illustration. One of the first things to do is to learn what kinds of chairs, stools, davenports, and benches are available. The variety is amazing, for seating can be: for one person or for two or more; hard or soft; high or low; with or without backs or arms; fixed or movable; rectangular, curved, even triangular; ornamented or plain; big or small (in actual bulk or in scale); light or heavy (in "visual" or in actual weight); of wood, cane, metal, plastic, or stone; sturdy or fragile in construction; easy or difficult to maintain; formal or informal; relaxing or activating; and unusual or commonplace.

This list might be continued for several pages if we considered that, for example, wood can be hard or soft, light or dark, red or brown, yellow or black, fine or coarse grained; upholstery can be of wool, cotton, mohair, silk, leather, fur, or plastic; and that the color and texture of upholstery, in particular, can vary infinitely. A thorough investigation would take a lifetime, which you do not have for one aspect of the problem, but do look carefully at all the chairs you see. You might well start with the one you are sitting in now!

You might prefer to begin your study with tables or chests, textiles or floor coverings, dishes or glassware, or lighting. Throughout this study, though, keep asking yourself: How well does this object meet the human needs for which it was produced? What degree and kind of beauty does it have? What are the materials from which it was made and how have they been used? Naturally, you will want to look at both historical and contemporary products. Question everything and in finding your answers use your eyes and your hands, your head and your heart.

5. *Consider your finances.*

Costs, original and continuing, are mighty factors never to be ignored. How much can you afford to spend? Over what period of time? What expenditures will give you greatest satisfaction?

If you are young and unmarried, about to be married, or just married,

HERMAN MILLER FURNITURE CO.   PHOTOGRAPH BY EZRA STOLLER

1-6   A corner of an apartment living room with furniture selected and arranged
to fit the space.   Simple, straightforward, and unified, it is thoroughly modern,
comfortable, and durable.

your financial resources are probably either meager or modest and every
penny must count.   Furthermore, the chances are against your being
permanently settled.   At first, you may be living in small rented quarters, possibly furnished, with no family; later you will probably move
to a larger, unfurnished, rented space or to a home of your own; and you
may well move to another city.   The typical American moves around
quite a bit before sinking permanent roots.   All of this, needless to say,
complicates the financial problem.

Although there is no single way to solve it, the writers have found the
following suggestions worth while:

- Get a few good basic objects, such as your bed, a comfortable davenport, and good storage chests that are durable, pleasing in character
  to you, and can be used flexibly.   Concentrate your spending on these.
- Fill in with frankly inexpensive, temporary things such as Chinese
  split cane chairs, fiber rugs, unbleached muslin draperies.

■ Avoid the moderately expensive things which are not quite what you want; not excellent in design, structure, or material; but which cost too much to discard easily later.

In short, hit high and low in the beginning, fill in the scale as you go along. As your tastes mature and your needs become more definite, you may change the general character on which you had decided. Never, though, go beyond your ability to pay.

6. *Continually remind yourself of what you are trying to achieve.*

It is surprisingly hard to keep clearly in mind what you set out to achieve, surprisingly easy to alter your course without realizing you have done it. Bargains that you could not resist, gifts that you never would have purchased, or simply failing to remember what you and your family want most can over the years lead you far from your intended route and land you in an environment not congenial to your deepest self.

Once you are really sure of your needs and tastes, repeat to yourself and your family at regular intervals, "What we want is ——, ——, and ——. What we do not want is ——, ——, and ——."

To be sure, it may well be necessary to change your ideas. You may move from California to Maine, or from the city to the country; your economic conditions may change; your family may increase or decrease; or your tastes may evolve in a different direction. Such things are real and normal and must be accepted. If they occur, make intelligent, considered modifications (after all, this is growth), but do not let the accidental or the incidental shift you off your course.

Interior design is far more than choosing a color scheme and arranging furniture. Its roots are in the plan and architectural shell that shape space for living, and its full development takes us out into the landscape, because today inside and outside are joined as they never have been before. In the next three chapters we will consider how living with others, private living, and housework can be made pleasant and satisfying.

CHAPTER 2

Living with Others

ONLY HERMITS AND RECLUSES live alone and they are rare, for people are naturally gregarious. But living with others, rewarding as it is, begets problems. Group activities are varied and often conflict with one another, and not always does everyone in a home want to participate in what the others are enjoying. Offhand it would seem that group activities are so well understood that people would naturally plan well for them. Such is not the case. In many houses reading, conversation, music, quiet games, study, small children's activities, and eating—plus miscellaneous traffic—are interwoven in a living and a dining room which are neither planned nor furnished with their uses clearly in mind. The result is far from the ideal that might be achieved through sensible planning.

In solving the problem of providing pleasant and adequate space for social activities, the logical first step is to consider specific group activities, the equipment and conditions desirable for each, and then to arrive at some suggestions and principles pointing toward successful solutions. Typical group activities include *conversation* with your family and friends; *reading* newspapers, books, and magazines when others are around; *games*—quiet and active indoor games and those played outdoors; *music* to which the group listens or in which it actively participates; *television, home movies,* and *slides* projected for several or more persons; *eating* with others; and the varied *small children's activities.*

18

The degree of emphasis given to each type of activity varies from individual to individual and from one family to another and, furthermore, changes for any one person or group as the years roll by. None save the very wealthy can provide equally well for all. Thus, most of us have to think carefully of what activities give us greatest satisfaction, then plan wisely. Our interests and preferences are, of course, determined in part by our original natures together with accumulated habits and influences, but they are also strongly if subtly directed by our environment. For example, only the avid will read much under conditions bad for reading, because most of us need the encouragement of comfort. Bear in mind that all facets of home planning not only should express the present but will affect your future patterns of living.

GROUP ENTERTAINMENT AND LEISURE

Conversation

Conversation is the major group activity, pervading all of the home and reaching greatest density in the living and eating space. Conversation can be as lively as a ping-pong ball, as unpredictable as a shuttlecock, or as dead as a last year's tennis ball, depending on the participants and their surroundings. In some rooms the talk always seems lively, in others it dies quickly. Basic needs are:

- *Space* sufficient for the normal number of persons. Each person in an easy chair requires a minimum space of 3′0″ by 2′4″ but with his feet stretched out he may take up to 6 feet. A sofa is usually 2′6″ to 3′0″ wide and may range from 4 to 7 feet in length or longer.
- *Comfortable* seats for each participant; a minimum of one good seat for each permanent member of the family and additional ones to accommodate guests.
- *Arrangement* of seats and tables in a generally circular or elliptical pattern so that each person can look at others easily and talk without shouting; arrangement should be ready for group conversation without moving furniture. A diameter of 8 to 10 feet is desirable.
- *Light* of moderate intensity with high-lights at strategic points; fire in fireplace adds varied patterns.
- *Surfaces* (tables, shelves, etc.) on which to put things.

Conversation thrives in a warm, friendly room in which the architecture, furniture, and accessories are spirited but not overpowering; distractions are minimized; and sounds are softened and mellowed (see Figs. 2-1, 2, and 3). It is the normal accompaniment of meals, for the dining furniture and its arrangement give ideal conditions for up to an hour or so. Well-planned porches and terraces are also natural conversation centers when they offer good seating and at least a degree of shelter.

Reading

Members of a literate culture take pride in reading and gain satisfaction if the reading material is stimulating and the reading conditions good. Minimum essentials are:

- *Good seat* for each reader, of comfortable height and width, giving adequate support to the back (and to the neck, arms, and legs if maximum comfort is desired); resilient but not soporific.
- *Good light* coming over one shoulder of the reader; daylight of moderate intensity or artificial light which both illumines the room and concentrates fairly strong, somewhat diffused light on the reading material.
- *Security from distracting sights and sounds,* especially miscellaneous household traffic.

Desirable extras are a chair-side table, accessible shelves to hold books and magazines, and enough space to "stretch the eyes" occasionally. Such conditions are good for looking at the Sunday newspapers or for a quiet family evening of reading and can be achieved in the typical living room. Reading makes little noise, results in minimum wear-and-tear. If, however, one or more members of the group do concentrated reading, greater privacy and seclusion are necessary and this is usually provided for in den, study, or bedrooms. People read in every room in the house; the places of greatest frequency deserve the best conditions.

Music

In most American homes music is limited to the radio and phonograph before and after the children go through their stint of music lessons. If, however, the family is one of the privileged few which enjoys making music, good provision should be made for this activity. Home music usually centers around a piano, an instrument whose sheer bulk, intrinsic interest of shape, and contrast of black and white keys makes it a dominant piece of furniture. Minimum essentials are:

- *Space* sufficient to take the piano (or other instruments) and the performers pleasantly. A large grand piano requires a space 9′ by 5′, while a small upright needs only 4′8″ by 1′7″.
- *Location* in living, eating, activity, or play space so that people can easily gather around or listen comfortably and so that the piano is protected from sharp changes in temperature (preferably placed against an inside wall out of direct sunlight) to keep it in good condition.
- *Light* of fairly high intensity directed on the music and instruments.
- *Acoustical* control to improve quality of sound and protect persons not in the music mood.
- *Seats* for participants and listeners.
- *Storage* cabinets for music and instruments.

Usually, the piano has to go against the only wall large enough to take it and still allow people to get around it. If space permits, a music center can be made in one part of the living area, preferably a corner, so that all musical paraphernalia is concentrated and organized, convenient but not in the way of other activities. Sometimes such a center can be created by standing the piano at right angles to the wall, thereby partially subdividing the larger space into pleasant units.

Good conditions for listening to a radio or phonograph are similar to those for group conversation—a workable arrangement of seats and their accessories, moderate illumination, and a minimum of distractions—except for a more serious interest in the quality of the sound. For best results, the speaker should be at approximately ear level or above and slanted down, facing the group, and at least some of the walls, ceiling, floor, and furnishings should be of sound-absorbing material. Separating the controls from the speaker gives the operator a better chance to get the desired balance of sound than if his ear must be a few inches from the speaker while his hands are on the controls; then too, placing the controls and especially the record player in a part of the room normally reserved for traffic, for example near a door, is better than having them in a hard-to-get-at corner. Notice that the controls for the radio-phonograph in the room in Fig. 2-2 have been placed inconspicuously yet accessibly. The speaker is mounted in the wall (not shown in the photograph) at the left side of the room. Acoustics are improved by the sloping ceiling and the sound-absorbing books and upholstered furniture.

Television and Home Movies

For some years a relatively few families have been aware of the problems raised by showing movies to family and friends, but with the coming of television this problem has become widespread. The novelty of television during its first few years caused considerable change in the households of those owning a television receiver, for it was prominently but awkwardly given the best spot in the living room so that the many friends it attracted could all see it at least moderately well. Now, like the radio, it is no longer an attraction of great group interest but is settling into the household as another source of entertainment and annoyance. Control of light and sound, efficient seating for the audience, and protection for those who are not amused are major considerations.

- *Seating* requirements differ from those for conversation in that all must face the screen and those in front should be low enough so that heads do not obscure the screen. Since few can or wish to devote one room entirely to TV, chairs which are easily movable or collapsible give flexibility to room arrangement and use; backrests on the floor enlarge the capacity.
- *Location of screen* should permit the desired number to see it well and should put it at the eye level of the audience.
- *Light* needs to be of low intensity, shielded so that it shines neither on the screen nor in the audience's eyes (a number of specially designed fixtures are available). Dark walls and furniture increase apparent brightness of image.
- *Acoustical control,* as for radio or phonograph, is needed.

Typically, the television receiver is placed in the living room, for only here can the minimum requirements be met, but while a program is tuned in, the room is all but unusable to persons interested in other diversions. Like the theater, a television program precludes conversation, reading, or almost anything other than smoking, nibbling at snacks, or knitting by touch. Thus, the television receiver is, after the novelty wears thin, frequently placed in the dining or activity space, or the den, so that individuals can take or leave it; and increasingly it is being mounted in a cabinet on wheels and pushed to where it is most wanted.

PHOTOGRAPH BY MAYNARD PARKER

2-1 Small or large groups could enjoy conversation, buffet meals, or television in this room. Additional seating is provided by the raised hearth, and the television receiver has been well placed.

BLUE RIDGE GLASS CORP.   PHOTOGRAPH BY MAYNARD PARKER

2-2   A symmetrical conversation center designed for a person who enjoys friends, books, and recorded music. Comfortable, built-in seats flank the fireplace, books are used as a major decorative feature, and the radio-phonograph is conveniently housed in the case at the left. Both natural and artificial light come through the ceiling panels of translucent glass. Harwell Hamilton Harris, architect.

Many of the newer sets have doors to hide the screens, which are otherwise a blank staring light gray spot when not in use.

Quiet Indoor Games

Cards, checkers, chess, and similar games demand concentrated effort and are most rewarding when played on a well-illuminated table of the

PITTSBURGH PLATE GLASS CO.

2-3 In contrast to the living rooms on the preceding pages, this one is light and open, has floors that will take punishment and furniture that can easily be moved for varied activities. Eating and living are combined in one L-shaped room for increased spaciousness and flexibility.

right height (dining tables are too high) while sitting on moderately high, straight, hard chairs in a spot free from distractions. Because most families do not indulge in such sports with any frequency, folding card or game tables and dining chairs set up in the living, dining, or activity space suffice. Serious gamesters, however, may want and deserve table and chairs permanently placed in a suitable spot. The space required for such a setup is at least 5' by 5', not counting the necessary circulation area around it.

Active Indoor Entertainment

Dancing, charades, and other active games for young and old require free and durable floor space, furniture easily pushed out of the way, illumination and equipment suited to the activity. A fairly rough and ready play or activity space or a basement rumpus room are ideal; the living room, probably combined with the dining space, is less good, not because the space is unsuitable but because the walls, floors, and furniture do not gracefully take punishment. An exception is the living room shown in Fig. 2-3 which has been deliberately and carefully planned for active, varied family living including children's activities.

Active Outdoor Games

Croquet, badminton, ping-pong, and all the less rigidly ruled outdoor sports provide healthful group exercise, and release youthful exuberance in suitable surroundings. First, of course, there must be enough outdoor space for the game, and second, there must be the necessary gear. But the frequency with which the outdoor space is used depends on its quality, the durability and pleasantness of the underfoot surface, the privacy and protection from wind given by walls or planting, the ease with which you can get at the necessary paraphernalia, and the comfort with which you can rest while others expend their energies. Outdoor space can be a wonderfully refreshing extension of the house, compensating handsomely for cramped enclosed quarters *if* it is thoughtfully organized.

Small Children's Activities

Varied and unpredictable (except possibly to the child psychologist) as life itself, the needs of small children range from active noisy play to

PHOTOGRAPH BY EZRA STOLLER

2-4 In a Sarasota, Florida, house for a family with five children, what would customarily be an unusable bedroom hall has been widened to 7′4″, transforming it into a play space that greatly relieves pressure on the rest of the house. Twitchell and Rudolph, architects.

quiet moments, from eagerness to be with others their own age to desire to be alone, from wanting to be with the family to carefully avoiding it. Of these, the varied noisy activities are the most distinctly characteristic and the most difficult to provide for in typical living quarters planned only for adults. Needed are: space sufficient for the discharge of abundant energy, convenient to a toilet and to the out-of-doors as well as to the kitchen, so that supervision is not burdensome; walls, floors, and fur-

FUNNY BUSINESS   By Hershberger

2-5   "We had these alcoves built so we wouldn't interfere with the children playing!"

niture that can take punishment gracefully and that lend themselves to change; light, warmth, and fresh air—and all of this segregated from what it is hoped will be the quieter parts of the house. In short, a small kindergarten.

Clearly the living room in which the parents try to put their best foot and furniture forward is unsuitable and the dining room only slightly better; the kitchen has the desirable durability but is usually too small to accommodate another activity in what is already the most intensively used room in the house and, furthermore, has the household's greatest collection of potential hazards; the fast-disappearing basements and attics offered the requisite space and ease of maintenance but were often cold, dark, or damp and were far from mother's supervising eye; garages and carports have obvious disadvantages. This leaves us with the bedrooms.

Of all conventional rooms, the children's bedrooms have the most advantages, for these already are, or should be, planned for children to make their own; but they are usually small and in two-story houses located on the second floor. These factors (plus adult needs for space in which to carry on hobbies, dance, show movies, or look at television) have led to a new type of room variously referred to as *activity, all-purpose, multi-purpose, combination, play,* or *recreation*. It bears somewhat the same relation to the living room that the old-fashioned living room had to the old-fashioned parlor. It has more flexibility and durability; it is nearer to the dining space (which it often includes) and has easier access to the kitchen and outdoors. Naturally, it is ideal for children—of all ages. A widened bedroom hall used as a play space that more than earns its slight additional cost in terms of family harmony is shown in Fig. 2-4.

Thinking about the character and demands of the above activities we see that they fall into three categories in terms of noise and movement:

- *Quiet, sedentary activities,* including reading, conversation, and quiet games, involve little physical movement; result in minimum wear and tear on furniture, floors, and walls; produce only a moderate amount of noise; and suffer most from distractions. Thus, they are logically grouped in the quietest part of the house—a living room well separated from other parts of the dwelling or the dead-end of the living space in an open plan.

- *Noisy, sedentary activities,* such as listening to or making music, looking at and listening to television, not only produce sound but suffer from conflicting noises; may require moving of furniture if the group is large; but involve little physical movement and little wear and tear. Ideally, they are centered in an acoustically treated portion of the living space separated as much as feasible from the space devoted to such quiet pursuits as reading and sleeping. In order of desirability, they may be in the activity room, an alcove off the living room, or one end of that room.

- *Noisy, lively activities* usually take as much space as can be found; are most satisfying in durable surroundings; and should be well insulated from quiet space. Few homes can make permanent provision for these, but they can center in the play or activity space and overflow into living and dining areas and outdoors as necessary. If the family regards them as important, the entire house may be planned with a minimum of fixed partitions and furnished with durable equipment.

The preceding analysis may appear to make an almost overwhelming number of requirements impossible for the average family to fulfill in its home. That is in part true—but no family is going to try to do all of this, and, as has been suggested, many activities have basically similar requirements. This, however, is not to say that the typical solution is all that we need, because in it almost nothing functions with complete efficiency and satisfaction. The sensible way to start toward a workable solution is to gain a good understanding of what promotes each phase of living with others, then come as close to the ideal as we can.

EATING WITH YOUR FAMILY AND FRIENDS

Eating is a lively part of group living, for man normally becomes even more sociable as he smells and tastes food. Often, meals are the only daily event that brings a whole family together with a single purpose, and thus they become much more than a mere stoking of the furnace. But in no aspect of home life has there been such abrupt change as in the preparation and eating of food. Gone, for most of us at least, are the days when a large, efficiently furnished room was reserved for those three hours a day in which servants served quantities of food and then took full charge of the cleanup. Under such circumstances the family was left to full, uninterrupted enjoyment of one another's company and the meal. As house-size shrank, household help found more rewarding employment, and food became more expensive, there was a tendency to minimize the importance of eating together, to accent efficiency rather than pleasantness, to treat it almost as a necessary burden. The dining room was retained in the house plan, the company dishes and glassware in the china closet, but these were seldom used. In adjusting ourselves to changed circumstances, it pays to take a good look at the requirements for meals of different types.

The requirements for enjoyable eating vary somewhat with the type of meal but all include:

- *Surface* on which to put food and utensils, ordinarily 28 to 30 inches above the floor but with considerable variation in size and shape and in type—tables, counters or bars, arms of chairs, and the like.
- *Seats* which give comfortable, upright support; may be chairs or stools, built-in or movable benches.

- *Light,* natural and artificial, which illumines food and table but does not shine directly in diners' eyes.
- *Ventilation* without draft.

To these minimum essentials we quickly add that *convenience to kitchen and dish storage* saves energy, *freedom from excessive noise and traffic* saves nerves and promotes digestions, and *pleasant surroundings,* preferably with a good outlook, raise spirits.

As noted earlier, there are many kinds of meals and many locations for eating. Few persons can provide equally well for all of these; therefore, decisions in terms of preferences, habits, and finances are in order so that you will get what you want most.

Family sit-down meals deserve first consideration, and for these there should be one adequately large, relatively permanent space planned so that the table can be prepared, the seating arranged, the meal served and eaten, and the table cleared with a minimum of interference to and from other activities. Typically, the family eats together in a special dining area, the kitchen, or in the end of the living or activity space nearest the kitchen. Such meals do not necessitate a separate room but are at their best if not tightly intermingled with other activities. In determining the size of the dining area needed, remember that each person needs a space 2 feet wide for minimum elbow room, that seated in his chair he projects at least 1'6" from the table, and that a space 2 feet wide or more is needed for circulation around the table. A table 2 feet wide is the absolute minimum, while one 3 feet wide is ample. A breakfast nook should be at least 6 feet wide and 4 feet deep to seat four people, but nooks are usually inconvenient for more than four people unless they are open on two sides.

Holiday celebrations are important family events but occur so infrequently that the large amount of space required can seldom be reserved for them alone. This suggests planning a family dining area so that at least one end opens into the living or activity space permitting the celebration to extend as the number of participants demands. The living-dining room in Fig. 2-7 is well planned in this respect.

Hurry-up meals in which all is sacrificed to speed and economy of effort have something to recommend them from the family point of view. Those who desire to eat some of the time in this way should look carefully at lunch counters where a counter with stools on one side and a food preparation center on the other function with a dispiriting effi-

2-6 A dining table with built-in seats on one side makes a pleasant dining corner in a living room. The decorative panel at the end of the table slides up and the table slides through into the kitchen, minimizing to-and-fro steps in setting and clearing the table. John Yeon, architect.

ciency. There is, however, good reason for having eating space in the kitchen, for it is a boon to the busy housewife bringing up a family. Usually, kitchen meals are more pleasant if the eating space is at least partially separated from food-preparation centers, as shown in Fig. 2-8, and better yet if it can be placed near a window. *Snacks* can be expedited at a stool-and-counter arrangement.

Buffet meals, like self-service groceries and cafeterias, permit one to see what he is getting and they distribute the labor of serving food. Also, they make it possible to use all of the group living space for eating and usually lead to a lively informality. If such meals are to be handled successfully and often, one should take a lesson from cafeterias where a good carrying-tray and not-too-precious dishes and glassware are provided; the food is served from counters near the kitchen; traffic is directed so that tray-laden people do not collide; and when dinner is in hand, there is a place to rest body and food. The serving bar shown in Fig. 2-7 is convenient to the dining space, the living space, and the terrace.

Formal meals in the home have become something of a rarity because of their cost in space, equipment, and labor. A well-segregated dining space, preferably a separate dining room, is highly desirable for these occasions because it is possible to set the table in advance, then give

REVERE QUALITY HOMES

2-7 Dining space convenient to the kitchen in one end of an L-shaped living space. The cabinets serve as storage, an efficient pass-through which can be closed, and a counter used for buffet meals or as an eating bar. Stopping the cabinets short of the ceiling and continuing the wood gives a spacious feeling.

2-8 Eating space in the kitchen is a great convenience, almost a necessity with small children. Here it is well segregated from other activities, gives comfort in minimum space. Richard Neutra, architect.

the guests a pleasant surprise with whatever table decorations are used, allow them to eat the meal with no disturbance and to get out of sight of the table when the dinner is over. One end of the living room can be used for such entertainment and often is, for it permits maximum use of available floor space and eliminates the crowded feeling often experienced when the capacity of a dining room is pushed to its limits. But the disadvantages are serious—the clutter, movement, and noise inherent in serving and clearing up destroy the smooth, apparently effortless quality of good formal dinners, and it is difficult to combine in one rectangular room furniture for formal dinners and furniture for before- and after-dinner conversation and entertainment (seating is undoubtedly the most difficult problem because the eight, ten, or twelve matched chairs suitable for formal dining seldom take their place comfortably in the room during all the time when they are not being used for their specific purpose). Hard as it may be for the persons who cannot afford the elegant dinners they would like to give in their homes, it is only sensible for most of us to give them up or take our friends to a good restaurant, a much less expensive procedure in the long run. Naturally, though,

the decision is yours and if formal dinners are high on your list of preferences, provide for them properly.

Outdoor meals can punctuate eating routines by giving a refreshing
change of surroundings, a different type of food, another eating pattern.
In all parts of the country outdoor eating could be much more frequent

PHOTOGRAPH BY JULIUS SHULMAN

2-9 A terrace designed for relaxation, cooking, and eating adds greatly to the
pleasures of living with others. Harvey Harwood, designer.

and enjoyable if thought were given to planning for it. Ideal conditions include tables and seating usable without undue preparation and standing on a firm, level, dry surface; protection from extreme heat, cold, wind, or glare as well as from the countless insects that food and people attract; convenience to the center at which the food is prepared; and durable table settings. At its best, outdoor eating takes place in space that is paved, roofed, solidly enclosed on two or three sides and screened on those that are open. But, of course, even without all of this picnics and barbecues at home can be happy family or guest affairs in which all present can participate, actively or as spectators, in what can be the fun of cooking, serving, eating, and even after-meal cleanup. Not incidentally, outdoor eating can be an effective way of encouraging the man and children of the house to help relieve the housewife.

Small children's meals are a vital part of home life and a part of the educational process often poorly handled. One might as well accept at the outset the fact that for small children eating is both an adventure and a problem. They will play, experiment, and make mistakes. Insisting on standards beyond the child leads only to scolding, crying, frustration. Far better to provide a place, preferably in the kitchen or play space, where children can spill, as they inevitably will, on durable, easy-to-clean surfaces. But at a surprisingly early age children want to eat with the grownups and quite rightly object to eating in conditions midway between those for adults and those for household pets. Eating with the family should be a socializing, not a "training," process; sturdy and durable chairs, tables, walls, and floors easily cleaned with a damp cloth, unbreakable dishes and non-tipping cups help the whole family.

PLANNING FOR GROUP LIVING

Home life with your family and friends is a varied, complex, and changing experience involving individuals of many age levels and diverse personal preferences and interests. The social quarters of any home should give each person a sense of security in the family group; provide an opportunity for expressing his own feelings and urges, of doing things the way he wants to; and encourage each to play his best role in the making of the family pattern. In short, group-living space should promote the *security, self-realization,* and *socialization* of each individual.

We can say at once that realizing these ideals requires as much space as can be afforded, and that even so this space should be planned for maximum flexibility; but how can we go about planning it wisely?

Clearly, the problem demands group action. Group-living space is for everyone, and all should share in its planning. Perhaps the most common mistake is to regard the living room as the woman's domain, possibly with one corner fitted up for the man of the house. It then becomes a "nice room" planned primarily to elicit admiration from women guests. Heartening family life does not thrive under such circumstances. Another mistake is to sacrifice everything for the children. Planning for all is not easy but it is healthy fun. One way is for each member of the family to retire into a corner and make a list of what he wants in the space, then bring them together and try to reconcile the inevitable conflicts. Another, probably better, approach is to get the family together for a series of discussions, trying to reconcile differences as they arise, and developing a plan of action. Applying the six steps discussed in Chapter 1, you would:

1. Make a list of all the things you now have for group living and a list of the things you want and expect to acquire.
2. List the group activities your family now enjoys and add those that you want or expect to come later.
3. Decide on the character you want your group-living area to have.
4. Learn the ways and means of making this part of your home useful, economical, beautiful, and individual.
5. Watch your spending.
6. Continually remind yourself of what you are trying to achieve.

Number of Separate Rooms

Fifty to seventy-five years ago many houses had four or five separate rooms of ample size for group living—an entrance hall, parlor, living room, dining room, and possibly a library or study. As building and maintenance costs increased, household help became scarce, families were smaller, and entertainment became less home-centered, group-living space changed. The parlor disappeared first and then the separate dining room. People began to think about flexible space for living rather than

PHOTOGRAPH BY JULIUS SHULMAN

2-10 In contemporary open planning, the entrance area and hallway often merge with each other and with adjacent rooms. A cabinet behind the built-in seat is the only separation between entrance and living room, but the brick floor and trellis overhead define without enclosing space for circulation. Carl Maston, architect.

of separate rooms for specific activities. The *open plan* (Fig. 2-10), with a minimum of fixed floor-to-ceiling partitions and a maximum of uninterrupted, flexible space in the group-living area, became popular. Its advantages include a sense of spaciousness, diversified use of the space, and recognition of the fact that family activities are not isolated events. But it has disadvantages: noisy activities interfere with those requiring quiet, and the retiring soul finds minimum refuge when he wants to be alone. If not well planned, the space may appear barnlike.

There are two major ways of compensating for these disadvantages. First is shaping the living space with walls and furniture so that different functions are segregated. L-shaped rooms, furniture at right angles to the walls, screens, and folding doors have all been tried. Second is adding to the house a *seclusion* room which is small, tightly enclosed, and planned for not more than two persons at a time. It is much like the older studies or dens, but it belongs to no one person and it often doubles as a guest room.

Size

Most of us want as much space for group living as is possible because here we want a real feeling of spaciousness. It is seldom wise, however, to have a living room so large that bedrooms, kitchen, bathrooms, and storage space are cubbyholes. In small houses, living rooms range from a meager minimum of 150 to an ample 320 square feet, dining space from about 100 to 200 square feet. Larger houses, of course, may allow more. The decision depends on how much space one can afford and how one wishes to allocate it, but apparent size can be greatly increased by the ways and means detailed in Chapters 5, 6, and 7.

PHOTOGRAPH BY ROBERT C. CLEVELAND

2-11 Equipped with a daybed, two comfortable chairs, a well-lighted desk and shelves and cabinets, this seclusion room is comfortable for one or two persons or an over-night guest. Paul Sterling Hoag, designer.

Shape

There is no "best" living-room shape, although today an L-shaped room with dining space in the smaller part is popular. Squares and rectangles, hexagons and octagons, circles and ellipses, and many less rigid floor areas are possible.

The shape of the floor is only part of the story. Although usually perpendicular, walls can slant inward or outward and can be opaque, translucent, or transparent. The ceiling can slope in one direction or two following the roof lines, can be curved like a section of a cylinder or domed like a section of a ball, or it can combine horizontal and sloping planes. With such thoughts as these we are getting near the heart of spirited interior design.

But we must return to the typical box-like room. At least until furnished, it is uninviting, lacks character, suggests no furniture arrangement ideas, and is acoustically poor. But it is familiar to all, easy and cheap to design and build, harmonious with rectangular furniture, and its inherent dullness is a challenge to do something. There are many ways to relieve the monotony of the box—broad openings into adjoining rooms, window-walls, or bay windows, recessed or projecting fireplaces, or variations in ceiling levels and shapes. Then, too, color and furniture arrangement can help. This sounds as though any deviation from the rectangle were an improvement, a statement not true because unless such deviations are grounded in need and skillfully handled, they may be only awkward affectations. The fact remains, though, that a simple rectangular parallelepiped is not a lively room shape.

Location

Group-living space at its best is near the main entrance to minimize guest traffic through the house; adjoins outdoor-living space to encourage use of the yard; and is near the kitchen to facilitate serving food. Usually, the group area is one integrated unit, at least partially segregated from private living space and to a lesser extent from the work areas.

Orientation

Because most of us are sun-lovers, living-room windows desirably face the south. Morning sun is pleasant but afternoon sun is usually welcome only in winter.   Also most of us want privacy and an outlook.   But this anticipates a fuller discussion of orientation in later chapters.

In conclusion, let us look at group activities and the spaces in which they can occur.   Perhaps the most important point to be derived from this list is that the varied group activities take place in many parts of the house and yard.   Group living is no longer confined to the living room, as not so long ago it was supposed to be.

Family Leisure and Entertaining	*Space*
Conversation	Living room
Reading	Activity, recreation, play space
Games: quiet indoor	Dining space
active indoor	Kitchen
active outdoor	Outdoors: porch or terrace
Music: active participation	lawn
listening	garden houses,
	pergolas, etc.

Eating	
Family meals	Dining space
Buffet meals	Living space
Formal meals	Kitchen
Snacks	Play or activity space
Small children's meals	Outdoors

Small Children's Activities	
Active, noisy play alone or	Children's bedrooms
with others	Play, activity, or recreation space
Quiet play	Living or dining space
Participation in family	Kitchen
activities	Outdoor play space

CHAPTER 3

Private Living

GREGARIOUS though we may be much of the time, all phases of home life do not fit into group patterns. As individuals we need and enjoy varying degrees of privacy for sleeping, napping, or just stretching out to relax; dressing and undressing; keeping ourselves clean; entertaining house guests who spend a night or two; working individually and pursuing hobbies; and just being by ourselves to collect our thoughts, rest our emotional equipment, enjoy our dreams—in short, to get to know ourselves as individuals again.

SLEEPING AND DRESSING

Sleep, that wonderful necessary complement to wakeful activity, can be undertaken anywhere under any conditions if you are sleepy enough. Primitive man slept on the ground, on rock ledges, in caves, or in trees, seeking only a place safely protected from the elements and his enemies. As civilization advanced and man began to build sheltering structures, he usually reserved in them a place for sleeping, although this was not always separated from other areas. Historically, man was late in isolating sleeping from other functions, and then he did not do so continuously. Thus, from the decline of the Roman Empire until the Renaissance, it was fairly common practice for all people of the household to

42

sleep in one room, often on the floor and frequently in the company of animals. Today we take for granted that seldom will more than two people sleep in one room and that some care will be taken to make their sleep effective.

Recent investigations of optimum conditions for sleeping make one wonder how medieval men, women, and children ever got really rested, huddled together as they were on cold stone floors in cold draughty rooms. Now we know that the rest given by seven or eight hours of sleep under ordinary conditions can be equaled in five or six hours if the room is absolutely dark and quiet; the air is fresh and pure; air movement is moderate and uniform; and temperatures are constant and warm enough so that only light coverings are needed.

This has led some people to recommend that sleeping be done in a cubicle containing only a bed, with air, light, and sound precisely and automatically controlled. The person seriously interested in the best possible sleep would do well to provide himself with such an environment, although he might worry about an electric power failure. It all sounds fine except that human beings are not quite this single-minded: sometimes it is pleasant to go to bed early and read awhile, occasionally glancing up at a picture or textile adorning the room; sometimes it is fun to wake up in a room, not a cubicle, and lie in bed a few minutes looking through a window, or listening to the call of a bird or the burbling of a baby; when conditions permit, it is relaxing to curl up or stretch out on one's bed in the afternoon; and, unfortunately, there are always those times when illnesses make it expedient to stay in bed. For reasons such as these, sleeping has for the past few centuries taken place in a moderate-sized, multi-purpose room.

The requisites for sleeping and napping are:

- A *bed* long and wide enough to accommodate one or two persons and give them resilient yet firm and supporting comfort.
- A *bedside table,* night stand, or small chest of drawers to hold whatever you want near your bed is not only a great convenience, but practically a necessity. Sometimes such facilities are part of an extended headboard or part of a built-in unit (Fig. 3-1).
- A *light source* preferably on the wall over your bed, less desirably on the bedside table or attached to the headboard where it is in the way, enables one to light the room in an emergency or to read in bed, bad though the latter is said to be for one's eyes. If used for reading, this

3-1 Well-designed headboards can be useful furniture.

light should illumine the reading material well, and some general illumination is needed in the room.

- *Control of natural light* is chiefly accomplished by draperies, shades, or blinds. We hasten to add, though, that the lightness or darkness of walls, ceiling, floor, and furniture is important: if these areas are dark in color, it is much easier to reduce the light intensity to a level good for sleep than when they are high in value.
- *Ventilation* is best when windows or ventilators are in two opposite walls to encourage through breeze in summer, next best in adjacent walls, least good when confined to one. Being able to let the hot air

out through a ventilator in the ceiling or through a window at ceiling height is a boon in summer heat.   But although air movement is desirable, sleeping in a draft is not; in fact, medical opinion places part of the blame for many respiratory disorders on too much cold, moving air in sleeping quarters.

- *Quiet,* like darkness, is a normal necessity for sleep, and every reasonable precaution should be taken to insulate sleeping areas from outside noises and to muffle sounds originating in the area.

Dressing and *undressing* consist of a variety of movements which demand conditions quite different from those best for sleeping.   They are:

- *Space* sufficient to stand, stretch your arms, turn around, and bend over, and also to see yourself in a
- *Mirror,* full length if possible.
- *Seating* for dealing with hosiery and shoes.
- *Storage* units for all types of clothes within the reach of an arm or the step of a foot.
- *Dressing table* with a well-lighted, three-way mirror and small drawers for small things.
- *Light,* artificial and/or natural, so that you can find what you want and see how you look in it.

Ideally, all of this takes place in a separate dressing room for each member of the family which adjoins his sleeping quarters and bathroom; practically, it takes place in whatever space the bed and other furniture leave in the bedroom.   Under these typical conditions, it becomes less arduous if a "dressing center" can be developed for each occupant of the room, probably in one corner where, if possible, all of his clothes are conveniently stored.   Certainly, each member of the household deserves his own closet near his chest of drawers; adding a mirror, good lighting, and a chair would provide an adequate "dressing center."

Planning Bedrooms

These are the physical requirements for efficient sleeping, dressing, storing your clothes, and reading in bed.   If you stop at this point, however, you overlook the possibility of bedrooms as one of the best places in the home to indulge your individuality.   Maybe bright, light colors are

3-2 Planned for a girl, a bedroom with appropriate furniture, wall coverings, and textiles. The combination dressing table and desk is a convenient space-saver.

not quieting, but if you yearn for them and the rest of your family does not, try them in your own room. Put the photographs that have sentimental appeal for you on the walls or the dresser, the collections you cherish wherever you can find space for them. There is usually space in terms of cubic footage but not in terms of suitable furniture, because the typical bedroom furniture makes allowance for nothing but clothing. You will have to add bookcases, shelves, or cupboards if you use your bedroom beyond its minimum functions.

Individual differences of all sorts, if not suppressed, lead to marked differences in the way bedrooms are furnished. "Boys will be boys" is an old saying, and the bedroom in Fig. 11-8 has youthfully masculine character. Girls deserve equal consideration. They tend to like soft colors, floral patterns in textiles, and a feminine character as illustrated in Fig. 3-2. For girls, durability is not paramount. Since ideas change as youth matures, and children's bedrooms are likely to undergo a series of transformations to take care of new needs and preferences, ease of change is an asset.

When man and wife share a bedroom, a new situation arises, for then clearly it should suit and express both. The bedroom illustrated in Fig. 3-3 is masterfully planned and furnished for two persons. Walls and furniture of fir, a harmoniously textured carpet, a bedspread subtly echoing the parallel lines and textures of both walls and carpet, and a bamboo window shade for light control set the character of quiet naturalism. Glass curtains diffuse the light and give partial privacy, the cane chair and stool are easy to move and desirably small in size and scale, and the lighting fixtures are on the walls. Through careful planning this bedroom of average size and shape has been made into much more than sleeping space, chiefly because the trim built-in furniture unifies equipment designed for many purposes. At the right is the man's desk with drawers beside it, then two storage chests of drawers. The left corner with its compact, convenient, around-the-corner combination of dressing table, desk, and bedside table belongs to the woman. Notice, too, how

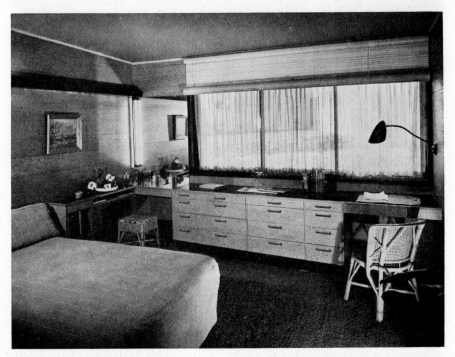

PHOTOGRAPH BY JULIUS SHULMAN

3-3 An unusually pleasant and livable bedroom. Much can be done conveniently in little space because it was thoughtfully planned in advance.

PHOTOGRAPH BY JULIUS SHULMAN

3-4 No one would ever mistake this for a hotel bedroom because the owners have expressed themselves in a spirited way. The contrasts are strong, the harmony richly complex. Burton Schutt, architect.

the well illumined mirror continues the line of the windows and greatly enlarges the apparent size of the room.

Striking individuality and charm characterize the bedroom in Fig. 3-4. Shutters attractively and efficiently unify one entire wall of windows, closets and cupboards. Their small scale rectangularity vigorously contrasts with the bold, curvilinear, conventionalized foliage patterns used as wall surface and drapery on the adjacent wall—but the repetition of the shutters relates the two walls. The fine, old-fashioned, reed chair, which at first glance seems to have nothing in common with anything else, actually provides a subtle link between the two walls because it is small in scale and open in design like the shutters, and curvilinear like the fabric. Notice, too, the comfortable set-up for reading. Fig. 3-5 shows a bedroom designed and furnished with the utmost simplicity because it commands a sweeping view of rugged hills. This bedroom opens itself completely on one side to a screened outdoor area to give an inexpensive, usable spaciousness far in excess of the room's dimensions.

In spite of this emphasis on individuality, one has to remember that bedrooms are units in the whole house and, unless a home is to look like a series of model rooms in a furniture store, thought should be given to over-all unity.   Achieving variety in unity, avoiding both monotony and chaos, is a challenge.   Moderation, give-and-take, and common sense are useful guides.

Bedroom Types.   Bedrooms vary in type in terms of the number of persons sharing them, the accommodations they offer, and the relative emphasis placed on each activity carried out in the room.   At one extreme is the sleeping cubicle, such as those in inexpensive hotels, in summer camps, or on trains and ships.   Then come those rooms with adequate space for the bed, a chest of drawers, one straight chair and just enough room to dress.   Better is the slightly larger type for one or two persons, but planned and furnished to provide for reading or relaxation in a comfortable chair and writing or working at a desk or sewing table.   Most desirable are those spacious rooms, maybe even suites of rooms, that are

PHOTOGRAPH BY JULIUS SHULMAN

3-5   A bedroom that takes full advantage of a view and a mild climate.   Raphael Soriano, architect.

3-6 Careful planning of bedroom storage brings a tremendous return. The racks and shelves on the backs of the doors facilitate keeping small things in order.

complete, private living units. Then there are living-bedrooms which provide for several phases of private living as shown in Figs. 2-11, 5-13. Much, however, can be accomplished in the bedroom of average size by selecting small scale furniture that fits tightly together and then by arranging that furniture to use efficiently every foot of floor space.

Number of Bedrooms. Size and economic status of the family determine the number of sleeping areas. The average family consists of two parents and two or three children, probably including a boy and girl. Thus, the typical family requires a minimum of three separate bedrooms. A room for each child is desirable but often not feasible if the family is large.

Location in Plan. Bedrooms are usually grouped together in the quietest part of the house, on the second floor of a two-story house or in a segregated unit of a house on one floor. Ideally, a person should be able to get from a convenient outside entrance to his bedroom without going through any other room. This means either a bedroom hall leading off from the entrance area or an outside door to each room. For some family patterns, separating the bedrooms from each other has advantages. A guest room, for example, is best when not too close to the family areas, and as children outgrow babyhood the parents may find greater peace if their room is somewhat isolated. These, however, are exceptions that do not invalidate the general desirability of grouping the bedrooms in one quiet zone.

Doors and Windows. In so far as compatible with other requirements, the doors, if there are more than one, should be close together and the paths from the most used door to the closet and dresser should be as short

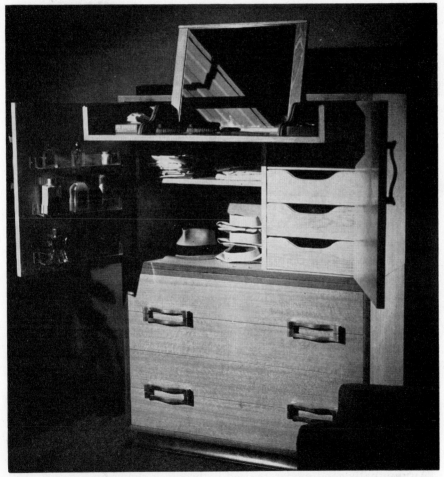

3-7   A chest of drawers designed after an analysis of a man's needs. The built-in mirror and the racks on the door are most sensible.

and direct as possible. If the doorway is not directly in line with the bed or dressing area some privacy is afforded even when the door is open. Grouping the windows makes the room seem larger and gives more usable wall space for furniture although the need for ventilation strongly suggests having windows in two walls. Finally, placing doors and windows close together is a major factor in unifying the background.

Storage. Almost as important as in the kitchen, storage in bedrooms is a much easier problem to solve, and yet good bedroom storage is not often found—closets are too small, poorly planned for anything but hanging full-length dresses, and often separated from the chest of drawers. The closets in Fig. 3-6 and the chest of drawers in Fig. 3-7 clearly demonstrate that a little thought can greatly simplify finding clothes and keeping them in shape.

HYGIENE

Bathrooms are the most standardized room in the house, and we have come to take for granted the three white fixtures arranged against the walls of the smallest room in the house. Plumbing fixtures and facilities as we know them today are, however, of very recent origin. The first real bath tub was put in our White House only about a century ago, and in the same year a New York hotel proudly advertised that it also had just installed one. Although toilets similar to those we know today were described in the 16th century, they were not common until well along in the 19th century.

Bathroom standardization makes it easy to summarize the essentials of good planning.

Types. Bathrooms can be categorized in terms of use, which of course affects their number, and the location, size, and arrangement of fixtures. Principal types include: private bathrooms for one or two persons entered only through the bedroom or dressing room; the semi-private planned for two or three members of the family, near the bedrooms and entered from the bedroom hall; the family type which serves all and therefore should be large and centrally located; and the half-bath (toilet and wash basin) usually located near the entrance for guests and family.

An unusually good moderate-sized bathroom is shown in Fig. 3-8. Setting the basin in a counter which goes around the corner, having fixed mirrors on two walls, and a place for toilet articles *not* behind a mirror

3-8 With durable surfaces in gray, red, and black synthetics, a bathroom is easy to keep clean. More important, though, is the efficient planning: a washbasin counter that goes around the corner to become a dressing table; mirrors on two walls; and a low storage compartment between toilet and tub.

are devices well worth noting, as is the cabinet separating the toilet from the tub. In Fig. 3-9 is a real family bathroom with two wash basins in a large space, the toilet and tub in compartments made private by sliding doors.

Number. Our desire to multiply bathrooms is checked only by their high cost. Ideally, a house for three or more persons should have two complete bathrooms, as should a house with sleeping quarters on two floors. As the family increases so should the plumbing, if the budget can stand it. The ideal number can be decreased, however, if the tub is in a separate compartment, wash basins are put in bedrooms, or a family-type room is planned.

Location in Plan. Convenience is the first factor, privacy the next; and finally we must consider installation economy. In a one-bathroom house, this important room should be conveniently reached from the bed-

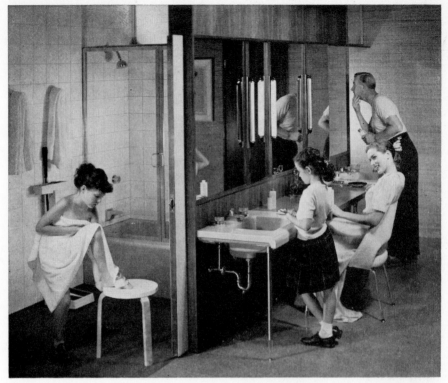

3-9 A family style bathroom with two basins connected by a counter. Tub and toilet are in compartments with sliding doors.

rooms without going through or getting in sight of the group living areas, but it should also be as near the kitchen and living room as feasible. This tough assignment is well handled in the plan shown in Fig. 18-1. If there is more than one bathroom, they can be side by side (for economy of installation) or separated (for convenience). Concentrating all plumbing (including that of the kitchen and laundry) reduces construction costs, but the amount saved is not worth life-long inconvenience.

Size. Minimum size is about 5′6″ by 6′0″, but these dimensions preclude use by more than one person at a time (often a necessary inconvenience), seriously limit storage space, and make the occupant feel unduly cramped. A few more square feet are usually well worth their cost. Beyond that, size limits are set by one's preferences and purse.

Doors and Windows. The door should be located so that when opened it will not hit a person using any of the fixtures, will shield the toilet, and can be left open for ventilation without giving a full view of the bathroom from any place where people are likely to be. Two doors may be indicated, for example when a bathroom is between two bedrooms, but forgetting to lock or unlock them becomes a big nuisance. Windows should ordinarily be high enough to give privacy and good ventilation and should not be directly over any of the fixtures. The best combination of light, ventilation, and privacy comes from a skylight or high windows.

Arrangement of Fixtures. Size and shape of bathroom, the number of people using it, location of doors and windows, and plumbing costs determine its arrangement—individuality and beauty are seldom considered. Plumbing costs are lowest if the fixtures are along one wall, higher if on two walls, and highest when on three: the cost differences, however, are almost negligible if convenience is affected. So accustomed are we to having the three fixtures in one room—a leftover from the days when plumbing was new and was put into the hall bedroom—that we seldom realize that they are quite different in function. Usability is increased by putting them in separate compartments, but this takes more space and more partitions, and you have to pay for both.

Wash basins in bedrooms are a convenient and economical way to lighten the load on the bathroom. They take about 1'6" by 2'0" of space, can be set into a small counter with storage space underneath, and can be hidden behind a door.

Storage. "Storage at point of first use" is the best guide here as elsewhere, and bath linens, soaps, tissue, medicines, hot-water bottles, and a miscellany of other things associated with hygiene should be conveniently and accessibly housed. Conventional medicine cabinets do about one tenth of the job: spacious cupboards, although needed, are seldom found.

Mirrors. Until used, the typical prefabricated medicine chest with a mirror on the swinging door located over the wash basin seems like genuine 20th century efficiency. However, when one watches a man shaving in front of one of them, their inefficiency is almost humorous. More likely than not, one of the needed articles in the cabinet is forgotten; this necessitates ducking out of the way of the open door. Then the posture necessary to bring one's face near the mirror while keeping one's stomach away from the wash basin is ludicrous. Finally, the hot water running into the basin often transforms the mirror into a good imitation of frosted glass. All of this can be remedied, as hinted at above, by having a mirror fixed to the wall at right angles to the basin as in Fig. 3-8.

Illumination. The most important requirement for bathroom lighting is that when one is standing in front of the mirror one's face should be illuminated evenly and without glare. This is usually accomplished by wall fixtures around the mirror in addition to general lighting from the ceiling.

Even though bathrooms are small, engineered for efficiency, and dominated by three bulky (usually white) objects more suggestive of the laboratory than the home, these rooms can have both beauty and individuality. Floor, walls, and ceiling can have color and texture; fixtures are made in soft or strong colors; and curtains, rugs, and towels are available in great variety. In the past about the only suitable surfacing materials were plaster and tile, and these were usually a pale color to minimize the fixtures' white bulk, to render water spots inconspicuous, to reflect light, and to make the room seem larger. Today there are many durable, interesting natural and synthetic materials. In the bathroom shown in Fig. 3-8, red, gray, and black plastics, some of which are textured, offer pleasant contrast with the white fixtures. In the family bathroom, waterproof, plastic-impregnated wood and cork, and wallboards with both grid and textile patterns are combined with glass and metal to produce a rich variety in unity. Wood, sealed against water, or brick can be used for walls, as can many waterproof wallpapers, textiles, and wallboards. From all of these you can select those most appropriate to the character of your home.

HOUSE GUESTS

The pleasure you and your house guests get from their visits is almost directly proportional to the manner in which you can put them up. They have exactly the same basic private-life needs as members of the family while they are with you: a secluded place to sleep and dress; clothes storage, but in lesser amount than the family; bathroom facilities; and the possibility of getting outside the family circle from time to time. As with other facilities for living, your preferences and purse determine the guest accommodations you will provide. Going from the ideal down to the minimum these are:

- A guest room which is a fully-equipped bed-sitting room with private bath, pleasantly separated from family sleeping areas and always in readiness because it is used for no other purpose.

A. SCHNELLER SONS

3-10 This ingenious bed-davenport quickly converts from good sitting to good sleeping facilities. The adjacent cabinet has storage space for bedding and serves as an end table by day, a bedside table at night.

- A seclusion room, study, or library doubling as a guest room, which is a sensible idea because a room well-planned for these purposes has many of the qualities of a good guest room (Fig. 2-11).
- A quiet alcove off the group-living space that can readily be made private by folding or sliding doors, curtains, or screens.
- A bed-davenport in the living room, such as the one shown in Fig. 3-10, or any of a number of other kinds.

Few can afford the first, but if you expect to have house guests with any frequency, effort should be expended to have the second or third; the bed-davenport is a make-shift, often necessary but seldom satisfactory.

INDIVIDUAL WORK AND HOBBIES

With today's emphasis on individuality, personal expression, and self-realization, space and equipment for satisfying such urges and needs have become increasingly important—and at a time when both space and equipment are very expensive. Few houses now have the luxury of "spare rooms," and basements, attics, and sheds in the backyard are becoming scarce. Since solving the problem is not easy, let us begin with some of the simpler activities.

We have already noted in Chapter 2 that reading, whether for pleasure, school, or one's business, requires only a comfortable chair and good light in some degree of privacy, for which provision can be made in an out-of-the-way corner of the living room, the seclusion room if the family has one, or the individual's bedroom. Writing requires a desk in or around which the needed paraphernalia can be kept conveniently. A family desk in a secluded corner of the living room may suffice for a small family, but it is far more satisfactory to have a desk for the housewife at the planning center in the kitchen, one for each child in his bedroom, and to give some thought to where the man of the house can readily put pen or pencil on paper.

Knitting and crocheting can be done wherever one can read, but family mending and sewing are not so easily disposed of. The collection of needles, threads, scissors, patches, and other "findings" seems to invite disorder and the fingers of small children to which they are a definite hazard. If we add to these a sewing machine and space for sewing, complications really set in. In order of their desirability, we mention a secluded sewing room which is nowadays a luxury, space in the master bedroom, or space in the already overloaded kitchen or in the usually minimum laundry. Wherever this is fitted in (and that is usually just the way it is handled!), well-planned storage is essential.

From such different work and hobbies as reading, writing, and sewing, we move into the miscellany of such handicrafts as weaving and woodwork, which require much space and specialized equipment and make as much noise as music makes. Important as these may be to the individual, such interests if seriously pursued can quickly and seriously endanger the composure of the rest of the household unless they are somewhat isolated from the group living space.

SOLITUDE

For those raising families—and perhaps for the members of the families being raised—solitude is a rare and precious commodity, seldom well-planned for in today's homes unless there is a seclusion room planned for *not more than two persons* at a time, or a bed-sitting room for each person. We hear much about the importance of the two-week vacation during which you "get away from it all." This is all to the good, but it is no substitute for the half-hour vacation most individuals need every day. A sheltered spot in the garden is ideal but this is a fair-weather proposition. If physically possible, give each person his spot and having given it to him, respect it.

These are the major private activities listed along with the parts of the home in which they may occur.

Activities	*Space*
Sleeping and Dressing	
	Bedrooms
	Dressing rooms
Hygiene	
	Bathrooms
	Lavatories in bedrooms
House Guests	
Relatives	Guest room
Children's friends	Study or den
Parent's friends	Children's bedrooms
	Living room
	Activity space
Individual Work and Hobbies	
Study or homework	Study, den, or studio
Crafts, painting, etc.	Bedrooms
Music	Play, activity, or recreation space
Sewing	Living or dining room, kitchen
	Workshop, garage, or basement
Solitude	
Parents	Bedrooms
Children	Study or seclusion room
House guests	Secluded garden

CHAPTER 4

House Keeping

HOUSEWORK AND MAINTENANCE include such varied tasks as getting meals, housecleaning and "straightening up," laundry, sewing, yard and garden work, and miscellaneous repairs. Though some of this work must be done throughout the whole house and yard, most major tasks are concentrated in the kitchen, laundry, garage, basement, and service yard. House keeping is an integral part of home life and can be an invigorating family enterprise *if* the house is planned and furnished sensibly and all members of the household do their share. It is tempting to digress on ways of making housework worth while to all, but our primary concern in this chapter is planning and furnishing for efficient operation.

The greatest labor-saving possibility at our command is *sensible planning of the whole house and yard for convenient, economical living.* This includes putting functionally related areas together, storing objects conveniently and accessibly at point of first use, selecting materials and forms that can be easily maintained, having no more furniture and accessories than you use and enjoy, and taking full advantage of labor-saving devices. None of this is intended to imply a Spartan existence, nor will it lead to a home that takes care of itself, but it can contribute to pleasant home life in which there is time and energy for other activities.

4-1 A pleasant, well-lighted kitchen divided by equipment and furniture into three zones—food preparation, eating and planning, and laundry. Although the room is spacious, equipment is arranged to minimize steps. At off-hours, the laundry zone could be used for small children's play and the dining table for games, homework, or suitable hobbies.

GETTING MEALS

No home activity has received such intensive study as has food preparation; no room in the house has changed as rapidly and drastically as has the kitchen. Home economists have studied every phase of the problem; manufacturers have poured their energies into the design of new equipment. This is no accident or whim: it grows directly from the fact that keeping a family well fed is a large-scale order which takes a good many hours every day. Major problems include: analysis of activities; the design of work centers; arrangement of work centers; size of kitchen; loca-

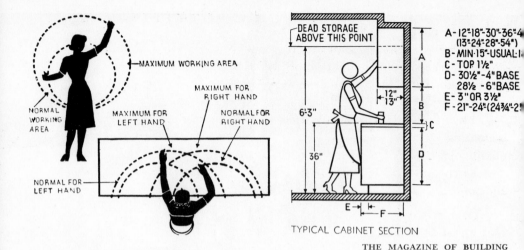

4-2 Kitchen dimensions should be based on the dimensions of the persons using that room.

tion in plan; and choosing suitable materials for floors, walls, counters, and cupboards. Study of meal-getting quickly shows that kitchen planning is more than spotting a sink, range, and refrigerator, filling the space between with cupboards, putting in some doors and windows, and then brightening it all up with paint and curtains. The kitchen illustrated in Fig. 4-1 combines an efficient U-shaped food preparation center with space for eating and a partially segregated laundry area in a design as convenient as it is pleasant.

Analysis of Activities

In chronological sequence, meal-getting involves planning, shopping, receiving and storing supplies, preparing food, serving, and after-meal cleanup. Preparing food is the most important operation, serving and clearing next, in terms of equipment and space needed. A thorough study [1] of these problems has given us new and needed knowledge.

1. The housewife's physical limitations show that work curves should not be more than 48 inches wide and 16 inches deep, and that the top shelf for active storage should not be more than 72 inches above the floor.

2. Storage should be in terms of *first use* rather than placing like things

[1] Conducted by Mary Holl Heiner and Helen E. McCullough at the College of Home Economics, Cornell University, and reported in the *Architectural Forum,* February and March, 1946.

together. *Clear visibility* indicates that stored items should be only one row deep except for such identical objects as tumblers. *Easy accessibility* suggests storing frequently-used or heavy items near counter level, and stacking only such identical objects as plates or cereal dishes.

3. The number and variety of things stored even in the modest kitchen is amazing: 75 to 80 packaged foods and 45 to 50 utensils are used first in mixing operations, and 300 or more items are used first in serving meals.

4. Kitchen activities suggest four work centers: *Mixing, Range, Sink,* and *Serving.*

Design of Work Centers

The *Mixing Center* is for all sorts of mixing—salads, desserts, breads, and pastries. It should have:

- A *counter* at least 36 inches long and not more than 30 to 32 inches high (in contrast to the standard 36-inch height) to lessen fatigue from mixing.
- *Wall cabinets* (16 inches above counter if an electric mixer is used) to store condiments, staples, and light-weight or shallow pans, bowls, etc.
- *Base cabinets* with drawers for small utensils, sugar, and flour, and lower drawers or sliding shelves for heavy items used in mixing operations.

Based on extensive research, these kitchen units are designed for easy assembly in varied kitchen layouts. They are based on a 2-foot module, have interchangeable parts, and include built-in appliances.

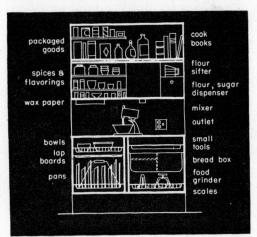

HOUSING RESEARCH CENTER, CORNELL UNIVERSITY, AND HOUSE AND HOME

4-3 A Mixing Center 4 feet wide in which everything used in mixing operations is conveniently and accessibly stored at point of first use. The work counter is adjustable in height.

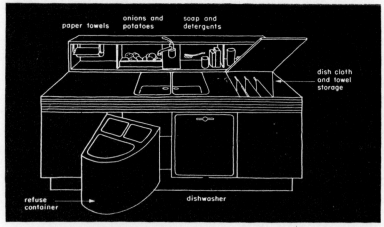

4-4 An 8-foot-wide Sink Center in which a useful three-compartment refuse container swings out to give knee room so that the housewife can sit while working. The storage space for onions and potatoes, soap and detergents is usefully placed.

The Mixing Center should be adjacent to the refrigerator in which many of the mix-first supplies are necessarily stored.

The *Range Center* is most efficient when it has:

- *Heat-resistant counters* on one or both sides of the stove.
- *Wall cabinets* for small cooking utensils, seasonings, and hot-food serving dishes.
- *Base cabinets* for heavy, range-first utensils.

Adjacent to the Sink Center, near the Mixing Center, and convenient to the eating space describes the most desirable location for this work center. Typical ranges come in one unit with ovens below the surface burners, but today separate surface and oven units are also available (see Fig. 4-8) which make it possible to place the oven at a convenient working height. A heat-resistant counter beside the oven is then particularly important.

The *Sink Center* is indeed multi-purpose, serving as it does for washing fruits, vegetables, dishes, and children's hands and providing water for mixing, cooking, freezing, and drinking. It is associated with garbage disposal and may spread into storage for tableware, although that is sometimes better at the Serving Center. The Sink Center needs:

- *Counters* at *both sides,* at least one of which is a waterproof drain-board.
- *Storage space* for dishes if it seems most convenient to put these away directly from the dishwasher or drainer, and for all sink-first items, such as packaged foods that need water (coffee, dried fruits, etc.); for utensils for food cleaning, straining, cutting, juicing, measuring, and surface-cooking; and provision for trash and garbage.

Because it is desirable to have the sink near both the Range and Mixing Centers it is often located between them.

The *Serving Center,* ideally a unit separating cooking and eating space, is used for storing tableware (especially silver and glassware), linens, accessories, and those foods (catsup, sugar, etc.) that go directly from storage to table. It may have sections accessible from either side and should include a pass-through to facilitate serving.

Arrangement of Work Centers

The cardinal principle of work-center arrangement is efficiency of operation. We know in general that:

- The *Sink Center* is the kitchen's busiest center with many trips from other work centers during all phases of getting meals.

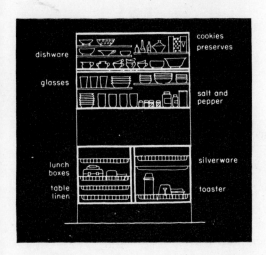

dishware

glasses

cookies
preserves

salt and
pepper

lunch
boxes

table
linen

silverware

toaster

HOUSING RESEARCH CENTER,
CORNELL UNIVERSITY, AND
HOUSE AND HOME

4-5 A 4-foot Serving Center holds all items used first in serving a meal. A counter 30 inches high can double as a desk or snack bar.

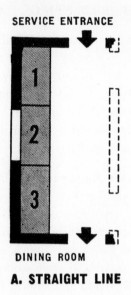

A. STRAIGHT LINE

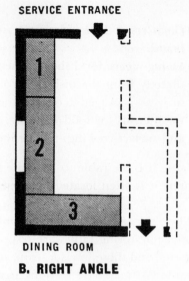

B. RIGHT ANGLE

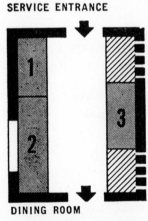

C. OPPOSITE WALLS

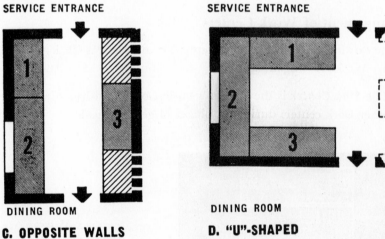

D. "U"-SHAPED

THE MAGAZINE OF BUILDING

4-6 The four typical kitchen plans.

- *Mixing Center* activities take much time, especially if there is much baking, dessert, sandwich, or salad making, but much of this can be done at slack periods.
- The *Range Center* usually becomes the busiest center for half an hour or so prior to serving the meal and it is also the danger spot.

- The *Serving Center* is heavily used during serving and cleanup times.
- Traffic around the work centers should be confined to that related to getting meals.

Further, we know that:

- Normal work sequence is from right to left for right-handed persons, and steps are saved if the Mixing Center is at the right and the Sink Center is next to the left, followed by the Range and Serving Centers.
- Distances between work centers should be as short and direct as possible and still allow the necessary work counters and storage space for each center; this usually means that the "work triangle" formed by stove, sink, and refrigerator measures less than 20 but more than 12 feet.

Typically, kitchen arrangements fall into four categories (Fig. 4-6) which have the following advantages and disadvantages.

Type	*Advantages*	*Disadvantages*
STRAIGHT LINE	Can be fitted into alcove and concealed when not in use.	Very wasteful of steps if equipment and storage is normal size.
	Equipment and cabinets can be purchased as a prefabricated unit.	Suitable only for "kitchenettes."
	Concentrates plumbing, wiring, etc., in one place.	
	No "dead" corners in cabinets.	
RIGHT ANGLE	Distance between work centers less than in STRAIGHT LINE.	Not as compact as "U"-SHAPED.
	Leaves remainder of room free for eating, laundry, etc.	One "dead" corner.
	Tends to divert traffic away from work centers.	

Type	Advantages	Disadvantages
OPPOSITE WALLS	Distances between work centers less than in RIGHT ANGLE. No "dead" corners.	Traffic between work centers if doors are at opposite ends.
"U"-SHAPED	Most compact, efficient layout. Minimizes traffic.	Two "dead" corners (which, however, can be well used with good planning).

Kitchen Size.   Kitchen size is determined by the amount of cooking done, which in turn is related to: the size of the family and the kind of entertaining; the amount of storage space needed or desired; the number and kind of other activities, such as family eating, laundry, child play; and family preferences and finances.   In small houses kitchen floor space varies from 50 to 180 square feet, with from 15 to 20 linear feet of wall for base cabinets and equipment; in larger houses the space may be conspicuously bigger.   Twenty or thirty years ago there was a marked trend to make the kitchen as small and compact as possible—a highly specialized laboratory for cooking only; today there is an equally marked trend toward making the kitchen larger to accommodate other activities. Nevertheless actual square footage is not the only factor, because kitchen efficiency and pleasantness are determined by shape, doors and windows, and location in the house plan as well as by size.

Shape.   Here, again, there are no ready-made rules.   Generally, a rectangle of approximately the proportions of 2 to 3 requires fewer steps than either a square or a long, narrow shape.   Very small kitchens, however, may be longer in proportion to their width, and large kitchens may approach the square, especially if space for meal getting is segregated from space for eating, laundry, and all those miscellaneous things that gravitate toward the kitchen.

Doors and Windows.   Doors in a kitchen are a necessary evil, necessary as entrances and exits, evil because they take space, determine location of work centers, and invite traffic.   The most efficient kitchen has two doors—one leading out to the garage and service yard and the other to the dining space—and between the two there is bound to be a traffic path. It is desirable, however, to have a short convenient path from the kitchen to the front door and also to a lavatory, and this may necessitate a third

4-7 An up-to-date living-kitchen segregates the work areas from the dining and lounging space, which has some easy chairs facing a fireplace. This kind of planning leads to wholesome family life and pleasantly informal entertaining. Allmon Fordyce, architect.

door. Whatever the number, keep them as close together as possible and with no major work center between them.

Windows make the kitchen light and pleasant and provide ventilation, but like doors they take space and often interfere with efficient disposition of wall cabinets and equipment. Minimum window space should equal 10 per cent of the floor area, but 15 to 20 per cent is better. If possible, at least one counter should be amply lighted by windows and afford an outlook; the usual practice of placing kitchen windows over the sink center seems defensible because it is the only major piece of kitchen equipment over which a window can be well placed, good light is essential at the sink, and the time spent there passes more quickly when one can see out of doors. Windows which reach to the ceiling provide better illumination than those which are lower and, if they can be opened at the top, help greatly in ridding the kitchen of cooking odors. Many contemporary designers, recognizing the demands of kitchen storage upon wall space, have introduced skylights or clerestory windows which fill the kitchen with cheery light without taking wall space.

Location. For efficient house keeping the kitchen should be the shortest possible distance from the dining and service areas and the garage;

4-8 Pine cabinets, walls, and ceiling, brick around the stainless-steel cooking units, and a tile-patterned linoleum floor give a kitchen a friendly warmth and all are easy to maintain.

it should be convenient to the main entrance and also to a lavatory; and desirably it should afford easy supervision of the play of younger children. To achieve this, the kitchen will usually be near the center of the house, not in an out-of-the-way place as though it were a somewhat embarrassing necessity.

A pleasant view and the effect of sunlight should be remembered too. Sunlight, particularly in the morning, helps get the household into a pleasant breakfast mood; but uncontrolled afternoon sun pouring into an already warm, busy kitchen toward supper time is invariably exasperating. Thus, take your choice of north, south, or east with preference for the northeast or east; avoid the west unless you are certain that you can mitigate the effect of afternoon sun.

Materials. The kitchen suffers the greatest wear and tear of any room in the house, has to be cleaned up most often, is a center of noisy activities, and is the center of the housewife's work. Thus, shapes and materials for floor, counters, cupboards, walls, and ceilings should be chosen for *wear-ability, clean-ability, sound-absorption,* and *pleasantness* to sight and touch. By *wear-ability* we mean shapes and materials that resist breaking, denting, and scratching; that do not show conspicuously the damage bound to occur; and that can be repaired or replaced easily; by *clean-ability*, things that can be quickly cleaned with ordinary materials; that do not call attention to such irritants as a few crumbs or water spots; and that do not get more or less permanently stained. *Sound-absorption* is simply soaking up rather than reflecting noise. *Pleasantness* to eyes, hands, and feet differs greatly from one person to another; suffice it to say that the kitchen ought to please the person spending the most time in it.

LAUNDRY

Provisions for doing laundry at home range from using the sink or wash basin for rinsing out little things to having a fully-equipped, separate laundry; this depends on the size and age distribution of the family, the size of the house, and how the family feels about sending laundry out. Of all household chores, laundry is the easiest to delegate to an outside agency which will call for it, handle it more or less the way you like, and return it in a neat package—but this tends to be expensive in terms of money, especially if the family is sizeable, and in greater wear and tear on linens and clothes. Two factors have greatly changed the picture of washing clothes at home: first, the development of automatic washers and dryers; and second, the trend toward getting laundry equipment out of the dark, damp, inconvenient basement and on to the main living floor of the house. On the other hand, the many self-service "launderettes" make it possible to wash and dry your clothes outside the home at small expense and moderate inconvenience.

Laundry activities, like meal getting, fall into four categories and consequently suggest four centers:

- *Receiving, sorting,* and *preparing center* which requires a work surface (a counter with drawers or bins, a table, or often simply the top of the washer).
- *Washing center* which includes laundry trays and/or washing machine plus storage for soaps, bleaches, and other supplies.
- *Drying center* which is ideally an automatic dryer but may be a drying yard; a small outside drying space is desirable even with a dryer.
- *Finishing* and *ironing center* which includes the ironing board and/or ironer, a place to put finished laundry, and, ideally, space and equipment for mending.

In smaller houses all of this is likely to be reduced to a minimum and compacted into whatever space can be found, a practice not to be commended but born of necessity. Since a separate laundry room is out of the question for most of us, laundry equipment is most often placed in the utility room,[2] basement, garage, or kitchen. The utility room is probably the best location because even at its best laundry work makes clutter, water and soap gets on the floor, and washers and dryers are noisy; getting it all out of sight and sound is comforting. The fast-disappearing basement also gets laundry out of the way but puts it in an inconvenient, generally unpleasant place. Doing laundry in the garage isolates it from other activities but puts it in a place hard to keep clean and seldom warm in winter. Combining the laundry with the kitchen often saves space, time, and steps, but adds noise and confusion to the busiest room in the house. We might as well face the fact that washing, ironing, and mending clothes are not much fun, but being able to do the work in a well-lighted place made cheerful with color and a view outdoors mitigates the unpleasantness.

KEEPING THE HOME ORDERLY AND CLEAN

The housewife spends a great many hours a week keeping the house orderly and clean; she works at it seven days a week (including holidays); and although she cheerfully accepts it as part of her job there are numerous ways to reduce this work. The amount of time spent on housework varies with the size of the living quarters, the size and ages of the family, the amount of help employed or received from the family, the standards of housekeeping adhered to, the general cleanliness of the environment, and the *design of and the materials used in floors, walls, ceilings, furniture, and accessories.*

Putting things back in place, an ever-present burden, can be lightened in several ways.

■ Plan conveniently located and well-equipped centers for each major individual or family activity with everything you need where you need it. This applies to reading, music, and hobbies quite as much as to preparing meals. If this is done, things are much more likely to be put away and clutter is reduced.

---

[2] The name given to the room, usually small, which houses the furnace and hot-water heater and which is usually adjacent to the kitchen, garage, and service yard.

4-9 Furniture that comes in a variety of small units fitting tightly together has many of the advantages of built-ins, plus flexibility. They can be combined in any room to provide work and storage facilities for varied activities and can be rearranged easily. Charles Eames, designer.

- Have a well-considered place for each object—chairs, tables, and lamps placed so that they seldom need to be moved, convenient and accessible storage for all things that need not be left out. In short, a good furniture arrangement with good storage.
- Have a maximum of fixed objects. Built-in seating, tables, storage, and lighting fixtures stay where they belong despite the whims of children and adults, thereby saving the endless pushing around of detached units. Fixed furniture and equipment in typical living quarters are limited to kitchen cabinets, bathroom medicine chests,

4-10 The Chinese cane barrel-type chair is remarkably comfortable and inexpensive, easy to move and to keep, and lasts a great deal longer than its price indicates.

linen shelves, and a few ceiling lights. The easiest-to-keep home has built-in sofas and tables, storage in or on the walls of every room, lighting fixtures that take neither floor nor table space and have no hazardous exposed cords, and a permanently attached fireplace screen. Alternatives to built-ins are units of furniture (Fig. 4-9) designed to look and act almost as though they were integral parts of the house— they fit tightly together and against the wall to save space and at least look permanently placed—and there are lighting fixtures that can readily be fastened on the walls.

■ Select movable objects with movability in mind. Those that have to be moved should be light in weight, easy to grasp, and resistant to the wear and tear that moving brings. For example, pull-up and dining chairs ought to be sturdy and easy to lift, not the kind that have to be given a floor-scraping shove. Similar criteria apply to small tables, portable lamps, and even ashtrays.

■ Put away or discard everything that you do not use often or really enjoy. Households have a tendency to get cluttered with everything from unneeded furniture to unappreciated bric-a-brac, and every object in your room takes housekeeping time. Sell or give them away if they are no longer important to you, store them if you are reasonably certain you will want them later, and use the time formerly spent keeping the unnecessaries clean and in order for more productive activity.

Cleaning, too, can be much less of a chore if furnishings are chosen wisely. Because this is not a book on housecleaning methods we will not go into such important matters as a sensible cleaning schedule or ways to clean a carpet without hurting your back or carpet; but we will say that storage for cleaning equipment and materials is necessary and that

PHOTOGRAPH BY MAYNARD PARKER

4-11   An outdoor chair of copper and redwood withstands weather and hard knocks, is proportioned and angled for comfort, and has a detachable arm which minimizes the need for little tables. Cliff May, designer.

it is usually located in or near the kitchen, probably better *near* than *in* that much-used room.   Our concern is with the selection of forms, colors, and materials that are easy to keep in good condition, on which dust and dirt do little harm until they are removed; liquids do a minimum of damage through penetration, staining, or bleaching or simply by leaving untidy water spots; and scratches, dents, and blemishes are reduced to a minimum but when they do occur, do not cause serious disfigurement and can be repaired simply.

Dust and dirt are unpleasant to see and touch, unhygienic, and tend to shorten the life of anything on which they remain.   They are most harmful if they penetrate or become embedded in the material and under such circumstances are difficult to dislodge.   This suggests:

- Forms that are broad and simple, that have a minimum of separate parts, moldings, carvings, or crevices into which dust and dirt settle and from which they are hard to remove.   This applies to walls, furniture, tableware, indeed to everything!
- Furniture that either comes solidly to the floor on all sides or is supported on a minimum number of legs high enough above the floor to make cleaning under it easy.
- Surfaces that are smooth and impenetrable such as well-sealed wood, linoleum, tile, and plastic textiles.   To be sure, almost everyone wants some place in the house the warmth and richness of textured rugs, upholstery, and draperies; these are hard to keep really clean, but compensate by not showing the "matter foreign to the article in its pure state," as dirt has been defined.
- Colors that are grayed and are neither extremely light nor dark. These are the colors in which nature abounds, the colors that are restful because they demand little attention; they are also the colors on which a little dust and dirt is not noticed.
- Surfaces that are patterned rather than plain.   Any color-varied surface is easier to maintain than is one of a solid color, but those easiest to keep looking well have small, irregularly varied patterns such as are found in natural patterns: the grain of wood, the grass in a lawn, crushed rock, the veining of marble, or cirrus clouds.
- Surfaces that are dull rather than glossy.   Mirrors and shiny metals give life and brilliance to any room and are welcome accents, but they show every fingerprint and speck of dust; mat surfaces with their lack of luster and gloss take such inevitables in their stride.

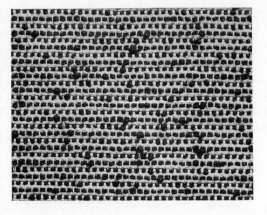

GOLDING DECORATIVE FABRICS

4-12 Textured weaves, available in many colors, camouflage the effects of use, look presentable with little care far longer than do plain weaves.

Spilled and spattered liquids are a constant threat to the housekeeper; water is the most common but least serious, while other liquids, all the way from beverages to ink, may stain or bleach any porous, non-colorfast material. To economize on work and possible replacement use:

- Waterproof materials wherever feasible. They are especially needed in the kitchen, laundry, and bathroom, but are also a convenience where food is served, especially to children, and in multi-purpose or activity rooms. Although glass, metal, and glazed ceramics are history's chief waterproof materials, we can now add to them a host of plastics (Fig. 9-12) and synthetics (Fig. 9-9) which are opening the way to easier housekeeping.
- Materials that do not show water marks. In general, shiny surfaces whether glass, metal, plastic, or wood show water spots which can only be removed by polishing, whereas on dull surfaces they are barely noticeable. If in addition to being shiny the material is transparent (and this includes, of course, clear glass), the nuisance value of a water spot is doubled. Many household waxes and polishes have the serious disadvantage of turning white or discoloring with water.
- Colorfast materials. These resist bleaching and expedite the removal of stains.

Even in the most careful households, surfaces will get scratched, dented, and blemished, and repairing or concealing the results of such accidents is part of routine housekeeping. In trying to solve this problem we quickly get into a mass of seeming contradictions, but these are the facts:

- Resilient materials such as rubber, linoleum, and cork take a blow or scratch and bounce back with scarcely a record of the event.

- Rigid materials such as masonry and heavy metal do not give a bit, but will crack, break, or dent under heavy blows; and if and when they do, repair is difficult, sometimes impossible. For example, metal kitchen cabinets do not often get dented, but if they do, repair is an expensive matter best trusted to an expert.
- Wood, especially the harder types, ages gracefully if finished to reveal its color and grain and like good silverware grows richer with use. It seems to make minor scratches and blemishes part of itself.
- Glossy finishes are almost always more resistant to scratching and abrasion of any sort than are "softer" finishes, but the blemishes are conspicuous. Thus, glossy paint or varnish is more durable from every point of view than are the dull-finish varieties, but you see every disturbance of the gloss.
- Patterns, especially those that are small and indistinct, conceal blemishes quite as much as they do dust, water marks, and stains.

Lest you begin to think that we are advocating a house monotonously medium brown and gray with a confusion of little texture-patterns everywhere and no plain, bright, dark or light colors, no sparkling surfaces, we hasten to say that this is by no means the whole story. But for easy housekeeping and for informal living it is a good part of the story of how to treat the *big surfaces of walls, floors, and furniture.* We have explained the facts; you will make the decisions. Concentrating single-mindedly on economical housekeeping necessarily minimizes consideration of beauty and individuality but it does not exclude them. A house can be easy to keep, pleasing, and express the personalities of its owners all at the same time. As a matter of fact, for most of us the three (together with use) go hand-in-hand, which explains the groundswell of interest today in the informal, natural house. Love of nature is one of our deepest feelings and, perhaps to balance the mechanization of much work, we are making our homes natural in the best sense of the word, not only because such homes mean less work and wear well but because we get positive enjoyment from the colors and textures of the out-of-doors.

Use, economy, beauty, and individuality have been brought together in a happy union in the room shown in Fig. 4-13. Because it is planned with people and furniture in mind, there is a good place for every object. Most of the furniture—the book and storage cases, sofa, end and dining tables—is built in, as are the concealed lighting fixtures; the few

PHOTOGRAPH BY JULIUS SHULMAN

4-13 The living-dining space in a small house which integrates to a remarkable degree use, economy, beauty, and individuality. Gordon Drake, architect.

movable pieces—the coffee table and the chairs—are easy to grasp and light in weight. All pieces either come to the floor or clear it sufficiently to allow easy cleaning underneath. All of the forms are broad and simple, but certainly are neither monotonous nor dull. Because almost all surfaces show natural colors and patterns they do not demand excessive maintenance. Were it not for the fact that this chapter is on housework we would discuss, rather than merely mention, the visual interest achieved in the ceiling variations, the band of high glass that brings light and lets one see the sky without demanding curtains for privacy, the lively contrast of textures, the painting that is large enough for the space it occupies, the high degree of unity, and the promise of good living that even a black and white photograph extends.

HOUSEHOLD REPAIRS AND MAINTENANCE

There is no better way to economize on the expenses of household repairs and maintenance than to have a handy man (or woman) in the house, but people with the necessary skills, tools, interest, and time are rare today. Thus the typical home rightly makes no special provision for this work other than a corner in the garage or basement where paints and tools are kept and where there is possibly space for a workbench. If, however, one or more members of the family can be inveigled into such pursuits, they deserve adequate space to keep supplies and do the work. A small shop near the garage or utility room, but segregated from both, is the seldom-found ideal.

YARD AND GARDEN WORK

A joy or a backache? Possibly both. Because landscape design is discussed in Chapter 20 we will only emphasize here that any yard requires maintenance and that the amount of maintenance is in large part determined by the design. Here are some ways to reduce the load:

- Storage for the mélange of garden tools, insecticides, fungicides, and fertilizers should be carefully planned and conveniently located, usually near the garage and service yard.
- Paved areas require a minimum of upkeep.
- Simple designs with relatively large areas of one type of planting are easiest to keep under control.
- Hard-surface "mowing" strip around lawns minimizes hand-clipping of edges.
- Weatherproof furniture does not have to be protected each time it rains.

Keeping the family fed, the house and yard in good order and repair, is a wholesome aspect of family life. It need not be disheartening drudgery. Fortunately for all of us, contemporary architects, designers, home economists, and manufacturers have developed many new concepts, materials, and pieces of equipment with this in mind. We repeat, however, that sensible planning is the greatest of all labor savers.

PART TWO

Design and Color

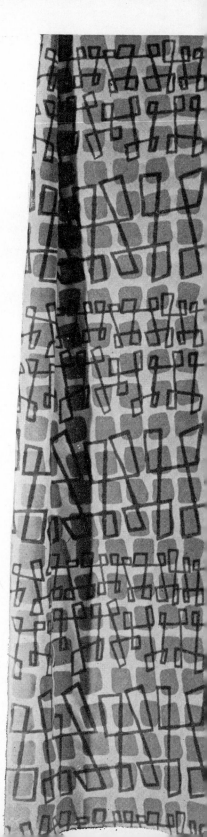

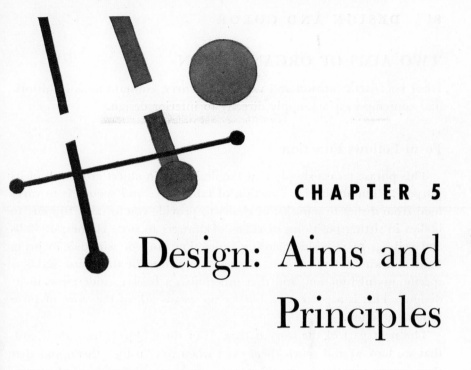

CHAPTER 5

Design: Aims and Principles

IN GENERAL USE the word *design* has several meanings: purpose, aim, or intention; plan or scheme; and selection and organization. Put together, they describe the entire design procedure. It consists of deciding on your purpose or aim, developing a suitable plan of approach, and then selecting and organizing the forms and materials best suited to your purpose. In this sense every decision you make about your home is a design decision.

In art, however, design usually refers to the selection and organization of forms, spaces, colors, and textures to produce beauty. In this chapter, we shall use the word in this limited sense while keeping in mind that use, economy, and individuality are not-to-be-forgotten aspects of design.

Design for beauty has no laws, recipes, or rigid standards to trouble or comfort us, as the case may be, because beauty and creative individuality are close partners. There are, however, useful observations and guides, aims, and principles.

TWO AIMS OF ORGANIZATION

FORM FOLLOWS FUNCTION and VARIETY IN UNITY, constant aims in historic and contemporary art, apply directly to interior design.

Form Follows Function

This phrase means simply that the design of an object grows out of its purpose. The utilitarian function of table forks and spoons is to carry food from dishes to mouths; of chairs to provide comfortable support to bodies in sitting positions, of chests of drawers to store clothes; of walls and ceilings to provide enclosing protection; and of windows to bring light and air into the house. Nearly everything in the house serves a specific useful function, and that function is a basic consideration in its design. This is a good part, but by no means all, of the story of form follows function.

The next part of the story is that all of these objects have their cost, that we look at and touch them even when not "using" them, and that they express our tastes. In short, they represent expenditures of money, time, and energy and they are possible sources of esthetic pleasure and individuality. A spoon or a chair is completely functional only when it is useful, beautiful, and economical to an individual; this lifts the design and selection of silverware and seating well above the mere supply of equipment that fits human anatomy. The tale of function concludes with those objects intended only for the spirit—paintings, sculpture, and accessories whose claim on us is their beauty. These are at the opposite end of the scale from the strictly useful furnace and garden hose, but they are of great significance to the whole man living a full life.

Designing and selecting for all functions is no child's play. Factor must be weighed against factor, and compromises made. Suppose, for example, that you are looking for a coffee table to put in a contemporary living room where adults relax and small children want to play. It is easy to find many that are functional in size, shape, and height: but it is not easy to locate one that is moderately priced; pleasing in itself and harmonious with the room; strong, durable, and easy to keep clean; has some storage space and has no sharp corners dangerous to the little ones. As a matter of fact, the writers are looking for just such a table now and have been for several years. The difficulty is that several of the above criteria are contradictory. Sooner or later they will have to give up the qualities of lesser importance and buy or make a table having those deemed most important. In the meantime, though, it is as challenging to search for the perfectly functional table as it is to dream about the perfectly functional home.

Variety in Unity

As inseparable as Romeo and Juliet, this classic pair sounds like a contradiction in terms, but it is no more so than is *E Pluribus Unum.* All nature and all art show variety in unity, our own bodies with their unified diversity being the examples best known to us. Your hand, for example, is an amazing unit in which each part differs from the others yet all are coherent parts of a whole. Study the different parts, and see how they relate to each other and to your whole hand.

Unity can be defined as oneness or singleness; variety as difference, diversity, or lack of sameness. Heed well that we say variety *in* unity, not variety *and* unity. This is an important difference, often overlooked. Variety should develop out of unity as an expansion or development of the central idea or purpose, just as an oak tree develops from an acorn. Start with an idea, purpose, or character from which unity and variety grow together, not with a series of ideas that have to be "pulled together." Very rarely can forceful unity be produced out of differences.

Unity is best achieved out of the strength and clarity of a motivating idea. In interior design, this is the general character, as discussed in Chapter 1, that you want your home to have. Why should a home be unified? Because a unified home satisfies our desire for wholeness, is a welcome restful relief from the confusion of contemporary life, and brings a peace and security not found in a furniture store or in a home that resembles one.

Unity is achieved by several specific means.

- Sameness or repetition is the surest and most obvious. Having all walls the same in color and texture forcefully establishes a unified background; having all furniture of the same material and design also makes for oneness.
- Similarity and harmony are but one step removed from repetition, and lead directly toward unity while introducing some variety. The walls in a home might be of one hue, gray or green for example, but

some could be lighter or darker, warmer or cooler, stronger or weaker, or have different textures. All of the furniture could be of either light or dark wood, but in neither case does all of the wood have to come from the same species of tree.

- Emphasizing those parts that most forcefully express the basic character strengthens the feeling of unity. Put in noticeable spots the furniture that has the character you want, relegate to secondary positions the other pieces.
- Enclosures or frames help unify parts of your home by separating them from their surroundings. A hedge or fence around a garden or a frame around a picture are examples, but watch lest in unifying a part you disunite the whole.

Variety protects us from the boring monotony of too much sameness. It arouses interest, heightens the total effect by being different, brings vitality through friendly opposition, introduces welcome surprise, and of course destroys unity if carried too far. Just as unity can lead toward monotony, variety can lead to anarchy.

The home in which and to which everything "belongs," in which all things (including people) are compatible, is a comforting haven, not a restless assemblage of doors, windows, floors, walls, draperies, furniture, and knickknacks fighting with each other and silently but constantly asking you to help settle their difficulties. Remember that we shape our homes and that they shape us.

Variety is produced by developing opposing or complementary ideas *out of* the basic unity. It is secured by diversity of materials, forms, colors, textures; by contrasts of all sorts. It can be as subtle as a scarcely noticeable difference between the textures of two pillows on a davenport or as clamorous as a polished copper hood on a rough stone fireplace. Because variety can be an attention-getter of the first order, use it full strength only where you want people to look hard and long, in dilution where you want merely to relieve the monotony of an unimportant, uninteresting part of your home.

Almost no homes have too much unity, and for those few that do the simple remedy of getting some marked variety suffices to give them life. For example, the room shown in Fig. 5-1 has good furniture well arranged, but there is too much of the same thing. One yearns for at least one piece of furniture not supported by tubular metal, for some pronounced enrichment, for a few more non-metallic accessories. Many homes have

5-1 Even well-designed furniture loses its effectiveness when monotonously repeated. Significant unity is not achieved by repetition alone.

too much variety, and here too the action is simple—eliminate some of
the not-needed variety. The dining room in Fig. 5-2 has, for the writers,
too much variety. With a window treatment as elaborate as this and
furniture as diversified, the effect of the whole would be greatly improved
by a simple, small-scale wallpaper (or plain walls) and a few significant
accessories. These easy, inexpensive changes are the kind that would
improve many houses.

A workable way of keeping variety and unity hand in hand is having
one dominant character pervade your home, then introducing a secondary and possibly a tertiary theme. Composers of symphonies have found
this a good way of sustaining interest in lengthy compositions. The first
movement of a symphony usually has a major theme which establishes
unmistakably the dominant character of the composition, then a secondary theme usually of contrasting character is introduced. These two
themes are developed individually and together, but there is no rivalry
for dominance. Still other musical ideas which either support or oppose
the major themes are introduced in the later movements. Out of this

5-2 Too much variety and too little dominance robs this room of satisfying wholeness.

procedure develops a rich complexity of harmony and contrast, lively yet unified. In homes a major theme might be informal simplicity coupled with a minor theme of intricately enriched accessories, or the major theme might be formal precision sparked by unexpectedly whimsical accents. Color schemes usually have a dominant and a subordinate color, possibly a third of still less importance, and then occasional accents of other hues. Do not think that unity is limited to sameness or that it limits you completely to only one kind of furnishing.

PRINCIPLES OF DESIGN

In the search for ways and means to produce beauty, man has evolved a number of principles of design based on observation of nature and study of the most satisfying art objects. Balance, rhythm, and emphasis are a simple but inclusive trio of design principles, useful to anyone concerned with the pleasantness of his living space.

Balance

Defined as equilibrium, balance is a major principle in all phases of living from furniture arrangements to bank accounts, diet, and personality. Through balance we get a sense of stability, steadiness, and equipoise, but this may range from static permanence through repose and suspended animation to objects in actual motion. It is achieved when interplaying forces, attractions, or weights are resolved. Nature abounds in objects illustrating these qualities. The Rock of Gibraltar typifies static permanence with changes too slight to be readily apparent. A sand dune is always in a state of equilibrium resulting from the interplay of the fine granular nature of sand, wind and moisture, vegetation, the lay of the land, and the force of gravity; it shifts and changes shape, without losing its balance, as these forces and conditions change; and except on windy days it is in repose. A tree, too, is always in a changing equilibrium because it grows and is affected by moisture, temperature, air movements, and gravity. In winter a deciduous tree is in a state of suspended animation waiting for spring to induce growth. On quiet days there is no visible motion, but in a gale the trees move violently as do clouds and ocean waves. Thus from nature, our most stimulating guide and inspiration in design, we learn that balance need not be a dull, dead-weight-against-dead-weight equalization, but that it can be an always-changing resolution of forces which gives the beholder a feeling of participating in a living process. In all of these examples, balance exists in four dimensions—length, breadth, height, and time. Nature is ever changing but is seldom caught off-balance, no matter from what angle we view it. To the degree that our homes capture this feeling of "balancing" rather than of "balanced," they too will seem to have life.

In balancing an interior we deal with the "visual weights" of architecture and furnishings, and these visual weights are primarily determined by three factors: importance in our patterns of living; size and physical weight; and their other powers to attract and hold our attention. Thus, doors and other openings which control our movements, chairs and beds which promise rest to our bodies, gain visual significance because they directly affect our life patterns; objects of large size and those made of stone, solid metal, or thick wood look heavy because we know that they are hard to lift; and the following are visually heavy because they demand our attention: bright colors, intricate detail, strong contrasts of all sorts, and anything that is unusual or unexpected. These are active forces, psychological and physical, and a well-balanced interior holds their interplay in poise.

Balance in an interior is as ever-changing as is nature's equilibrium, but in different ways. The first factor is light. The natural illumination of any room is altered every minute of the day, changes markedly with sky conditions and the seasons, and only within small limits can we control its effect on our interiors. For example, subtle nuances of color and very fine detail can be readily appreciated in moderately bright light, but very strong sunlight or dusk all but obscures them. Artificial illumination can, of course, be precisely controlled, but has to be flexible to meet varied needs, and flexibility brings change. People are the second factor, for the design of a room is never complete except when they are using it. The people in a room move and in so doing see the room from different angles and locations; also they vary in number and they wear clothes chosen to fit themselves, not the room. All of these introduce change in equilibrium. The third factor is the composite of all the little things that happen to a room in the course of a day—the reading material and other portable paraphernalia brought in and left—as well as the changes that come with the months and years—the scarcely noticed fading of textiles and mellowing of wood, to say nothing of the replacement of outworn or unwanted objects. What does all of this mean to us? Simply that in view of all these changes, many of them beyond our control, the fundamental pattern of equilibrium had better be strong enough to take these onslaughts in stride, to absorb them rather than be destroyed by them.

Three Types of Balance. It is customary to differentiate three types of balance: *symmetrical, asymmetrical,* and *radial.*

Symmetrical balance, also known as formal or passive balance, is that type in which one side of the object is the exact reverse or mirror image of the other half. There are countless examples of symmetrical balance in the world around us: where and, more important, why?

- The bodies of animals (when viewed from the front or back) and the leaves, flowers, and fruits of a great many plants are symmetrical because symmetry in these smaller aspects of nature appears to have importance in the struggle for survival.

- Our clothes, furniture, and equipment (forks and spoons, for example) are nearly all symmetrical because then they fit our symmetrical bodies.
- Classical architecture—Greek, Roman, Renaissance, and American Colonial—is almost always symmetrical because symmetry brings stateliness, dignity, and reserve, qualities dear to the hearts of Classicists.

Thus, symmetrical balance is found in many relatively small objects of nature and art for reasons of utility, and in many examples of Classical architecture for reasons of effect.

Symmetrical balance is easy to appreciate and to create. Anyone can see quickly and without effort that one side is the reverse replica of the other and, therefore, the two must be in equilibrium. The effect is quiet and reposed, probably because it demands little effort from the observer. Its overtones of stateliness and dignity are not easy to explain, but certainly we stand or sit as symmetrically as we comfortably can when we wish to appear dignified. The center is a logical focal point for something one wishes to emphasize, but calling attention to the center and dividing the space into two equal parts reduces the apparent size of a room or wall.

Symmetrical balance is as simple as *a b a*, the formula from which it is developed, and this simplicity contributes to its popularity. Although few entire homes or rooms are completely symmetrical (utility rules this out), many have symmetrical parts—a centered fireplace flanked by bookcases or niches (Figs. 1-1 and 2-2) or a davenport with identical end tables and lamps at both ends. These are easy to plan and give satisfying stability and repose to parts of the home. Often, however, symmetry is forced arbitrarily or comes out of habit or laziness when there is no real need for it. Frequently then it interferes with convenience. For example, the center of a wall is seldom the best place for a window because a centered window often prevents a logical furniture arrangement, and the center of a wall is almost never the logical place for a door because that leaves two spaces of equal size which may be difficult to furnish unless the room is very large, and it brings traffic into the room's center. Symmetrical balance is indicated (but not dictated) when—

- a formal, reposed effect is wanted.
- focusing attention on something important is desirable.
- use indicates symmetry.
- contrast with nature is sought.

5-3 Symmetrical balance seems formal and static.

It is a good way to achieve orderly organization. Use it when it comes naturally and easily, but do not force it because you believe it to be "correct." Combine it with asymmetrical balance for variety and utility, but have one or the other dominant.

Asymmetrical balance, also known as informal, occult, or active, is that type in which the visual weights or attractions on each side are equal but not identical. Here we apply the principle of the lever or the teeter-totter—weight multiplied by distance from center—and place heavy visual weights near the center to balance those of lesser attraction further from the center. There are countless examples of asymmetrical balance around us:

- Our own bodies (and those of animals) when seen from the side or in almost every position we normally assume, and all of the larger aspects of nature—trees, hills, rivers, lakes and clouds.
- Buildings or gardens designed to harmonize with their natural surroundings.
- Buildings planned with careful attention to efficient use of space.
- Furniture arrangement in a room planned for convenience.

The effects of asymmetrical balance differ markedly from those of symmetry. It stirs one more quickly and vigorously, arousing one's curiosity to see what makes the object well-balanced. Because it is less obvious than formal balance, it tends to attract attention and to set the observer thinking. It suggests movement, spontaneity, informality, or even casualness, and may well be filled with surprise. Being subject to no rigid rules, asymmetry allows full freedom and flexibility in arrangements for utility as well as for beauty and individuality. In a somewhat contradictory fashion we like asymmetry because our bodies are almost always in informal positions and we enjoy freedom from restraint; we like symmetry because we are basically symmetrical and it gives us a reassuring sense of established order.

Asymmetrical balance is indicated when—

- an informal, flexible character is desired.
- an effect of spaciousness is wanted.
- use suggests asymmetry, as it does in house and room plans, landscape design, and furniture arrangement.
- harmony with nature is a goal.

Contemporary trends toward informal, relaxed living find apt expression in homes planned asymmetrically just as those of the 18th century favored symmetry as a background for the formality of their occupants.

Radial balance is that type in which all parts are balanced and repeated around a center as in the spokes of a wheel or the petals of a daisy. Thus, it is really a type of symmetrical balance in which a number of identical elements meet at a central point. Its chief characteristic is a circular movement out from, toward, or around a center. In the home it is found chiefly in such circular objects as plates and bowls, lighting fixtures, flower arrangements, and textile patterns. It is of lesser importance than the two major types but makes its own special contribution in many small objects.

Remember that balance—

- Establishes equilibrium, which is a fundamental of order and design.
- Can be symmetrical (formal and reposed), asymmetrical (informal and active), or radial (movement around a center).
- Should be predominantly of one type in each home and the dominant type should be the one best suited to your needs and wants; but have

MATT KAHN

5-4 Asymmetrical balance suggests informality and movement.

no hesitancy in introducing the other two when utility, beauty, economy, or individuality make them appropriate.

■ Is complete only when it is four-dimensional.

Two Textiles

The two textile patterns, "Round Dance" and "Square Dance" (Figs. 5-5, 6), provide an opportunity to summarize the preceding discussion of design and to anticipate the next. Both textiles are based on American folk dances and capture their lively spirit. They have a strong sense of recurrence but not the rigid repetition of a military march. "Round Dance," one might surmise, is that moment when partners join hands, poise, and bow to each other. "Square Dance" expresses a lively part of the dance when the dancers weave intricate patterns against the steady beat of the music.

Form Follows Function. Both are drapery textiles for hanging at windows in vertical folds to add interest and softness to a room. Both have patterns that keep their character and over-all design quality when draped.

Variety in Unity. Each pattern is based on one dominant form (or *motif*—a theme or dominant feature) further unified by being joined in horizontal bands, and each has a sub-dominant motif of regularly recurring spots. In both, the dominant forms represent the dancers' figures and movements, the spots express the rhythm of the music.

Variety comes with the slight or marked variations of the two motifs. In "Round Dance" not only do the individual shapes differ from one another, but what appears to be the white "left-over" background is an upside-down repetition of the black forms. Keeping the forms constant but changing the direction and color gives variety *in* unity.

Balance. Textiles by nature are large pieces of material continuous in length and breadth and, with minor exceptions, their design movements should be balanced in all directions. "Round Dance" has horizontal bands of figures counterbalanced by the verticality of the figures themselves. What might have been an excess of up-and-down and crosswise movements is balanced by the diagonal outlines of the figures, their slight diagonal lilt, and the punctuating pauses of the round spots.

"Square Dance" employs much the same means. The horizontal force of the linear patterns is balanced by the longer, thicker vertical lines, and

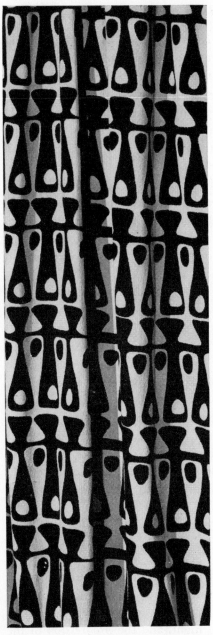

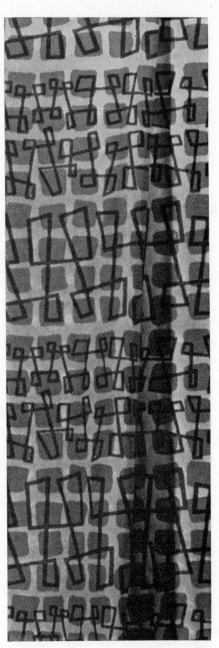

KONWISER FABRICS

PLASTRON, INC.

5-5 "Round Dance," a printed cotton textile designed by Matt Kahn, has a steady, poised rhythm with a lively punctuation of round spots.

5-6 "Square Dance," a printed plastic fabric, has a more vigorous rhythm than does "Round Dance," but the limited range of dark and light makes it less dominant. Angelo Testa, designer.

balance of motion in all directions is strengthened by the background spots which align vertically, horizontally, and diagonally.

Rhythm. As in almost all textiles, these are "repeat" patterns. At first glance the figures in "Round Dance" seem identical, but closer inspection shows that the exact repetitions are many inches apart. Between the repetitions are a series of subtle alternations and progressions. The same is true of "Square Dance" although the shape variation is more quickly noticed.

That the rhythms of the two differ goes almost without saying. The first, based on curves, is poised, slow in tempo, somewhat formal, and each form is distinct. Based on straight lines and angles, "Square Dance" is faster, more active, and the shapes are strongly related to each other.

Emphasis. In textile patterns for draperies, we seldom want strongly concentrated emphasis on parts because that is likely to destroy continuity, but we usually want some parts more dominant than others. The dark forms in "Round Dance" are more dominant than the white and emphasis is slightly concentrated around the white spots.

"Square Dance" when examined from a short distance has three levels of emphasis, the larger linear forms being dominant, the small linear forms secondary, and the spots take a background position. Interestingly, though, at a distance the background spots are most conspicuous and the linear patterns become a subdued tracery.

Over and above such rather academic analysis, both textiles embody in the quality of the lines and forms a vitality that expresses living. Although the designs stand up well under logical study, they are lifted out of the commonplace by the designers' abilities to make forms live—and that is the essence of art.

Rhythm

Rhythm, which we define as continuity, recurrence, or organized movement, is our second major principle of design. It is exemplified in time and in space by everything around us: in time, by the *repetition* of our heart beats, the *alternation* of day and night, and the *progression* of the four seasons; in space, by the repetition of leaves on a tree, the alternation of dark and light stripes on a zebra, and the sequences and transitions of the curves in a river. It is basic in music, poetry, and the dance; in painting and sculpture; and in interior design where it helps "lead the eyes"

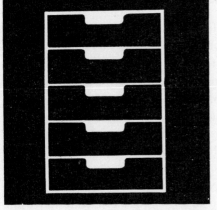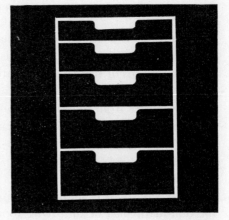

5-7 A chest of identical drawers illustrates repetition of size, shape, and direction.

5-8 Progression of size and shape comes when the drawers decrease in depth.

easily and pleasantly around a room or through a house. Rhythm contributes to the beauty of our homes in a number of ways: unity and harmony result in large part from rhythmic repetition and progression; seeing and understanding what we see are facilitated by the regularity and "expectedness" of a clear strong rhythmic pattern of recurring elements; the character and individuality of a home are in part determined by the character of the fundamental rhythms—slow and heavy, fast and light, regular or variable—and all objects from chairs to houses gain the generally desired quality of "aliveness" through the implied movement and direction that rhythm gives.

Repetition and *progression* are the two primary ways of developing rhythm. *Repetition* is basically as simple as repeated squares or triangles, colors, or textures; but it can be given more intriguing complexity by *alternating* shapes, colors, or textures. Even the most commonplace home is full of repetition, evidence of its universal appeal and also of the fact that simply repeating anything anywhere is not very effective. Some useful guides are:

- Repeat strongly and consistently the forms and colors that underline the character you are trying to establish.
- Avoid repeating that which is ordinary and commonplace.
- Too much repetition, unrelieved by contrast of some sort, leads straight to monotony.
- Too little repetition or progression leads straight to confusion.

Progression is a sequence or transition produced by increasing or decreasing one or more qualities; it is ordered, systematic change. There are progressions of size, shape, and directions; of color from light to dark, dull to bright, or from one hue to another as in green, blue-green, blue; and of textures from rough to smooth. Because progression indicates not only movement but changing movement toward a goal, it is more lively and dynamic than is repetition. It is also a little more difficult to manage and more likely to attract notice, both of which suggest that it be used in important parts of your home.

Progression of size, shape, and direction are handsomely dealt with in the dominant part of the living room in Fig. 5-10. The wall above the fireplace is the largest expanse of unbroken wall and it is horizontal in shape. Next comes the wall to which the vine clings, smaller in size and moderately vertical in feeling. Finally, this progression is brought to a conclusion by the smallest unit, the decidedly vertical pier behind the end table. Accompanying these size and shape changes is one of direction, for these walls show a progression of angles. Notice, too, the way in which the lowered ceiling seems to originate in the fireplace wall, just touches the middle wall, and appears to carry through the vertical pier to the wall beyond. Also, how the ledge and seat begin by paralleling the center wall but then angle out into the room. The regular grid pattern of the concrete blocks emphasizes each change much more than would walls of smooth plaster. Progressions of size, shape, and direction are

MATT KAHN

5-9 A Windsor chair illustrates many kinds of repetition (front legs, back legs, stretchers, size of spindles in back) and many kinds of progression (all of the curves, the direction of the spindles, and the heights of those above the arm rests).

5-10   The walls in this living-room corner have a pronounced progression from large to small size, from horizontal to vertical shape, and in their angular placement.   The uniform concrete blocks set up a steady, quiet repetition.   Blaine Drake, architect.

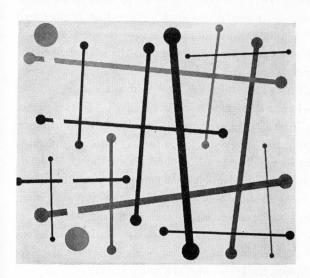

5-11   Progressions from long to short, thick to thin, black to light gray, horizontal and vertical to diagonal, bring life to this variation-on-a-theme design for a textile by Angelo Testa.

diagrammatically illustrated in "Stirs," the textile pattern in Fig. 5-11. Fifteen similar shapes, none duplicating any other, progress (but not with perfect consistency) from large near the center to small toward the edges. This pattern equally well demonstrates some of the possibilities of variations on a theme, a kind of diversity in oneness.

One should decide on the dominant rhythm in house, furniture, and garden just as he should on the dominant type of balance, then follow it consistently but not slavishly. Call your tune and then dance to it, varying the step only when there is good reason. Some people prefer the gay, light, whimsical rhythms found in the curves of 18th-century Rococo furniture (Fig. 6-14) while others prefer the more sturdy measured sweep of the Renaissance (Fig. 6-13). Some feel most at home with the clear undisguised strength of straight lines and right angles, others want to temper this rectangularity by rounding some of the corners and edges. Each of these approaches sets up a rhythmic pattern, no one of which is universally better than the others; choose your dominant rhythm to emphasize the dominant character of your home.

Emphasis

Emphasis, our third principle of design, is often referred to as dominance and subordination. It is concerned with giving just importance to each part and to the whole, calling more attention to the important parts than to those of lesser consequence. It has to do with centers of interest, focal points, and "rest areas." Without emphasis, our homes would be as monotonous as a pea-soup fog, and without subordination as clamorous, chaotic and competitive as New York City's Times Square. As a matter of fact, most interiors suffer as much from lack of dominance and subordination as from any other single cause. You have undoubtedly been in many rooms in which everything had about the same dead-level, dispirited quality of non-importance, and you have probably been in rooms in which everything shouted loudly for your attention. Neither is satisfying. Less often, you have certainly seen rooms in which your attention was clearly directed to a few important parts—a substantial fire-place, a fine large piece of furniture, a window with a view—shown to good advantage against quiet backgrounds. In such instances, you feel that the room was planned with conviction and you are neither bored nor overstimulated.   Your attention is held and then released in a pleasantly alive way.

Two steps are involved: first, deciding how significant each part really is; and, second, giving it the visual importance (or unimportance) it deserves.   Determining significance is like separating the flowers from the weeds, but in interior design the problem is not as simple as in this instance because we are not dealing with only two categories—important and unimportant—but with a scale of degrees of importance, such as most important, very important, moderately important, of minor importance, and unimportant.   In planning an interior it might be worth while to list everything in a room under one of these headings.   Here is an example:

Most Important	Very Important	Moderate Importance	Minor Importance	Unimportant
Fireplace	View of garden	Wall treatment	Ceiling	Floor
	Major furniture group: davenport, chairs, end and coffee tables, lamps, large pictures	Radio-phonograph	Draperies	
		Desk	Plants and flower	
		Smaller pictures	arrangements	

If this were your list, you would then consider carefully all the ways and means of making the fireplace dominate the room as a forceful center of interest and of making the floor inconspicuous.   You might make the view of your garden attractive by having a large, quietly curtained window; the major furniture group would direct attention toward the fireplace but also allow you to look at the garden.   The radio-phonograph and desk would be placed for convenience and good light and related to some of your smaller pictures.   The ceiling would be simple, possibly white to reflect light; the draperies would be unobtrusive but perhaps of interesting weave and subtle color to act as a frame for the garden view; and plants and flower arrangements would find their place not too conspicuously throughout the room.   The floor would have a minimum of attention-demanding color, texture, and pattern.   Other conditions would lead to different approaches.   If one were lucky enough to have an extensive view and windows large enough to appreciate it, the view would undoubtedly be rated the most important item in your planning. A collection of good antique furniture might justifiably lead you to concentrate interest on it, or fine Oriental rugs might become the focal center of a room.

Many, however, do not have an impressive fireplace or view, a collection of noteworthy furniture or rugs. What then? A wise procedure under such circumstances is to concentrate your spending on one large, important piece of furniture, locate it prominently and augment its attractiveness by grouping smaller furniture and accessories around it. Funds permitting, purchase one or two other good articles not quite as emphatic as your major piece and make them the centers of secondary groups. If you are just beginning and cannot afford even one good piece of furniture, you might place emphasis on an out-of-the-ordinary color scheme achieved inexpensively by painting walls, ceiling, furniture, and maybe the floor, so that the color harmonies and contrasts of the whole room become noteworthy. The essence of all this is: emphasize a few things, subordinate the remainder.

This has been done in the room shown in Fig. 5-12. A simple but well-proportioned sofa has been made important by placing it in front of an intriguing map of Paris on the wall, behind a distinctive coffee table, beside an end table holding a sparkling lamp, and then covering the floor with a long-pile, cotton rug. Inexpensive geodetic survey maps of your area or cost-free road maps could be substituted for the Paris map, but if they are to do the job, they must cover enough wall space to be impressive.

What are some of the ways and means of establishing emphasis?

- Decide on the levels of importance of different parts of your home. Play up the strong points and subordinate the others.
- Limit the number of interesting centers. One dominant and two or three sub-dominant centers are about as much as the typical room can take. Do not have every room, every wall, every furniture group equally exciting.
- Arrange the parts to emphasize the important ones. Central positions are conspicuous. Also, an object gains importance if "built up" with others less important, a practice widely followed (for beauty as well as use) in relating tables, chairs, lamps, and pictures to a sofa.
- Use the attraction of visual weights wisely. Large forms, intense colors, bright lights, contrast or opposition, and anything unusual or unexpected compel our attention.

5-12 A large wall map helps greatly to make this part of the room dominant. The map, however, does not overshadow the furnishings.

THE STYLIST MAGAZINE

5-13 Dominance also comes when furnishings, perhaps subordinate as individual pieces, are grouped in a strong pattern.

- Repeating anything increases its importance. Repeating one color or one form makes it more dominant, not in the "center of interest" sense but as an impressive total.

Two day beds with assorted pillows, a corner storage unit, a distinctive lamp, and a row of framed prints join their individualities to make a corner of a room worth looking at, as in Fig. 5-13. Here the emphasis is less on one piece than on a carefully related group.

Other Principles

If the forms follow their intended functions, exhibit variety in unity, balance, rhythm, and emphasis, an interior will more than likely be esthetically satisfying. There are, however, several other concepts or principles that deserve discussion.

Harmony, defined as consonance, concord, or agreement among the parts, is almost indistinguishable from unity and springs from the same sources, such as emphasizing a single motivating idea and making good use of repetition and similarity.

Proportion is generously defined by Webster as "the relation of one portion to another, or to the whole . . . symmetry; harmony; balance." If used to indicate relationships of all sorts, proportion is undoubtedly the most important design principle, but it attains this importance by becoming so all-inclusive that it is difficult to apply. We can, however, limit its meaning to *shape relationships,* as is frequently done in art discussions. Then we are faced with defining pleasant shape relationships. Enormous amounts of time and energy have been expended in trying to reduce pleasant proportions to an easily applied formula. It would be a great convenience if a foolproof system that would hold good in all cases could be developed. Up to the present, however, it is abundantly clear that there is no set or system of proportions which either experts or laymen find consistently to be the "most pleasant." True it is that the so-called Golden Section often gives safe, pleasant effects. It is achieved by dividing a line, area, or form so that the smaller segment has the same ratio to the larger as the larger has to the whole. The progression $1:2:3: 5:8:13:21$ . . . (in which each term is the sum of the two preceding) approximates this relationship. For those who want formulas this is as good as any, but its possible applications are limited and its effects uncertain.

All admonitions and efforts to find "perfect proportions" fall into their true insignificance when we deal with real problems involving use, economy, individuality, and materials. Few persons complain that a fork or a floor-lamp base is poorly proportioned because it is long and thin, that a soup bowl or a sofa is ugly because it is low and broad: they are shaped that way for very good reasons which we all know. Do we throw the whole concept of proportion out the window because some writers have ossified it? No, because it is clear that the most pleasantly proportioned shapes are those characterized by *moderation, simplicity,* and *comprehensibility*—those that are not extreme, complicated, or difficult to understand—qualities worth remembering in anything we do. But it does lead us to look with great suspicion on any rules or formulae.

Scale, referring to *size relationships* between parts or between the parts and the whole, is closely allied to emphasis. Scale is based on the physical dimensions of our bodies and on our spiritual needs; it is expressed in the actual size of objects and the size and character of their detail. In interior design, our most important consideration is this "human scale." Physically, the typical person stands between five and six feet tall and weighs between 100 and 200 pounds, and these figures act as a yard-stick for basic sizes of rooms, furniture, and equipment. Well-scaled homes make us look and feel like normal human beings, not like midgets or giants, because they are in human scale. Scale helps us appreciate size by clues, contrasts, measuring sticks. Thus, a great plain really looks larger if there is one tree on it, a sandy beach if there are a few rocks. These, we say, give it scale. Homes need this, too. Patterned or textured draperies and upholstery can give scale to windows and furniture. A small window or chair looks larger if the pattern is small, smaller if it is large. Accessories are usually the final notes in scale.

Consistency of scale is a prime virtue in any interior; deviate from it only with good reason. High building and maintenance costs have made today's house considerably smaller than the house of fifty years ago, and to compensate for this reduction in size it is smaller in scale. So is the great majority of contemporary furniture. Massive chunks of wood heavily carved, and bulbous upholstered chairs and sofas which crowd a small room are rapidly giving way to slender unadorned wood and metal supports, upholstering that is light in weight and small in bulk. It is a normal process of suiting the scale of our homes to their size. Watch the scale of your home as carefully as you watch your weight. Do not crowd your space and your family with overpowering furniture and accessories, but do not go to the other extreme either of having every-thing minute and delicate. In short, be sensible.

The illustrations up to this point have shown rooms and furnishings in moderate scale. We adapt ourselves readily, however, to a range of different scales *provided all elements are consistent.* Look carefully at the two rooms shown in Figs. 5-14 and 15. Two rooms for contemporary Americans could hardly be less alike, yet each is excellent in its way, for its intended purpose. The difference in scale is startling. Contrast the two fireplaces. The first is made small in scale by the delicately detailed tile border, the refined and graceful wood panels and moldings, and the charming little firescreen. The second is a massive block standing boldly out in the room. Large, textured concrete blocks and vigorously rough stonework stand for what they are with no additional detail. Every detail in each room is consistent, even the bouquet of tulips in one and the banana plant seen through the glass wall of the other. Imagine—if you can—the lamps or the coffee table from the first room in the second. It would be hopelessly overpowered, pathetically out of scale.

5-14 Everything in this delightfully cosy room is very small in scale.

5-15 Everything in this vigorous structure is appropriately very large in scale. Anschen and Allen, architects.

Scale, however, is only one of the factors that so sharply differentiate these two rooms. Some of the others are tabulated below.

	SITTING ROOM	LIVING SPACE
Form Follows Function	Small, intimate, secluded, formal room for a few persons. Forms are delicate, refined, richly detailed.	Large, free, open, informal space for groups. Forms are large, vigorous, rough, and without ornament.
Variety in Unity	Unity through consistent, small scale, curvilinear refinement.	Unity through large areas of a few materials treated naturally; straight lines predominate.
	Pronounced variety of size, shape, material, and ornament. Decided contrast of scenic wall pattern.	Limited diversity—but strong and compelling. Strong contrast of solidity and openness.
Balance	Symmetrical	Asymmetrical
Rhythm	Easy, graceful, and flowing but self-containing.	Strong and direct, angular, continuing from one object to another and beyond.
Emphasis	Many emphatic areas and small spots.	Emphasis is on whole or large units, almost no concentration in small areas.
Harmony	Consistency of all parts.	Consistency of all parts.
Proportion	Slender.	Blocky.
Scale	Small.	Large.

Design is a matter of relationships, and the aims and principles we have discussed are all concerned with the relations among all the parts and the whole of the house. *Form follows function* describes the relationship between shape and purpose; *variety in unity* deals with diversity as related to oneness; *balance, rhythm,* and *emphasis* refer to the ways in which various components are selected and related as means to equilibrium, continuity, and dominance and subordination. Taken altogether they help us achieve beauty and, since they are guides rather than rules, offer us ample opportunities to express our individuality. At one time beauty was regarded as being closely akin to uselessness, individuality was associated with freakishness. Utility and economy, substantial practical partners, were on the other side of the fence. We realize now that such thinking was unsound, that no one of our goals is at odds with the others, that the design of our homes can relate utility, economy, beauty, and individuality if the problem is grasped and solved realistically. But in this chapter we have consciously concentrated on design for beauty.

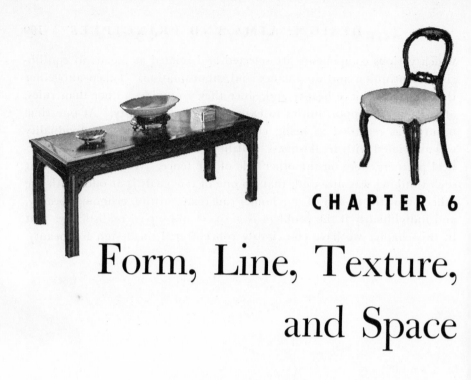

CHAPTER 6

Form, Line, Texture, and Space

WRITERS use words, mathematicians numbers, and musicians sounds to express their verbal, mathematical and musical ideas. In interior design our vocabulary is form, line, texture, space, light, and color, which are conveniently referred to as the plastic elements. Much as chemical elements—oxygen, hydrogen, nitrogen, and carbon—make up the compounds of our physical world, the plastic elements combine to make up our visual environment.

FORM AND LINE

Form, defined as three-dimensional shape, mass, or structure, is the most inclusive and unchanging element of our visual world, and therefore deserves first consideration. Area defines the extent of any figure and is usually thought of in two-dimensional terms, as the floor area of a house or the wall and window areas of a room. Line has but one dimension and in interior design is customarily used to describe the outline of a shape or space.

Form shapes the space in which we live by establishing its limits.

Stripped to their barest essentials, the forms around us can be reduced to a few basic geometric solids—cubes, pyramids, spheres, cones, and cylinders and their many variations. These primary, geometric shapes are a good beginning.

Straight, Angled, and Curved

Perfect cubes are seldom found in interiors, but three-dimensional rectangles are the most common forms and spaces in interior design today. So general is this boxlike shape, so deep in our thinking, that it seems strange we have no term to describe it unless it is because the word *room* has come to mean this shape for most persons. In part, our homes have this rectilinear character because the right angle, so easy to handle on designers' drafting boards, is well-understood by carpenter and mason and one of the simplest for machines to produce. Right angles also always fit snugly together, a fact of some importance under a system in which the multitudinous parts of a building come from many sources to be assembled on the job, when the furnishing of a house including replacements is a long-time process, and when space for living is becoming increasingly expensive. To be sure our rooms and furniture could be based on the circle or ellipse as is the Eskimo igloo or the African grass hut, or on some many-sided shape as was the American Indian tepee. Contemporary designers have experimented with shapes other than rectangular and produced stimulating results, but only exceptionally have they been made the nucleus of interior design; on the other hand, landscape design is a natural field for diagonal lines and freely curved shapes.

Not only is the right angle a great convenience to designer, builder, and owner, but it has other qualities that strengthen its universal acceptance. A right angle is a sturdy secure relationship of 90 degrees, no more and no less, and we subconsciously share in its certainty. Further, it is the angle at which active men and animals meet the earth in the most efficient adjustment to the force of gravity. It is in a way fortunate that rectangular forms are so widely accepted and used in our homes, because their repetition sets up an incipient unity and rhythm in even the humblest abode.

In spite of its definiteness, rectangularity can encompass great variety. Cubes can vary in size, color, and texture, and they can rest stably on one side, insecurely on one edge, or precariously on one corner; rectangular

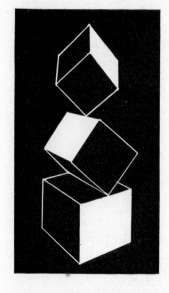

MATT KAHN

6-1 Cubes can rest stably on one side, insecurely on one edge, and precariously on one corner.

forms can do all this and range in shape from an almost linear thinness to an almost cubical fullness. If you want a feeling of motionless stability, you might use a cube; if you want a feeling of motion directed along one line, perhaps toward an important part of a room, consider using a slender rectangular solid; or if you want an effect between these extremes, use an intermediate form. This may seem far afield from our problem of getting livable homes, but on the contrary, it is at the heart of learning how to achieve the character you want in your home. Look sharply at all the rectangular forms you can see from where you are sitting, ignore all of the qualities except shape, and note the differences in visual effect among them.

It is the very qualities of clarity, stability, and rigidity that combine to give rectangular forms widespread acceptance but also give them the harshness we often want to alleviate. History abounds with houses characterized by rambling, unpremeditated plans, or formally combining diverse geometric shapes, roof shapes of great ingenuity, and rooms which are not boxes; historical furniture usually shows clear recognition of the rectangle in its basic design but seldom adheres to it slavishly or flaunts it in our faces. Today there is a tendency away from unthinking rectangularity toward a freer approach to shape. We know, as Frank Lloyd Wright and a few others have long known, that a modern house does not have to look like a shoebox inside or out: roofs can be pitched to add impact to the exterior and considerable spatial interest to the interior if ceilings follow the lines of the roof; wings can meet the main body of the house at angles other than 90 degrees, as they frequently do in the so-called Ranch house; and one or more walls of a room can be oblique. Davenports, chairs, and tables, but not as yet beds and storage units, can be effective with a minimum of right angles. But—and it is a large one—in nearly every instance these deviations from conventional practice are expensive and unless handled with sensitivity and certainty may look merely awkward or weak. The right angle has a pure, strong, absolute character, its own qualities of beauty, which make it extremely useful and pleasant if, as with everything else, it is not overused. Naturally, it does not have to be used alone.

MATT KAHN

MATT KAHN

6-2 Actually rigid, triangles seem flexible.

6-3 Curves are the most variable of all forms.

MATT KAHN

6-4 Circles and spheres ordinarily serve as small-sized accents.

The pyramid and triangle, also angular, differ most notably from recti-linear shapes in their pointed, dynamic character. Although from a struc-tural point of view the triangle is one of the most stable forms known (its shape cannot be altered without breaking or bending one or more of its sides), it seems to express greater flexibility than does the rectangle—chiefly because the angles can be varied to suit the need. Used occa-sionally and at large size as in the gable end of a pitched-roofed house, it contributes a secure yet dynamic character; used frequently and at smaller scale it is likely to seem nervous and jagged like the cutting edge of a saw. Familiar as they are in an abstract way, triangles find their way into our homes so seldom that when used they assume marked impor-tance, attracting attention and becoming dominant out of proportion to their size. This suggests that when used, they should be used well.

Curved forms remind us of nature—it has been said that "nature ab-hors a straight line"—and bring together continuity and constant change, a lively combination if ever there was one. Curves seem sympathetic to us humans, who live with our curvilinear bodies. Their variety is al-most overwhelming. Circles and spheres are man's and nature's most conservative and economical forms, since they not only enclose the great-est area or volume with the least surfacing but strongly resist breakage and other damage; they are as rigidly defined geometrically as squares and cubes but they do not seem as "set," probably because we cannot forget that balls, hoops, and wheels roll easily; they have an unequaled unity because every point on the edge or surface is equidistant from the center and, especially when accented, this center is a focal point. In our homes, dishes, lamps, a few tables, and some textile patterns mark about the only appearances of circles, an occasional lighting fixture being one of the few true spheres unless one happens to have a crystal ball in the living room or a gazing globe in the garden. In short, circles and spheres ordinarily take their place as small-sized accents welcome for their variety; but rooms with circular bays, curved stairways, and gardens laid out on circular motifs give a pleasant, expanding effect.

Cones have the peakedness of pyramids, but with the angles knocked off; cylinders are substantial, useful, and economical shapes. Much as cones and cylinders resemble each other, there is an important basic difference in that the cone reaches a climactic terminal peak whereas the cylinder could continue forever. Thus the cone is more emphatic and concentrates attention on its focal point. Both are thoroughly familiar to us because they are like the trunk, arms, and legs of our bodies; they are also the basic shapes of the arms and legs on most of our furniture.

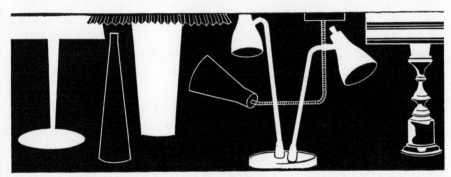

MATT KAHN

6-5 Cones and cylinder are often used for lamp bases and shades.

MATT KAHN

6-6 Furniture legs, too, are usually cones or cylinders, pure or modified.

Furniture legs of wood or metal often taper toward the bottom—making them truncated cones, a refinement that gives them visual lightness and grace—and may or may not terminate in toe- and dust-catching feet. Metal cylinders, pipes, or rods, are becoming increasingly common furniture supports because of their great strength in relation to their size and weight, their durability and ease of cleaning, and the freedom with which they can be bent into pleasing curves (Figs. 4-11, 5-1, and 9-9). Cylinders and cones, the latter usually truncated, are found frequently in the bases of table lamps, the supports of floor lamps, and in vases.

Once we leave the more or less geometric curved forms we encounter limitless variety and uncounted possibilities in the "language of vision." Curves can have the big sweeping force of ocean waves, the large but somewhat gentler drift of clouds, or the relaxation of the course of rivers; they can have the concentrated energy of spiral snail shells, buds of roses about to open, or a snake coiled to strike; they can have the substantiality of the shell of a squash; and they can be as flaccid and spineless as a quiet angleworm. They can be large or small, active or quiet, ascending or descending—in fact, they can express almost anything you can think of. More important, they do! Watch your curves, for they are lively and get out of control easily.

By nature, curves seem best suited to supple, plastic, or malleable materials. The softness of textiles gives them an affinity for the unbroken continuity of curvilinear patterns *if* you want to emphasize the pliability of cloth (but if you want to de-emphasize that softness, to relate textiles more closely to the rectangularity of architecture, angular patterns are in order). Wood is also amenable to rounded forms because they are its natural growth shape and it can be readily rounded by hand or machine. All of the plastic (which means capable of being molded or modeled) materials such as clay, glass, or the synthetic "plastics" conform more naturally to round than to angular forms and, equally important, are more durable without sharp edges. Metal, too, will assume the shape of any mold into which it is poured, hammered, or bent. Although we tend to think of masonry in rectangular terms and see it most often in those shapes, stone can be cut and/or laid, bricks molded, and concrete poured in curves. Every home contains a good many curved shapes and lines, but one begins to wonder why there are not more. It may be that we like the man-made character of straight line shapes as evidence of our ability to create something not found in our environment, and that these non-natural shapes complement and strengthen by contrast the freely curved shapes of nature.

Size and Direction

Form and its counterpart, space, are the basic factors in the expressive character of our homes. In the above paragraphs we have pointed out some of the more important differences in the expressive effects of angular and curved forms. Now we look at size and direction. Large objects, regardless of shape, tend to fill our field of vision, proclaim their importance through sheer bulk, and at least imply strength and power. But they succeed in expressing power only when their shape is as forceful as is their size; otherwise, they are contradictory and express disunified weakness. For example, a coffee table might be designed with curves which *at that size* express grace, but if these same shapes were enlarged three or four times on a large dining table, what was graceful might become elephantine. Perhaps you have seen circus elephants costumed as dancers performing a ballet. The converse is equally ludicrous, as in the too-frequent small houses that display, sometimes almost at paperweight size, the shapes developed for mansions. For maximum pleasantness, the power of the shape should be in agreement with its size, a matter of good scale.

Direction and position also determine expression and pleasantness. Vertical forms and lines express a stabilized resistance to gravity, are upright and upstanding, seem poised; if high enough, they evoke feelings of aspiration and ascendancy. Horizontals tend to be restful and relaxing, expressing a minimum of force, pull, and tension, especially when long; but if they are short and interrupted, they become a series of dashes. Compare the upstanding sense of the vertical in the Haarlem and Philadelphia rooms (Figs. 6-13 and 14) with the relaxing sense of the horizontal in the Japanese and contemporary designs (Figs. 6-15 and 16). Diagonals are as active as a runner's body; unless well supported they seem to be in a never-ending search for equilibrium. Big upward curves, tall ascending vertical lines, and angles neither strongly obtuse nor acute suggest power and uplift; big horizontal curves and long horizontal lines suggest gentleness and quietness; large downward curves and lines express a range of feelings including sadness and seriousness, laziness, weakness and deadness; and small upward or horizontal curves or angles induce feelings of playfulness, merriment, agitation.

6-7 This room brings all types of forms together compatibly. Each one is suited to its function and position.

Emphasize verticals—high ceilings, tall doors and windows, upright furniture—if you want to have people feel like standing straight and tall, behave with at least moderate decorum, and enjoy a suggestion of loftiness or lift. Emphasize horizontals—low ceilings, broad openings, stretched-out furniture—if you want them to lounge comfortably, relax and act informally. Emphasize diagonals—sloping ceilings, oblique walls, furniture and textiles based on diagonal lines—if you want your family and friends to be active and sparkle. Each of these emphases is pleasant if it suits your individuality. Generally, we try to combine horizontals and verticals to secure a degree of balance between uprightness and repose, a balance in which either one may be dominant and the other subordinate, and we vitalize this relationship with diagonals or curves.

Diversity of forms helps give the room pictured in Fig. 6-7 above-average interest. The rectangular outlines of the compactly grouped sofa, daybed, and end tables give this furniture group a solid framework, but with the exception of the flower container no other rectangles are to be seen. Even these pieces are not defiantly angular. Upholstery and pillows have rounded edges and their supporting frames are curved, the recessed finger slots on the drawers have circular ends, and all these pieces are supported on truncated cones. Truncated triangles are unobtrusively but functionally used in the bolsters. Circles make good centers, an observation exemplified by the coffee table with its round top and cylindrical base. The nearly spherical lamp bases are substantial, restful pauses; the shades repeat, but in quite different size and proportion, the shape of the daybed legs. The frames of the pull-up chairs progress from straight to curved lines without a break and the upholstery with its stylized foliage relates to the bouquet. The total effect is restfully horizontal but is counterbalanced by the many, although subordinate, verticals. Not many rooms show such agreeable diversity of forms.

So far our discussion has centered on pure, unadorned form in an endeavor to get you to look beyond the manifest attractiveness of color and beyond the intriguing character of ornament, because basic form is the fundamental of interior design. From time immemorial, however, man has felt the need to enrich form through ornament, and we now turn our attention to that phase of our problem.

Enrichment of Form

Anything as widespread and persistent as ornament must arise from a number of reasons, quite possibly underlying them all being the irresistible human urge to "do something" to a blank surface: many adults doodle on pads of paper and a few have been known to embroider wire-mesh fly swatters; children draw, paint, and scribble on walls, floors, and furniture even without encouragement; savages paint and tattoo their bodies. These are examples of self-expression pretty much for its own sake with little concern for utility, economy, or beauty. One short step removed from this individual creativity is the desire to embellish our environment with patterns or decorations, if not of our own making at least of our own choosing. Other important reasons for ornament are:

- To emphasize and clarify basic form—the form of a cylindrical lamp can be emphasized by carved ridges parallel to the base.

- To bring out potential beauty in materials—ornament on silverware may show to good advantage the way in which silver can reflect light.
- To contribute to the utility and economy of objects—a ribbed handle on a screw-driver gives the user a good grip, patterned floors are easier to maintain than are those of solid color.
- To establish points of emphasis so that our eyes do not monotonously and fatiguingly rove around, but come to rest on points of attachment—decoration around the rim or in the center of a dinner plate.
- To produce variety sufficient to arouse interest and hold attention—the ornamentation around a Colonial fireplace as in Fig. 1-1.
- To develop rhythmic interest—patterns on draperies and upholstery.
- To arouse associations and emotions—the popular floral draperies and dinnerware apparently remind many persons of the beauty of real flowers.

Other reasons for ornament, quite indefensible but so common that they merit mention as warnings, are:

- To disguise poor workmanship and poor materials.
- To minimize the unpleasantness of insensitively designed forms.
- To make evident one's ability to pay for and maintain objects that took long to produce and are hard to keep up.
- To keep otherwise idle fingers busy, thereby relieving simple nervousness, as epitomized by the embroidered fly swatters.

Types of Ornament.   There are two major types of ornament, each having sub-types.

Structural Ornament	*Applied Ornament*
Fortuitous	Naturalistic
Factitious	Stylized
	Abstract

Each kind has its special piece to speak in our interiors.

Structural ornament comes from the materials and processes employed in making an object.

Fortuitous ornament comes from the materials, as in the grain of wood or the veining of marble.

Factitious ornament comes from the process, such as the patterns of woven textiles originating in the weaving process.

6-8 *Left:* This Finnish platter by Tapio Wirkkala takes full advantage of the fortuitous enrichment of wood grain. *Right:* James Prestini's platter employs the wood grain more casually.

In many objects, braided rugs for example, the two kinds of structural ornament are combined.

Structural ornament is integral with the object it enriches and has a frank, natural, fundamental character. Usually it is less subject to physical deterioration such as breakage or fading, and it is less likely to go out of fashion than is applied ornament. These qualities endear it to many contemporaries. Designers and craftsmen sensitive to materials realize the full value of structural ornament. Thus, workers in wood can take full advantage of grain by selecting wood and shaping the piece so that the grain fortifies the form, as it does in the Finnish platter in Fig. 6-8, or the grain can run where it will as in the other platter. Both are interesting, but one looks thoughtfully planned while the other seems accidental. Structural ornament deserves the same kind of planning as does that which is applied.

The range of structural ornament is much more limited than is that of ornament added to the object. Generally, structural ornament is quiet and unobtrusive, qualities which make it appropriate for such large areas as floors, walls, drapery and upholstery materials. Rare and costly are the exceptional highly figured woods and beautifully grained stones. Thus, there are good reasons for applied ornament.

MATT KAHN

6-9 The blossom of an iris can be rendered naturalistically, in stylized manner such as the French fleur-de-lis, or it can be taken as a point of departure for an abstract pattern.

Applied ornament is that added to an object—patterns printed on cloth, plates, or wallpaper, carved in wood or stone, or etched on glass. Its range and variety are limited only by the nature of materials and the imagination of designers. It can be precisely suited to the object's use, form, and material—and it can be distressingly inappropriate.

Naturalistic ornament closely imitates natural, less frequently man-made, objects.

Stylized or *conventionalized* ornament is based on natural or artificial objects but modifies them in the interests of appropriateness to form and material and expressiveness of character.

Abstract ornament is clearly man-created and shows little specific relation to the forms around us.

Three treatments of one motif, an iris, are shown in Fig. 6-9 to point up the differences between naturalistic, stylized, and abstract ornament. Waste no time, though, trying to draw superfine lines between intermediate examples of these sub-types, because they merge imperceptibly with each other. A hair's breadth separates an almost stylized from an almost naturalistic floral pattern, and many motifs are so completely stylized that they verge on the abstract.

Naturalistic ornament, like much painting and sculpture, is representational. It arouses strong associations with the subject-matter represented —flowers, fruit, animals, fish, landscapes, etc.—and the subject-matter becomes a major source of pleasure or displeasure. · Also, the subject-matter largely determines the ornament's character: it is difficult to make fish formal and impressive but easy to get that effect with roses. Further, subject-matter and use should be compatible. This need not rigidly limit marine subjects to the bathrooms, fruits and vegetables to eating and cooking spaces, and flowers and birds to the living rooms, but certainly objects represented many times ought to bear some relationship to the room's use. Whether or not you like to see meat and potatoes put on dishes ornamented with naturalistic flowers and landscape scenes is for you to decide. Naturalistic ornament is likely to be lively and informal and is often seen in large scale bunches of foliage and flowers loosely arranged on textiles. Many naturalistic patterns have little design merit, all effort having been expended in getting a realistic picture of the object. These seldom have more than passing appeal because they have neither the changing intricacy of nature nor the ordered design of art.

Stylized ornament draws inspiration from nature but modifies and organizes the subject-matter to make it compatible with use, form, and material; to emphasize such expressive qualities as dignity or gaiety; and to integrate the forms into designs of lasting appeal. Simplification, conventionalization, exaggeration, and re-arrangement make the natural rhythm more pronounced, emphasize what is most important to the ornament's purpose, and bring all into equilibrium. In general, stylized designs "wear better" than do naturalistic designs because they have been consciously planned to give lasting satisfaction. At its best, stylized ornament penetrates the superficial surface aspects of nature to reveal more fundamental qualities; at its poorest, it merely substitutes smooth curves or meaningless angles for nature's complex richness.

Abstract ornament is clearly man-created. Inevitably much of it is reminiscent of the forms in the world around us, but not of any particular one. Circles, triangles, rectangles, stripes, plaids, free-curves—these are some of the ingredients. Abstract ornament has been used throughout history whenever people wanted pure form that did not remind them of something else. Historically, abstract ornament has tended toward the formal and static, as in the Greek frets and the intricate interlacings of the Mohammedans, but many contemporary abstract patterns are informal and dynamic. Abstract ornament is liked by many people today because it is frankly and sincerely what it is: a man-made design for man's enjoyment. Also, it is an excellent foil for natural forms—people, plants, and live flowers.

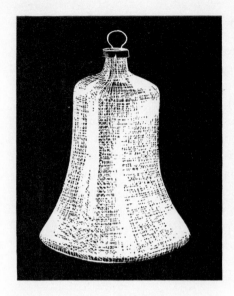 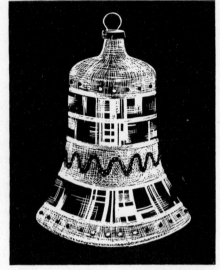

6-10 Unornamented forms have the beauty of simplicity. Ornamented, the same form gains complex richness.

Criteria for Ornament. Ornament should fit function; it should suit form, size, and material; and it ought to be worth while in itself. More specifically:

Ornament frequently touched by the body should be pleasant to feel.
   Resting our arms or back against sharp carving on a chair and handling utensils unsympathetic to our hands are unpleasant experiences.
Association aroused by ornament should be in harmony with function.
   The foliage patterns often used on stoves and radiators some years ago seem unsuitable for anything that gets hot. Naturalistic flowers seem less in harmony with the functions of floors than they do with draperies.
Expressive qualities should be harmonious with use.
   For bedspreads, quieting patterns, not rousing diagonals, are indicated, and the patterns in upholstery materials that suggest comfortable sitting look soft, not hard.
Ornament should enhance form.
   At its best, ornament develops out of the underlying form to strengthen and enrich it. Notice how in the lamp shades in Fig. 6-7 the converging ribs reinforce the up-and-down movement of the truncated cones, while the concentric, horizontal rings remind us that this shape can also be thought of as a series of progressively smaller circles. All

of the furniture in the Powel Room, illustrated at the end of this chapter, is carved to strengthen its curving lines.

Ornament should be related to size and scale of the form.

Boldly patterned draperies can be effective on large windows in large rooms but are usually unsuitable for those small in size and scale. Large pieces of heavy pottery are suitable for bold ornamentation, but after-dinner coffee cups of porcelain are not.

Ornament should be appropriate to the material.

Compare the ornamentation of the chandeliers in the Dutch and Powel rooms. The differences come in good part because one is sturdy, burnished metal while the other is delicate, sparkling crystal. Think of how effective fine, linear decoration can be on smooth, light-reflecting metal or glass; on wood it might look merely scratchy. Or consider how elegant a precise, detailed pattern is when woven in fine silk yarns, and how its character would be lost in coarse wool.

Ornament should be vital in itself.

Ornament can be perfectly appropriate, can exemplify, perhaps slavishly, the aims and principles of design, and still lack spirit and character. Everyday we see much of this listless, inert kind of ornament. In some designs a few rectangles are treated so that they do something for man's spirit. In others, what might have been vital forms are killed outright. No rules can be laid down, nor can this quality be precisely defined. But it makes the difference between the ordinary and the significant, between those patterns in which one loses interest after a look or two and those that are rewarding year after year.

Therefore, the final questions are:

Is the ornament sensitive and alive?

Does it kindle your imagination and raise your spirits?

To say now that applied ornament is not necessary may sound like an anti-climax, but it is true because a genuinely beautiful form skillfully made of handsome materials often needs nothing more. A coffee table topped with handsome marble or fine wood needs no carving *if* it is of excellent shape and workmanship, nor does beautifully woven fabric of good fibers need applied pattern. Regrettably, these are rare and usually expensive, and since most of us have to live with things well this side of perfection, applied ornament can contribute the richness lacking in the unadorned piece. Even so, beware of ornament, because it is often seductive and misleading, blinding us temporarily to basic form; and if it is of poor quality or used injudiciously, it produces a cluttery, frittery impression. That is why many contemporaries shy away from it and believe that it is better to use unbleached muslin at their windows and furniture of unadorned wood rather than run the risk of having their rooms look cheaply overdressed. This, however, does not rule ornament out. Select and place it wisely.

TEXTURE

Texture refers to the surface quality of materials, how they feel when we touch them and how they affect the light that hits them. Run your fingers over your cheek and your hair, the clothes you are wearing, the pages and the cover of the book you are reading, the chair on which you are sitting, and you will get an idea of the variety of textures within your reach. Try some or all of these first with your eyes closed so that you can concentrate on touch alone, then with your eyes open so that touch and sight are fused, as they usually are, into a single experience. Far too often this aspect of our environment is ignored; that we cannot afford to do in interior design.

The texture of any material is chiefly determined by the degree of roughness or smoothness and the difference between the height of the high and low points. But other factors enter in and these are: the distance between the highs and the lows; the shape of the peaks and of the valleys; the hardness and resiliency of the material; and the regularity of the up-and-down pattern. This gives us quite a vocabulary just for textures in our search for pleasantly livable interiors. The infinite combinations possible give us the complex differences between striated or ribbed plywood and smoothly sanded wood; smooth, frosted, and ribbed window glass; cork and sponge rubber; brocade, leather, and bricks.

Texture serves us in a number of ways. *First,* it affects our sense of touch and therefore is of great importance in everything we touch. Upholstery fabrics are good examples. If rough and harsh, they can be actually irritating. If too smooth and shiny, they feel and look slippery and cold. Those most generally liked are neither excessively rough nor smooth. *Second,* texture affects light reflection and thus affects an object's appearance. Very smooth materials—satin, mirrors, and polished metals—reflect light brilliantly, attracting our attention and making their colors look clear and strong.   Moderately rough-surfaced materials—burlap or unglazed earthenware flower pots—absorb light unevenly because of their textures; this makes their colors look less intense and darker and tends to make the object unobtrusive.   Very rough surfaces set up vigorous patterns of light and dark which change markedly with changing illumination.   *Third,* texture is a factor in household maintenance: remember that smooth, shiny surfaces are easy to clean, but that they show everything; rougher surfaces call less attention to foreign matter but are harder to clean; and smooth surfaces with a textural pattern combine most of the good qualities of both.   *Finally,* texture is a type of ornament and a source of beauty.

Because texture is ornament, the same criteria apply to both.   *Use* comes first—deep-pile carpets can serve well in living rooms, not at all well in activity rooms or kitchens.   Generally, one expects harmony of texture with *form, size,* and *scale* unless contrasting textures have been deliberately chosen for a specific effect.   Each *material,* too, has its own textural possibilities and limitations.   Silver, for example, can be rough, but it then loses much of its distinctive beauty.   Because texture is a source of beauty, the aims and principles of design are useful guides in selecting and organizing it in our homes.

Moderate and harmonious are the words to describe the textures in the living room in Fig. 6-7, but they vary from smooth to moderately rough. Smoothest of all is the glass table top.   Smooth, also, are the wood (but one *sees* the grain), the metal legs (but they have a spun finish), and the ceramic lamps (which are smooth but not glistening).   The upholstery fabric on the chairs is quite smooth, the rug slightly textured, and the sofa and daybed upholstery and the pillows have more pronounced tactile qualities.   Now, look carefully at the selection and distribution of textures in Figs. 6-13, 14, 15, and 16.   Then, when you read Chapters 8, 9, and 10, keep in mind that texture is one aspect of materials.

Our tale of texture would stop here if materials had exactly the textural effect we want plus many other qualities—but chiefly ease of maintenance.   Ease of maintenance is closely allied with smoothness and hardness, neither of which always warms the heart or satisfies the eyes. To remedy this, contemporary designers have given us many materials that have applied designs with a simulated textural effect.   Linoleum, vinyl tile, and plastic-impregnated wall and furniture surfacings are frequently seen in patterns resembling textures.   The same is true of carpets, drapery and upholstery fabrics. The best of these are abstract applied art, not imitative of specific natural objects, but in them one is far less conscious of "pattern" as it is generally defined than of a surface made lively or rich—and easier to keep that way—with color and shape variation as illustrated in Figs. 13-6, 7, 8, and 9.

Getting Inside of Form

Our discussion has dealt with form as though it were always solid and viewed or felt from the outside, because this provides us with an easy introduction. But a moment's reflection tells us that there are very few solid forms in our homes (most of them are hollow) and that their hollowness is what concerns us most. To be sure we can look at the exterior of a house and appreciate its masses, outlines, and textures with no thought of what happens inside, and we can look at a chest of drawers in the same way. Looking at form from the outside is important, but far less so than studying form from the inside, because it is there that things really happen. We live inside the house and garden, store our possessions inside the chest of drawers; the outside is primarily a series of enclosing surfaces, a protecting shell. Once we get inside of form, we are dealing with space, and this brings us back from ornament and textures to the most important plastic element in contemporary interior design.

SPACE

Space extending and enclosing are combined in furniture-designer and architect Charles Eames' own experimental home (Figs. 6-11, 12). A light steel framework, not unlike a boy's Erector set, gives a structural system that permits great freedom in the location of walls and choice of materials because their only function is to subdivide space. Glass, wood, and prefabricated-cement panels left their natural gray color or painted white, black, and primary colors are fastened where transparent or opaque planes are needed. No ordinary structural system would have allowed this kind of liberating spatial effect.

The major portion of the group-living zone is a lofty, unimpeded volume from which one not only can look in almost every direction but finds it pleasant to do so. Although protected from the elements, one is not inhibited. In contrast to this space opened for activity is the adjacent

PHOTOGRAPH BY JULIUS SHULMAN

6-11 Charles Eames' moderate-sized home appears tremendously spacious because one can see in so many directions.

6-12 The conversation center of Eames' house provides desirable enclosure in contrast to the extending space around it. Notice the unusually handsome fortuitous ornament in the wood panel.

compact sitting area screened by storage walls. Its low ceiling and different floor treatment add to its feeling of quiet relaxation. Daylight floods the activity area, but the sitting zone is only moderately bright. They supplement each other in satisfying two basic spatial needs of man—for the open and the enclosed.

Architecture has been aptly referred to as "space enclosed for a reason" and interior design might well be called "space enclosed for living." The space enclosed literally shapes our lives. In cramped or poorly planned space family frictions develop, tensions find no release. Adequate, efficient space is no guarantee of successful home life but it contributes toward that goal.

Form and space are inseparable because space is defined or modeled by the forms enclosing it. Thus, all that has been said about form applies to space. It can be small or large in actual size and it can be large or small in scale; straight, angled, or curved in shape; static or dynamic in feeling; predominantly horizontal or vertical in direction; emphasized by making the enclosing forms unobtrusive, subordinated by making them rich in interest. The space inside our homes can flow openly and flexibly throughout, it can be sharply divided into separate rooms, or, most sensibly, it can be open in group living areas, closed in those planned for private life. Indoor and outdoor space can be merged with large windows and doors, sheltered terraces and gardens, or the two can be rigidly separated. It is a vocabulary without limits.

How to enclose space inexpensively and well has always been a fundamental problem of architecture, and it has seldom been more acute than now with today's high construction and maintenance costs. While waiting hopefully for some epoch-making discovery, we might as well settle down to making the space we now have or expect to have as effective as possible. How can we design space for maximum livability? First comes analysis of activities and possessions as the basis for enclosing amount and kind of space needed for your pattern of living. Second, consider carefully original cost and upkeep. Third, give serious thought to making that space beautiful. Fourth, be yourself and you will achieve the kind of individuality you need.

The chances are that having done the above you will want to make your space look every bit as big as it is, probably bigger than its actual dimensions. In general a sense of spaciousness is gained through:

- Unity and harmony
- Asymmetrical balance
- Continuity and recurrence
- Minimizing emphasis and contrast
- Subordinating form and ornament
- Small-size and small-scale furnishings
- Receding colors

And here are some specific ways and means, purposefully stated in extremes, from which you can select those best suited to your needs.

Form and Line

- Limit the number of pieces of furniture to those really needed. Avoid crowding too much furniture into a small room. Many rooms seem crowded because they have too much furniture, leaving too little free space. Buy or keep only what you really need.
- Select small-size, small-scale furnishings. Buy furniture that is no larger than necessary for comfortable use, has supports no thicker than needed to hold it firmly, ornament that is small and unobtrusive. Avoid oversized, overstuffed, boldly patterned chairs and davenports, coarse designs on draperies and rugs (except where these are needed for contrast).
- Arrange the furniture thoughtfully. Organize it in compact, useful groups related to the walls. Keep the center and the space in front of large windows open by limiting the quantity and having the few necessary pieces light and open in design. Put the heavy furniture against the walls, back in corners. Avoid equal spaces between pieces of furniture or furniture groups. Push some of it tightly together, then enjoy a noticeable expanse of free wall space. Avoid symmetrical arrangements and those that look complicated.
- Keep form and line simple and continuous. Cover the floors in one room, or better in several rooms, with the same material from wall to wall; treat the walls in most or all of your home the same way or with only minor variations; use as much of one drapery material as is feasible. Select furniture with a minimum of interrupted lines or forms. Avoid breaking up areas or forms into small unrelated pieces, and minimize small vigorous contrasts. Beware of dominant enclosing frames around pictures, doors, or windows, borders around rugs.
- Emphasize horizontals. Since we are walking rather than flying creatures, horizontal space is of most importance to us, and interiors emphasizing horizontal lines in walls and windows, furniture and draperies seem to gain size. Diagonals, however, are always the longest dimension of an area, and calling moderate attention to them extends apparent space: furniture or a painting placed near the corner of a room and corner fireplaces are examples. Emphasis on verticals gives a lofty sense of airiness very welcome in a large room, but a high ceiling, vertical furniture, or vertical stripes on a wall reduce the apparent size of small enclosures. Avoid equal emphasis on both horizontals and verticals, since it tends to reduce size.

Texture

- Use small-scale textures. Closely woven textiles (including rugs), fine-grained wood, and smooth plaster call attention to the whole area they cover, not to parts of it.
- Have unobtrusive textures predominate. Almost all large-scale textures attract attention to themselves and thereby distract from the space they enclose. So do some of small scale: highly polished metal or smooth opaque glass are insistent and therefore seem to come forward.

Space

- Emphasize spatial continuity. Large windows and glass doors lead the eyes through enclosing walls; large unadorned openings between rooms encourage the eyes to explore the distance beyond, especially when the same material or color carries through. Avoid small openings wherever feasible, except as contrasts.
- Place centers of interest at the ends of vistas. A colorful painting at the end of a hall, an unusual shrub at the end of a garden path make one notice long dimensions.
- Expose as much of the floor as possible. Furniture supported well off the floor on slender legs allows one to see more floor than does furniture with an enclosed base.
- Have one wall in a room deviate from the right angle. A wall curving outward seems to make the room swell out, a diagonal wall lessens the enclosing rigidity of the rectangle. Avoid extremes, though, if you want attention concentrated on space, not tricks.
- Employ illusionistic devices. Mirrors, paintings with deep perspective, and some scenic wallpapers suggest distance.

Light and Color

- Plan for moderately bright general illumination with focal accents. Light should be neither so bright that you see everything at once nor so dark that you fail to notice corners; pools of light can direct attention where you want it.
- Use receding colors. Hazy blues, pale dull greens, smoky lavenders and neutral grays are "distance colors"; hot bright reds, oranges, and yellows seem nearer to you than they are.
- Have one wall different in color or material from the other three. Differentiating one or two walls from the others seems to open the

room.   A wall of glass is the most effective because it really opens the room; next in effectiveness comes the wall of mirrors, but somewhat the same result comes when one wall is covered with wood, cork, wallpaper, or simply painted another color.   Tight, boxy enclosure can also be minimized by having one wall strongly related either to the ceiling or floor in material or just in color.   Avoid contrasts so strong that they call attention to themselves and dispel the intended illusion.

If you are in the unusual spot of having too much space, do just the opposite of what has been suggested above: fill the space with big furniture arranged out in the room away from the walls; emphasize individual elements by frames, centers of interest, varied large-scale ornament and texture; use strong contrasts of vivid colors, call attention to the centers of your walls with paintings or hangings, to the center of your ceiling with a chandelier, to the center of your floor with a table or a rug with a center medallion; and have a predominant scheme of static symmetrical balance—but not all of these in one room at once, please.

Using all the ways and means of emphasizing spaciousness in one room would give a simple, open and cool effect, probably excessively so.   It would verge on the monotonous and lack what most of us think of as home-like qualities.   By no means is this what we advocate.   For one thing, a room so planned and furnished might fail to give the desired effect because it would provide no contrast, no yardstick by which to estimate.   Cool receding colors, for example, have these characteristics exaggerated when seen near small areas of warm advancing colors.   The actual size of small furniture is most readily appreciated when one or two larger pieces or a few large accessories are introduced.   This will become clearer as we look at some historic and contemporary organizations of form, line, texture and space.   Frequently, as the following examples show, they seem to oppose, almost contradict, one another, to gain variety, contrast, and richness.

FOUR ROOMS

From 17th-century Netherlands, 18th- and 20th-century United States, and 20th-century Japan come the four rooms in Figs. 6-13, 14, 15, and 16. They have much in common.   Each is a unified expression of a way of living, and in each the character is so clear that one can readily imagine the manners and clothes of the owners.   In each the architecture is a

6-13   Robust, rectangular vitality and vigorous contrasts characterize the form, line, texture, and space of this room from Haarlem, the Netherlands, dated 1608.

vital part of the whole and contributes as much to the character as do the furnishings.   Each is beautiful in its own way.

Seventeenth-Century Netherlands

Hearty and robust as a Dutch dinner, the Dutch room was designed in Haarlem around 1608.   Form and line are predominantly large size and large scale, vertical, and substantially rectangular in all of the bigger aspects, but many and varied curves together with small scale, intricate detail complement the massive solidity.   The large forms meet each other with abrupt contrast as though each wanted to maintain its independence—the wood paneling hits the plaster wall without transition, the fireplace mantel stands by itself, and even the chairs do not snuggle up to the table.   Within (but not between) these units, there is considerable progression and transition such as the moldings on the panels, the carving on the chair arms, and the whole chandelier design.   Conventionalized, applied ornament is concentrated on important areas and generally is closely related to material and process. The wood paneling and carving has a woody quality, the carved fireplace columns are in the nature of stone, the sculptural enrichment on the metal hollow ware and fireplace utensils has the feel of metal, and the textile pattern is woven in. On the ceramic tiles and dishes, the painted designs are less integrated with the material but are perfectly appropriate.

Textures, like the large forms and materials, are concentrated and contrasting. There is much textural interest at the fireplace but not on the wall behind. The entire paneled wall and the ceilings are large areas of subordinate textural interest, the table with its cover and accessories and the chairs are almost as lively as the fireplace.

Space is handled in the same forthright manner as is form. The contrast of wood and plaster walls opens the room a little, the dark heavy ceiling makes the room appear lower, and the strong similarity of ceiling to wood wall establishes continuity between top and one side. On the whole, though, the space is organized as though the designers said, "This is it. Let it be."

Asymmetric balance characterizes the room as a whole, but the individual units are symmetrical. The dominant rhythms are slow and chunky, but a few subordinate rhythms (chair arms and chandelier) are more rapid and graceful. Large units or areas—the whole fireplace, the whole wood wall, and the major furniture group—are emphasized against the plain plaster walls and inconspicuous floor, but there are no centers of interest to fix one's attention. Each object in the room states its character without apology or compromise. Why, then, are they compatible? In part they are unified by their forthright individualities and in part because deep down under their differences they all belong to the same family.

Eighteenth-Century United States

One hundred and sixty years after the Dutch room, the room from the Powel house (Fig. 6-14) was designed in Philadelphia. Elegant, graceful, and "refined," it epitomizes the living quarters of a few American colonists in 1768.

Form and line here, too, are predominantly vertical, but their size and scale are small, and delicate, graceful, continuing curves come into full swing. The rectangular room shape and wood paneling give a stately, measured rhythmic background against and with which the curves play.

6-14 This room from the Powel House, Philadelphia, dated 1768, shows the refinement and ordered gaiety of 18th-century American design at its height.

Although the room is spacious, only the scenic wall design and the fireplace (notice how small the chair near the fireplace looks) are large. Harmony (through repetition, progression, or similarity) among the parts is much more marked than in the Dutch room. Throughout there is a feeling of forms going beyond their confines—chair legs curve out at the bottoms and chair backs out at the top; mirror and painting frames expand more than they enclose their contents; the broken pediment above the painting opens toward the ceiling; and the plaster ceiling ornament and effervescent crystal chandelier can scarcely contain their gay movement. Applied ornament is used liberally but judiciously, always with sufficient quiet areas. Structural ornament is found only in the wood grain of furniture and floor, the veining of the fireplace stone.

All textures are smooth to touch. Roughness and sharp corners are minimized for fundamental unity of one plastic element. That they do not look monotonous is because the shapes are intricate and varied and the materials are many. Thus the room has quite a range of visual but not tactile (touch) textures.

As with the Dutch room, there was no reason to expand or contract the visual space, but the light colors, small size and scale, repetitions and continuing rhythms make one appreciate every inch. The ceiling ornament certainly expands this area by inviting one to follow the curves near its boundaries. What does the scenic wall covering do? Having one wall treated differently, you will recall, tends to enlarge a room, but this design intriguingly combines two somewhat contradictory qualities. Its complexity and the large (for wall patterns) size of the buildings makes one look at it and would bring it well forward, *but* the lines and forms recede diagonally into the distance. We might say that attention starts in front of the wall and ends behind it to give an expanding feeling of movement in space. By the rule-book we would condemn this as inconsistent, as falsifying the wall's basic flatness, but if we look at it with eyes and minds unclouded by rules the effect is superb.

Strict, almost insistent symmetrical balance marks every large form and would make the room passive were it not for the abundant curves. Informal balance is confined to the painting, small sculptures, and wall covering. The flowing, slender rhythms are stabilized by the rectangular paneling. This room clearly has a center of interest—the family portrait. Between it and the unobtrusive floor are many transitional steps of dominance and subordination. Unity comes with a hundred big and little repetitions plus countless progressions, but basic to the unity is the idea from which all these sprung.

Twentieth-Century Japan

The Japanese room, Fig. 6-15, has a remarkably calm serenity. Essentials alone, and these selected and organized with a subtle perfection, make one feel like taking a long, deep breath. There is no trace of hurry or tension, clutter or confusion, insistence or demand. A word or a gesture here could be fully appreciated.

Simple rectangles, beautifully proportioned and sensitively varied in size and shape, dominate. Rounded forms in the upright poles, wood jar, circular disc, and the lamp shade complement them. Diagonals and free forms have been carefully saved for the flower arrangement and scroll. Size and shape are small. Structural ornament is almost everywhere, applied ornament is minimal because the varied materials, sizes, and shapes are meant to be seen. Textures are those that come in the

6-15 Simple dignity and repose describe the general character of this Japanese room.

materials used, and they are predominantly but not conspicuously smooth and refined.

The very small space seems free and open because the scale has been adroitly handled and the forms efface themselves to let you see what they enclose. The enclosure is not boxy but is modulated in three dimensions. The built-up units, horizontal panel behind the light, modular (a *module* is a repeated unit of measure) floor mats defined by black strips make each enclosing plane significant. Informal balance brings spaciousness and movement, the rhythms are quietly straight line repetitions and progressions, and dominance is unequivocably held by the scroll and flower arrangement.

No better example of unity arising from a way of living could be found.

Twentieth-Century United States

From and for our country and period comes the living room designed by Gordon Drake (Fig. 6-16), illustrating some leading contemporary

6-16 Straightforward forms, continuing lines, and natural textures enclose space for living today in this house designed by Gordon Drake.

trends. It has a substantial forthrightness something like that seen in the Dutch room and there is more than a hint of the peaceful continuity of the Japanese. With the 18th-century Philadelphia room it has almost nothing in common, but it is fundamentally similar to our 17th-century interiors.

The forms and lines are youthfully vigorous, simple and angular, continuing, and dominantly horizontal. When contrasts come, as they do in the verticality of the fireplace or the openness of the wall beyond the sofa, they come with decisive force. The pitched ceiling and floor pattern introduce harmonious (angular) diversity (diagonals). Comparatively moderate in scale, it is somewhat larger than the Japanese or 18th-century rooms but it is smaller than the Dutch. This medium scale makes sense because a larger scale would crowd the available space and a smaller scale would separate it sharply from the outdoors. Ornament is entirely *of* the material, or the process, or both. Textures, too, are natural or structural, but they range from the smooth uniformity of the light-reflecting ceiling panels through wood and floor covering to the vigorous brick-work. Running through the center of the house is a backbone-like beam which supports the roof, contains lighting fixtures and heating conduits, and unifies the house's skeleton as do our own spinal columns. From it the ceiling beams spread like ribs.

This is a moderately small room and there was need to make the space seem more extensive. The means used are horizontality of walls and furniture; integration of major furniture and walls; pitched ceiling of contrasting color; asymmetric balance; long, uninterrupted lines and continuity with outdoor space. Although enclosing planes hold interest and

PHOTOGRAPH BY JULIUS SHULMAN

6-17 Indoor and outdoor living areas when merged give a feeling of great spaciousness. Richard Neutra, architect.

have their moments of dominance, the real emphasis is on space for indoor-outdoor, informal, contemporary living.

There are other contemporary ways of organizing form, line, texture, and space—but this is one kind of living space for us today. Another approach is illustrated in Fig. 6-17. Two glass walls visually join living room, terrace, and view. Wide, sliding glass doors physically open the inside to the outside. Although all of the enclosing surfaces are of handsome materials, they are subordinate to the volumes they envelop—they are simple planes shaping space for living and are appreciated after the space itself has been enjoyed. The hardly noticeable glass with its minimal frames is a transparent screen against the weather, and the wood ceiling of the living room continues over much of the terrace. On the floors, however, there is a clear distinction between the soft, textured, wall-to-wall carpeting and the durable flagstone paving.

In comparison with Gordon Drake's design, the one by Richard Neutra is simpler and smoother, somewhat more formal and precise. Which do you prefer?

CHAPTER 7

Light and Color

LIGHT AND COLOR are inseparable. Without light there is no color, and light is always colored. Our world is made visible through light entering our eyes, and despite the importance of our other senses, most of us still hold that "seeing is believing."

Although color has always been considered a fundamental of interior design, only recently have we become fully aware of the importance of light as a design factor in our homes. In the past few decades the lighting of homes has undergone a major revolution. Window walls, clerestories, and skylights flood rooms with natural light, and the tremendous advances in lighting fixtures make possible effects scarcely dreamed of in our grandmothers' age—but we are anticipating the discussion in Chapter 12 of natural lighting as a major phase of window design and the treatment of artificial illumination in Chapter 15. In this chapter we simply introduce the subject of light to emphasize its importance along with form, line, space, texture, and color as one of the major plastic elements.

Light is a form of energy. Physicists do not know as yet whether this energy is some kind of wave motion, some kind of tiny particles, or both of these combined. Of importance to us, though, are these known facts:

- Light travels in straight lines until it hits something.
- Light varies amazingly in brightness, the light from strong sunlight being approximately 400,000 times that from the full moon.

- White or apparently colorless light is composed of all the colors of the spectrum.
- When light strikes an object, it may be reflected, absorbed, or allowed to pass through it. Usually all three of these happen but in differing amounts depending on the degree of transparency or opacity of the material and its surface qualities.
- Light reflected from smooth surfaces is bright and sharp, diffuse when reflected from rough surfaces.
- Objects illumined by small, sharp light-sources show strong contrast of light and dark, less contrast if the source of light is broad and diffuse, and almost no contrast if evenly lighted from all sides.
- Shadows from objects lighted by small, sharp beams are usually hard, sharp and dark; soft and spread-out if the light source is broad and diffuse; and multiple and overlapping if the light comes from more than one direction.
- Strong contrasts of brightness and darkness are dominant and dramatic, but fatiguing to the eyes; uniform illumination is unexciting to the spirit but easy on the eyes.
- Bright light is stimulating, low levels of illumination are quieting.
- Good lighting illuminates objects, but the light source does not intrude on our vision.

Because color and light are closely allied, we turn now to color.

COLOR

The colors of objects we see are the result of two factors: first, the way in which the object absorbs and reflects light; and second, the kind of light that makes it visible.

When light strikes an opaque object, some of its hues are absorbed and others reflected. Those that are reflected give the object its color quality. A lemon, for instance, absorbs almost all color rays except yellow; yellow paint does the same thing. White objects reflect almost all of the colors in light while black objects absorb most of them. We have to say *almost* because pure colors are very seldom found. The true color quality of an object is revealed when it is seen in white light. Usually, however, light is not completely colorless, and this brings us to the second factor.

The color of light depends on its source and whatever it passes through before coming to our eyes. White (or apparently colorless) light such as that from the sun at noon contains all of the hues of the spectrum—violet, indigo, blue, green, orange, and red—balanced and blended so that the effect is colorless. Light from the moon is bluish while that from open fires or candles is yellowish as is light from typical incandescent bulbs. If the glass of the bulb is colorless, the light remains yellowish; but if the glass is blue, some of the yellow rays are filtered out and the light is white. This should make clear that there are two sources of color in light. In our homes we take advantage of this when we alter the color of daylight with thin, colored curtains or of artificial light with translucent shades that are not white.

Color Theory

Organizing facts and observations on color into a systematic theory is a first step in understanding color relationships and effects. Three different kinds of theories have been developed: physicists base theirs on light; psychologists on sensation; and artists on pigments and dyes. Our interest is chiefly with the latter, but even here a choice must be made among the three widely accepted pigment theories. We shall follow that developed by Brewster, often called the *three primary* or *red, blue,* and *yellow* pigment theory, because it is the simplest and most familiar and leads to effects indistinguishable from those growing out of more complex systems.

The Dimensions of Color

To describe any color you need to tell about three of its characteristics, and these are *hue, value,* and *intensity.*

Hue is the name of the color—red, yellow, blue, green, orange, violet and so on. It indicates warmth and coldness—reds, oranges, and yellows seem warm, blue is cold, and green and violet are moderately cool. Hue also tells the position of the color in the spectrum or on the color wheel.

Value describes only the lightness or darkness of a color, or the quantity of light it reflects. White is the lightest value, black is the darkest and between these extremes you can get as many grays as you wish. But value is not limited to black, gray, and white. Red can be dark, as it is in maroon, light as it is in pink, or some place in between as it is in scarlet or cerise.

Intensity describes the degree of purity or strength of a color, its brightness or dullness, or the quantity of the dominant hue. It refers to the amount of the predominant hue which we see: pure red is completely intense with redness, dull or weak red gives us the sensation of only a little redness. Red can be pure, strong, and bright as it is on fire engines, or it can be neutralized, weak, and dull as it is in old, over-cooked beets.

Let us try describing one of the reds, yellows, and greens from each of the columns in the List of Color Names on page 155.

Color Name	Hue	Value	Intensity
artillery	red	middle	full
baby pink	red	high light	full [1]
Harvard crimson	red	high dark	two-thirds intensity
African brown	red	low dark	two-thirds neutral
golden glow	yellow	low light	full
cream	yellow	high light	full [1]
buff	yellow	low light	two-thirds intensity
olive green	yellow	dark	two-thirds neutral
peppermint	green	middle	full
seafoam	green	low light	full
apple green	green	low light	two-thirds intensity
evergreen	green	low dark	two-thirds neutral

[1] Value is so high that it does not seem to be full intensity.

You can see from this table that "artillery" differs from "baby pink" primarily in *value* but that it differs from "Harvard crimson" in both *value* and *intensity*. Similarly, "golden glow" and "cream" differ principally in value, but both value and intensity distinguish "cream" from "olive green." Unless one uses an accepted term, such as "cream," that is pegged to one color, it is necessary to describe the three dimensions of a color precisely.

HUE

Hues are often classified as primary, secondary, and tertiary.

Primary hues are yellow, blue, and *red* (in the Brewster system) and they are labeled (1) on the Color Wheel, Fig. 7-1. They are called pri-

7-1 Color Charts.

VALUE SCALE   COLOR WHEEL   **INTENSITY SCALE**

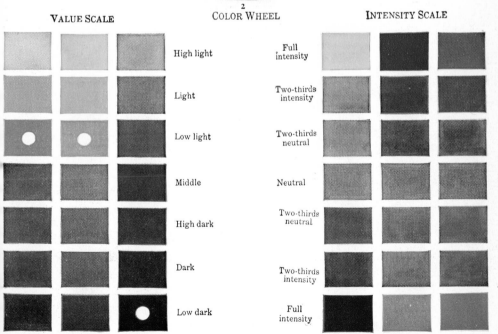

The color wheel shows a sequence of hues in the following order, beginning with yellow at the top and proceeding clockwise: yellow, yellow-green, green, blue-green, blue, blue-violet, violet, red-violet, red, orange-red, orange, yellow-orange.

The value scale shows seven values each for the three hues: green, orange, and violet. Those containing white disks are at full intensity.

The intensity scale shows two different degrees between full intensity and neutral for six hues. The intensity is lowered by mixing the hue with its complementary, the hue on the opposite side of the color wheel. The dimensions are approximate only. (From *The Art of Enjoying Art* by A. Philip MacMahon as

mary because they cannot be produced by mixing other hues, but when mixed properly they will produce nearly every other known hue. When the three are mixed, the result is theoretically gray but in practice it is brownish.

Secondary hues are green, violet, and *orange* and are labeled (2) on the Color Wheel. Standing midway between the primaries, they result from mixing approximately equal amounts of the two primaries between which they stand.

Tertiary hues are yellow-green, blue-green, blue-violet, red-violet, orange-red, and *yellow-orange.* Labeled (3) on the Color Wheel, these are produced by mixing a primary with either of the nearest secondaries.

The manner in which secondaries and tertiaries are created demonstrates that hues are changed by adding neighboring hues. Red, for instance, became red-violet when it was combined with violet. If more violet were added, the hue would be changed again. The twelve hues on our Color Wheel are the merest beginning because there can be an almost infinite number of hues.

Two other terms need definition.

Complementary hues are those directly opposite each other on the Color Wheel. Yellow and violet, green and red, orange and blue are examples.

Analogous hues are those next to each other such as yellow, yellow-green, and green; or red, red-violet, and violet-blue.

With our basic terminology in order we are now ready to look at the ways hues affect not only each other but our feelings, as well as the apparent size, distance, and outline of an object.

How do hues affect one another? How are harmony and contrast produced?

What happens when complementary hues are brought together? That depends on *how* they are brought together.

- Red and green mixed in proper amounts produce gray.
- Red mixed with a little green becomes duller, grayer, or lower in intensity.
- Red placed next to green brings contrast: both seem more intense and the effect is strong, bright, and sometimes harsh.

Generalizing from these examples we can say that mixing complementary hues neutralizes the color; putting them next to each other intensifies each hue and leads to contrast.

What happens when analogous hues are brought together? .

- Green and blue mixed produce blue-green, the exact hue being determined by the proportions of each.
- Green next to blue produces harmony.

Thus, mixing related hues produces another hue; putting them next to each other leads to harmony.

This is the basis for producing with hues sharp contrasts, soft harmonies, and the infinite number of intermediate effects.   Place blue against orange, red against green, or yellow-green against red-violet and there is immediate feeling of excitement, vibration, lively opposition— and also of full, well-rounded balance.   Blue, blue-green, and green are restful because they are closely related.   Similarly, yellow, yellow-orange, and orange introduce no sharp conflict but their harmony is not as quieting as with the cooler hues.

Intermediate degrees of harmony are produced when hues neither adjacent to nor opposite each other on the Color Wheel are combined. Yellow and blue-green, for example, give an effect midway between harmony and contrast because blue-green is midway between yellow and its complementary violet.   Yellow and green, being closer together, bring a little more harmony; yellow and blue, which are further apart, introduce more contrast.

Thus hues, when placed side by side, can produce effects ranging from close harmony to strong contrast depending on the distance between them on the Color Wheel.

What are warmth and coolness of hue and what are the effects?

Each hue has its own "temperature" because the rays at the red end of the spectrum are physically warmer than those at the violet end.   The effect is reinforced by our association of reds, oranges, and yellows with the sun and fire, of greens and blues with water and ice.   "Red hot" and "blue with cold" are familiar sayings.   Green and violet, however, seem intermediate in temperature because green combines the warmth of yellow and the coldness of blue, and violet appears to have some of the heat of red and the coldness of blue.

Warm hues are *advancing,* cool hues are *receding*.   This has both a physiological and a common-sense basis.   Physiologically, the red rays register behind the eye's retina, and in bringing them into good focus the eye pulls them forward whereas the cool rays register in front of the retina and are pushed back. Everyday experience proves that faraway objects look bluer because of the atmospheric haze than do those nearby, and this leads us to associate cool colors with distance.

The qualities and effects of warm and cool hues can be tabulated as follows:

Warm Hues	*Cool Hues*
Conspicuous, stimulating, cheerful.	Attract less attention, restful, sometimes cold and depressing.
Seem to come toward you.	
Appear to pull objects together.	Seem to recede.
Make objects look larger.	Separate objects seen against them.
	Make objects look smaller.

All such generalizations require qualifications: a very dull or very pale yellow is less conspicuous than a full-intensity blue; noticeably cool colored objects seem less separated against a cool background than against one that is definitely warm; and while red generally makes objects seem larger this would not be true if the background were also red.

Good use can be made of hue warmth and coolness in your home. A too cold, north room can be warmed and cheered by yellow walls or ceiling and curtains, tan or brown rugs, and dull orange or red upholstery; a room can be quieted and cooled with blues, greens, violets, and grays. Miscellaneous furnishings will seem more related to one another against warm walls than against cool, and a sofa upholstered in red or yellow will seem larger than if upholstered in green or blue. Shapes, especially outlines, of objects are emphasized when object and background contrast in hue, an observation you can easily check by placing a blue vase against a blue background and then against one of orange or yellow.

VALUE

The lightness or darkness of a color, the quantity of light it reflects, is called value. White is the lightest value possible, black is the darkest, and between these extremes come the neutral grays and the chromatic hues.

The steps between black and white can be as numerous as one wishes, but seven is a convenient number; adding black at the bottom and white at the top gives a total of nine value steps. Values above the middle are called *light* or *high* (and are often referred to as *tints*), and those below the middle are referred to as *dark* or *low* (and are often called *shades*). The Value Scale in Fig. 7-1 shows the seven value steps for green, orange, and violet.

If you look carefully at the Color Wheel, you will notice that the hues differ in value. Yellow is very light, violet is very dark, and the other hues are graded from the light yellow down to the dark violet. The values in which the hues are shown on the Color Wheel are known as *normal values;* that is, the values most characteristic of each hue. To be sure, yellow can be made so dark that it is almost black and violet can be so pale that it is almost white, but when so treated, yellow and violet lose much of their typical qualities. The normal values of the twelve primary, secondary and tertiary hues correspond to the seven steps in the value scale. Starting at the top and going down both sides, we get:

Value Step	*Hue*	*Hue*
White		
High light	Yellow	Yellow
Light	Yellow-orange	Yellow-green
Low light	Orange	Green
Middle	Orange-red	Green-blue
High dark	Red	Blue
Dark	Red-violet	Blue-violet
Low dark	Violet	Violet
Black		

A moment's reflection will show that we ordinarily think of hues in somewhat this way: yellow, for instance, usually comes to mind as a light, bright yellow—the color of a lemon or a dandelion. Violet usually is thought of as a dark color—the color of a violet or grapes or plums.

How is the value of a hue changed? When we *raise* the value of a hue, we make it capable of reflecting more light. If we wish to *lower* the value of a hue, we reduce the light it reflects. With pigments this is most readily done by adding white or black (although the process of raising or lowering the value of pigments is apt to be accompanied by unavoidable changes in hue and intensity).

How do different values affect each other?

The story here is the same as with hue. Black looks blacker when seen against white than it does against gray, just as red looks redder when seen against green than when seen against orange. In short, strong value contrasts make the dark values seem even darker and the high even higher than they really are, while smaller contrasts tend to reveal values in their true character. Strong value contrasts also tend to separate objects, minimum contrasts unite them.

How do different degrees of lightness and darkness affect our feelings?

High values raise the spirits and stimulate us to be active (as do warm hues) unless they are all so monotonously high that they seem weak and pallid; middle values are relaxing and comforting (as are the intermediate hues); and dark values give one a serious, dignified, perhaps somber feeling. Strong value contrasts, like contrasts in hue, are stimulating. Closely related value patterns are quieting.

What effect does value have on the apparent size of an object?

Usually, but not always, the higher the value the larger the object seems to be. Painting the walls of a room in high values makes it seem to gain in spaciousness; painting a house white makes it look larger than it would if painted dark brown. *But* the value contrast between an object and its background is important because great contrast makes the object stand out, and what stands out seems to gain in bulk. Thus, against a white background a davenport or chair upholstered in dark material will probably look larger than it would if covered in lighter material.

What is the relation between value and apparent distance?

Generally, objects high on the value scale seem farther away than do those that are darker. Faraway trees or mountains are invariably lighter than those in the foreground (and we should not forget that they are bluer in hue). Also, they show less contrast among their different values. Thus, if you want to get an effect of distance with values, keep them high and of minimum contrast. A ceiling painted white or a light color seems considerably higher than does one of a dark color.

How do value contrasts affect the outlines of objects?

Contrasts emphasize them. If you have a piece of furniture, a vase, or a lamp that has contours you wish people to notice, place it against a background of strongly contrasting value. If, on the other hand, you want to minimize its outline, place it against a wall of the same degree of luminosity.

If your rooms look spotty and disconnected, the chances are that there is too much contrast in the wrong places. Frequently the walls are light and the furniture is dark and, in consequence, each piece stands alone. Lighten some of the furniture and/or darken some of the walls. Maybe, though, your room looks lifeless. Introducing a few strong value contrasts at important places—white or light-colored accessories if the room is predominantly middle, or dark ones if its high values predominate—can bring at least a breath of life.

INTENSITY

Colors vary in purity and strength—in the degree to which they are different from gray; this quality is called intensity. Pink, for example, is always red in hue and high in value: but it can be vivid, pure pink or dull, grayed pink—this is intensity.

Scales of degrees of intensity can be as long or short as you wish, but for convenience we have adopted one which has two degrees between full intensity and complete neutrality. This is shown in the Intensity Scale in Fig. 7-1 for the primary and secondary hues. The steps are described as *full intensity, two-thirds intensity, two-thirds neutral,* and *neutral.*

Intensity of a hue can be changed in either of two ways. First, mix a hue with its complement. You will notice on our Intensity Scale that yellow is grayed by the addition of violet, violet by yellow, red by green and so on. This is the practice followed by most artists because hues grayed in this way appear to have a complex liveliness and vary one from another. Should you mix a hue with one adjacent to its complement, you will also lower its intensity but in so doing you change the hue. Second, mix any hue with white, gray or black; this reduces its intensity with less trouble and mistakes than when complements are used. They literally "gray" the hue. If all the colors in your home are grayed with black, a harmony or monotony, depending on how you feel about it, is developed.

Every time you change one dimension of a color you almost inevitably change the other two, because pigments are never pure except under laboratory conditions. Available blacks and whites tend to be either warm or cool, and thus they always alter the hue with which they are mixed. It is possible to change intensity without changing value *if* you use a gray which absolutely matches the value of your color, but this is almost never done. We can, of course, alter one of the dimensions much more than the other two, but in all practical situations we cannot change one and hold the others constant.

The apparent intensity of a hue can be heightened in three ways: placing it next to its complementary hue; next to neutral gray, black, or white; and next to a color of the same hue but lower in intensity. Suppose, for example, that you have a faded green sofa and you want to make it look brighter without a re-upholstering charge. Put some terra cotta, maroon, or rose gray pillows on it; place it in front of a gray wall, on a gray rug, or both—or substitute for gray a green of a very low intensity; or introduce some cherry, white, or black accessories into that part of the room, but keep these a little removed from the sofa because if too close, their brightness might make its dullness more noticeable.

If the sofa were too intense in color, it would look grayer if you put bright green or blue pillows on it, hung a brilliantly colored picture above it, or placed black, white, or any pure-hued accessories as close as possible.

How do different intensities affect each other, our feelings, apparent size and distance, and distinctiveness of outlines?

You can probably guess the answers because they are so much like those above. Colors of high intensity usually make one another look even brighter *if there are nearby neutral colors to give a point of reference;* if all colors are equally strong, they all lose in brilliance. A room in which everything is full-intensity red, blue, and yellow would certainly be an intense color experience, but the hues themselves would not seem as brilliant as they would against a background of gray, white, or black.

Intense colors:

- Stimulate, exhilarate, and compel the observer's attention.
- Increase the apparent size of an object.
- Decrease its apparent distance from the observer.
- Often distract interest from an object's outline by concentrating attention on the hue itself.

Colors of low intensity have opposite effects. Strong feelings are likely to come with strong colors: neutralized red is pleasantly warm and cheering but pure red is exciting; grayed green is quietly relaxing but pure green is positively refreshing.

Summary of Effects of Hue, Value and Intensity

	Hue	*Value*	*Intensity*
Feelings	Warm hues are stimulating, cool hues quieting.	High values are cheering, low values restful to depressing; contrasts are alerting.	High intensities are heartening and strong, low intensities are peaceful.
Attention	Warm hues attract more attention than cool.	High values tend to attract the eyes; but contrasts or surprises are even more effective.	High intensities attract attention.
Size	Warm hues increase apparent size of objects; but on walls decrease apparent size of room.	High values increase apparent size of objects; but strong contrast with background is equally effective.	High intensities increase apparent size of objects; used on walls decrease apparent size of room.
Distance	Warm hues bring objects forward, cool hues make them recede.	High values increase distance, low values advance. Sharp contrasts in values also bring objects forward.	High intensities decrease apparent distances.
Outline or Contour	Warm hues soften outlines slightly more than do cool hues; contrasting hues make outlines clearer than do related hues.	Value contrasts are most potent way of emphasizing contours.	Moderate intensities sharpen outlines more than either extremely high or low.

COLOR NAMES

The names given to colors are great fun because the sky is the limit (there are more than 6,000 names of colors) and the names chosen call up pleasant associations, but they are confusing because the names do not describe one specific color. What, for example, is "moss green" supposed to make us think of? Some moss in shady woods is an almost full strength, middle value green; other moss may be reddish or brownish; and Spanish moss is so nearly gray that you have to look twice to see the green in it. "Peach" is another example. If you go into a fruit store in peach season, you will see many kinds of peaches for sale and each variety is a different color. Furthermore, each peach is more than likely to show one side of pale yellow-orange while the opposite side may be strongly reddish, and in between the two are subtle transitions. The

varied colors described as "peach" are not really very much like any peach
the writers have ever seen. Inaccurate and confusing as they are, color
names are intriguing and carry in them some of the thrill and impact
that one gets from the colors.

Many attempts have been made to standardize color names in an effort
to minimize confusion, and one of the most thorough is the *Dictionary
of Color* by Maerz and Paul. In this work, moss green is stabilized as
a yellow-green light in value and approximately two-thirds intensity.
Peach, however, has been divided into peach, peachbeige, peach bisque,
peachbloom, peach blossom, peach blow, peace blush, peach red, and
peachwood.

The following list of accepted, common color names gives some idea
of the range and also shows how these colors are made from the primary
and secondary hues with the addition of black, gray, or white.

List of Color Names

Hue	High Intensity	With White	With Gray	With Black
red	artillery	arbutus	American beauty	African brown
	Castilian red	baby pink	cardinal	chestnut
	poppy	coral blush	cerise	chocolate
	scarlet	crushed strawberry	cherry	cordovan
		cupid pink	cobweb gray	garnet
		fiesta	coral	maroon
		peach blossom	Harvard crimson	mauve taupe
		shrimp	iris mauve	rose gray
		strawberry pink	lacquer red	seal
		watermelon	muscade	sepia
			peach bloom	
			raspberry	
			rose beige	
			ruby	
			terra cotta	
orange	cadmium orange	carrot red	adobe	autumn
	flame	Chinese orange	amber glow	bronze luster
	golden poppy	chrome orange	caramel	brown sugar
	marigold	orange peel	goldbrown	burnt umber
		paprika	leather brown	cocoa brown
		Princeton orange	mandarin orange	coffee
		pumpkin	oak	olive wood
		scarlet vermilion	Ponce de Leon	raw umber
		sunkiss	raw sienna	Russian calf
		Tokyo	sorrel	sherry brown
			tan	
			tawny	
			titian	
			Windsor tan	

List of Color Names (Cont.)

Hue	High Intensity	With White	With Gray	With Black
yellow	cadmium yellow	chrome lemon	beige	asphalt
	chrome yellow	cream	bisque	beaver
	dandelion	ivory	buff	bronze green
	golden glow	jonquil	canary yellow	ivy
		lemon yellow	chamois	olive drab
		maize	chartreuse	phantom
		peach	cinnamon	rose taupe
		popcorn	cork	smoke brown
		primrose yellow	ecru	taupe
		straw	fawn	
			flesh	
			gold	
			nude	
			sand	
			toast	
green	arsenate	aqua green	apple green	bottle green
	harlequin	Chantilly	grass green	chrome green
	peppermint	emerald green	lettuce	cypress green
	spearmint	ocean green	Ming green	evergreen
		Paris green	mistletoe	forest green
		seafoam	moss green	hunter green
		sky green	Nile green	jungle green
		spring green	pea green	lichen
		sulphate green	pistachio	Lincoln green
		watersprite	Quaker	wintergreen
			sage green	
			sea green	
			shamrock	
			surf	
			willow	
blue	blue turquoise	Adriatic blue	ash gray	Annapolis
	cobalt blue	Dresden blue	baby blue	ensign
	grotto blue	love-in-a-mist	cadet	Flemish blue
	Niagara blue	lupine	Ch'ing	glacier blue
		Nile blue	delft	midnight
		Sèvres	delphinium	navy blue
		sky blue	Empire blue	Oxford
		sky gray	forget-me-not	Quaker blue
		spray	French gray	slate
		tourmaline	opal	teal blue
			peacock	
			robin's egg blue	
			sapphire	
			sistine	
			smoke gray	
violet	artificial ultra-marine	cameo pink	amythyst	burgundy
	fuchsia	cornflower	dark Wedgwood	charcoal gray
	pansy	cosmos	Della Robbia	egg plant
	Persian rose	hyacinth	dove gray	gunmetal
		lilac	heliotrope	mulberry

List of Color Names (Cont.)

Hue	High Intensity	With White	With Gray	With Black
		orchid	hollyhock	plum
		purple heather	lavender	raisin
		thistle	magenta	sooty black
		wistaria violet	mist	steel
		wood violet	moonbeam	turtledove
			pearl gray	
			periwinkle	
			royal purple	
			smoked pearl	
			Yale blue	

TYPES OF COLOR SCHEMES

Planning a color scheme is one of the most exhilarating parts of home planning. You can assert your individuality to the hilt and enjoy the freedom that comes from knowing that pleasing color costs no more than does that without character or appeal.

There are two major categories of color schemes and each has sub-types.

Related	*Contrasting*
Monochromatic	Triad
Analogous	Complementary
	Split-complementary

Monochromatic (literally, one hue) color schemes are those based on one hue. A room or a house might have a color scheme of different values and intensity of brown or green. The advantages of mono-chromatic schemes are:

- Unity and harmony are firmly established.
- Spaciousness and continuity are emphasized.
- The effect is quiet and peaceful.
- Success is almost assured in advance.

The major danger is, as you have probably guessed, a tendency toward monotony. This possible pitfall can be avoided by emphasizing

- Different values of the hue.
- Different intensities of the hue.
- Varied forms and textures.
- Diversified spatial relationships.

■ Liberal use of black, gray, and white.
■ Accents of other hues.

Having eliminated one of the dimensions of color, we make full use of all other devices as compensations.

A monochromatic living room in browns (which is neutralized orange) might have walls of natural wood or be covered with textured, tan wallpaper; a floor of wood, brown concrete, or cork, or covered with a tan, gray, and brown textured rug; the ceiling and the draperies could be white or a pale beige; upholstered furniture covered in plain tans, browns, burnt orange, or grays, in tweed weaves, or in printed materials in these colors; and accessories might well be primarily of copper, brass, or bronze, of clear glass, and of gray, white, or orange ceramics. Some accent colors would come inevitably with the sky, foliage, or buildings seen out the windows; plants and flower arrangements; pictures on the wall; books and magazines; and, never to be forgotten, the clothes you and your friends wear. It would be a restful room but by no means a lifeless one. In similar fashion a room, possibly a bedroom, could be done in blues, in greens, in yellows or, if you want a rosy warmth and cheer, in suitable pinks and reds most of which would be quite neutralized—any or all of these enlivened with grays and whites, textures and patterns, and contrasting accents.

Monochromatic color schemes are finding increasing favor today because they let us see the room and the people in it, they are undemanding, and are good foils for whatever can be seen through large windows, for distinctive furniture, or for collections of anything especially important to you. As backgrounds for living, monochromatic schemes make people the foreground.

Analogous color schemes are composed of a few hues lying near each other on the Color Wheel. Thinking in terms of the Color Wheel with twelves hues, they can be:

Three adjacent hues such as

blue-green, blue, blue-violet
yellow, yellow-green, green.

Three hues each separated by one step such as

blue-green, blue-violet, red-violet
yellow-green, blue-green, blue-violet.

Three hues with unequal steps for variety such as

blue-green, blue, violet
yellow-green, blue-green, blue.

Analogous schemes usually have three hues, but there is no law against using two or four. These, too, are basically unified color schemes because all of the colors have one hue in common, but they start you off with more variety because you begin with more than one hue. We could make the monochromatic living room described above into an analogous scheme by introducing yellows and yellow-greens into the walls, draperies, and upholstery. Then we would need less variety of textures and forms. Analogous color schemes have somewhat more life than do monochromatic, but neither of them gives a balance of warm and cool hues as do those schemes based on contrast. Even so *related* color schemes, as monochromatic and analogous are called, make thoroughly livable interiors.

Contrasting color schemes are the *triad, complementary,* and *split-complementary*. All of the contrasting schemes give a pleasant full-bodied balance of warm and cool sensations, call attention to the different hues through contrast, are vividly brilliant if the hues are highly saturated, and have lasting appeal. But in comparison with related schemes, they are somewhat more difficult and more likely to get out of hand, and what they gain in variety and balance is lost in unity and harmony. Nothing is both easy and perfect.

Triad schemes are those using any three hues equal distances apart on the Color Wheel—red, blue, and yellow; green, orange, and violet; or blue-green, red-violet, and yellow-orange. In case such combinations sound shocking, remember that fully saturated hues are seldom used in homes. Red, blue, and yellow might be translated as mahogany, French gray, and beige; green, orange, and violet could be sage green, cocoa brown, and dove gray.

Complementary schemes are built on any two hues directly opposite each other on the Color Wheel. Green and red, yellow and violet, or yellow-orange and blue-violet. These are strong but balanced contrasts, said by some to be the most psychologically satisfying and the best to live with, for they combine stimulation and relaxation. That, of course, is more or less a matter of personal opinion, but one can safely say that a complementary scheme does not seem lopsided, only half there, or unseasoned. Certainly, some of the fancier suggestions such as crushed strawberry and mint green, pea green and shrimp, lemon and burgundy, or seafoam and peach sound appetizing.

Split-complementary schemes are composed of any hue and the two hues at each side of its complement. Yellow with red-violet and blue-violet is an example. Violet, the complement of yellow, was split into red-violet and blue-violet, making the contrast less violent than in the simple, complementary scheme. It also adds a little richness and variety.

These are the color schemes usually listed. They are good to know and to use. But by no means do they exhaust the possibilities of combining colors. We have mentioned black, white, and gray somewhat incidentally, but often they become integral components, functioning quite as strongly as any hue. Gray-green and chartreuse with accents of vermilion become quite another matter if you add large areas of gray; black and white will lift strawberry and mint green out of the soda-fountain class. Do not overlook the neutrals. And do not cast aside a good combination merely because it does not fit one of the categories.

No matter what your color scheme, you will do well to heed the following:

Law of areas
- Keep the large areas quiet in effect and limit your intense colors and strong contrasts to smaller areas.

Form follows function
- Choose individual colors and combinations with use, economy, beauty, and individuality in mind.

Unity in variety
- Use one, two, or three hues to unify the whole.
- Wake it up with one or two contrasting accents.
- Do not use too many colors—it is easier to get variety than to maintain unity.

Balance
- Combine warm with cool or neutral hues to get a warm-cool balance.
- Distribute the colors to establish color equilibrium throughout the room.
- Balance areas of heavy or bright colors with larger areas of light or dull colors.

Rhythm
- Distribute your colors so that continuity comes through repetition and progression.

- Use sharp accents in more than one place so that they do not look like accidents.

Emphasis

- Vary the amounts of different colors so that one is clearly dominant, one subdominant, and any others are progressively subordinate.

Remember that there is no such thing as a color bad in itself but that any color can be used badly and can be awkwardly related to its neighbors. The most common errors in color schemes are these:

- Lack of any discernible color plan, which makes a room look haphazard.
- Use of too many colors in too-nearly equal areas, giving a cluttered, spotty effect.
- Selection of ordinary, stereotyped colors, which makes your home monotonously like your neighbors'.
- Combining colors so that they distract from, rather than enhance, one another.

DECIDING ON A COLOR SCHEME

Developing your color scheme is great fun, perhaps more fun than any other part of interior design. Often, though, it is hard to get started, and here are some suggestions that may be helpful.

1. Start a scrapbook or clipping file, putting into it everything that shows color combinations you like. Do not limit yourself to home interiors, but include advertisements, magazine covers, reproductions of paintings, and so forth. Include some color combinations that you do not like. They will remind you of what you want to avoid—and you may get to like some of them.

2. Collect swatches of cloth, samples of wallpapers, and paint color cards; and buy a package of assorted colored papers. With these you can try out combinations of your own.

3. Visit furniture stores, art museums, and model homes with notebook in hand and make notations of what you especially like and what you dislike.

4. Look at original paintings or reproductions, because painters working freely with pigments for expression often achieve effects that would not occur to you.

Chart c

ROOM	WALLS	FLOORS	CEILING	FURNITURE AND UPHOLSTERY
Entrance Hall	1 of autumn brown paneled wood; 3 of sage green; opens into a room paneled in blue spruce green.	Sage green shag rug.	Sage green.	Oak; no upholstery.
Living Room 1	1 of Empire blue; 3 of ecru.	Sand shaggy rug.	White.	Bamboo and reed, su green upholstery.
Living Room 2	Redwood (burnt umber in color).	Sage green shaggy rug.	Sage green painted wood.	Oak built-ins, chairs wi lacquer red seats a backs; mistletoe green te tured upholstery.
Dining Room 1	3 of Lincoln green; 1 of pearl gray brick.	Plywood squares stained mahogany.	Pearl gray.	Mahogany; upholstered deep chrome green.
Dining Room 2	Lichen green.	Cinnamon, bottle green, and smoke brown Oriental rug on oak floor.	White.	Mahogany with chestnu ivy green and bla needlepoint upholstery.
Kitchen 1	3 of ash gray wood; 1 of salmon pink plaster.	Reused brick and navy blue linoleum.	Terra cotta.	Terra cotta cabine stainless steel tops, o black and white marl top, stainless steel ran units, white refrigerat
Kitchen 2	Peach bloom; Yale blue and white figured tile behind range.	Rose gray jaspe linoleum blocks, black cove.	Cobweb gray acoustical tile.	White metal cabinets a appliances, dark cardir red linoleum and o counter tops, black la quered chairs, oak dini counter with pearl gr top.
Bed-room 1	3 of plum; 1 of mist.	White shag rug.	Iris mauve.	Antiqued white wood a walnut, old rose uph stery; robin's egg bl bedspread.
Bed-room 2	1 of emerald green; 2 of willow green; 1 of grass green.	Old ivory and black jaspe lino-leum blocks and old ivory shag rug.	Willow green.	Black iron, wicker, a glass; chamois and em ald green upholste deep chrome yellow a old ivory bedspread.
Bath-room	Upper walls bisque, lower walls French gray tile, molding of peach bloom tile.	Garnet linoleum with gunmetal border.	Bisque.	Peach bloom cabinets w dove gray counter top white fixtures, chrome tings.

DRAPERIES	ACCESSORIES	COMMENTS
ne.	Oak driftwood, copper bowl, large-leaved plant.	Green and orange; welcoming and natural.
tachio green and white age print.	Black iron lamp base with chartreuse shade; peacock blue glass ashtrays.	Analogous scheme (blue, green and yellow); relies chiefly on impact of green against blue for interest.
aw-colored, rough-textured pes.	Brass lamps with bronze shades; brass clock, plants, pewter vases; lacquer red ashtrays and cigarette box.	Analogous scheme (green, yellow, and orange) as restful as a shady woodland.
rl gray, black and sage en geometric pattern.	Charcoal gray stone sculpture, green plants.	3 basic colors are green (fairly high intensity), red (very low intensity), and gray; strong, rich contrasts.
stilian red damask.	Silver chandelier and hollow ware, white porcelain bowl, gold-framed portraits.	Complementary scheme based on green and red; balanced, gracious, cheering.
urmaline blue, white, and ck printed linen.	Stainless steel and copper pans and bowls, white electrical appliances, clear glass jars.	Monochromatic red-orange relieved by grays; varied textures add much interest.
e blue plastic.	Dark cardinal red and white canisters.	Triad (red, blue, and yellow) with much white; fresh, lively, and balanced.
bin's egg blue.	White iron flower container, white lamps and shades, white pottery.	Analogous scheme of blue, violet, and red; white contrasts with harmonious hues.
llow green fishnet.	White pottery breakfast dishes, white picture frames, brass lamps with white shades, brass vases.	Greens and yellows, black and white; sparkling and invigorating.
rnet drapes and shower tain.	Garnet and white towels.	Monochromatic (red) with gray; pleasant relief from antiseptic or pallid colors.

5. Study the color scheme you now have and those of your friends. Pay attention to your first impressions and to the more important lasting impressions.
6. Make a list of your favorite colors—and those you find least appealing.
7. Look at a list of color schemes such as the one on the preceding pages.
8. When you are reasonably certain that you know what you want, get the largest samples you can lay hands on—a full length of drapery material, a piece of upholstery large enough to cover a good portion of a chair or davenport, a roll of wallpaper—most of which can be borrowed. It may well be economical to go to the trouble and expense of buying a piece of wallboard and painting it the color you think you would like for your walls; then place it against *all* the walls on which you might use it, study it by daylight and at night. Large samples are important because:

- Increasing an area of color often changes its apparent hue, value, and intensity.
- Color quality is influenced by the amount and kind of light that makes it visible.
- Color combinations at small scale only hint at the full scale effect.

And here are a few don'ts.

- Do not copy any ready-made color scheme unless it exactly meets your needs. You may, however, find one that can be modified.
- Do not build your scheme around a mediocre painting of which you may soon grow tired.
- Do not develop your color scheme around some things you have but do not really like and hope to get rid of.

In the preceding chart are some color schemes, tried and found satisfactory *for specific people in specific rooms.* All of the colors are in the LIST OF COLOR NAMES. They are in no sense "suggested color schemes" for you to apply (a color scheme *should not be applied* but *should develop* and *grow*) indiscriminately in your home, but they may start you thinking.

Factors to Consider in Selecting a Color Scheme

Color schemes ought to be related to you and your family, your possessions, your rooms, and your environment.

You and your family. The people using a home every day always come first in sensible interior design.

- Active, vigorous families and young people often like strong, contrasting colors.
- Quieter or older persons generally prefer somewhat cool, neutralized, harmonious schemes.

Your possessions. The furniture and accessories you now have, or intend to get, deserve sympathetic consideration.

- A collection of antique furniture, good paintings, or individualized accessories might determine your colors.
- A miscellaneous set of furnishings can often be pulled together by a related scheme of warm, middle value, low intensity colors.
- If you are starting from scratch, your favorite color scheme might be the guide in selecting furnishings.

Your rooms. The walls of your rooms, including the windows and their treatment, the doors and fireplaces, are the largest color areas. Floors and ceilings come next in size, then furniture and accessories. Typical color relationships are as follows.

- Floors are moderately low in value and intensity to give a firm, unobtrusive base and to simplify upkeep, and they are warm in hue because cold floors are seldom liked.
- Walls are lighter in value than floors to provide a transition between them and the ceilings, quite neutral in intensity to keep them as backgrounds, and are more often warm than cool.
- Ceilings are very high in value and very low in intensity for a sense of spaciousness and efficient reflection of light; frequently they are white but may be tints of either warm or cool hues.

This standard approach resembles nature's pattern of colors and gives a satisfying up-and-down equilibrium. Although it has much to recommend it, there is no need to follow it unthinkingly. Light floors, for example, make a room luminous by minimizing heavy shadows. Dark walls give comforting enclosure, make rooms seem smaller, and unify miscellaneous dark furniture; intense colors are stimulating and refreshing deviations. Dark ceilings, lessening apparent height of walls, make rooms seem more intimate.

Use of rooms is much less important today than it was when certain colors were deemed appropriate only for certain rooms.

- Entrance areas can be in any colors that welcome visitors and introduce them to the character of the house.
- Group living space we expect to be cheerful and hospitable. Because this space is used by many persons for various activities, it is seldom the best place for overwhelming, aggressively individualistic colors.
- Dining space, if a separate room and used only a few hours a day, provides opportunities to experiment without much suffering if the experiment is a failure.
- Kitchens have no limitations other than the three large pieces of white equipment, the constant cleaning kitchens require, and their tendency to get overly warm. Aside from these, any colors the kitchen worker likes are suitable.
- Bathrooms are small and used only for short periods. They, too, are a good place to experiment.
- Bedrooms are the individual's refuge, and it is out of place to recommend colors for this sanctum.

Room use is a very general factor in color schemes, and specific guides are useless unless one wants to repeat the stereotypes that make many houses dull.

Room size and shape seem to change with different color treatments, as discussed earlier.

- Cool hues, high values, and low intensities make rooms look larger.
- Rooms too long and narrow can be visually shortened and widened by having one or both end walls warmer, darker, and brighter than the side walls.
- Rooms that are too square and boxy seem less awkward if two adjacent walls are treated differently from the others, or if one wall and the ceiling or the floor are the same color.

Windows and orientation affect the character of rooms and have a bearing on color schemes.

- Rooms well lighted by large windows do not distort colors. Those less well lighted make colors seem darker and duller. Very bright sunlight raises values but lowers intensities. A bright red, for

example, loses much of its brilliance in a dark room and also in
one flooded with sun.

■ Rooms facing south and west get more heat and more light (of a
yellowish hue) than do those facing east or north. These differences
can be minimized by using cool colors in south and west rooms, warm
in east and north; they can be maximized by putting warm colors in
warm rooms and cool in the others; or the differences can be left as
they are by using the same colors in all rooms. No rules can be given
because it is up to you to decide which effect you want.

Architectural character of a sort positive enough to be a factor in color
selection is a rarity, but if your rooms have such, regard it as an asset and
reinforce it with your colors. If you are planning a home, make certain
that the interior has character and then enhance it with an appropriate
color scheme.

Your environment is a subtle factor, often overlooked, and how much
attention you want to give to it is a personal decision. Positive, specific
suggestions are extremely risky, but it does seem that one color scheme
would not be equally appropriate for an apartment in New York City
and a ranch house in California, or for homes in Louisiana and in Seattle.
Study your environment to see what it suggests, what leads it offers, so
that your color scheme will not seem completely foreign to its total
setting.

Regarding the rooms separately has grave dangers because a home is
a unit, not a collection of rooms. Unified color schemes recognize this
and bring harmony and continuity; they increase visual spaciousness and
make it possible to shift furnishings from one room to another without
disturbing color schemes. This makes sense. But what about monotony?
That is a matter of personal opinion—and the colors you use. After
living for some years in houses with unified color schemes, the writers
find the unity less monotonous than is the variety in most houses. This
approach almost necessitates using neutral browns, tans, grays, or greens
as the basis. If one total color scheme bothers you, give thought to
having one color carry through all the floors, the walls, the ceilings, or
the draperies. Or you can have a more complex carry-through like this:
Mellow grays, pinks, and greens of a patterned fabric in the living room
are the basic colors and spread out into walls of gray, a ceiling of very
pale pink, and a blue-gray carpet. The dining room has the same carpet

and ceiling but one of the greens in the fabric becomes the wall color and the pink is modified into cedar for the draperies. The master bedroom has the same carpet, three walls of gray, and the fourth wall and ceiling of pink, a bedspread of green, and curtains of soft yellow. Devices such as these create a sense of consistent wholeness.

ASPECTS OF COLOR

As the final round-up on color, we will summarize briefly some facts about color weight, stimulation and efficiency, pleasantness and symbolism.

Color Weight

The apparent weight of a color is primarily determined by its value, high values seeming to be light in weight and low values heavier. But hue, if high in intensity, also enters in. Red and yellow are heaviest, green next, and blue and violet are lightest. This corresponds nicely with our experience, for the heavy earth is mostly low intensities of red, orange, and yellow; the lighter-weight foliage is green, and the weightless sky is blue. If we wish to be in harmony with nature's scheme, we would make our floors warm hues, our walls intermediate, and our ceilings cool. As hues are neutralized, differences of weight diminish.

Color Stimulation and Efficiency

Red is stimulating and exciting and over short periods of time red light or walls can stimulate people to greater efficiency in simple tasks; it is not, however, a satisfactory way of increasing work output. Orange and yellow have similar effects but of lesser degrees. Green is tranquilizing, blue and violet are subduing—and lead to less work.

Color Pleasantness

Many experiments to determine the pleasantness of single colors or combinations lead to the general conclusion that not only do people differ widely one from another but over even short periods of time change their own minds. Under laboratory conditions in which use, shape, materials, and the like are excluded, red and blue are usually at the top of the preferred list and orange and yellow-green are at the bottom, but these have little application to our problem. We mention it only to disabuse you of any thoughts that some colors *per se* are better, more pleasant, or more popular than others. Pleasantness is a matter of relationships.

Expressiveness and Symbolism

Colors have come to have a rich, confusing symbolism based on their inherent qualities of hue, value, and intensity; the immediate context in which they are observed (a wedding or funeral, a classroom or theater); the persistent contexts such as sky, foliage, and fire; traditions which persist even though they now seem arbitrary because their origins have been forgotten; and the mood of the observer. It is no wonder that the same color can express many things.   •

Red. The stimulating effect of red makes us associate it with bravery and strength. Because it is the color of blood, it is a symbol for health, danger, tragedy, anger, cruelty, and war. The blush of love or shame makes it the color of ardent passion. If diluted with white or mixed with violet, it may stand for truth, beauty, and love; and when it becomes purplish, it stands for royalty.

Yellow and Orange. When bright, yellow and orange are symbols of light and warmth, harvest and fruition. The Chinese use yellow as a sacred and regal hue; it is said to be the favorite hue of intellectuals, and is associated with the preciousness of gold. In this country, it is also the standard symbol of cowardice. The darker shades are often associated with such undesirable feelings as deceit, distrust, and decay—but browns in the home do not call up such ideas, for then they become strong, solid, earthy, vigorous, and just a little melancholy because they are the colors of late autumn.

Green. The color of growing plants, green is associated with spring, vigor and youth, life and plenty, and immortality. The laurels of victory were, of course, green. When not too brilliant, it expresses solitude and peace. For those religions based on nature worship, it is a sacred color. The Irish have made shamrock green their own.

Blue. The color of sky, shadows, water and ice, the most striking quality of blue is its coldness, its strongest association is with sky and heaven. With this in mind, it is easy to see how it has become related with constancy and serenity, intelligence, truth, and hope. "Blue-blood" has come to mean thoroughbred, learned, or aristocratic, and in religion its association with serene conscience, sincerity, and piety makes it the traditional color for the Madonna's robe. Its shadowy nature suggests melancholy, but curiously it seems to have no connotations of intrigue or crime.

White. Perhaps because white light combines all hues it has a tremendous range of associations. The Orient regards it as the color of mourning, but the Christian religion associates it with peace and the rejoicing of Easter. Its infinite capacity to reveal dirt gives it overtones of purity as in the uniforms of nurses, barbers, and cooks. It may stand for bravery or for cowardice, humility or integrity. Finally, it is the color of ghosts.

Black. Although black pigments combine all others, the range of symbols is limited probably because it is the darkest possible color. It expresses dignity in the robes of judges and priests and in men's evening clothes, mourning in funeral cars, and perhaps extravagance in other automobiles because it makes them so hard to keep looking well. It signifies woe, gloom, darkness, dread, wickedness, and crime in part perhaps because it is the color of night.

ECONOMIES WITH COLOR

Let us not end the chapter of color with the dread and gloom of black but with a look at the bright economies which color can bring.

- A coat of paint on one or more walls of a room will change the atmosphere more cheaply than any other single device.
- Old, battered, nondescript furniture takes on new vitality with new paint.
- Bands of color painted around windows are inexpensive substitutes for draperies; floors painted in suitable colors, possibly textured with spatter-dash, lessen the need for rugs.
- A preponderance of high value colors can cut your electric bills and probably let you see better.
- Warm colors in your home make you feel comfortable at lower, probably more healthful temperatures.
- Cheering colors lessen the apparent need for vitamins and tonics.
- Colors that do not fade, or that fade gracefully, minimize replacement.

■ Nature colors, especially if patterned, not only reduce daily and weekly maintenance but remain passably good-looking longer than do most clear, sharp colors.

■ A unified color scheme throughout the house makes for economical interchangeability of furniture, draperies, and rugs.

PART THREE

Materials

CHAPTER 8

Wood and Masonry

OUR HOMES are built with materials, a truism that we would not repeat were it not often forgotten. With them, we put into use what we know about planning areas for living and organizing the plastic elements in terms of the aims and principles of design. Each material has its own potentialities and limitations which distinguish it from others and which indicate forms and uses appropriate for it. One cannot go far toward realizing a home for pleasant living without understanding something of the nature of the materials from which it is built. Together with planning and design, materials determine the usefulness, economy, beauty, and individuality of homes.

WOOD

Wood, which from time immemorial has been one of man's most useful materials, holds its own today in spite of the great advances in plastics, glass, and metal. In fact, the newer materials, having relieved wood of some uses to which it was not really suited, have made us see more clearly how wonderful wood is. Much as we admire and respect metal, glass, and plastics, they seldom arouse the deep responses—love, if you will—that wood generates. It is the major structural material in most houses and greatly favored for exterior walls and roofs; the chief material for garden fences and pergolas, doors and window frames, floors and furniture; and a material well suited to varied small household objects such as wooden bowls, salad forks and spoons, and lamp bases. The qualities that bring about such extensive and varied use are:

- availability in most parts of the world in readily usable shapes and sizes
- strength in relation to weight and bulk
- ease with which it can be worked with simple or complex tools; fastened together with nails, screws, dowels, or glue; and maintained and repaired
- economy—original, continuing, or both
- good insulation against heat and cold
- versatility of shapes and finishes to which it is suited
- variety of grain and color, hardness, etc.
- pleasantness to our sense of touch
- organic beauty.

Wood is a useful, economical, beautiful, and individually varied material. That it can be used for so many purposes and in so many shapes is in part because of its remarkable strength in relation to its weight and size. Most notable is its *tensile* strength, which means that it resists breakage when bent or pulled, as anyone who has handled a bamboo fishpole knows. This tensile strength makes wood useful for spanning gaps as in arbors, floors and roofs, or the arms of many chairs. Also, it suits wood to cantilever construction (non-vertical members supported at only one end) seen in those roofs that project beyond house walls and table tops that project beyond the legs. Wood also has considerable strength in *compression* (retains its shape under pressure), which makes it useful for upright posts—the 2 x 4's in house construction and the legs of chairs and tables.

In all countries where trees grow abundantly, wood is comparatively inexpensive in original cost, and for many purposes it is the least expensive material over the years. Interior walls of wood, for example, originally cost more than plaster, but in ten years the total cost of the two is about equal, and from then on wood is less costly to maintain. Hard wood furniture takes relatively little maintenance, and it takes scratches and dents in stride—or should we say in grain?

Even were it not for all the other good qualities of wood, we would use it for its beauty and individuality. Wood grain and color show a perfect union of variety and unity: no two pieces are ever identical, the two ends or sides of one piece are never exactly alike, and yet there is a powerful, organic unity in each piece and among many pieces. The beauty in its pattern of grain has for us a special appeal because it is a record of the way the tree grew, a statement that wood belongs to our living world.

Its limitations are like those of other organic materials: it burns, rots, decays, is attacked by insects: also it swells, shrinks, and warps with changes in moisture content. The first step in overcoming these limitations is giving due consideration to other materials that might be more suitable for some uses: masonry or metal where there is a fire hazard; or masonry where there is excessive dampness. The second step is selecting the best wood for specific conditions, because woods vary greatly in many respects: redwood and cedar, for example, resist rot and decay; and mahogany and walnut have high shape and size stability. The third step is proper drying of the wood. This reduces the high moisture content of living wood to minimize rot and decay, shrinkage and warpage. Woods, however, will always vary in moisture content and shrink or swell with variations in humidity, the soft woods more than the hard. Wood finishes protect the material from sudden changes and from great differences between the moisture content of the surface and the interior, but they do not affect the long-time amount of absorption. The fourth step is designing and making an object of wood with sensitive regard for the nature of the material, its limitations as well as its potentialities. The fifth step is applying an appropriate preservative or finish as discussed later in this chapter. Finally comes sympathetic, sensitive care and maintenance of the object as it is used.

Selecting Woods

Wood comes from plants ranging from pencil-slender bamboos (really giant grasses) to Australian eucalyptus up to 400 feet in height and California redwoods up to 100 feet in circumference. Wood structure is a complex organization of fibers and pores: concentric *annual rings* which develop every year increase the tree's girth; *vertical fibers* and *pores* run parallel to the trunk; and *medullary* rays radiate from the center to the bark at right angles to the vertical fibers and pores. This complex structure gives wood its strength, porosity, and pattern of grain.

Somewhat arbitrarily, wood is often classified as *hard* if it comes from broad-leaved trees which drop their leaves in winter (maple, oak, and

Qualities of Different Woods

NAME	SOURCE	COLOR AND GRAIN	CHARACTER	USES
Alder (Red)	One of few native hardwoods in Pacific northwest.	Pleasant light colors from white to pale pinks, browns. Close, uniform grain.	Light-weight, not very strong; resists denting, abrasion; shrinks little.	Chairs, other fu ture.
Ash (White)	Central, eastern U. S.; Europe.	Creamy white to light brown. Prominent grain resembling oak; pronounced elliptical figures in plain-sawed or rotary cut. Burls make decorative veneers.	Hard, strong, wears well; intermediate to difficult to work; intermediate in warping.	Furniture frames requiring strength exposed parts of moderate-priced niture; cheaper t most durable ha woods.
Beech	Central, eastern N. America; Europe.	White or slightly reddish. Inconspicuous figure and uniform texture similar to maple.	Strong, dense, hard; bends well; warps, shrinks, subject to dry-rot; relatively hard to work, but good for turning; polishes well.	Middle-quality, country-style furn ture; good for cur parts, rocker runners, interior part requiring strength also floors, utensil handles, woodenw food containers taste or odor). O stained or painte natural wood pl ant.
Birch	Temperate zones; many species, yellow birch most important.	Sapwood, white; heartwood, light to dark reddish-brown. Irregular grain, not obtrusive; uniform surface texture; undulating grain called "curly."	Usually hard, heavy, strong; little shrinking, warping; moderately easy to work; beautiful natural finish; stains, enamels well.	Plywoods; structu exposed parts fu ture, usually natu rally finished (esp. Scandinavian); ca be stained to imit mahogany, walnu
Cedar	North Pacific coast, mountains.	Reddish-brown to white. Close grained.	Rather soft, weak, light-weight; easily worked; little shrinkage; resists decay; holds paint. Red cedar repels moths, has many small knots.	Shingles; siding; porch, trellis columns; vertical gr plywood; cabinet work; interior pa ing.
Chestnut	Eastern U. S.; Europe; Asia.	Soft grayish-brown. Coarse, open grain much like oak.	Soft, light; splits easily; warps little; resists decay; easy to glue.	Core stock in ply-wood; cheaper fu ture; interior of fi furniture.
Cypress (Southern)	Southeastern coast U. S.; southern Mississippi Valley.	Slightly reddish, yellowish-brown, or almost black; weathers silvery gray if exposed. Open grain.	Moderately strong, light; resists decay; holds paint well.	Doors, sash, sidin shingles, porch m terials; occasional outdoor furniture

AME	SOURCE	COLOR AND GRAIN	CHARACTER	USES
	Europe and U. S.	Light grayish-brown tinged with red to dark chocolate-brown; white sapwood. Porous open oak-like grain, delicate wavy figure, many unusual figures.	Hard, heavy; hard to work; shrinks; swells; bends well.	Somewhat sparingly in furniture; curved parts of Provincial types; extensively used now for decorative veneers.
;las)	Pacific coast U. S.	Yellow to red to brownish. Coarse grain, irregular wavy patterns, esp. rotary-cut plywood, "busy."	Rather soft, quite strong, heavy; tends to check, split; does not finish well.	Plywood (some given striated surface or textural pattern) for interior walls, doors, cabinet work; interior, exterior trim, large timbers, flooring; low cost furniture, esp. interior parts.
(Red eet)	Eastern U. S. to Guatemala.	Reddish-brown, often irregular pigment streaks make striking matched patterns. Close-grained figure much like Circassian walnut.	Moderately hard, heavy, strong; tends to shrink, swell, warp; susceptible to decay; easy to work; finishes well.	Most used wood for structural parts, with or imitating mahogany, walnut, also exposed as gumwood.
·gany	Central, South America; Africa.	Heartwood pale to deep reddish-brown, exposure to light darkens. Adjacent parts of surface reflect light differently giving many effects, small-scale, interlocked, or woven grain, to ribbon, stripe, or distinctive figures.	Medium hard, strong; easy to work, carve; shrinks little; beautiful texture; takes high polish; always expensive.	Most favored wood for fine furniture in 18th century; much used in 19th century, today in expensive furniture finished naturally, bleached, stained dark.
·pine ·gany a true ·gany e- les it)	Philippines.	Straw to deep reddish-brown according to species; pales when exposed to light. Pronounced interlocking grain gives conspicuous ribbon figure.	About as strong as mahogany, less easy to work; greater shrinking, swelling, warping; less durable, harder to polish.	Extensively used for furniture past few decades; also plywood wall panels.

Qualities of Different Woods (Cont.)

NAME	SOURCE	COLOR AND GRAIN	CHARACTER	USES
Maple (Sugar, and Black, both called hard)	Central, eastern U. S.	Almost white to light brown; small, fine, dense pores. Straight-grained or figures (bird's-eye, curly, wavy).	Hard, heavy, strong; little shrinking, swelling; hard to work; has luster, takes good polish.	Early Am. furni but not stained pleasantly hot r brown used in i tion pieces toda Now used as sol wood for sturdy durable, unpret tious, moderate priced furniture Good material f hardwood floors
Oak (many varieties, two groups, White and Red)	All temperate zones.	White oaks: pale grayish-brown, sometimes tinged red. Red oaks: more reddish. Quite large conspicuous open grain, fancy figures rare.	Hard, strong; workable, carves well; adaptable to many kinds of finishes.	Long popular f furniture, solid veneer; standard wood in Gothic period, early Re sance in norther Europe, continu used in U. S. F wall panels, plyw etc.
Pine (many varieties similar in character)	All temperate zones.	Almost white to yellow, red, brown. Close-grained.	Usually soft, light, relatively weak; easy to work; shrinks, swells, warps little; decays in contact with earth; takes oil finish especially well, also paint. Knotty pine originally covered with paint.	Throughout wor for provincial, r furniture, notab early Am. settler Early Georgian niture for ease o carving, also pa walls. Often all painted or decor patterns here an Europe. Now i pensive cabinet-v doors, window sa frames, structura members; some niture.
Poplar	Eastern U. S.	White to yellowish-brown. Close-grained, relatively uniform texture.	Moderately soft, weak, light-weight; easy to work; finishes smoothly, holds paint well.	Siding; interior, terior trim; inex sive furniture, network, especia when painted or enameled.

Qualities of Different Woods (Cont.)

AME	SOURCE	COLOR AND GRAIN	CHARACTER	USES
...ood	Pacific coast U. S.	Reddish-brown; lightens in strong sun; becomes gray or blackish if allowed to weather. Inconspicuous parallel grain in better cuts, contorted in others; highly decorative burls.	Moderately strong in large timbers, but soft and splinters easily; resists rot and decay.	Exterior siding, garden walls, outdoor furniture; some use for interior walls, cabinetwork.
...wood ...al spe- ...grouped ...se of ...ance)	India, Brazil	Great variation from light to deep reddish-brown. Irregular black, brown streaks in fanciful curves.	Hard, durable; takes high polish.	Extensively used in fine 18th-century furniture, chiefly veneers, inlays; 19th-century solid wood. Today chiefly in piano cases.
...lo Gum	Southeastern U. S.	Pale brownish-gray heartwood merges gradually with white sapwood. Interlocking grain, lack of luster makes inconspicuous; no figure of importance.	Hard, heavy, strong; good stability; moderately easy to work; tendency to warp.	Same purposes as red gum, but somewhat weaker, softer.
...ut ...rican ...ck)	Central and eastern U. S.	Light to dark chocolate-brown, sometimes dark irregular streaks. Distinctive, unobtrusive figures of stripes, irregular curves; stumps, crotches, burls give intricate, beautiful figures.	Hard, heavy, strong; warps little, moderately easy to work, carve; natural luster; takes good finish.	In America from earliest times for good furniture, but especially in 19th century; now in high-grade furniture, paneling.
...ut ...ssian) ...alled ...sh, ...n, ...ean, ...an,	Balkans to Asia Minor, Burma, China, Japan. Planted Europe for wood, nuts.	Fawn-colored, many conspicuous irregular dark streaks give elaborate figures; butts, burls, crotches add to variety.	Strong, hard, durable; works, carves well; shrinks, warps little; takes fine polish.	A leading furniture wood since ancient times; Italian, French, Spanish Renaissance; England, Queen Anne, 1660-1720 called Age of Walnut; imported for American furniture.

walnut) or *soft* if it comes from trees with needle-like leaves retained throughout the year (pine, cedar, and redwood). In general, wood from the second group of trees is softer, less good for furniture, not as attractively figured, and costs less, but there is enough overlapping between the two categories to make it necessary to study the qualities of each wood rather than merely relying on the category in which it is conventionally placed. For example, southern yellow pine is harder than chestnut, gum, basswood, or poplar, although the latter four are broad-leaved and deciduous and thus classified as "hard"; redwood and Douglas fir, both needle-leaved evergreens, are approximately as hard as chestnut and gum. On pages 178-181, the significant characteristics of wood used often in our homes are tabulated, so that you can see for yourself what the qualities of the different kinds are and make your decisions wisely.

In looking at this chart keep in mind that every piece of wood does not have to be top quality in every respect. All wood should be strong enough to do its job, but many jobs are adequately handled by woods that are relatively weak. Hardness is an advantage if the wood is to be subject to wear, no advantage otherwise. Capacity to take a high finish is a desirable quality for furniture woods but is not needed for exterior work. Beautiful grain and figure, in moderation, are often desirable where they can be seen and enjoyed, but they are pretty much wasted outdoors and may become distracting if used too extensively in interiors. And it is unimportant if the woods used in household objects are subject to decay in very damp locations, because such dampness would be bad for us, too.

Shaping Wood

As we all know, wood can be worked with ordinary saws, knives, chisels, planes, and sandpaper and can be fastened together far more readily than can metal or stone. This makes it the ideal material for the home builder and craftsman, but it submits equally well to machine fabrication. Further, it lends itself to a great diversity of shapes and kinds of ornamentation, as is well exemplified in the photograph of the Medieval room. Flat boards form the wall panels, bench, and chair seat; round poles form the legs, arms, and back of the three-legged chair. The chair supports are simply but pleasingly shaped by turning, and the panels are beautifully carved. Especially interesting is the almost lacelike tracery

8-1   A section of a Medieval room in which wood and masonry have been used in many ways.   Notice the delicately carved paneling, the turning on the chair; the sturdy, carved stone supporting the fireplace hood; the brick and tile patterns; and the comparative delicacy of the metalwork.

at the top of the paneling in contrast to the more vigorous carving on the bench.

We hear much today about respect for materials and about preserving the qualities of each material we handle; this is a thoroughly defensible philosophy.   Bored with the insincerity of imitations, with the early excesses that came with only a partial understanding of the machine, we now say: Be frank and sincere.   Express yourself—and let the materials you use express themselves.   How does our treatment of wood fit this philosophy?

The greatest respect we can give a tree is to leave it alone, except when we can help it with water, fertilizer, or surgery.   Merely look at it, enjoy

PHOTOGRAPH BY BERTON W. CRANDALL

8-2 Roughhewn posts and rails give an arbor a pleasantly rugged, natural character and blend well with informal planting and irregular flagstone.

its beauty, its shade, and its flowers or useful fruits, if any. The next step would be to let it stand but put it to some use: hang a hammock between two trees or possibly build a tree-house for the children. But in terms of real use of the wood, we are almost forced to cut the tree down and strip off its branches. This gives us long pole-shaped trunks and branches (cones tapering so slightly that they are almost cylinders) covered with roughish, irregular bark which attracts insects and rather quickly peels off. Trunk and branches are peeled of bark and cut into usable lengths, and with only minor removal of troublesome irregularities can then be used as framework for tents covered with bark or skins, or huts covered with slabs of bark or bundles of grass; the logs can be used either vertically or horizontally as the walls of a house in typical log cabin fashion; or the branches can be made into rustic furniture. They can be split into rails for fences or pergolas. If the poles are further refined in shape, they can be used as posts and pillars, lamp bases and rolling pins, the legs of chairs and tables (which, not incidentally, are often tapered in a manner similar to the original shape of the wood).

Another step away from the trunk and branch shape is to square the log—and at this point the roundness is replaced by a rectangularity which is still a long, relatively slender shape. Continuing in this direction we can saw it into smaller beams (2 x 4's, for example) or into thinner planks and siding. Or the tree trunk can be sawed into round blocks and used as such for rustic seats and tables or turned into bowls and plates; here we lose the long, slender quality but preserve the roundness. We can also take another direction and literally "unwrap" the log, peeling it into very thin continuous sheets which are then mounted on thicker wood as veneer, on paper as Flexwood, or combined with other thin sheets to make plywood. In one sense this is a reversal of the process by which the tree grew through adding its annual rings. There is one more step: the wood can be ground up and pressed into wallboard; ground up, softened and bleached, and made into paper; or dissolved and made into synthetic fibers.

Anyone who has looked at tennis racquets and skis knows that wood, especially when thin, can be bent and kept in that shape. Furniture

HERMAN MILLER FURNITURE CO.

8-3 Chair seat and back are molded plywood, legs and back-support are laminated. Charles Eames, designer.

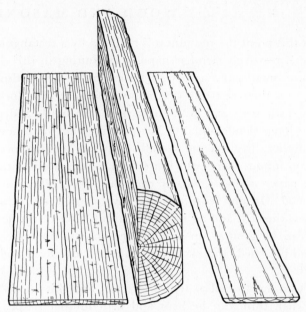

U. S. FOREST PRODUCTS LABORATORY

8-4 Quarter-sawed board at left differs noticeably in grain from plain-sawed board at right.

designers take advantage of this characteristic. Windsor chairs gain much of their characteristic shape from bent wood, and the chairs designed by Charles Eames are based on plywood and laminated strips bent and molded into curved forms.

We have become so accustomed to all of these forms of wood that none seems inappropriate, but the pole seems a little more "in the nature of the material" than does the slab, which in turn seems much more wood-like than does paper or rayon. This demonstrates the great virtuosity of wood, the variety of shapes it will take without open rebellion. Not every kind of wood is equally suitable for all these shapes, but one or more is nearly perfect for each.

Plain-Sawed and Quarter-Sawed Wood. The way in which wood is sawed in relation to the annual rings and medullary rays produces notably different results.

Plain-sawed or flat-grain lumber is cut at right angles to the rays or tangentially to the annual rings. Cut with less waste, it is usually cheaper than quarter-sawed and the grain pattern is likely to be irregular parabolas and ellipses, less often stripes.

Quarter-sawed, also referred to as radially-cut or edge-grain, lumber is cut parallel to the rays and across the rings. It shrinks less in width than does plain-sawed and also checks, twists, and cups less. The grain-pattern usually shows predominant longitudinal stripes together with transverse markings which are short and interrupted in black walnut, red gum, and mahogany but are large and conspicuous in oak.

Solid Wood, Veneer, Plywood, and Laminates. Solid wood needs no explanation. Its advantages are:

- the satisfaction that comes from knowing that all of the wood is the same as the surface
- the edges of table tops, chair seats, etc., do not expose the layer-cake construction of veneers
- the wood can be carved or turned
- the surface can be planed in case of damage, or thoroughly sanded for refinishing, without fear of going through to another wood
- the surface cannot loosen or peel off (as it may in improperly constructed veneers).

Veneers are thin sheets of wood (customarily ⅟₂₈″ thick for hardwoods) glued on to thicker lumber or on to other veneers (in which case they are usually called plywood or laminated wood). They are cut in one of three different ways: *slicing* in which a sharp-edged knife pares off the thin slices of wood; *sawing* in which a fine-toothed saw cuts off thin slabs, usually quarter-sawn; and *rotary-cutting* in which the log is cooked for several hours in hot water and a sheet is then peeled from the surface of

8-5   Black walnut. End surface at left, plain-sawed in center, and quarter-sawed at right.

PHOTOGRAPH BY JULIUS SHULMAN

8-6 Plywood is used in large sheets on the table, in smaller sections on the wall. The fiber floor covering and bamboo chairs emphasize the natural, informal character. Willard Hall Francis, architect.

the log as it is rotated in a huge lathe. *Plywood* is composed of an odd number of veneers glued together with the grain of adjacent sheets at right angles to each other. *Laminated* wood is a type of plywood in which the grain of the successive layers goes in the same direction. Its chief use in furniture is for those parts which are bent and in which the greatest stress and strain are in one direction, as in the bent legs of chairs or tables (Fig. 8-3).

The popular notion that veneers and plywoods are cheap substitutes for the real thing is in part a misconception. To be sure, they are usually less expensive than solid wood, especially in the better grades of hardwood, because the expensive wood goes much further when used as a veneer. But they also have other advantages:

- readily available in much larger pieces (4′ x 8′ or 4′ x 12′) than is solid wood
- greater strength in many respects than a single board of the same thickness and weight
- less likely than solid wood to shrink, check, or warp excessively
- less liable to splitting by nails or puncturing by sharp objects
- give almost identical grain on several pieces which can then be matched to produce symmetrical figures
- permit use of fragile, highly figured woods which, if solid, might split apart or shrink irregularly
- lend themselves readily to curved and irregular forms.

Plywood is extensively used for such hidden parts as drawer bottoms, the sides and backs of dressers and cabinets, and also for such exposed parts as cabinet doors, table tops, interior and exterior wall panels, garden walls, and even floors.

Used in ancient Egypt and Rome, veneering was revived in the Renaissance, considerably improved in the 19th century, and greatly improved during the past few decades. The major drawback—the possibility of the veneer separating from its base—has been practically eliminated by new glues. The development of plywood bonded with waterproof adhesives has extended its uses where moisture is a problem—exterior walls, kitchens and bathrooms, and boats.

Ornamentation in Wood

Wood comes with built-in ornament in its grain and figure. Grain can be emphasized or minimized by the way in which the wood is cut, as you can see in the photograph showing the irregular curves of plain-sawed walnut and the quiet rectangular pattern revealed when it is quarter-sawed. The grain of wood is almost always made more conspicuous by any transparent finish because this increases the contrast of lighter and darker parts. In addition to the beauty of typical grains, some woods show amazingly intricate deviations of figures which have long been cherished by furniture designers. *Stripes* and *broken stripes*; *mottles* of irreg-

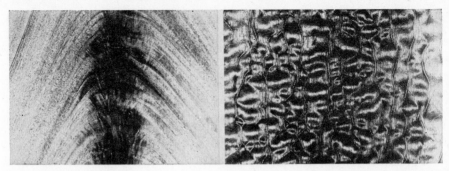

U. S. FOREST PRODUCTS LABORATORY

8-7   Figures in woods can be rich and varied.   Both of these are mahogany, at left a crotch figure and at right a blister figure.

ular, wavy shapes; *fiddle-back; rain-drop; curly;* and *bird's-eye* are but a few, to which must be added all of the figures found in *stump* or *butt wood, crotches, burls,* and *knots.*

Texture of the surface is also a kind of ornament and largely determines the effectiveness of the grain.   *Roughly sawn* wood, which has a rough, light-diffusing texture that minimizes the grain, is not pleasant to touch and is used for exterior work where a rustic character is wanted; *re-sawn* wood is considerably smoother, with a soft texture something like a very short-pile fabric, and reveals but does not emphasize the grain; *smoothly finished* wood reflects light, emphasizes the figure, and is good to touch.   Two new surface treatments add other possibilities: *striated* (also called ribbed, combed, or "cat-scratch") plywood (Fig. 11-11) has a varied arrangement of parallel ridges and grooves something like very small folds of cloth which give a subtle light-and-dark stripe overlaying and almost obscuring the grain; *etched* plywood (Fig. 11-11) is treated to lower the softer portions of the wood and leave the harder "islands" raised, as on a relief map or as occurs naturally when wood weathers, making the grain a conspicuous three-dimensional ornament.

Joints.   Flush joints create no pattern of consequence and are best used when one wishes to center attention on the form of the piece or the grain of the wood and to provide a smooth, usable, easily cleaned surface, as on a table top or built-in furniture (Fig. 8-6).   In many cases, however, wood is brought together in such a way that the joints create a pattern: overlapping shingles and siding, exterior or interior walls in which the flush boards meet in a small V-shaped groove.

Moldings.   Long, narrow strips not flush with the surface are called moldings, and they serve many purposes:

- protecting walls from marring and chipping (base moldings help keep furniture from rubbing against the wall)
- covering the gaps left when wood shrinks—or the workmanship is imperfect
- framing one element and separating it from another (the frame separates the picture from the wall)
- providing transitions between two planes (picture moldings relate wall and ceiling)
- providing size- and shape-transitions between different elements (moldings typically used to frame doors and windows give a pause between the large static wall and the smaller more active door or window)
- emphasizing a direction or movement (in board-and-batten walls the narrow battens covering the joints between boards gives an emphatic vertical or horizontal movement)
- dividing a large area into smaller units (panels on a wall or door—seldom seen today because of our desire for continuity)
- providing a beauty of their own through subtlety of form or more elaborate pattern.

Although moldings can be made from stone, plaster, metal, and plastic, today they are usually of wood. In terms of upkeep it is worth noting that if moldings are deeply-enough cut to give a worth-while pattern of light and dark, they are also deep enough to collect dirt and dust.

Turning. Ever since man invented the lathe, and that was a long time ago, he has enjoyed the diverse ways in which a rapidly rotating piece of wood can be shaped with a chisel for furniture legs, feet, rungs and stretchers, balusters and columns (see furniture in Figs. 6-13 and 8-1). At least from the great days of the Egyptians, furniture designers of almost every period have produced turnings with distinctive profiles: the spirals of India and the European Baroque; the 15th- and 16th-century melon bulbs; the 17th-century balls or sausages; and the spool, ball and reel, bead and ball, knob, vase, and so forth. Elaborate turning is seldom found today because good turning takes time to produce and finish, wastes wood because the piece has to be as thick as the broadest portion but is only about as strong as the thinnest, and increases household maintenance noticeably—but it can be beautiful as we have seen in the furniture of the Haarlem Room in Chapter 6.

Carving. The nature of wood has suggested carving from the very earliest days in every part of the world. The great periods of furniture, such as the Italian Renaissance or 18th-century English and American, are known as much for their carving as for their more fundamentally important approaches to design, because in all of these carving was an essential ingredient. Gothic carving in oak, Renaissance in walnut, and 18th century in mahogany each developed an effective enhancement of form out of the spirit of the age and the type of wood used. Good carving, like all ornament, fits the size, shape, and function of the object and is in harmony with the nature of the material. · It is clean, crisp, and spirited. In wood it can range from delicate to robust (but not as delicate as the ornament effective on glass or metal, and not quite as robust as that suitable for stone), can sometimes reveal in an impressive way the beauty of the grain, and certainly enriches the surface.

When wood is carved the size and character of the grain and the density of the structure are controlling factors. Oak with its fairly open coarse grain was suitable for the strong carvings of Elizabethan furniture and interiors, but the refinement of 18th-century furniture would have been impossible without such close-grained woods as mahogany and satinwood. It is disturbing to see a wood grain larger in scale than the carving done on it, something which often happens in cheap imitations of historic pieces, because then the forms of the carving tend to be lost in the pattern of grain. But good carving is expensive, hard to care for, and is often unpleasant to touch. For these reasons, one sees little contemporary carving in wood.

Inlay, Intarsia, Marquetry, and Parquetry. These are ways of combining different woods, metals, ivory, shell, and other materials so that the contrasting colors and textures make patterns in a plane surface. *Inlay* has come to be a somewhat general term covering them all; *intarsia* refers to that type in which the pieces are inlaid in solid wood; *marquetry* is used when the design, usually representational in nature, is inlaid in veneer and then glued to a solid backing; and *parquetry* refers to geometric patterns, especially in floors. As with carving, this type of ornamentation is seldom used today because of its cost and our desire for simplicity.

Wood Finishes

Anything done to a freshly sanded piece of wood takes away some of its clear, satiny beauty, but that will soon disappear even if you put no finish on it. All but a few woods used in a few ways need some protective finish to keep the surface from absorbing dirt and stains; to give an easy-to-clean smoothness; to minimize excessive sudden changes in moisture content; to protect the wood from rot, decay, and insects; to keep it from drying out and to replace the lost oils; to minimize fading or darkening of color; to emphasize the grain with oil, change the color with stain, or hide both color and grain with opaque paint—in short, to protect and embellish. Finishes can penetrate or stay on the surface; be transparent and colorless, transparent but colored, or semi-opaque or opaque; and they can vary from a dull mat to a high gloss. To say that any one of these is better than the others, except for a specific purpose, would be to fly in the face of facts. To be sure, today a good many people like to see wood changed as little as is compatible with its use and therefore prefer transparent, colorless, dull finishes. Few of us like the finish to be more noticeable than the material underneath, as it often is on heavily varnished cheap furniture. And we can also say that, *generally speaking:*

- opaque finishes hide the wood character, give a smooth uniformity, and offer great possibilities for color
- transparent finishes reveal the character of the wood and do not emphasize minor damage that comes with use
- penetrating finishes (except plastics which impregnate the wood and also give a surface coating) produce a soft surface through which stains may penetrate, but do not chip, crack, or show scratches
- glossy finishes reflect more light, are more durable because of their hard dense surface, are easier to clean, but show blemishes more than do dull finishes
- gloss can be reduced by adding more thinner to the paint, rubbing with sandpaper, steel wool, or pumice—it will also dull with age and use
- quick-drying finishes are often hard to apply evenly with a brush, and usually wear less well than those drying more slowly
- many thin coats of any finish, sanded or rubbed between coats, give a more durable, pleasant result than one or two coats applied thickly.

But since that is about as much as can be said on general matters, let us look at some of the ways in which wood can be treated, as summarized in the following chart.

Wood Finishes

NAME	COMPOSITION	APPLICATION	RESULT	USE
Bleach	Various acids, chlorine compounds.	Brush (if bleaching agent is strong enough to affect wood, will also affect skin).	Lightens wood, neutralizes color, usually makes grain less conspicuous; not dependably permanent; wood loses some of luster.	Widely used few years ago to ma furniture pale, blond, bleached- reaction to dark stains popular w previous generation. Occasiona used on outdoo siding, furniture give weathered look.
Enamel	Varnish mixed with pigments to give color, opaqueness.	Brush or spray over undercoat since enamel has less body, covering power than most paints.	Generally hard, durable coat, like varnish; usually glossy, may be dull; rubbing with pumice, oil gives satiny surface. Wide range of colors.	Used chiefly on furniture, cabin walls getting ha use and washing Also on floors.
Lacquer	Cellulose derivatives, consist of resin, one or more gums, volatile solvents, a softener, and a pigment (if colored).	Regular lacquer best applied with spray as it dries rapidly (15 min.), brushing lacquers dry slowly, make brush application feasible.	Harder, tougher; more resistant to heat, acids, less elastic than paints, varnishes; costlier, but time saved, durability offset this. Not suitable for outdoor wood because of expansion, contraction. Usually glossy, may be rubbed to satiny finish; dull lacquers also available.	Transparent lacquers much use on furniture, wa opaque used on furniture.
Oil	Boiled linseed oil, or varied other oils; usually thinned with turpentine.	Brushed or wiped on, excess wiped off, allowed to dry, sanded or rubbed, between 5-30 coats, more the better. Hot oil sinks into wood, brings out grain emphatically.	Penetrating, very durable finish with soft luster; darkens and yellows wood somewhat at first, considerably in time. Protective, not conspicuous. Must be renewed yearly.	Oil, often mixe with beeswax, u in Europe from early times to 1 cen., also in Am ica in 17th cen. Now used on informal indoor, o door furniture, siding. Also un satisfactorily on softwood floors.

Wood Finishes (Cont.)

NAME	COMPOSITION	APPLICATION	RESULT	USE
int 4)	Pigment suspended in vehicle; most paint ⅓ solvent (usually linseed oil) which hardens on exposure to air, ⅔ pigment to give body, color, small amount of drier to hasten hardening. Turpentine often added to thin paint, make spread; but reduces gloss, wearing power.	Brush or spray.	Opaque coating, varies from hard, durable gloss to softer dull finishes. Hides character of wood.	Long used to protect, embellish wood indoors, outdoors. Painted furniture popular in ancient Egypt, Orient, in Europe since Middle Ages; much Early Am. furniture painted. Widely used now on exterior, interior.
ellac	Resinous secretion of insect of southern Asia, dissolved in alcohol. Varies from lemon yellow to pale orange when pure; made white by bleaching with alkalies.	Brushed, rubbed, or sprayed; dries rapidly; many thin coats, each rubbed, gives best finish.	Changes character, color of wood very little, especially white type. Rubbed to soft satiny finish or high brittle gloss (French polish). Fragile finish, wears, badly affected by heat, moisture. Water spots. Good as filler or undercoat for varnish, wax.	Used today primarily as an easily applied, quick-drying undercoat.
ain	Dye or pigment dissolved or suspended in oil or water.	Brushed, sprayed, or rubbed.	Changes color of wood without covering grain (often emphasizes grain or changes surface noticeably); usually darkens wood to make look richer.	Frequently used to alter color of furniture woods thought unattractive, or in imitation of expensive woods. Now decreased interest in dark wood. Used outdoors to compensate for weathering.
arnish	Various gums, resins dissolved in drying oils (linseed, tung, or synthetic), usually combined with driers. Gums, resins make hard, lustrous, oils make elastic, durable. Dye or pigment makes varnish-stain.	Brush or spray, many thin coats best. Dries slowly or fast, depending on kind, amount of thinner used.	Thin, durable, brownish skin coating, little penetration; darkens wood, emphasizes grain. Ranges from dull mat to high gloss. Best when not thick, gummy.	Known by ancients, not used again until middle of 18th cen. Widely used today on furniture, floors, walls, chiefly interior.

NAME	COMPOSITION	APPLICATION	RESULT	USE
Wax	Fatty acids from animal, vegetable, mineral sources combined with alcohols. Usually paste or liquid. Vary greatly in hardness, durability.	Brushed, sprayed, or wiped on, usually several coats. Often used over oil, shellac, varnish, but may be used alone.	Penetrates raw wood, especially liquid waxes. Darkens, enriches, brings out grain; gives soft to high luster depending on type and amount of polishing. Must be renewed often, surface wears, washes off; many show water spots, make floors slippery. Difficult to remove entirely, cannot use other finishes over wax.	Very old way of finishing wood. Generally used today easily renewed surface over more durable undercoat, some liquid waxes used alone on wall, floors, furniture.

More than any other material, wood ties the typical home together structurally and visually. Although we may or may not see it, wood is usually underfoot, overhead, and around us in walls and furniture. It is not too far-fetched to say that wood (along with much smaller amounts of masonry) forms the skeleton and muscles, sometimes the skin too, of our shelters; metal comprises most of the nervous and circulatory system; and glass may be compared to our eyes.

MASONRY

The materials of masonry are stone, brick, tile, concrete, plaster, and mortar—materials made of mineral products found in the earth's crust. In comparison with wood these are hard, dense, and heavy; do not burn, rot, decay, or harbor insects and vermin; are of crystalline rather than fibrous structure; will retain their shape under great weight (are strong in compression), but have little resilience and tensile strength.

Most of the buildings we call "great historic architecture" are of masonry, chiefly stone but with some brick and concrete, because masonry construction was the most solid, strong, and long-lasting building method known to man. Generally, these are large public or religious edifices, but also throughout the world there are countless humble houses and barns built of stones and bricks.

The essence of historic masonry construction (with the exception of the Roman work in concrete) was piling blocks on top of one another so that they defied the force of gravity. Usually the blocks were joined together with mortar, occasionally with metal clamps, and sometimes they were held in place simply by their own weight and the pressure of those above them. Walls built this way must be very thick and have very solid foundations, and they are expensive. They do not lend themselves to large unobstructed openings, unless these are arched, and they offer no space for ducts, pipes, and wires. Today, pure masonry construction is almost never used. Instead, masonry is reinforced with metal to decrease its weight and bulk without lessening its strength, or a masonry veneer is fastened to a wood or metal frame. Nowadays, masonry is chiefly used for foundations, basement walls and floors; some exterior and interior walls; fireplaces and chimneys; and exterior paving or those interior floors that rest on the ground.

The chief advantages of masonry are:

- abundance of materials all over the world in readily usable form
- strength in compression
- resistance to damage by fire, insects, and moisture
- permanence and ease of upkeep
- variety of ways in which it can be used
- feeling of strength, solidity, and security
- beauty of color and texture.

Masonry's major disadvantages are its high initial expense, which comes from its weight and the skill needed to handle it well, its poor insulation against cold and dampness, and its coldness to hands and eyes.

Masonry can be divided into two major categories: the *block* materials —stone, bricks, blocks, and tiles—which are used as structural and/or surfacing materials are delivered in their finished form, and are put together with mortar; and the *plastic* materials—concrete and plaster—which are used at the building in a semi-liquid state.

Stone

Stone, a concreted earthy mineral matter, has so many desirable qualities that it would undoubtedly be widely used were it not for its very high original cost. Resisting weather, it makes durable exterior walls. Resisting fire, it seems naturally associated with fireplaces either as the material from which they are built or as a decorative surfacing. Belonging to the earth, it seems at home when used for floors subject to hard use and for outdoor paving. Wherever used, it is most effective in honest, solid masonry construction of relatively large size. Often, though, its high cost limits it to small spots, such as the "stone rashes" that used to break out around front doors and along foundation lines, and then more often than not it looks patchy or ragged.

The four types of stone most commonly seen in homes are:

Limestone, which includes a great variety of sedimentary rocks containing lime, is relatively soft and easy to cut, varies in color from almost white to dark grays and tans, and is used chiefly for exterior walls.

Marble, a compact crystalline limestone, takes a beautiful polish, is used around fireplaces or for table tops, is often variegated, and comes in white, grays, pinks and reds, greens, and black.

Sandstone, a natural concrete of sand grains held together by cementing materials which therefore looks and feels sandy, is used for exterior walls and paving, and is usually tan but may be reddish, greenish, or black.

Slate, a sedimentary rock, splits easily into thin sheets, has a smooth surface, is used for floors or outdoor paving, was once used for roofs, and is usually bluish-gray but may be green, red, or black.

Stone can be cut and joined in several ways, each of which has a name and expressive character.

Rubble refers to untrimmed or only slightly shaped stones laid irregularly. It is the least costly, least formal kind.

Random ashlar is laid with stones more or less rectangular in shape but neither horizontal nor vertical joints are continuous.

Ashlar has precisely cut, usually rectangular, stones in regular patterns. Horizontal joints are continuous, vertical joints are discontinuous but in alignment. It is formal and expensive.

The homes illustrated in Figs. 8-8, 9, 10, and 11 (as well as those in Figs. 5-10, 11-3, 5, and 15) demonstrate some of masonry's possibilities. The Gondi Palace shows ashlar stonework progressing from heavy rustication at the ground floor to smoothness at the top, with sensitively scaled moldings framing doors and windows as well as dividing the building into three horizontal sections. Ashlar masonry is indeed appropriate in this highly formal composition. In the entrance hall illustrated in Fig. 8-9 large piers of rubble stonework contribute to the naturalness sought in this home. They are in decisive contrast to the regularity of the wood ceiling and the thinness of the unframed glass, but their texture is in harmony with the carpet laid over a concrete floor. The two houses shown in Figs. 8-10, 11 are basically similar in their asymmetrical regularity, expanding character, and integration with their sites—but here the similarity stops. One is a smooth, precise, formal composition executed in long thin bricks laid to emphasize the horizontal joints, smooth bands of stucco, and rectangular flagstones in an orderly pattern. The other, less formal, is marked by vigorous contrasts and rough textures. Random ashlar masonry and irregular flagstones are largely responsible for the effect. In each of these four examples, masonry materials were thoughtfully chosen, sensitively designed, and handled with appropriate skill to express an idea. How different the ideas and how expressive the materials!

Brick (Clay)

Why have bricks, the oldest artificial building material, maintained their popularity continuously? They are easily made by hand or by machine from clays found practically everywhere; resist weather, wear, and fire; are relatively light in weight in relation to their strength (in spite of the saying "heavy as a brick"); can be made in a variety of sizes, shapes, textures, and colors; and can be laid in many patterns. What is wrong with bricks? Not very much, but brick walls are expensive and transmit cold and moisture quite readily.

Typical clay bricks are blocks of clay hardened by heat in a kiln; adobe bricks are clay (usually combined with a cement or asphalt stabilizer) blocks simply dried in the sun. A standard size of clay brick is $2\frac{1}{4}"$ x $4"$ x $8\frac{1}{4}"$. Although "brick red" is a common phrase, brick colors range from almost white, pale yellow, and pink through oranges and reds down to near browns and purples. Surface texture and resistance to breakage, moisture, and fire give several brick types.

Common or *sand-struck* bricks, made in a mold coated with dry sand, have slightly rounded edges and are used for exposed side walls or as a base for better-quality brick.

Face bricks, usually formed by forcing clay through a rectangular die and cutting with wire, have sharp edges and corners, and are more uniform

8-8 The Palazzo Gondi, a Renaissance palace in Florence, Italy, is a beautiful example of *ashlar* stonework. Giuliano da San Gallo, architect.

8-9 *Rubble* masonry piers in the entrance establish the informal character of this house.

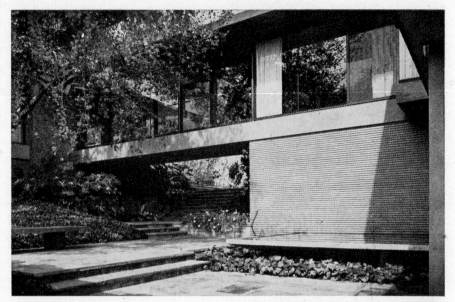

PHOTOGRAPH BY JULIUS SHULMAN

8-10 An outstanding contemporary example of precise, refined masonry. Everything, except the plants, is rectangular, but there is great variety of size, shape, direction, and material. Thornton Ladd, designer.

8-11 The *random ashlar* stonework of this house continues in raised planting beds and steps. The boldly projecting cantilevered trellis is of wood. Anschen and Allen, architects.

in color and texture and more resistant to weather than are common bricks.

Paving or *flooring* bricks are those made harder by firing at higher temperatures to withstand abrasion and to lessen absorption of moisture.

Fire bricks are usually yellow, and are used for places subject to great heat, such as the backs of fireplaces.

Today brick is used for fireplaces and chimneys because it is fireproof and decorative; for exterior walls (usually veneer) because it is long lasting and good to look at, and takes almost no maintenance; and for garden pavement because of its durable non-slip surface, and its color and texture which give a glareless surface and pleasant contrast with foliage. Wherever used, bricks with their regular patterns give an orderly rhythmic background of a scale appropriate for homes, their color variations (best when not pronounced) add interest, and their texture, midway between rough and smooth, is satisfying.

Concrete Blocks

These have many of the characteristics of brick, but they are made with cement, are not fired (although drying may be hastened with low heat), are usually quite a bit larger than bricks so that a single thickness of block makes a sturdy wall, and are almost always hollow. The standard concrete block is heavy, strong, gray, and approximately 8" x 8" x 16" in size. More popular today are the *light-weight-aggregate* blocks made with light-weight, porous materials such as cinders, pumice, or volcanic ash, instead of sand and gravel. Weighing about half as much as the typical blocks, these are less expensive to transport, are better insulation against heat and cold (because of their porous aggregates), and come in neutral earth colors and in several sizes (4 x 8 x 16 inches being one of the preferred); but they are not as strong as those made with sand and gravel. In mild climates, a wall of these blocks needs no interior or exterior treatment other than waterproofing, although they can be painted or plastered inside or out. If left exposed inside (Fig. 5-10) and out, they give a pleasantly rugged texture and have considerable appeal for those who like to know that nothing is covered up, that the structure, the interior wall, and the exterior wall are one and the same thing frankly revealed. Such use of material stresses indoor-outdoor relationships.

Glass Bricks

These are hollow blocks of glass which can be set together in mortar to make a fairly strong wall; in short, they are structural glass. They come in a diversity of size and shape and vary in the amount of light they transmit. They are the only material now available which transmits light, gives a degree of privacy, affords reasonable insulation against heat and cold, and makes a supporting wall of any strength. This is a rare combination. Further, they have their own decorative value in the manner in which they diffuse light and create interesting, multiple abstract patterns out of objects seen through them; and they surely relate the indoors to the outdoors. They have been used in homes to illumine entrance areas, bathrooms (Fig. 11-9), and kitchens or any other part of the house where natural light combined with privacy is wanted, and less often as "dividers" between two areas of a house used for different purposes.

In spite of their virtues, they have not been widely used in homes. It may be that they have come to seem "commercial," that they are a little too brittle and glittery to make one feel "at home," or that subconsciously we do not like to see light coming through something that is or could be holding up part of our home. It may, of course, simply be that they are expensive.

Tile

Clay tiles set in mortar serve as durable surfaces for floors and walls. They can be made in the same profusion of sizes, shapes, colors, textures, and decorations as can pottery. The Persians, Italians, Spanish, Portuguese, and Mexicans have long used them as rich permanent embellishment, but until recently those generally available in this country have been limited to slickly finished, pallidly colored little squares associated with bathrooms and kitchens. New life has recently been given to this product and this is encouraging because tile is a good material; lasts a very long time; is not damaged by water or heat; does not scratch noticeably; is easily cleaned with a damp cloth; and looks cool, crisp, and clean. Tile is somewhat expensive to install, has no resilience, which means that it will break under sharp impact and may be tiring underfoot, and it reflects noise. In Figs. 11-9 and 13-1 it is well used.

These are the major block masonry materials. Because they are expensive it pays to consider ways of making them earn their cost. In general this means emphasizing strongly the special qualities of block masonry to differentiate them from wood or composition sheet materials:

- Simple, massive forms seem more in the nature of these materials than do complex, attenuated shapes.
- Rectangular forms seem normal, especially for bricks and blocks, although other shapes are possible.
- All masonry, being of the earth, is most convincing when it is substantially related to the ground.
- The degree of regularity of the pattern ought to emphasize the character of the house.
- Large areas are invariably more effective than small spots.

We now turn to the masonry materials used on the job in a semi-liquid, plastic state. When they harden, they develop characteristics similar to block masonry, but they can be poured, molded, and modeled as can clay, glass, or metal.

Concrete

Concrete is a kind of stone made by man from cement, sand, and gravel. One volume of cement to two of sand and four of gravel is the usual mix for concrete, which begins its existence as a thick slush, takes the form of any mold into which it is poured, and hardens into artificial stone. Since the Romans used it extensively concrete is not new, but in the past century the variety of ways in which it has been employed, especially in large structures, makes it seem like something quite different. Its great virtues are its plasticity before it sets and its durability after it hardens. No other material combines these two qualities to the same degree. Although often unnoticed, it makes an extremely important contribution to our homes in foundations, basement floors and walls, walks, terraces, and driveways. Recently it has come to notice as the material used for the floors of one-story houses. Also, it has been used in a limited way for house walls since some early experiments made by Thomas Edison.

Concrete has not been widely used in homes for four reasons: the original cost is rather high, not so much for the material but for the expense of the forms into which it is poured; it is a poor insulator against

8-12 Masonry (and glass) effectively bring indoors and outdoors together. The terrazzo floor, marked in diagonal squares, continues from living room to terrace, as does the brick planting box.

cold and moisture; ordinary concrete is not attractive in color or texture; and it is associated with basements and sidewalks. Here are some of the ways that these disadvantages can be minimized:

- Concrete can be prefabricated in blocks or slabs under efficient mass-production methods, using the same forms over and over.
- Concrete can be made from materials other than sand and gravel to improve its color and texture as well as its insulating qualities.
- The surface can be varied by adding colored pigments, troweling it smoothly, or giving it any number of possible textures.
- The gravel used in the concrete can be exposed in either of two ways—*terrazzo* is the term used for concrete made with marble chips and ground and polished to reveal an irregular mosaic-like pattern; *broom-finished* describes the pebbly-surfaced concrete made with round pebbles from which the surface coating of concrete has been brushed off (frequently used in garden terraces).
- Paints and dyes of special types to withstand the strong alkaline reaction of concrete can be applied to the surface, the paints usually

being thick enough to smooth the surface while the dyes are transparent and penetrating.

■ Plaster or stucco can be applied as a surface coating.

Plaster

Extensively used all over the world as a surface coating for walls, plaster is a pasty composition of lime and water to which sand is sometimes added. It is usually applied to *lath,* a term now used to describe thin strips of wood, sheets of expanded metal, or specially prepared gypsum boards, but it may also be applied directly to any masonry surface rough enough to hold it. For interior work, two coats are generally used—a rough sandy undercoat and a smooth white finish coat which can be left in its pristine beauty or which can be painted, papered, or covered with canvas or other fabric as embellishment and protection. *Stucco* refers to waterproof plaster used on exteriors.

Plaster has been popular for ages because it is not costly, can be applied without visible joints to surfaces of almost any shape, smoothly hides anything behind it, and is an excellent background for varied surface treatments. Its disadvantages are minor, but it does crack, is more costly and has less insulating value than many wallboards, is so commonly used that it escapes attention, and often chips when you hang a picture or fasten shelves or lamps to the wall. Stucco is an excellent exterior finish provided precautions are taken to prevent cracking and the air is clean enough so that it is not soon streaked with soot and other dirt.

Here is a quick review of masonry:

The materials of masonry are the mineral products of the earth's crust. They can be used as they are found (stone); ground up, purified, combined and mixed with water to form substances that harden on exposure to air (concrete and plaster); or purified, combined, and mixed with water to form substances that are hardened by heat (bricks and tile).

Masonry is strong, long-lived, and necessitates minimum maintenance because it does not burn, corrode, rust, decay, or encourage insects—but it has high original cost, offers poor insulation against cold and moisture, and is difficult to alter or remodel.

It has its own special appeal—a permanent, substantial, but somewhat cold security.

Masonry is of the earth and *in today's homes* makes its most effective contribution when its solid, earthy character is revealed—but this is certainly no condemnation of the soaring spires and lacelike tracery made in stone by the Gothic builders, the rich polychromy of Persian and Spanish tile work, or the slender and graceful contemporary bridges of concrete which seem to spring from the ground.

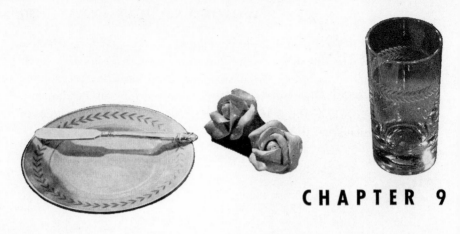

CHAPTER 9

Ceramics, Glass, Metal, and Plastics

CERAMICS, GLASS, METAL, AND PLASTICS have been grouped into one chapter because they have important characteristics in common. Since all are shaped while in a plastic or liquid state the diversity of forms to which they will submit is tremendous; all are subjected to heat in their processing; and, with the exception of a few synthetics, all are inorganic, which means that they will not burn, rot, decay, or appeal to insects and vermin.

CERAMICS

Not only bricks and tiles but dishes used at the table or for cooking, vases, ashtrays, and lamp bases, plus chimney flues and drain pipes, are made of clay. Taken together, they are called *ceramics,* which is a short way of saying "objects made of clay and hardened by heat." No one knows the who, when, and where of the invention of ceramics, but we do know that early in his history man in many spots on the earth learned that clay can be easily shaped when it is moist and that when it is exposed to heat, it becomes hard and more or less waterproof. The essential steps in the process are:

- Finding a suitable clay or combination of clays.
- Moistening the clay sufficiently to make it workable.
- Shaping the clay by hand, on the potter's wheel, or in a mold.
- Allowing the pieces to dry slowly and evenly until they are "leather hard."
- Firing or baking the pieces at temperatures sufficiently high to harden them permanently.

The process could stop at this point, and often does in primitive work, but usually involves two other steps which are:

- Decorating the piece with carving or painting.
- Glazing it with a glass-like coating.

Ceramics differ widely from one another in terms of the *body* which is the clay from which they are made, the *glaze* which is a glass-like surface coating, the *form,* and the *ornamentation.*

Body

The clays used for the body of ceramics vary greatly in color before and after firing, in texture, in the way they react to different temperatures, and in the type of glazes for which they are suitable. Colors range from white through tans, grays, and reds to black. Textures range from fine, even, and dense to coarse, irregular, and open. Each clay has its melting point (the temperature at which it loses its shape), but among the clays commonly used this range is almost 1000 degrees Fahrenheit. In general, those clays which hold their shape at high temperatures make stronger objects because the separate particles fuse together or vitrify into a dense, homogeneous, glass-like, waterproof mass which often becomes translucent, and the glazes which can be used on them are hard. There are four major types of ceramic bodies.

1. *Earthenware* includes bricks, floor tiles, flower pots, terra-cotta sculpture, and also some vases, bowls, and dishes which are sometimes referred to as *majolica.* It is made from surface clays and shales which are usually coarse in texture. Fired at from 1841 to 2030 degrees

Fahrenheit it retains its rough, porous earthlike quality because the clay particles are not fused. It is not waterproof, has very little resistance to shock, is not translucent, and is usually covered with an opaque tin glaze which is soft and easily scratched. Its earthy qualities suggest simple and vigorous shapes and ornamentation such as are found in peasant wares.

2. *Stoneware* is extensively used for decorative pottery and for the better grades of so-called "pottery" tableware. It is made from clays which hold their shape at temperatures of 2129 to 2300 degrees Fahrenheit. The clay particles are fused together and the body becomes waterproof, stronger and more durable than earthenware but, like it, opaque. The medium soft glazes can usually be scratched with a knife. It can be treated boldly or with considerable refinement.

3. *China* is a somewhat general term used to describe vitrified translucent ware with a medium hard, scratch-resistant glaze. It might better be called "semi-porcelain" because its qualities place it between stoneware and porcelain, but *China,* originally given to the European ware imitating true Chinese porcelain, has persisted as the most used name. It is made from clay mixed with bone ash or powdered glass; and it is vitrified, waterproof, and from medium to high in translucency. Its general refinement and translucency suggest refined shapes and ornamentation.

English China or *bone China* has a white, highly translucent body, a soft but brilliant glaze, and although durable does not withstand hard use as well as some American wares.

American vitreous China has unusual resistance to breakage and chipping, has glazes and decorations that resist scratching, and comes in three weights—double thick for restaurants and hotels; single thick rolled edge, which is often a long-run economy in homes; and single thick or American Household China which is of the same weight as imported dishes but is more durable.

4. *Porcelain* is used for high-grade, expensive dishes and ornamental wares. The genuine type is made from a high grade of clay called Kaolin mixed with feldspar. Fired at 2300 to 2786 degrees Fahrenheit, it is completely vitrified and highly translucent, has an extra hard glaze, and a medium-to-high resistance to chipping and breaking. The material strongly suggests precise, refined shape and ornament.

Glazes

These are glassy coatings fused at high temperatures to the bodies of ceramics for the two reasons that you should come to expect by now: use and beauty. They make a protective film which is easily cleaned and usually waterproof, is good to touch, and comes in all the colors of the rainbow plus a good many not found there. Glazes can be thick or thin; smooth or rough; shiny or dull; transparent, translucent, or opaque; and textured or plain. They also vary in the degree to which they join themselves to the body: on a broken piece of glazed earthenware you can easily see the difference between the glassy coating and the porous earthy body, but if you look at the edge of a piece of broken porcelain, you will find that the glaze and body are almost if not completely indistinguishable one from the other. If you look at Oriental ceramics in a museum or even at some of the dishes in your own cupboards, you will notice that glazes can develop cracks, which means that the glaze and the body do not fit each other perfectly, that they contract and expand in different degrees, or that the ware was rapidly cooled after firing. Sometimes, as in some Oriental bowls and vases (Fig. 9-2), this was an intentional way of ornamenting the piece, and it can be very attractive; but often in household dishes it is the result of poor workmanship, a result which may not appear until the piece has been used several or many times and which not only allows the body to absorb foods but may shorten the life of the piece.

Form in Ceramics

The shape possibilities and limitations of any material are determined by its physical properties, the methods by which it is formed, the use of the object—and the skill and sensitivity of the designer. These are the physical properties of clay: before firing it is composed of small, powder-like or granular particles which can be mixed with a little water to make a plastic mass or with much water to make a creamy liquid called *slip;* but, after firing, clay is hard and brittle, has little tensile strength and therefore breaks quite easily when hit or dropped, especially at the edges or on any parts which stick out (think of the teacups with broken handles and the plates with chipped edges). Thus, for durability one looks for shapes which are not only easy to hold but are strong and compact in shape and so have a minimum of edges.

9-1 A vigorous shape and a deep-lustered brown glaze give this Japanese bottle enduring quality. The tool marks made while this pot was being fashioned on the potter's wheel can clearly be seen, especially in the lower portion.

Clay when shaped is either plastic and therefore responds easily to any pressure applied to it, or is liquid and will take the shape of any mold into which it is poured. This gives us no definite clues concerning appropriate shapes, but the long association of clay and the potter's wheel makes us think of rounded forms. In terms of use, the dishes on our tables come to mind first, and for centuries round forms have been the standard shape. Why? Because round forms come naturally from the potter's wheel and the mass-production jigger and jolly; are good to hold in our rounded hands; harmonize with round cups and glasses— the only shapes pleasant to drink from; have a minimum of edges to chip; and are pleasant deviations from the basic rectangularity of our homes. Ceramic vases and bowls are usually round and compact, too, for similar reasons. This may seem like a long way of saying that rounded forms, simple in outline, seem most appropriate to clay, but we list these reasons because you are bound to see clay objects that are square or triangular or have outstretched parts. There is nothing wrong with these latter forms *if* they are pleasant to look at and handle, and if their use does not lead to frequent breakage. Think, however, a little while before you buy any of them.

Ornament

Often the basic form plus the glaze of ceramics make other ornamentation redundant, as is made abundantly clear in much of the better Oriental work (Fig. 9-1) and in contemporary American pieces. There is, however, that previously mentioned urge to do something to a plain surface, and ceramics have received perhaps a little more than their share of decoration. The medium almost seems to invite it: soft clay suggests modeling of rounded ornament; slightly harder clay is easy to carve; and

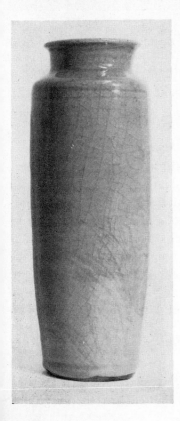

STANFORD ART GALLERY

MORTIMER C. LEVENTRITT COLLECTION

9-2 Almost cylindrical, this beautifully formed Chinese vase is enriched with a hardly noticeable incised foliage pattern and a crackled, Celadon green glaze.

9-3   Graffito (or scratched) decoration in varied rhythmic patterns enlivens the surface of these simple ceramic shapes.

clay takes certain pigments well. Thus, modeling, carving, and painting are the three basic ways of enriching ceramics. All can be done by hand and reproduced by machine.

Modeling and carving which give a three-dimensional play of light and shade range in character from scarcely noticeable incised bands or floral designs, through the low embossment sometimes seen on dinnerware, to the vigorous, sculptural handling of natural subjects on large urns. Graffito (literally *scratching*) has from the time of the earliest potters up to today been a favorite way of adding interest. While the clay is soft, it can be scratched with almost any sharp or blunt tool. Often an over-coat of a differently colored clay is put over the body and the design reveals the color underneath (Fig. 9-3).

Colored pigments may be applied by hand with a brush, transferred from decalcomanias, or printed mechanically as concentric bands, stylized foliage and flowers, or naturalistic representations of pastoral scenes or famous buildings. Colored decoration may be *underglaze* or *overglaze*. *Underglaze* decoration is applied before the final glazing, which protects it from scratches and wear; it was formerly limited in color range but now comes in considerable variety. *Overglaze* is applied to the surface of glazed ware and fused with it at a low firing temperature. Although not protected, it can be durable if well done. The process encourages variety of color and is the cheapest and most common type of ceramic enrichment.

SYRACUSE CHINA

9-4 Dishes, glassware, and silverware are appropriately ornamented with conventionalized foliage patterns to produce a harmonious table setting. On all, the ornament is well related to use, form, size, and material. That on the silverware is smallest and has most detail, the glassware comes next, and the dishes have the largest, in keeping with their size.

With such possibilities, it is easy for inventiveness and technical skill far to exceed taste. That is why we sometimes see dinner plates with rectangular plaids, scenes reproducing paintings, a single blossom or bunches of flowers dropped or sprinkled with almost complete indifference to the form on which they land. Once in a while these are refreshing surprises if sensitively done—but plaids are better in textiles, paintings on the wall, and single or bunched flowers in vases. A dinner plate is a shallow, circular dish used to hold food at meals. Suitable enrichment emphasizes these qualities. That is why the decoration on almost all dinner plates is circular in movement, dominantly rounded rather than angled, flattish rather than heavily modeled, and does not compete with food.

What, then, is suitable enrichment for ceramics? It fits the function, form, size, and material. Clay is either plastic or liquid when shaped but hard and brittle when used, and the best ornament has something of each of these qualities. It is neither oozy or syrupy, nor is it hard or angular. It makes you feel as though a material once soft or flowing had been permanently shaped. This applies to form as well as to ornament. Look again at the handsome pieces in Figs. 9-2 and 3.

GLASS

The development of glass from a semi-precious material available only in small pieces to a material that can be bought anywhere and installed in large sheets has altered our homes as much as any other single factor. One of its most fascinating properties is that, technically speaking, glass always remains a liquid, never crystallizing or changing its physical properties. Therefore, even when rigid as it is at ordinary temperatures, it is actually an "undercooled liquid."

Its history is one of the most intriguing stories in man's progress. The making of glass apparently grew out of the development of glazes for ceramics. Green glazed beads found in Egypt have been dated as early as 12,000 B.C., and the oldest known pure glass is a deep-blue molded amulet from about 7000 B.C. For centuries Egypt was the glass center of the world, although the technique may well have been brought from the Orient, and from 1400 B.C. glass making was a continuous, stable industry. Very early the Egyptians displayed a remarkable knowledge of chemistry and produced glass in many colors, but rarely transparent and colorless, because glass was treated purely as an ornament equal to precious stones and clear glass was extremely difficult to make. The first hollow ware was made by laboriously combining hot softened glass rods around a core, usually of sand, but by 1200 B.C. the Egyptians had learned how to press glass into molds. The blowpipe, which has changed almost not at all from its first form, was invented shortly before the birth of Christ, caused a revolution in the industry, and made glass much more widely available. The Romans made vases of such beauty, ornamented with mosaics, threads, painting, gilding, and cutting, that the best were regarded as more valuable than vessels of gold or silver. Little was done with glass in Europe during the Dark Ages but by the 15th century the glass industry flourished, especially around Venice, but in other places as well.

Glass for windows was known to the Romans, who cast it in sheets on large flat stones, but for long periods the typical householder had to put up with paper, parchment, horn, or nothing at all, while the wealthier experimented with silk, alabaster, and mother-of-pearl. In England window glass was not available until the 13th century and did not become common in small houses until the end of the 18th century. Its first important architectural use was in the stained glass windows of Gothic cathedrals.

Today glass is an everyday material, but we seldom realize the limits to which it can be pushed: at one extreme are glass fibers only .00022 inches in diameter, while at the other extreme the Mount Palomar telescope has a single piece of glass 201 inches in diameter, 26 inches thick, and 20 tons in weight. It is a truly versatile material.

Glass is a product of sand, or silicates, and is closely related to the glazes on ceramics. It is made by the melting and fusing at very high temperatures of sand and some alkali, such as sodium or potassium, as the basic ingredients, but other materials give special qualities: crystal, the finest glass made, contains lead; and color comes from minerals—red from gold and copper, blue from copper and cobalt, yellow from cadmium or uranium. Other effects—opacity, bubbles, or crystallization—result from chemicals or the way in which the glass is treated.

The general characteristics of glass are as follows:

■ transparency unrivaled until recently by any other common material
■ capacity to refract light in a gem-like way
■ wide range of colors, degrees of transparency, and textures

- plasticity, malleability, and ductility which permit a great variety of shapes from thread-like fibers to large sheets
- unaffected by water and most acids and alkalies
- does not burn (but will melt at high temperatures)
- moderately high resistance to scratching, but
- low resistance to breakage through impact, twisting, or bending, and sudden temperature changes.

For convenience, we can divide glass into three categories: *architectural glass; textiles* and *insulation;* and *household glass.*

Architectural Glass

Glass used for windows is made by *drawing* or *rolling.* In *drawing,* the method by which most of our window glass is made, molten glass is drawn from furnaces in never-ending sheets, flattened between rollers and cut into usable sizes. Although quite satisfactory for most purposes, drawn glass is generally not as strong, thick, and free from flaws as is plate glass. In *rolling,* the method by which plate glass is made, molten glass is poured on an iron casting table, distributed and smoothed by iron rollers, and then ground and polished. Today sheets of plate glass more than fifty feet long can be made.

Although we usually think of architectural glass as transparent, color-less, and smooth, it can be frosted or pebbly, ribbed or corrugated, or colored to control light and vision; have a core of metal mesh or plastic film to reduce breakage hazard; or be of special composition to admit ultra-violet rays or to stop heat rays. Glass can be tailor-made to meet special requirements, and although the newer types of glass have been more widely used in commercial and industrial architecture than in homes, they are a delight to designers who wish to divide space with translucent materials. In the past, one had to choose between opaque walls and transparent windows and then cover the windows with blinds, shutters, or curtains for protection. Now we can easily have with one permanent material an entrance area (Fig. 11-10) or bathroom (Fig. 11-9) well lighted by natural light without sacrifice of privacy, a screen between rooms which divides without sharply separating, or a room in which the natural light is pleasantly diffused.

Insulation and Textiles

Spun glass has been used by the Venetians and others for centuries for purely decorative purposes, but not until about 1893 were its utilitarian uses really appreciated. Then neckties and dresses made of spun glass and silk were exhibited pretty much as curiosities because they were heavy, scratchy, and too stiff to fold. Soon after, ways of making glass fibers were improved and today these fibers are widely used for insulation against heat and cold, electricity and sound. As discussed in Chapter 10, glass textiles have come a long way since 1893. Another development is foam glass, made by introducing a gas-producing agent into molten glass: it is black and opaque with a rough, sparkly surface; has about $\frac{1}{15}$ the density of ordinary glass and will float on water; can be sawed, drilled, or shaped with hand tools; and has high insulating value.

Household Glass

Our tumblers, bottles, and baking dishes are made by one of two processes: *blowing* or *molding*. In the well-known process of glass blowing, the glass blower dips a hollow metal rod into molten glass, withdraws a mass of the consistency of very thick molasses, rolls it on a slab and then blows it into a bubble, and rolls, twists, and shapes the hot and malleable material into the desired shape. Stem, feet, handles, or ornaments are "dropped" on, and the finished product is slowly cooled. In contrast to this expensive, handmade glass is molded glass, made by the process by which almost all of our household glass is made. In this method, molten glass is blown or pressed by machinery into cast iron or wood molds.

Glass has come to be the standard material from which to drink water and other cool liquids because glass:

- allows you to see what you are drinking and enjoy the crystal clarity of water, the color of lemonade or wine, and the pattern of bubbles in ginger ale or champagne.
- makes immediately apparent any foreign matter on the glass or in its contents.
- gives an exciting play of reflected and refracted light.
- is non-absorptive, tasteless, and odorless.
- feels pleasantly cool and smooth to hands and lips.

- is not harmed by anything you can safely drink.
- is inexpensive.

Fragility is its only drawback, a small price to pay for its other good qualities—unless you have small children, eat outdoors or casually in various places in your home, or your storage space is limited and inconvenient. Under these conditions you might well consider tumblers of anodized aluminum, stainless steel, or some of the more durable plastics.

Glass is also used for other food receptacles with varying degrees of satisfaction: glass salad bowls and plates are refreshing when filled, but when the meal is over look less attractive than opaque wares; glass cups and saucers can hold hot tea or coffee but seem less suitable for hot liquids than do ceramic containers, and, if they are colored—green especially—do frightful things to the appearance of the beverage; and glass cooking utensils, although widely used, are harder to clean and less durable than metal. Glass (along with metal) is particularly appropriate for candlesticks because of the way in which it sparkles. It makes attractive flower containers if you can find good-looking flower holders, arrange the stems under water attractively, and keep the water very clear. It is the standard material for mirrors and is also used for table tops. Remember, though, that glass loses most of its beauty if not kept polished and that finger and water marks and specks of dust are more conspicuous on clear, shiny glass than on most materials.

Form in Glass

What was said about form in ceramics might almost be repeated here because, in both, form is given to an amorphous material while it is plastic or liquid; the finished product is hard, brittle, and breakable; and process, material, and use lead naturally, although not exclusively, to rounded forms. As the bowl is the normal shape for clay, the bubble is the normal shape for glass. Michelangelo is reported to have said that a good stone statue could be rolled down a hill without suffering greatly, and even though we do not expect to give glass such treatment, it is a good thought to keep in mind. Simple, compact, and round are the three key words to describe the most expressive and useful shapes in glass. Sharp edges, angular forms, and extended parts can all be made—but they are far better from all points of view when done in metal.

No discussion of form in glass is complete without mentioning that

9-5 The bubble is the most characteristic form for glass, and transparency is its unique quality. With shapes as beautiful as these and glass as perfect and clear, these Orrefors pieces need nothing more.

with this material one can achieve an almost perfect union of form and space. One looks less at a glass bowl or tumbler than through it to the space it encloses and to the space beyond it. Windows give a similar result. Contemporary designers and architects who are greatly interested in form-space relationships have a special feeling toward a material which so closely unites the two.

Ornament in Glass

Notice that we say ornament *in* glass, not *on* it, because with one exception glass ornamentation is not a skin treatment. There are innumerable ways of ornamenting glass—adding color or substances which

9-6 Glass can be shaped and formed, cut and engraved, to bring out a variety of exhilarating patterns of light.

make it cloudy or translucent or are suspended, like opaque particles; filling it with bubbles or crackling it; combining and fusing together small pieces of colored glass to make variegated mosaic, striped, or swirling patterns, cutting, engraving, or etching the surface; and applying colored enamels or gilding. Some of the major techniques used today are discussed below.

Hand-blown glass. The skilled glass blower can do many things to enrich the piece while it is still soft. He can, for example, make it fluted or ribbed, crimp the edges, or combine glasses of different colors, textures, or degrees of opaqueness in the body of the piece. Bases on stemware or vases can be twisted, or made into urn or baluster shapes; handles, knobs, and purely decorative additions can be abstract shapes or conventionalized representations of natural objects.

Molded and pressed glass. In its molten state, glass can be blown or pressed with a plunger into cast-iron molds and will emerge shaped and ornamented as was the mold. This is the common way of making household glass. Formerly, this too was a hand operation, but machines now transform continuous ribbons of glass into as many as 700 pieces per minute. The ornamentation, if any, is almost inevitably derived from hand-made types and may resemble cut or engraved ware. Usually, though, the pattern is raised slightly above the surface and has slightly rounded edges.

Cut glass. Although glass was beautifully cut and carved by the Romans, the technique was given new life about 1600 when a court jeweler in Prague applied gem-cutting techniques to glass. Glass is cut by slowly revolving sandstone or steel carborundum wheels which if convex make rounded hollows, if flat produce lowered panels, and if V-shaped make shallow to deep grooves; the latter were the most popular in our grandmothers' cut glass. Since the cutting leaves a frosted surface, it is usually polished or etched to restore brilliance. Handsome effects result when the design is cut through an outer coating of colored glass to reveal colorless glass beneath; but in colorless crystal, cutting gives many surfaces to catch and break up the light in a diamond-like manner.

Engraved glass. As with cut glass, engraving is done with wheels and abrasives, but the wheels are of copper in as many as 50 sizes and shapes, the abrasives are finer, and the engraving produces a shallow intaglio which by optical illusion seems to be in relief. Firmness of form, sharpness of edges, and easy, flowing curves distinguish engraved glass from that which is pressed, cut, or etched.

Etched glass. A Swedish chemist discovered in 1771 that hydrofluoric acid readily attacks glass, and since that time etched glass has been popular. Today etching is also done by sandblasting. When glass is to be etched with acid, the parts not to be eaten away are covered with an acid-proof substance (like paraffin) and the piece is exposed to acid fumes or spray—or the acid may be applied with a rubber stamp. The etched surface is usually frosty, but combinations of acids or polishing bring smooth transparency. Etching is frequently used in imitation of engraving, but the designs are never as sharp or subtly modeled. It is, however, a legitimate process in its own right when it does not imitate others. Usually shallow and delicate, etching may be as much as two inches deep, as it is in some handsome heavy French pieces.

Enameled glass. After looking at the cheap enameled glass frequently seen today, one is tempted to call this process an invention of the devil, for most of it is in harsh colors and trite forms unrelated to the object. But in the past, some very beautiful glass was made by burning into the surface opaque colored enamels.

9-7   Polished plate glass one-quarter inch thick rests in a slender, strong, welded steel frame in this strikingly simple, small-scale coffee table. Visually it takes almost no space.

Gilding. Glass is often decorated with ornament of gold or silver, usually in bands but sometimes in ornate patterns. This is a formal type of decoration that is at its best when both the glass and gilding are of high quality, the design is precise and refined, and the workmanship is of high quality.

The most effective ornament, no matter how it is achieved, is that which exploits what the material does with the light that hits it and makes clear that glass is an "undercooled liquid" which was once a viscose fluid—but this suggests more possibilities than limitations. Glass ornamentation can be as vigorous and bold as that suitable for wood or ceramics, but, since the pieces are usually small, heavy ornament is atypical. Its generally smooth surface texture and its fine, non-granular composition make very delicate, refined, precise decoration not only possible but worth while. In wood any carving that tells its story has to be coarser than the grain; in ceramics any carving or modeling must show through the glaze; but in glass (and metal, too) very delicate engraved or etched lines are easily appreciated, chiefly because of the manner in which they catch the light. Not all glass decoration has to be of this sort, but it is a type to which few materials are suited.

Wherever you use glass, exploit its unique qualities—the way in which it transmits, reflects, and refracts light in fantastically varied and changing patterns, the way in which you can see through thin transparent glass and into translucent or thick pieces, and its general air of almost liquid buoyancy—in contrast to the opaqueness, solidity, and strength of wood, masonry, and metal.

METALS

How do metals compare and contrast with other materials used in our homes? As with masonry, ceramics, and glass, the raw materials of metal are inorganic, hard and unyielding, do not burn, rot, or decay; but they differ markedly from these in two important respects—they rust and corrode (with a few exceptions) when exposed to moisture and air, and they have great tensile strength. Like glass, ceramics, and plastics, metals are subjected to heat in their processing, and they are first shaped when in a liquid state; like glass they are shaped when hot and can readily be softened, melted, and re-shaped. Like most glass and ceramics, they usually have a shiny, light-reflecting, non-absorbent surface. Somewhat surprisingly, they share two qualities with textiles (as well as with plastics and glass), for they can be made into very fine continuous filaments or large thin sheets of indefinite length. They far exceed any other material in capacity to transmit heat, cold, and electricity.

This unique complex of qualities—tensile strength; resistance to fire and decay; malleability, ductility, and meltability; and conductivity—make a house built without metals hard to imagine, even though we may not be very conscious of them when the house is finished. Metals are more or less hidden when used as reinforcing in masonry; conductors for water, heat, and electricity; weatherproofing for doors and windows, flashings for roofs and metal foil insulation; and nails and screws. They are thinly concealed by protective coatings of enamel in stoves, refrigerators, and washing machines. They become noticeable in hinges, handles, and doorknobs, water faucets, window screens, radiators, and hot air vents, and they really come to our attention in metal tableware, cooking utensils, lighting fixtures, decorative accessories, and metal furniture. They are being used more frequently every day for window sashes and frames, Venetian blinds, and as shingles, strips of siding, sheets and tiles for surfacing roofs, and exterior and interior walls. Generally, they are used thoughtfully because they are expensive.

Metals are extracted by heat and chemicals from ores found throughout the earth's crust, purified and generally mixed with other materials to produce the special qualities needed, and then given their first shape in a mold while in a hot liquid state. After this first processing, they can be rolled, pressed, turned on a lathe, hammered, bent, drilled, or cut with saws and torches while solid, or they can be melted and molded again into final form. Metal pieces can be joined together with bolts or rivets or welded together. No other material (except possibly the whole group of synthetics) takes kindly to such a variety of treatments.

Following is a brief description of the metals most important in the home.

Aluminum. Not until 1885 was it feasible to extract aluminum for general use even though it occurs in all common clays. Since then, its popularity has increased almost daily. It is a whitish metal, light in weight and easily worked; it rather quickly oxidizes to a soft gray, but it does not deteriorate indoors or out. Thus it is a valuable metal for cooking utensils, tumblers and pitchers; furniture that is easy to move and requires genuinely minimum maintenance; lamps and lighting fixtures; window frames and screens, siding, roofing, and insulation; gutters, drainpipes, and architectural ornament, especially when alloyed with small amounts of other metals to increase its strength. The surface can be highly polished, brushed to a silvery softness, or bedeviled with unconvincing imitations of oversize hammer marks. It can also be *anodized* with a hard surface of aluminum oxide which resists further oxidation, and this surface can be treated chemically to give a great range of bright metallic hues of a character unobtainable in other materials. In comparison with such other white metals as chromium, aluminum has a pleasant softness.

Chromium. This blue-white metal which takes and keeps a high polish is widely used as a thin plating where durability, ease of maintenance, and bright shine are wanted. Thus, it is found on water faucets, handles and doorknobs, toasters and cocktail shakers, kitchen forks and spoons, lighting fixtures and tubular metal furniture, as well as the gewgaws on automobiles and ranges. It is very hard and resistant to corrosion and therefore requires minimum maintenance, except that every finger mark and speck of dust are conspicuous. In its typical form, it is cold, hard and glittery, assertive and contrasting rather than harmonious; it is not "sympathetic" and does not, as yet at least, seem to have been domesticated except when it is given a brushed finish. But where hardness and brilliant shine are wanted, it is hard to beat.

Copper. Polished copper is a beautiful orange color and has a lustrous surface but quickly oxidizes to a dull greenish-brown, or sometimes to a lively blue-green; the oxidation, however, causes no serious deterioration. It was probably the first metal to be used by man and finds many uses today. It is soft and easily shaped but durable, qualities which make it excellent for pipes carrying water, and next to silver it is the best conductor of electricity, which explains its widespread use for wiring. It has a disagreeable taste and odor but conducts heat quickly and evenly; thus, some cooking utensils have copper bottoms, but food should not be brought into contact with the material. Because of its weather resistance, it is a long-lived but originally expensive metal for gutters, drainpipes, and roofs. Its color and luster give a sprightly richness to plant containers and the like—if they are often polished. Inside the house, the color and luster of copper have a warm friendliness not a little reminiscent of a fire in the fireplace.

Dirylite. This is an alloy of 16 metals used for tableware. It is gold in color and tarnishes slightly to yellow—not to black as does silver. It was originated 50 years ago in Sweden but now is made only in Indiana (by the same firm which originally discovered it). Dirylite is always solid—not a plate—and has no false weight. The knives made from this metal alloy are cast in one piece, and the edge is so hard that it can be sharpened on an ordinary kitchen knife-sharpener. Although much harder than silver, Dirylite will scratch slightly.

Iron. A grayish metal which has been used for thousands of years, iron is the most commonly used metal, although almost never in its pure state. It is inexpensive, widely available, and strong, but relatively easy to work either when *cast* in liquid form or *wrought* with tools. Freshly polished iron is a pleasant gray with a soft luster, a quality which is of little importance because it changes so quickly. Its great disadvantage is the speed with which it rusts, but in spite of this it finds favor for cooking pots and pans, and also for indoor and outdoor furniture, which must be well protected with paint or enamel. It is often *galvanized* with a zinc coating which gives a characteristic surface pattern and protects unpainted pails and nails from rust. Iron, of course, is the basic ingredient of steel.

Pewter. The word pewter brings to mind old dishes and candlesticks of a dullish, soft, bluish-gray metal which was an alloy of tin and lead. Nowadays, the word pewter is used to refer to varied alloys of tin, zinc, antimony, and copper. Britannia, Hanover White, Dutch White, Queen's, and Ashbury are but a few of the names for different pewter alloys used for food containers, tableware, and the like. In general, these are serviceable but rather soft metals which resist tarnish and are pleasant if not exciting to look at.

Silver. It is no whim or happenstance that silver has long been cherished as the most desirable of metals for flat and hollow metal tableware: it is the whitest of metals, reflects almost twice as much light as stainless steel and noticeably more than chromium, and takes a really beautiful polish. Furthermore, it is a workable metal, so soft when pure that it must be hardened, usually with copper—Sterling silver contains 7.5 per cent copper. Its one great drawback is that it tarnishes rapidly and soon becomes blackish if the coating of silver sulfide is not removed; but this, unlike iron rust, causes no serious damage. Silver is frequently plated over an alloy base, and if the plating is heavy enough, it will last a long time; but, of course, solid silver will remain in good condition indefinitely.

Steel. Iron made hard with chemically dissolved carbon is called steel. Its development has made possible the erection of skyscrapers, suspension bridges, and radio towers, and it is the structural material in metal kitchen cabinets, refrigerators, dishwashers, furnaces, and chrome-plated tubular furniture; it is also used for window frames and sash and occasionally in homes for beams to span large openings. Because steel rusts like iron, it is invariably painted or enameled. *Stainless* steels are another matter, for they have been rendered resistant to rust and staining through the addition of chromium. Hard, durable, and pleasantly blue-gray, stainless steel makes the most lasting, easiest to keep, and inexpensive (in the long run) of all cooking utensils as well as thoroughly satisfactory, nontarnishable knives, forks, and spoons.

Form in Metal

Were it not that metal is heavy and expensive, one would almost have to say that any form that man can design is good for metal. It will take and hold any shape that can be given to wood, masonry, ceramics, or glass; and that is why in the 19th century it was often cast to look like wood or pressed to imitate stone. Its unique quality, though, is its great

9-8 Metal takes many shapes gracefully. No other material could be used for such slender handles or such boldly projecting spouts. Few other materials, if any, are suitable for ornament as delicate as the incised pattern on the tea pot or the finial on the coffee pot.

9-9   The tubular metal frame of this outdoor-indoor chair is light-weight, strong, weatherproof, and maintenance-free. The same can be said for the synthetic fiber webbing.

tensile strength, which makes possible, as well as durable, shapes that are thin and strong. Forks and spoons, kitchen pots and pans, pitchers with usefully extended handles and spouts, slender legs for furniture or supports for lamps are obvious examples; the bodies of automobiles, stoves, and refrigerators are equally noteworthy. Furthermore, forms with sharp edges are more durable in metal than in any other material. When expressively used, it contributes a precise thinness, in pleasant contrast to the comparatively heavy solidity of wood, masonry, and ceramics. Then, too, one must not forget that metal along with glass is the chief source of brilliant sparkle in our homes.

Ornament in Metal

Highly polished metal gives mirror reflections, interestingly distorted on rounded surfaces; softly polished metal mellows and diffuses them; ornament adds to their complexity, producing bold to delicate patterns of high lights and luminous shades and shadows. Since polished metals are likely to attract attention in any room outside the kitchen, it is only logical if one wants to heighten their interest to add ornamentation. As with form in metal, there are really no limitations on ornament; it can project boldly from the surface and be deeply undercut to give cool dark shadows, or it can be so delicately engraved that it looks like a slight surface variation; it can preserve some of the soft flowing quality of the material in its molten state or emphasize the hardness of the cooled product. This leaves us with only three suggestions: first, very delicate, small-scale ornament in metal can show to good advantage; second, linear or angular decoration is more at home with metal than with other materials (although rounded forms are more pleasant to handle); and third, relatively formal, controlled, and precise ornamentation seems appropriate. Metal, however, does not suggest the free spontaneity found in

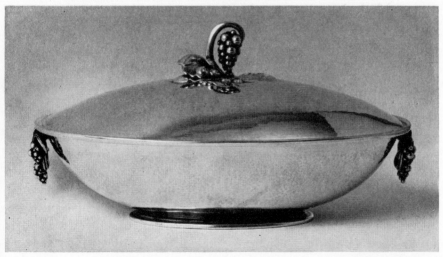

GEORG JENSEN, INC.

9-10 In 1920 Georg Jensen designed this covered vegetable dish which has become a "contemporary classic." Handmade, it shows the slight texture from the craftsman's hammer. The richly modeled grape motifs add striking notes of contrast.

the designs on peasant pottery, for example, nor does it lend itself to the somewhat casual exuberance often attractive in printed textiles. It is an expensive, fine-grained, hard material which lasts too long for whimsical or spur-of-the-moment enrichment.

PLASTICS

Chemistry, it is often said, was born with the medieval alchemists' unsuccessful attempts to transmute base metals into gold. Today chemists transform wood, coal, milk, and a variety of other materials into new substances tailor-made for specific purposes. The essence of this miracle is as old as the universe, for nature is constantly forming compounds out of chemical elements—hydrogen and oxygen combine into water, and carbon, oxygen, nitrogen, etc., are transformed by plants and animals into vegetable and animal tissue having little obvious relation to its components. The wonder of plastics is that man is now able to control this process on an enormous scale to produce materials in many instances better suited to our specific needs than those nature provides. The magnitude of this operation is indicated by the facts that in 1949 about 1,500,000,000 pounds of plastics were produced, and that the Manhattan Classified Telephone Directory has 16 pages under the heading Plastics.

Where are plastics used in the home? Almost everywhere, although as yet not conspicuously. We recognize them at once in clock and radio cases, vacuum cleaner parts, tumblers, dishes, and a variety of small objects, as well as in kitchen and bathroom curtains, durable upholstery, and permanent floor coverings. We are less conscious of them when they are combined with natural materials, such as plastic-impregnated textiles or wood. And we do not see them when they perform some very important functions, such as do electric insulators, the working parts in mechanical appliances, and the glues used in wood furniture.

What are plastics? According to the Society of the Plastics Industry, the definition is: "any one of a large and varied group of materials which consist of, or contain as an essential ingredient, a substance of high molecular weight and which while solid in the finished state, at some stage in its manufacture has been or can be formed into various shapes by flow usually through application singly or together of heat and pressure." In short—heavy molecules, shaped under heat and pressure while in a flowing state, and solid when finished.

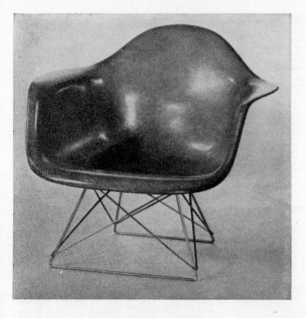

HERMAN MILLER
FURNITURE CO.

9-11 Molded plastic embedded with glass fibers make seat, arms, and back continuous in this molded chair. A thin metal understructure supports it. It is light-weight, durable, easy to maintain, colorful, and comfortable for *some* persons.

The history of plastics is short, and is generally said to begin when John Wesley Hyatt, an inventive printer in Albany, in 1868 combined cotton linters, nitric acid, and camphor to provide a substitute for the scarce ivory used in billiard balls. Called celluloid, this material was also used for readily cleaned collars, cuffs, and fronts of men's shirts; the flexible, transparent window curtains of early automobiles; and the plates for false teeth. The next fifty years brought only four important advances: in 1895 shellac, the natural resin long used for wood finishing, was made into phonograph records; in 1909 Dr. Leo H. Bakeland produced a resin from carbolic acid and formaldehyde that could be cast or molded under heat and pressure into a wide variety of forms; in the same year, bitumin plastics were made from asbestos, asphalt, coal tar, stearin pitches, and natural and synthetic resins and oils which could be molded at or near room temperatures and then baked to retain their shape; and in 1919 casein plastics were made from milk and formaldehyde. Since 1925 advances have come so rapidly that chronology becomes a mass of technical details, but the products have greatly changed some of the objects we live with—and consequently the way we live.

Plastics Most Used in Homes

Most plastic objects used in homes are made from the nine resins discussed in the following paragraphs. Three points should be noted:

Madagaska

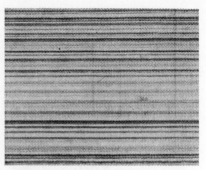

Woodtex

Palmetto

Bouclé

L. E. CARPENTER AND CO.

9-12 Textured and patterned plastic fabrics such as these can be used as wall-coverings, upholstery, table tops and door fronts because they are flexible and durable. They come in 28 fadeproof colors; resist stains, soil, fire, cracking, peeling, and scratching; can be cleaned with a damp cloth.

- Each name refers to a family of plastics, the members of which may differ considerably from one another.
- *Thermoplastics* are formed under heat but after hardening can be melted down and reformed, while *thermosetting* plastics are formed under heat and pressure in permanent shapes.
- The terms *plastic* and *synthetic* may be applied to the same resins. Thus nylon in molded form is called a plastic, but nylon threads are referred to as synthetic.

Acrylics (Thermoplastic) [1]   *Uses*

Acrylic plastics will withstand normal household usage.   dresser sets
They are unaffected by water, alkalis, salt, vinegar, and   brush backs

[1] Quoted by permission from *Better Design,* March, 1952, published by Better Design Magazine Company, East Stroudsburg, Pennsylvania.

Uses

window-cleaning solutions. Acrylics do not become brittle at low temperatures—are warm and pleasant to the touch, and are fairly hard and rigid. They possess exceptional optical clarity and the "piping" of light is one of their important characteristics.

combs
picture frames
lamps
clock housings

Cellulosics (Thermoplastic)

Cellulosic plastics retain a bright, lustrous finish under normal conditions. Among the toughest of plastics, they are resistant to most household chemicals, but may be stained by medicants, iodine, and some foodstuffs. They will withstand normal usage at low temperatures without damage—are pleasant and warm to the touch. They perform satisfactorily in water temperatures up to 130° F. Cellulosics are available in a wide variety of colors, ranging from clear transparent to opaque, including variations and simulations such as marble, wood grains, reptile finishes and mother-of-pearl.

vacuum cleaner
  parts
piano keys
soap dishes
cutlery handles
flashlight cases
radio housings
appliances
electric clock
  housings
containers
toys

Melamines (Thermosetting)

Melamine plastics have excellent heat resistance, will not support combustion. Melamine is the hardest plastic, is fully resistant to water and household detergents, is available in a full range of translucent and opaque colors. (Formica, Micarta, etc., are melamine laminates.)

furniture surfaces
tableware
kitchen cabinet
  tops

Nylon (Thermoplastic)

Nylon plastic is very resistant to abrasion—can, however, be scratched with sharp kitchen utensils. It is resistant to all common chemicals except mineral acids—may be stained by coffee, tea, beet juice, and other colored foodstuffs. Nylon can be used at freezing temperatures, and is a relatively hard, rigid material. It has a very high resistance to heat, can be boiled or steam-sterilized without harm.

tumblers
dinnerware
combs
soap dishes
brush bristles
brush backs
chair webbing

Phenolics (Thermosetting)

Phenolic plastics are light in weight, have a good surface appearance and excellent electrical properties. They are resistant to alcohol, water, mild acids and all common solvents, oils, greases, soaps and detergents. Phenolics are hard, strong, and rigid over a wide range of temperatures—are a poor heat conductor and are, therefore, cool to touch when used as handles for cooking utensils. They are, in fact, the principal plastic used in insulating parts of household electrical equipment and appliances.

coffeepot handles
containers
knife handles
radios and television housing
drainboard tops
telephone sets
electric-iron
  handles
toaster handles

Polyethylene (Thermoplastic)

Polyethylene plastics are a flexible and translucent material. They are lighter in weight than most plastics, have excellent electrical properties, toughness and low moisture transmission. Polyethylene plastics have an unusual resistance to chemicals and are unaffected by all household solvents at room temperatures. Water up to the boiling point may be poured into polyethylene products, but these objects should not be boiled or used on an open flame or heating element.

Uses

refrigerator trays
nesting bowls
soap dishes
ice-box dishes
  with air-tight
  covers
squeezable bottles

Polystyrene (Thermoplastic)

Polystyrene plastics have a lustrous surface, an exceptional color range, are hard and rigid. Various surface effects are secured through different manufacturing processes. Polystyrene products can be immersed in water and allowed to come in contact with almost all foods and drinks for almost an indefinite period of time without danger to the plastics or the foodstuffs. Their use is not recommended where severe impact or bending conditions are likely to be encountered. In addition, the use of abrasive household cleaning powders, steel wool, and metallic scrapers should be avoided.

kitchenware
refrigerator parts
bottle closures
measuring spoons
  and cups
ice-box dishes
wall tile
combs

Ureas (Thermosetting)

Urea, combined with formaldehyde, is an odorless, dimensionally stable plastic—has a high resistance to all organic solvents, weak acids, and alkalis. Urea provides a hard, scratch-resistant surface and an unlimited color range. Molded urea products are rigid, light in weight. They are not meant to be used outside the house, are subject to cracking upon exposure.

molded chair
  seats
radio housings
gas and electric
  range control
  knobs
luminous switches

Vinyls (Thermoplastic)

Vinyl plastics are available in clear, transparent forms— have an unlimited color range. They are water, acid, alkali, and fire resistant. Flexible vinyl products are strong, tear-resistant, are pleasant to the touch, and drape well. They can be formulated for dimensional stability, but it is not an inherent quality. Rigid vinyl is tough, also pleasant to the touch, and is dimensionally stable. A wide variety of surface effects can be obtained by embossing and printing. Vinyls may be used at temperatures ranging from those found in food-freezing units to 130° F. Moth repellents should not be allowed to come in contact with vinyl—which, for example, might happen where it is used for a garment bag or other storage container.

shower curtains
bathroom curtains
kitchen curtains
tablecloths
draperies
upholstery
bedspreads
closet accessories
lampshades
floorings

Forming and Fabricating Plastics

Plastic molding compounds come to the forming machine as powders or granules, compressed tablets, or liquids capable of taking under heat and pressure practically any shape the designer wishes. Basically, the processes are much like those used in shaping clay, glass, and metal although they are by no means identical. Powder or tablets can be compressed in steel molds or liquids can be forced through dies to form continuous sheets, rods, filaments, tubing, or pipes. Molding materials can be drawn into thin sheets or blown into molds by air or steam pressure just as glass can be drawn into thin sheets for windows or blown into molds for vases and tumblers. They can be made into foams for light, strong insulation and into buoyant materials by blowing them full of air or gas.

In laminating, layers of cloth, paper, wood, or glass fibers are impregnated with uncured resin, or alternated with uncured plastic film, then pressed into a single piece as in the making of plywood. Film and sheeting for shower curtains, upholstery, and photographic film are made by spreading plastic solutions on to wheels from 6 to 25 feet in diameter, which are heated to dry the plastic; by extruding the compound through a wide die; or by calendering—passing it between a series of three or four rollers to get the desired thickness and surface texture. In coating other materials, plastic compounds are spread on to the base material by means of rollers.

With this variety of processes available, it is no wonder that plastics come in every shape man wants.

Design in Plastics

When you think of the fact that a single member of this large family of materials—nylon—can be made into sheer stockings, durable carpets, toothbrush bristles, tumblers, and dinnerware, it becomes clear that one cannot generalize much about design as determined by the nature of the molding compound. About all we can do is look at a plastic object and ask: does the form suit the purpose, is it pleasant to see and touch, and is the material attractive in itself? Although plastics can be ornamented as easily as any other material, as yet the majority are relatively simple.

This is all to the good because it focuses attention on basic form and material. Undoubtedly more ornamentation will come as the novelty of newness wears thin. Let us hope that when it does, it will fulfill the suggestions for ornament discussed in Chapter 6.

Two questions remain to be answered.

First, are plastics to be thought of as substitutes for such materials as ceramics, glass, metal, and wood? Again the answer is that academic irritant—yes and no. In some respects they are and in others they are not. Their tremendous potential lies in man's ability to formulate them for specific purposes, to tailor them to our needs in a way that cannot be done with wood or stone. As yet, though, they are not perfect. Plastic floor coverings, for example, are said to combine durability, ease of maintenance, and resilience in a way not found in any other material, but the first cost is high. Laminated plastics for table and counter tops resist stains and scratches, but they are expensive, cannot be refinished, and no one knows what they will look like in twenty or thirty years. Plastic handles on kitchen utensils are light-weight, colorful and inexpensive, but they break more readily than hard wood; plastic vacuum cleaner attachments weigh and cost less—and have a much shorter life— than those of metal; and plastic dishes and tumblers, available in a wide price range, may or may not outlast those of clay and glass—but no plastic tumbler to date will last as long as one of aluminum or stainless steel. In some cases, plastics have indisputable advantages: plastic cases for the less expensive radios, phonographs, and television are cheaper than wood or metal and will undoubtedly outlive the usefulness of what they hold; plastic sheeting for bathroom and shower curtains has marked advantages over other materials, and lamp shades of vinyl and fiberglas are flexible, pleasantly translucent, easy to clean, and last well. In a few instances they are distinct improvements over natural materials, in some they are about equal to them, and in others they are clearly inferior. It pays to know what you are buying.

Second, will plastics ever replace all natural materials? Risking future embarrassment, we say they will not. Fine furniture will continue to be made of wood, sparkling tables will be set with glass and silver, and lighting fixtures will use metal, glass, clay, and wood. There is no question that many plastics are ideal in the short run where one or more of the following is paramount—low cost, low maintenance, and light weight. Today, however, they are not the materials most of us look forward to

9-13 The bowl and candleholder are ceramics, the cigarette box is enameled metal, the tray is plastic with varied material embedded between layers, and the belt buckle is metal. In each, the materials are well chosen for use and shape and appropriately enriched.

cherishing or giving as heirlooms to our children. They are good for their utility, but are expendable and should be accepted in those terms.

Much of the present confusion and uncertainty about plastics will be lessened as new developments take place, their properties are understood, and objects made from them are clearly labeled for the consumer's benefit.

CHAPTER 10

Fabrics

FABRICS are made by weaving, knitting, felting, or lacing together natural or man-made fibers and now also by fabricating plastics into thin, non-fibrous sheets. *Fabric* is a general term referring to anything manufactured by hand or machine, but it has come to be applied especially to cloth. *Textile* refers only to *woven fabrics*. *Textile* and *texture* are both derived from the same Latin word, an indication of the importance of texture in textiles.

Very early in his history, man in widely separated parts of the world found that animal skins, leaves, and bark were not always available in pieces of suitable size, weight, and manipulability and set about to improve on nature. He wanted something to protect his own body, to make his living quarters more comfortable, and to satisfy his need for spiritual stimulation and satisfaction—and he produced fabrics. More than anything in the house—except the people—fabrics humanize our homes because of their pliant responsiveness to our needs. They serve many utilitarian needs such as controlling and modulating light coming through windows, giving privacy without solid walls, insulating us and our homes against extremes of heat and cold, absorbing noise, providing easily removable and cleanable protective coverings for our tables and beds, and pleasant-to-touch coverings for our chairs and davenports. Beyond these utilitarian functions, fabrics are a primary source of beauty.

Today we accept fabrics as inevitable and often fail to appreciate what

241

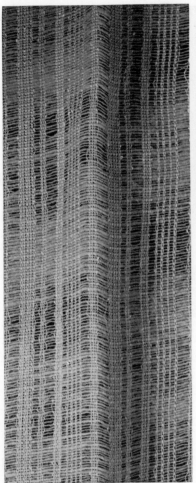

10-1 Fiber and weave make these textiles decorative. *Left:* Casement cloth woven with warp of spun rayon, rayon ratiné, and metallic thread and filling of mixture of acetate and spun rayon. *Right:* Woven of plastic fibers, this upholstery material remains soft even in extreme cold, is colorfast, water- and stain-resistant, durable, and cleans with soap and water.

they do for us. Of their many characteristics, three are outstanding. *First,* they are uniquely pliable and manipulable, for they can be rolled, folded, pleated, draped, or stretched without damage; and they can be cut, sewn, or glued together with simple equipment found in every home. *Second,* no other material comes in such wide widths and long lengths and can be used that way—paper tears and suffers from folding, metal is heavy and relatively uncompromising, and wood (even veneer) is either heavy and nonpliable or fragile. *Third,* they link together people, furniture, and architecture as no other material does. Carpets and other fabrics fastened to floors and walls adhere strictly and flatly to the "architecture" of the house; upholstery, slip-covers, and table linens adapt themselves to the seating or table on which they are used and at the same time relate those pieces to us and our clothes; and curtains and draperies (at their best) partake of the architectural quality of the window, relate the opening to the enclosing structure, to the furniture, and to us. Because they are used in quantity in every part of the house fabrics not only are connecting links, but become a dominant factor, secondary only to the people, the architecture, and the major furniture which they supplement, enrich, and emphasize. They can well be thought of as a counterpoint playing with and against, relating to and contrasting with, the organic forms and activities of the people and the architectonic forms of the structure and furniture.

Clearly, they are a subject deserving some time. We can look at the sources, history, and characteristics of different fibers; at the processes by which they are transformed into fabrics; and at a list of some of the more important ones used today. Then in the following chapters on walls, windows, floors, and furniture we will consider how they can be most effectively employed in relation to the character and functions of these parts of the home. Thereby, we hope to avoid treating textiles in the home as items separate from the whole house and to see them as integral with the floors, furniture, beds, and tables they cover as well as the openings they enhance.

The qualities of a fabric are the product of four factors—the *fiber,* the *yarn,* the *process* by which the yarns are fastened together, and the *finishing,* which includes applied decoration—and each of these will be discussed in the following sections.

FIBERS

Specifically, the term *fiber* is defined as a threadlike object or a filament, but it has also come to mean that which gives substance and texture, and both of these meanings apply equally to the fibers of fabrics. Nature provides an abundance of fibers which in their natural state suggest weaving, such as reeds, grasses, small twigs and branches, the wool and hair of animals, the fibers enclosing the seeds of some plants, and the filaments insects spin for their cocoons; and also a goodly number which need only a little processing, such as the wood of some trees which splits easily into thin strips, or the stems of such plants as flax, ramie, jute, and hemp. To these, man is almost daily adding fibers of his own invention. For our purposes, however, there are relatively few fibers of

Textile Fibers

FIBER	SOURCE	HISTORY	QUALITIES	USES	TYPES AND SPECIAL TREATMENTS
Acetate	Cellulose and acetic acid.	Only recently distinguished from rayon, but has many different characteristics.	Acetate is the "beauty fiber," rayon the "utility fiber." Soft and luxurious; drapes well. Good wrinkle-recovery; does not stain; dimensionally stable. Resists mold, mildew, moths. Retains heat-set pleats, etc.	Clothing is major use to date, but combined with other fibers is beginning to be used for draperies, upholstery, and rugs.	Celaperm is a very new yarn in which color is integral part of fiber; strongly resistant to fading from sun, washing, or dry cleaning.
Acrilan	Acrilac fiber; cousin to nylon, orlon, dacron, dynel.	Recently put on market after 12 years of research.	Bulky; warmth without weight. Apparently strong and durable. Resists moths and mildew; sheds wrinkles. Washable and fast drying. Semi-dull luster resembling wool in appearance and feel. Retains heat-set pleats and creases.	Chiefly blankets to date.	Too new for any of proven significance.
Cotton	Fibers from bolls of cotton plant grown in many parts of world; about 40% now grown in U. S.	Used at least as early as 3000 B.C. in India, very early in South and Central America; not raised in Europe until 2nd century A.D.	Extremely versatile fiber. Moderately strong and durable; shrinks when washed. Soils, stains, and wrinkles easily; also washes and irons easily; can be boiled. Pleasant, soft, dull surface good to look at and to feel.	Bed and table "linens," towels, draperies and slip covers; also upholstery and rugs but does not resist soil and wear as well as wool or synthetics.	Mercerizing increases luster, softness, strength and capacity to absorb dye. Starching and weighting make cloth heavier, crisper, and more resistant to soil but usually wash out. Raising nap gives light or deep pile by brushing fibers to upright position. Can be made water-repellent; resistant to creases, shrinkage, mildew and fire; and with a permanent high glaze.

Dacron	Polyester fiber.	Very new.	Strong and durable; resists stretching and shrinking; exceptional wrinkle-recovery. Unaffected by moisture, retains creases when wet. Easy to care for. Bulk leads to light-weight, warm textiles with pleasing soft hand.	Upholstery.	None as yet.
Dynel	Salt and air.	Released in 1950.	Fire-resistance and resilience are outstanding qualities. Does not shrink or stretch. Resistant to acids, alkalis, moths, and mildew. Washes well: thick textiles retain their softness, sheer nets their shape, after repeated launderings. Somewhat like wool in feel and appearance; blends well with other fibers to improve strength, shape-retention, and washability of textiles.	Fire resistance, washability, and resilience make it exceptionally good for draperies, bedspreads, upholstery. Resistance to moths and mildew makes it excellent for blankets.	Range from thick pile textiles which retain their softness after repeated washings, to sheer nets which will not shrink or stretch.
Fiberglas	Same as glass.	Spun glass used for centuries as decoration for glassware; used for textile fibers in 1890's but little done with glass textiles for homes until recently.	Moderately strong but sheds short fibers if subjected to abrasion. Does not deteriorate with age. Resists most chemicals, stains, sun, rot, mildew, moths, and fire; unharmed by moisture. Does not hold dirt and is easily cleaned. Often cold, hard, and slippery.	Window curtains, shower curtains, draperies, lamp shades; tablecloths, bedspreads. Serviceable when no abrasion.	Improved types better hand, look; limited color range in dyes, printed many hues. Embedded in plastic for lamp shades, wall panels, etc.

Textile Fibers (Cont.)

FIBER	SOURCE	HISTORY	QUALITIES	USES	TYPES AND SPECIAL TREATMENTS
Linen	Silky fibers, 2 to 3' long from inside bark of 1000 species of flax plant.	Probably oldest textile fiber; 5000 B.C. in Egypt; followed civilization up into Europe; North America too in prehistoric times.	Strongest, most pliable vegetable fiber; durable and non-elastic. Wrinkles easily but washes and irons beautifully, even after many years; can be boiled. Desirable soft, silky appearance and feel. Lintless; absorbs moisture readily; does not stretch.	Towels, tablecloths, napkins; curtains, draperies; slip covers, upholstery; durable rugs. Essentially same uses as cotton but superior, more costly.	Range from some of sheerest fabrics and laces made to tough rope and rugs. Treatment similar to cotton.
Orlon	Coal, air, limestone, natural gas, petroleum, water.	One of the newest synthetics; just coming on market.	Outstandingly resistant to sun-rot, also resistant to heat, gases, and soil. Resilient; holds shape and size. Almost as strong wet as dry. Feels warm, soft, and dry, something like wool. Drapes very well. Weaves and colors limited as yet.	Outdoor awnings, curtains; draperies; blankets; suitings.	As yet limited weaves and colors.
Nylon	Coal, wood, natural gas, petroleum, air and water.	Discovered 1928 in experiments combining small molecules into large molecules. Extensive experimentation by 1930.	Outstanding strength and lightness, resistance to abrasion. Strongest fiber—one strand will support 75 pounds. Great elasticity and resiliency, always returning to original shape if yarns are tightly twisted and fabric is heat-set. Resists moths, mildew, and stains; non-inflammable. Deteriorates in strong sun—but less rapidly than silk. Slow to soil, easy to clean; dries quickly. Has pleasant	Resistance to abrasion suits it to rugs, upholstery, draperies. Strength, sheerness, slow soiling and easy cleaning make it serviceable as glass curtains.	Can be heat-set to keep shape permanently.

	Source	History	Properties	Uses	
Rayon	Cellulose (major component of woody parts of plants) from wood, cotton, etc.	Discovered 1890's by Frenchman making study of way silkworms produce silk. First called artificial silk; officially rayon in 1924.	Most types not noticeably strong, durable, or resilient. Wrinkles easily, washes well if properly done, and dries quickly. Often feels slippery and "unsympathetic." Relatively inexpensive.	Low- to moderate-cost glass curtains and draperies, upholstery, table "linens," and rugs.	May be glossy or dull, sheer or heavy. *Bemberg* —named for system of "stretch-spinning"; can be made to feel, look somewhat like cotton, wool, silk; heavier cloths usually have other fibers added.
Silk	Filaments of cocoons of 500 kinds of Asian worms which spin 1 foot per min.; softest fibers from cultivated worms fed on mulberry leaves; coarser (Tussah, wild) fibers from worms fed on oak.	Known to Chinese by 3000 B.C.; kept secret until details leaked out to Japan in 300, India 400, and Europe 700 A.D. Continuously sought and cherished.	Greatest tensile strength of any natural fiber; elastic; resists abrasion but not sun. Luster and unique crunchy softness retained over long period of time. Drapes and folds luxuriously. Takes dye brilliantly. Expensive.	Chiefly high-quality draperies and upholstery although less costly synthetics have all but usurped the market.	Often *weighted* to give it heavier body and better draping qualities.
Wool	Fleece from 250 crossbreeds of sheep; also from camel, llama, vicuña, kashmir, alpaca. Produced in most parts of the world.	One of most ancient fibers—man first wore sheepskin, then made fibers into coat; spun and dyed in British Isles at least 2000 years ago. Continuously and widely used throughout world.	Great capacity for hard wear, especially when of worsted yarns. High elasticity—single fiber can be stretched 30% without breaking—and high tensile strength; as strong as gold thread of same size. Attacked by moths, mildew, sun, and moisture. Holds shape, resists wrinkles; does not stain and soil as readily as cotton. Soft, pleasant to touch. Dyes penetrate deeply to produce unequaled richness and subtlety of color.	Excellent, all-round material for rugs and upholstery; also handsome for draperies (but deteriorates rather quickly in bright sun).	Great range of weights and degrees of smoothness or roughness. *Mohair* (Angora goat) soft, smooth, durable, lustrous, a little slippery; for heavy pile, textured fabrics. *Worsted* yarns, made of long fibers laid parallel, tightly twisted into smooth, strong yarns, differ from *woolen.*

Textile Fibers (Cont.)

FIBER	SOURCE	HISTORY	QUALITIES	USES	TYPES AND SPECIAL TREATMENTS
Vicara	Protein fiber of field corn.	Very new.	Good tensile strength, superior resilience and recovery, highly resistant to wrinkles and creases. Resistant to moths, mildew, and dew. Promises to be best mixer of any fiber; drapes well; adds sheen and does not mat on napped surfaces. Easy to launder with little shrinkage. Luxuriously soft but strong enough for upholstery.	Draperies and upholstery (when blended with other fibers).	

importance: cotton and linen from vegetable sources; silk and wool from animal sources; and acetate, acrilan, dacron, dynel, fiberglas, orlon, nylon, rayon, and vicara from man's laboratories and factories.   The table on the preceding pages gives the significant facts about the qualities of these fibers and the uses for which they are most suitable.   In studying it, you will notice that fibers differ from one another in many ways: strength; elasticity; resistance to abrasion, sun, moisture, mildew, and fire; and tactile and visual qualities.

A few other natural fibers deserve brief mention.

Jute is a woody, somewhat harsh vegetable fiber occasionally combined with wool, linen, or cotton for draperies and rugs and often used as a durable backing for carpets.

Ramie is an exceptionally strong vegetable fiber which is little harmed by moisture or atmosphere, takes color readily, does not stretch, has a pleasant luster and can be woven alone or with other fibers into very fine or heavy materials.

Sisal is a hard, strong, flexible vegetable fiber often used in rugs.

Kapok, a soft silk fiber from the seed pods of several tropical trees, is not woven but is frequently used for stuffing and padding in furniture and pillows.   It is lighter in weight, more resilient, and lasts longer than cotton.

There are also several synthetic fibers, not widely used as yet, but with potentialities for the home.

Casein fibers made from milk are soft, resilient, drape well, and are frequently combined with cotton, rayon, or wool.

Chromspun is a color-locked fiber which is not faded by salt, sunlight, atmospheric gases, detergents, or bleaches.   Fast-drying, resistant to mildew, soil, and deterioration, chromspun holds great promise for draperies and slip covers.

Saran resists chemicals and stains, absorbs very little water, is non-inflammable, durable, flexible, easy to clean, comes in a wide color range, gives unusual service as upholstery and window screens, and is being increasingly used in carpeting, drapery, and upholstery fabrics.

Soybean fibers have great resilience, can be very thin, and are sometimes blended with wool, cotton, or spun rayon.

Velon is much like Saran and the fibers can be transparent, translucent, or opaque, while the colors, integral with the filament, can be rich, brilliant, or soft. Upholstery and awnings are among its uses although it can also be very thin and sheer.

Vinyon is strong, flexible, waterproof, resists shrinking and mildew, and does not burn, making it suitable for fire-resistant draperies and upholstery, and for shower curtains, awnings, and umbrellas.

No one fiber is ideally suited to every purpose because each has its strengths coupled with its weaknesses. Three paths are open to those who search for fibers for specific situations: find an existing one that has the desired qualities; combine two or more different fibers into one yarn or two or more different yarns into one fabric; or develop one tailored to specifications.

How do man-made fibers compare with those nature provides? Generally, the natural fibers are far better understood, having served for thousands of years and, all things considered, are more nearly multipurpose—but among the synthetics one can find fibers better suited to one or a few sets of conditions. For example, nylon holds its shape and stands abrasion wonderfully well, giving it unusual merit for indoor upholstery. Saran can be used indoors or out where extremely durable, weather-resistant upholstery is wanted. All of the man-made fibers share some highly desirable qualities: the fibers are of unlimited length in contrast to the shortness of cotton and wool; they repel moisture, stains, and dirt rather than absorb them, and thus are remarkably easy to maintain; and they give no foothold to insects, mildew, and fungus. Each, however, has its limitations. Nylon, for example, sometimes deteriorates in sunlight and soot, may sag in dampness. Orlon is resistant to sunlight and dampness but is difficult to dye. Sometimes a fiber's toughness can be a drawback: there have been complaints that one man-made fiber used on auto seats wears out trouser seats! But because synthetic fibers are made by man they can be improved by man, and continued fiber research will doubtless eliminate many minor disadvantages.

Man-made fibers now comprise 21.6 per cent of the textile fibers used in the United States (their production increased tenfold from 1930 to 1951), while cotton accounts for 71.2 per cent, wool 7.1 per cent, and silk 0.1 per cent. Of the man-made fibers consumed, 83 per cent is rayon or acetate. The new synthetics are important not only for what they can do now, but even more for what they will do tomorrow. More and more the two kinds of fibers, natural and man-made, are being combined to eliminate weaknesses; some natural fibers are even being impregnated with man-made resins to produce completely new fibers from the old.

Fibers are, of course, only a portion of the fabrics story, because their usefulness and beauty also depend on the way they are transformed into fabrics, the first step being the making of yarns.

YARNS

Yarn is the term used to describe fibers that have been twisted together to give them sufficient strength and length for weaving or knitting into fabrics. Yarn making involves many steps but, in natural fibers, it consists basically of cleaning the fibers of foreign matter, drawing them out so that they are more or less even and parallel, and spinning or twisting them into a yarn; in man-made fibers which are already clean, continuous, and parallel as soon as they become filaments, the process is simply one of twisting them together. Yarns vary in the kind of fibers used, the type and tightness of twist, and the size of the finished product.

Fibers from one source may be used alone or combined to adapt the yarn for special needs. For example, nylon used alone gives a yarn that combines strength and lightness, retention of shape, ease of care, and wear resistance; nylon and silk combine the good feel of silk with the stability and wear of nylon; nylon with wool feels like wool but is lighter in weight, longer wearing, and resiliently retains its shape and resists wrinkles.

Long fibers laid parallel to each other and tightly twisted give yarns smoother and stronger than do short fibers somewhat randomly arranged and loosely twisted. Nature provides only one long continuous fiber—silk—while all of man's fibers have that characteristic; any of them, however, can be cut into short pieces for different effects. Length of fiber and tightness of twist lead to the following types of yarn:

- *Cotton.* *Carded* yarns have only the very short fibers removed and the remaining ones somewhat straightened; *combed* yarns are composed entirely of long fibers laid parallel to one another before spinning, which makes the yarn stronger and smoother; *lisle* is hard twisted from smooth, long, combed, mercerized fibers.
- *Silk.* Most high quality silk is made from long, continuous filaments, but *spun* silk is made from the short fibers that cannot be unreeled from the cocoon.

- *Wool.* *Woolen* yarns are soft, fuzzy, loosely spun from fibers only partially straightened; *worsted* yarns are tightly twisted from long, combed fibers and are smooth and strong.
- *Man-made.* These fibers all originate as continuous, parallel, more or less smooth strands called *filaments,* which are usually twisted into ply yarns; but they may be cut into short lengths, blown apart, then brought together in a mass something like cleaned but uncombed cotton or wool, and these *staples* are twisted into soft yarns known as *spun* rayon, nylon, etc.

Twisting fibers tightly or loosely has already been mentioned, but this is only a beginning of the variations: the fibers can be given a right-hand or left-hand twist and these can be variously put together in two-, three-, or four-ply yarns; and there are many special twists, of which crepe, slub with thick and thin, nub, snarl, ratiné, and bouclé are only a few. Then, too, a rubber core can be covered with different fibers to give elastic yarns, and fibers can be wrapped with metallic wires.

Size of yarn ranges from spider-web single filaments to silk yarns of 200 strands and on to rope-like cords. Fabrics can be entirely of one size or may combine several to many sizes as the need and desire indicate.

FASTENING THE YARNS TOGETHER

There are four basic ways of fastening fibers and yarns together to make fabrics: felting, knitting, twisting, and weaving.

Felting, probably the first of the processes discovered by man, consists merely of matting fibers together with heat, moisture, and pressure. Under these conditions, wool and hair fibers bend and interlock, and cotton and some of the spun synthetics react similarly, to produce a dense, somewhat fuzzy and resilient fabric of no great strength. Felts are used chiefly today as rug cushions.

Knitting, an old art probably first used by prehistoric man in making fishnets, is done by interlacing one yarn in a series of connecting loops by means of a long blunt rod or needle. Patterns are produced by combining the well-known plain, rib, and purl stitches, plus a number of fancy stitches. Knitted fabrics generally have quite a bit of stretch and are more suitable for clothing than household use.

Twisting, the process by which laces are made, is the twisting together of yarns that run crosswise and those that run lengthwise. Usually thought of as an aristocratic luxury, lace-making may well have started when some frugal housewife twisted together the threads around a hole in a woven fabric, or it may have had its beginnings in knotting yarns together to make nets.   Rightly or wrongly, lace curtains, bedspreads, and antimacassars have fallen from favor, and the only appearance of lace in today's home is likely to be in seldom-used tablecloths and napkins. This seems somewhat strange when we think of the great possibilities of using laces which half reveal and half conceal only moderately pleasant views through windows.

Weaving is the interlacing of yarns at right angles to each other to produce textiles.   Before we discuss the process you should have two important definitions fixed in mind: *warp* threads run lengthwise on the loom and in the fabric; *filling* or weft threads run crosswise to fill and hold together the warp.   Weaving is also an ancient art with a rich history of accomplishment, and although we do many wondrous things with yarns and looms, we have by no means surpassed the technical excellence or the beauty of some very old textiles.

The apparently enormous complexity of weaves can be simplified into five basic types.

- *Plain* weaving is simply one filling thread over one warp thread and under the next (or groups of filling and warp threads regarded as one).   Variations are *basket weaves* in which two or more warps are crossed by two or more filling yarns as in Monk's cloth, and *rib weaves* such as rep and poplin in which a single filling yarn passes over and under groups of warp, or several filling yarns pass over and under single warp yarns, in regular alternation.
- *Floating yarn* weaves include twill, satin, piqué, and honeycomb or waffle.   They differ from plain weaves in that filling yarns float over and under several to many warp yarns or the warp yarns may float over the filling.   *Twill* is typified by diagonal lines, *satin* by long floats which minimize the over and under texture of most weaving and give a marked smoothness of surface, *piqué* by pronounced ribs or cords resulting from exposed warp threads, and *honeycomb* by square or rectangular designs on both sides of the fabric.
- *Woven-in-pile* weaves are distinguished by having (in addition to the flat-lying warp and filling) another set of warp yarns that stand up in loops.   If the loops are not cut, we get such textiles as terry cloth,

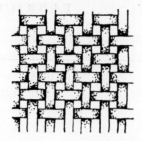
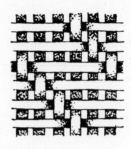

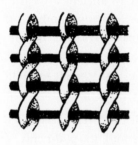
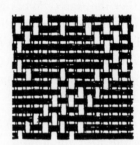

10-2 Diagrams of principal weaves: plain; floating yarn; woven-in-pile, cut and uncut; leno; and Jacquard.

tapestry and tapestry carpet, and frieze; if the loops are cut, velvet, plush, and the like are produced; or if some are cut and others uncut, a pattern is produced. In making Axminster rugs, tufts of cut pile are inserted rather than weaving in a pile warp yarn.

■ *Leno* weaves give more or less open, lacy effects by locking warp and filling yarns in figure eights. Marquisette and many other porous textiles are leno weaves.

■ *Jacquard* weaves are produced on a Jacquard loom, a complex machine in which punched paper cards control hundreds of levers to produce patterned fabrics. The fabrics may be flat damasks, raised brocades, cut velvets or uncut loops. This is not a type of weave (all types are done on Jacquard looms) but a mechanized way of producing pattern.

Weaves, like fibers, affect durability and maintenance.

- Loose weaves of any kind, but especially diagonal, and textiles woven of different fibers are likely to pull out of shape.
- Loose weaves, such as monk's cloth, or satin weaves with long floated yarns on the surface are likely to catch and break if used on furniture.
- Ribbed or corded textiles are likely to show wear on the raised portion more quickly than are flat or pile weaves.
- Loose weaves, unless specially treated, are highly susceptible to shrinkage.
- Napped textiles show wear and dirt quickly, pile textiles do not.
- Napped or pile textiles show spot cleaning less than do flat weaves.
- Smooth weaves show spots more readily than do rough.
- Soft, cut-pile textiles get mussed-looking easily.

FINISHING THE FABRIC

The fibers are found or made, spun into yarns, made into fabric; but when it comes from the loom, it is far from ready for use. Then various kinds of finishing give the fabric its final appearance and qualities. For us, the most interesting part is the application of designs, but it is of some interest to know that *beetling* or pounding with steel or wooden hammers gives cotton and linens luster; *brushing* removes short loose fibers; *calendering* rolls the fabric into a smooth finish and tightens the weaves and may also polish the fabric to a highly glazed sheen or emboss it with moiré, crepe, or other pattern; *crabbing* tightens and sets the weave in wool and *fulling* shrinks and compacts the textile; *gigging* and *napping* raise the fibers to give such textures as those found in flannel and fleece, which more or less conceal the weave and give a soft surface; *shearing* and *singeing* remove surface fibers, fuzz, and lint; *starching* makes cotton lustrous and stiffer; *shrinking* lessens the tendency of most fibers to contract when exposed to moisture; and *weighting* compensates for gum lost by silk in the cleaning process. By such means, lifeless, sleazy, grayish textiles are transformed into usable, attractive materials.

There are also some finishing processes which notably change the behavior of fiber and fabric. Textiles can be made:

- *Crease-resistant* by impregnating the fibers with resins, which also makes dyes more permanent, gives the textile more firmness and better draping qualities, makes it pleasanter to touch, and controls shrinkage in spun rayons, light cottons and linens, and velvets.

- *Fireproof* and *flameproof*, a worth-while safety quality even in the home, by treating them with chemicals which also usually make the textile heavier and stiffer, resistant to weathering and sometimes to insects and mildew, and longer lasting.
- *Glazed* with resins, a treatment usually limited to finely woven fabrics used for curtains, draperies, and slip covers, which give a permanent smooth, lustrous surface that resists soil and improves draping qualities.
- *Mildew- and moth-resistant* in varying degrees of permanence.
- *Shrink-resistant* chiefly through carefully controlled shrinking of the textile, although in some processes chemicals supplement moisture, heat, pressure, and tension.
- *Starched* by coating the surface with cellulose chemicals which do not wash out and keep the textile crisp and firm, give it a smooth lintless surface and better wearing qualities.
- *Water-repellent* by coating or impregnating the fibers with wax, metals, or resins which make the fabric feel better and hold its shape better as well as keeping dirt on the surface.

Since all of these processes not only do one specific job but make the textile generally better, one can only wonder why so few available textiles have been given these treatments. Undoubtedly they will become more common, but in the meantime, even if you have to look hard for them, you will be rewarded if you can find them.

Dyeing

Textiles can get their dye colors when they are unspun fibers, spun yarns, or woven textiles; and in some synthetics (chromspun and celaperm acetate) the dye is mixed with the liquid from which the fiber is made. Although generalizations about dyeing are risky, the synthetics in which the dye is united with the fiber seem to be the most permanent; next comes the fibers or yarns dyed before weaving; and last come the textiles dyed after weaving; but there is less difference between the latter two than there was in the past. The kind of dye and also the hue affect color-fastness, but almost all will fade in time if exposed to sun, washed, or cleaned, although some are more permanent than others. Unless you want to protect your fabrics from sun and use at the probable expense of happy family living, your best bet is to get the most nearly fadeproof textiles you can find; and since you know from the beginning that time will change them, select those that will mellow gracefully rather than those that will look tired and worn-out when they fade.

The following characteristics mitigate the results of fading:

Color. The colors most abundant in nature—grays, greens, browns, soft yellows and oranges, and the complex colors found in dull metallic ores—retain a pleasing appearance longer than do the brighter, more spirited, and stimulating colors of high intensity. Mixtures such as are found in tweeds and the like do not become as listless as faded solid colors. Dark colors lose much of their richness and depth when they fade even a little. Blues seem unusually susceptible to fading.

Texture. Fabrics with a definite texture compensate for the loss of color brilliance with their vibrant play of light and shade.

Pattern. Those whose interest lies chiefly in precision, clarity, and brilliance hold up less well than those of a softer, more diffused character.

This, however, is no condemnation of bright, solid, dark colors or decisive patterns—but you will probably more quickly feel the urge to replace them.

Printing

The easiest, least expensive way to enrich fabrics is by printing designs on the finished fabric or on the yarns prior to weaving, a process known for at least 5000 years. Printing is done with pigments mixed to the consistency of thick pastes applied to certain parts of the textile. If you have ever made a block print and cut a stencil, you know the essentials of the basic methods.

Roller printing is by far the most commonly used method, the pigment being applied to the textile from a copper roller engraved with the design. One roller is made for each color, but an effect of more colors than rollers can be obtained by engraving different parts of the roller to different depths and by printing one color over another. In warp printing, the yarns are printed before weaving, giving the design the somewhat soft diffuse quality such as is found in cretonnes and in tapestry and velvet rugs.

GREEF FABRICS, INC.   FORTUNY, INC.

10-3   Three printed textiles with notably different treatments of basically similar forms. *Left: Naturalistic* roses against a ferny background; chintz; American, 1850. *Center: Conventionalized* foliage also on chintz, American, and dated 1850. *Right: Abstract* pattern, derived from an ancient Peruvian design, on cotton.

Block printing is done by hand from blocks of wood often surfaced with metal or linoleum. Block-printed fabrics have the slight irregularities found in most of the handcrafts and are expensive.

Screen printing, done either by hand or semi-mechanically, is really a type of stencil printing especially suitable for large, vigorous, richly colored patterns produced in small quantities.

Stencil printing, chiefly used for rugs, is done by brushing color over a paper or metal stencil plate from which the pattern has been cut out.

COATED FABRICS AND PLASTIC SHEETING

Oilcloth and shower curtains of plastic sheets are examples of two types of fabrics that do not fit into other categories. Oilcloth, that humble and easy-to-keep material which still covers thousands of kitchen tables, is cotton muslin with an opaque coating of turpentine and resin; heavier versions used on floors have a stronger backing and are varnished. They are textiles given a coat of special paint and then too often printed with mediocre designs. In spite of their generally poor design quality, coated fabrics have much to recommend them, combining as they do the strength and flexibility of their textile backing with the impervious durability of their coating. Recently they have been much improved chiefly by using vinyl plastics as the coat. Heavier grades are made by squeezing the coating into the backing with hot rollers, joining the two inseparably, while in the lighter grades the coating is spread on and then baked in. They deserve consideration wherever water, dirt, and danger of tearing are present. Both coated and sheet fabrics can be somewhat elastic, a help in keeping upholstery in place and shape.

BAKELITE

10-4   This textured Vinylite plastic film can be used for draperies or tablecloths. Thinner versions are suitable for window or shower curtains. Regrettably, the designs *imitate* weaving.

Vinyl plastic sheeting comes in varied thicknesses from thin films for window and shower curtains to the heavy weight used for upholstery. Its fairly complete indifference to weather, moisture, dirt, and rough use make it well suited to windows or furniture not carefully protected. It has been known, however, to lose its lustrous surface with use; it lacks the friendly texture of most textiles when touched; it feels very cold and may stiffen notably in a cool room; it gets uncomfortably hot in the sun; and it may stick annoyingly to you if the air is humid. Even so, it is a good material to add to our repertory because it is durable and decorative: it takes all colors, either integral with the substances or printed, painted, or baked in; it can be metallized in interesting colors; it takes any embossed texture from narrow ribs and delicate wave-like scrolls to the roughness of straw and elephant hide; and the surface can be glossy, dull, or made fuzzy like flannel and velvet. It is versatile, durable, and quite expensive in the better grades. These upholstery fabrics invite comparison with leather, which they often imitate. They are less costly and come in a much greater range of colors and textures, but as yet few if any are as pleasant to touch. The comparison is much like silk as compared with synthetics: many synthetics perform specific functions better than does silk, but none of them has the feel of that amazing fiber for which the silkworm gives his life.

FABRIC DESIGN

All that was said in Chapters 5, 6, and 7 is generally applicable to fabric design, which can be structurally part and parcel of the fiber and weave, applied to the finished cloth, or can be a combination of the two. But fabrics have their unique characteristics from which their design should grow: all are pliable; all come in large sheets; almost all of them can be thought of as two-dimensional because, even though they may have textures or raised patterns, the up-and-down dimensions are minor in comparison with the length and breadth; and those that are woven, knit, tied, or laced have a clearly discernible design structure. What kinds of ornamentation do these qualities suggest?

Pliability suggests patterns, whether printed or woven, that are supple, pliant, plastic, and responsive to bending and folding unless the fabric is intended only to be stretched flat like rugs or some upholstery. This does not rule out angularity, but it makes questionable rigidity or hard-

10-5 Three drapery textiles illustrating differences in scale and activity. *Left:* "Syncron" is a woven pattern small in scale and quiet in effect. *Center:* "Fugitive Stripe" is a moderately large scale, active print. *Right:* "Suspension" is large in scale and active in movement.

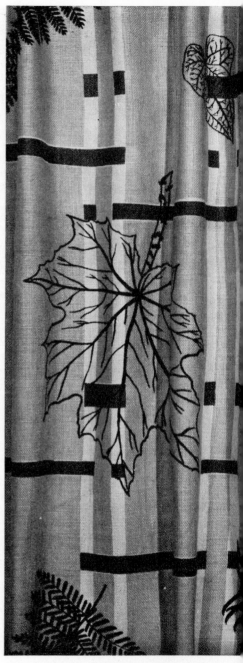

10-6 *Left:* "Branches," a screen print on Orlon, is delicate, in keeping with the textile on which it is printed, and is informal in character. *Right:* "Celeste," handscreened on heavy linen, has leaves floating in rhythmic repeat across a broken plaid background. It is heavier and more regular in character.

ness unless one wishes to set up a conflict between material and design. In general, however, it is better to get effects of unyielding strength in masonry and metal and allow fabrics to express their unique suppleness. Think carefully before you buy a fabric that looks as though it would break or fall apart if rolled, draped, or stretched.

The continuous, sheet-like character of fabrics (and wallpapers) is your best opportunity to get an uninterrupted, endless pattern without definite beginning or conclusion; in other words, over-all patterns that really take over all of the material, that lead you easily in all directions over the surface. Does this mean that separated medallions or other motifs are unsuitable? Strictly speaking, yes, for they make spots which interrupt the fabric's expanse. To be sure, such designs can be handled so that they do not stand as isolated centers of attention (Figs. 10-6b and 12-13g) in which case they function as means of holding and then releasing attention. Occasionally, though, fabrics with isolated spots can contribute variety, emphasis, or sparkle to a room.

The flatness of fabrics intimates that strongly three-dimensional enrichments are out of place, but beyond that statement this is a tough problem to handle. The extremes are easy to take care of: few people want bunches of fruit or flowers or abstract shapes that appear to protrude from the surface of their rugs, draperies, or upholstery, nor do they want designs raised high enough on rugs to catch toes and lots of dirt (handsome and rich as they may look in photographs) or so pronounced on upholstery that the occupant of the chair gets embossed; and not many like designs that seem to poke deep holes in a surface when everyone knows there are no holes there. But printed designs with no sense of depth often look flat and uninteresting, and woven fabrics that are absolutely smooth sacrifice the usually welcome vibrancy of many little lights and darks and show wear and soil quickly. Enough indication of in-and-out to bring life to printed fabrics and enough up-and-down to make woven designs spry and durable are generally desirable.

The pattern established in fastening the fibers together plus the qualities of the fibers may give all the enrichment needed. If more is deemed necessary, the weaves and fibers of the fabric are the starting point. The scale of the three, for instance, ought to be closely related for the simple reason that delicate print or stencil patterns lose their delicacy on coarse materials and large bold patterns usually seem clumsy rather than vigor-

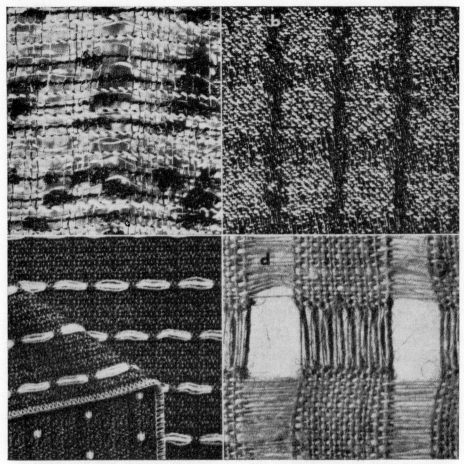

10-7 Four woven textiles depending on weave and fiber for their beauty. *Top left:* Bright rayon nubs enliven an open weave. *Top right:* Cotton, rayon, Lurex metallic thread, and wool are combined in a weave with irregular squarish shapes. *Bottom left:* This all-cotton textile is reversible. *Bottom right:* A casement plaid that gives an open-and-closed effect.

ous on fine cloths. In general, the coarser the yarn and the rougher the weave, the bolder the pattern.

In the above paragraphs we have purposely talked about fabric design with no mention of specific use and background because it will save you time to get a general "feel" for good fabric design before trying to select those rugs or draperies that you hope will do well in your own house.

When the problem is that specific, think in terms of our four objectives—use, economy, beauty, and individuality; look through the list of fabrics, and then read about the fabrics or other materials suitable for windows, floors, and furniture in the following chapters.

LIST OF FABRICS

The fabrics listed and described below are among those most frequently used in contemporary homes. They have been divided into five categories based primarily on thickness, which is of course important in determining their use. There is, however, quite a range within each category and some overlapping between categories. Most of the fabrics can be woven from a number of different fibers, but a few such as *ninon* are woven from only one. Fabric names are a strange miscellany being based on: the fiber, such as *linen,* which has come to mean a special kind of linen fabric; the weave, such as *satin;* the early use, such as *monk's cloth;* or the trade name, such as *Indian Head.*

Fabrics

VERY THIN	Almost transparent fabrics suitable for glass curtains, sometimes for summer bedspreads, dressing-table skirts, table coverings as well. Most of them can be made of cotton, silk, a synthetic, or even wool.

Bobbinet Fine and sheer to coarse and open plain lace with hexagonal meshes. Soft yet with character; most effective when very full; coarser types are best for straight folds; sheer well suited to tie-backs and ruffles. White, cream, ecru, sometimes pale colors.

Cable Net A coarse bobbinet.

Cheese-cloth Cotton in loose plain weaves, very low thread count. Very inexpensive; short-lived; informal. Usually off-white in color.

Dimity Fine, tightly twisted, usually combed cotton; plain weave with thin cord making vertical stripe or plaid; often mercerized. Fine, sheer, crisp; straight folds or tie-backs. Usually white; occasionally tints or printed patterns.

Dotted Swiss See Swiss Muslin.

Filet Square-mesh lace knotted at intersecting corners. Fine to coarse but usually

Fabrics (Cont.)

giving a bold, heavy effect. White, cream, ecru, and plain colors.

Marquisette Leno weave in many fibers. Sheer and open; soft or crisp; fine to coarse. Very serviceable; launders well. Usually white, cream, or pale colors; sometimes printed or woven patterns.

Ninon Acetate in plain voile-like or novelty weaves. Very thin; smooth, silky, pleasant sheen; replacing silk gauze. Best in straight folds. Plain colors, self-colored stripes, or shadowy figures.

Organdy Cotton in plain weave; like sheer, crisp muslin. Sheer and crisp, but crispness washes out unless specially treated; folds keep their place. Often used without draperies; frequently tied back. Many plain colors; also printed or embroidered designs.

Point d'esprit Variation of bobbinet with dots which give it a little more body. White, cream, and pale colors.

Scrim Cotton or linen loosely twisted yarns in an open, plain weave. Somewhat fuzzy; durable, but may thicken when washed. White, cream, or ecru; sometimes with woven patterns.

Swiss Muslin Cotton in plain weaves; usually embroidered or patterned in dots or figures. Fine, sheer, slightly crisp. Can be used alone, usually draped; effect generally informal. White and plain colors, usually light; figures may be colored.

Tarlatan Cotton in open weave; thin and stiffened with sizing. Cannot be laundered. Wide range of plain colors.

Theatrical Gauze Linen or cotton in a loose, open, crisp weave with a shimmering texture. Often used without draperies for colorful, informal effect. Wide range of plain colors, often two-toned.

Voile Open, plain weave, sheer and smooth. Drapes softly; gives more privacy than scrim; wears well. Many textures; many colors, usually pale; sometimes woven patterns.

Fabrics (Cont.)

THIN

Translucent fabrics suitable for glass curtains or for draperies, with sufficient body to be used alone and give a measure of privacy, although not at night. May also be used for dressing-table skirts, table coverings, and summer bedspreads.

Casement Cloth
Almost every known fiber in plain or small-figured weaves. Flat and lustrous. Usually ecru, but in a few other colors.

Osnaburg
Cotton yarns, coarse and uneven, in an open, plain weave; similar to crash. Usually medium weight, natural color, but can be light or heavy weight, any color, and with printed patterns. Strong and long-lasting; rough textured; informal.

Muslin
Cotton in a soft, plain weave; light to heavy qualities. Usually bleached or unbleached; also dyed and printed. Inexpensive, durable, informal; often used alone at windows.

Pongee
Wild silk in plain weave with broken crossbar texture caused by irregular yarns; also imitated in cotton and synthetics. Fairly heavy; often used without draperies; shrinks unless treated. Usually pale or dark ecru, but can be dyed.

Sheeting
Cotton in a smooth, plain weave, medium to heavy weights. Inexpensive and informal. White and pale colors.

Silk Gauze
Plain weave with a slight irregularity in threads, making an interesting texture. Hangs well; is never slick. Wide range of colors.

LIGHT WEIGHT

Fabrics suitable for draperies, and for bedspreads, dressing-table skirts, pillows, screens, wall coverings, table coverings, and slip covers; sometimes for upholstery in the heavier grades. Almost all come in a wide color range, and can be washed.

Antique Satin
Variation of smooth satin with a dull, uneven texture. Variety of weights but usually heavier than satin. Widely used for upholstery and draperies.

Armure
Silk, cotton, linen, or synthetic in a ribbed weave with a raised satin pattern. Designs are usually small, inconspicuous, conventional figures in

Fabrics (Cont.)

isolated, all-over design. Good upholstery material.

Broadcloth Cotton, rayon, or silk in plain or twill weaves; *and* spun rayon or wool in twill weaves. Varies greatly in terms of fiber and weave. Cotton and rayon types used for draperies, bedspreads, tablecloths.

Bunting Cotton or wool in a loosely woven, thin, plain weave. Usually white or off-white, but can be dyed. Cotton bunting usually neither durable nor colorfast; wool used for draperies.

Calico Cotton in a plain weave, printed with small-figured pattern. Inexpensive and informal.

Challis Wool, a synthetic or cotton in a soft, plain, firm weave. Usually printed with small floral designs but sometimes a plain color.

Chambray Cotton or linen in a smooth, close, plain weave. White frosted appearance on wide range of colors.

Chintz Cotton in a close, plain weave, usually with a printed design, and often glazed. Washing removes glaze in many types. Wrinkles when used for slip covers.

Drill Cotton in diagonal twill weave. Firm, heavy, very durable textile. Typical color is gray but other colors available.

Faille Silk, a synthetic, or cotton in a plain weave with decided flat crosswise ribs. Difficult to launder but wears well if handled carefully. Varies from soft yet firm to quite stiff.

Gingham Cotton in light to medium weight, plain weave; woven from colored yarns. Strong, launders well. Checked, striped and plaid patterns.

Homespun Cotton, rayon, or wool irregular yarns woven in loose, plain weave. Texture is somewhat rough and irregular; informal character. Plain colors; dyed; or woven of mixed yarns.

India Print Printed cotton cloth from India or Persia and with characteristic, intricate designs in clear or dull colors. Inexpensive and durable.

Indian Head Cotton in a plain weave, firm and smooth. Trade name for a permanent-finish cotton, vat-dyed, colorfast, shrink resistant. Inexpensive and durable.

Jaspé Cloth Cotton or rayon in plain weaves; varied yarns give unobtrusive, irregular, blended stripes. Gener-

Fabrics (Cont.)

ally firm, hard, and durable. Can be in any color but usually fairly neutral, medium dark, and monochromatic.

Linen Flax in a plain firm weave. Cool touch, good body, launders well; wrinkles easily unless specially treated. Often has hand-blocked designs.

Moiré Silk, a synthetic, or cotton in a ribbed, plain weave with a watermarked appearance. Most moiré finishes can be steamed or washed out —more permanent on synthetic fibers.

Oxford Cloth Cotton in a plain basket or twill weave, light to rather heavy weights. Durable and launders well.

Piqué Cotton, a synthetic, or silk in a plain weave with narrow raised cords running in one direction, or at right angles to each other (waffle piqué). Durable; interesting texture.

Poplin Cotton, silk, a synthetic, or wool in a plain weave with fine crosswise ribs. Firm and durable.

Rep Silk, a synthetic, wool, cotton, or combination in a plain weave with prominent rounded ribs running crosswise or lengthwise. Reversible.

Sateen Cotton, usually mercerized, in a satin weave; flat and glossy, with a dull back. Durable, substantial, but with a tendency to roughen. Often used for lining curtains.

Satin Silk, cotton, or a synthetic in a satin weave. Smooth, delicate fabric with very high sheen. Durable; somewhat slippery.

Seersucker Cotton or a synthetic in a plain weave with woven crinkly stripes. Durable, needs no ironing.

Shantung Silk, rayon, or cotton in a plain weave with elongated irregularities. A heavy grade of pongee.

Taffeta Silk, a synthetic, cotton, or wool in a close, plain weave, slightly crossribbed. Crisp; sometimes weighted with chemical salts; cracks in strong sunlight. *Changeable taffeta* has warp and weft in different colors. *Crackle taffeta*, sometimes changeable, has a slight crinkly effect. *Antique taffeta* has unevenly spun threads. *Strié* or *jaspé taffeta* has indefinite vertical stripes.

Fabrics (Cont.)

| MEDIUM WEIGHT | Fabrics suitable for heavy draperies and upholstery as well as for wall coverings and pillows, some also suitable for slip covers, bedspreads, screens and table coverings. Most are available in a wide color range, few are washable. |

Brocade Cotton warp yarns, silk or a synthetic filling in a variety of weaves but with a raised design achieved by floating the filling yarns. Woven on Jacquard loom. Usually has a multi-colored floral or conventional pattern.

Brocatelle Silk, linen, a synthetic, or cotton in a satin weave against a thinner twill background. Similar to damask but with much heavier design and thick padded figures. Usually self-toned or with one additional color. Used mostly as upholstery on large sofas and chairs.

Burlap Jute, hemp, flax, or cotton in a loose basket weave. Heavy and coarse; interesting texture. Often fades quickly.

Canvas Cotton in a plain diagonal weave. Heavy, firm, and durable. Strong solid colors, as well as stripes or printed designs. Often used for awnings, outdoor curtains and upholstery.

Crash Linen, cotton, a synthetic, jute, wool, or mixture in a plain weave with a rough texture caused by uneven yarns. Often hand blocked or printed.

Cretonne Cotton in a firm, plain, rep, or twill weave. Fairly heavy texture and bold design. Similar to chintz but heavier, never glazed, and patterns are usually more vigorous.

Damask Linen, silk, cotton, wool, mohair, a synthetic, or combination in any combination of two of the three basic weaves; flat Jacquard patterns. Firm, lustrous, reversible. Similar to brocade but design is not in relief. May be referred to as "figured satin." One or possibly two colors used.

Denim Cotton in a heavy close twill weave. Warp and filler often in contrasting colors; can have a small woven pattern. Inexpensive; washable; sanforizing prevents shrinking; reasonably sunfast.

Duck Cotton in a close, plain or ribbed weave. Durable; often given protective finishes against fire, water, mildew. Similar to canvas.

Fabrics (Cont.)

Hopsacking Cotton, linen, wool, a synthetic, jute or hemp in a loose, plain weave. Coarse and heavy. Inexpensive and durable.

Mohair Hair of Angora goats (or now often mixture of cotton and wool) in a plain, twill or pile weave or with a woven or printed design. Most resilient and durable of all fabrics. Novelty weaves now available from sheer to very heavy.

Monk's Cloth Jute, hemp, flax, usually mixed with cotton or all cotton in a loose, plain or basket weave. Coarse and heavy; Friar's cloth and Druid's cloth similar but coarser. Not easy to sew, tendency to sag. Usually comes in natural color.

Sail Cloth Cotton, linen or jute in plain weave. Heavy and strong. Similar to canvas or duck. Often used on summer furniture.

Serge Silk, wool, cotton, or a synthetic in a twill weave with a pronounced diagonal rib on both face and back. Clear, hard finish.

Terry Cloth Cotton or linen in a loose uncut pile weave; loops on one or both sides. Very absorbent; not always colorfast; may sag. Not suitable for upholstery but useful for draperies and bedspreads.

Ticking Cotton or linen in a satin or twill weave. Strong and closely woven. Durable; best known in white with colored stripes but may have simple designs. May not be colorfast but is washable.

HEAVY Fabrics suitable for upholstery because of heavy weight and durability; in lighter grades for draperies, pillows, bedspreads, slip covers, wall coverings, even table coverings. All come in a wide color range; few are washable.

Bouclé Wool, cotton, silk, linen, or a synthetic in a plain or twill weave. Flat, irregular surface, woven or knitted from specially twisted bouclé yarns; small spaced loops on surface.

Corduroy Cotton or a synthetic in a pile weave, raised in cords of various sizes gives pronounced lines. Durable; washable; inexpensive.

Frieze (Also called frizé.) Linen, cotton, mohair, a synthetic, or combination of these in a heavy-pile weave. Loops uncut or cut to form a pattern;

Fabrics (Cont.)

sometimes yarns of different colors or with irregularities used. Usually has a heavy rib. Extremely durable.

Matelassé   Silk, cotton, or a synthetic in a double-woven fabric with quilted or puckered surface effect caused by interweaving to form the pattern. Needs care in cleaning, but otherwise durable.

Needle Point   Originally handmade in great variety of patterns, colors, and degrees of fineness. Now imitated on Jacquard loom. At best, has pronounced character ranging from delicate to robust; at worst, looks like weak imitation.

Plush   Cotton, silk, mohair, a synthetic, or combinations in a cut-pile weave. Similar to velvet but with a longer pile. Sometimes pressed and brushed to give surface variations; sculptured by having design clipped or burnt out of pile leaving motif in relief; or made to imitate animal fur.

Tapestry   Cotton, wool, silk, or a synthetic in a weave with two sets of warps and wefts; woven on a Jacquard loom. Heavier and rougher than damask or brocade. Patterns usually pictorial and large, but not necessarily.

Tweed   Wool, cotton, or synthetic fibers; weave can be plain or patterned. Yarns dyed before weaving; often several to many colors combined. Soft, irregular surface.

Velour   Mercerized cotton, in a velvet weave with short, heavy pile. Slight luster, and indistinct horizontal lines. Durable.

Velvet   Silk, linen, cotton, mohair, or synthetic in a pile weave with loops cut or uncut. Luxurious but often shows wear quickly. Lustrous or dull, light to heavy grades, plain, striped or patterned.

Velveteen   Cotton or a synthetic woven with a short, close, sheared pile. Strong, durable, launders well.

PART FOUR

Elements

CHAPTER 11

Walls and Fireplaces

WALLS are the major vertical elements in the house, screening the gap between floors and roofs and usually supporting the latter. They give protection and privacy; govern room shape, size, and character; determine our movements and vistas; affect light and sound; and form the background against or with which we live. In addition, they are large and directly in line with normal vision. Walls are, however, seen and used in relation to the windows, doors, and fireplaces which are part of them; the floors and ceilings which complete the enclosure; and the furniture, accessories, and people. All of these are—or should be—considered together. The minute one begins thinking of windows, for example, as features separate from the walls and rooms in which they exist, all sorts of foolishness creeps into the "treatment," as curtains and draperies are so often rightly called. Let us then, while paying especial attention to walls in this chapter, think of walls, windows and doors, floors and ceilings, and fireplaces as unified parts of a whole.

WALLS MAKE ROOMS

Eighteenth-Century Formal Elegance

So accustomed have we become to thinking of 18th-century American homes primarily as formal, orderly exteriors and graceful, strong furni-

275

ture that an analysis of the Daphne Room (Fig. 11-1) in the Raleigh Tavern, Williamsburg, will help us understand the importance of the walls and fireplace in the total unity. The space enclosed by the walls, ceiling, and floor is simple, rectangular, of ample size, and with a generously high ceiling. One of the long walls is broken by a fireplace and by two doors leading to living rooms, the opposite wall by a door to the service quarters, and the end walls each have two windows giving cross light and through ventilation. Because all openings are symmetrically located the room has an easily understood and secure equilibrium. Although they provide access to other parts of the house and some contact with the outdoors, both the doors and windows do this in a guarded way: their relatively small size, formal placement, and elaborate treatment offer ways without inviting you to get out or look out of the room. Enclosure, not openness, is emphasized, but a great deal has been done to make the room worth staying in.

Time-honored materials, all in general use today, surface the enclosing planes. The medium-dark, oak-plank floor with a transparent, penetrating finish takes wear well and gives the room a dark base, and the plain plastered ceiling gives a light, unobtrusive top. The walls are wallpaper over plaster, combined with painted wood. Why is this wood painted? Because the smooth uniformity of opaque paint clearly reveals the delicately refined details derived from forms originally developed for stone. If visible, the free, organic grain of ordinary wood would weaken the clean, crisp, precise geometry of this ornament.

The walls are divided into three horizontal bands of markedly different proportions and these bands bring into balance what might have been an excessive verticality. A dado (the lower, decorated part of a wall usually between two and three feet high) surrounds and unifies the lower space and the furniture seen against it. Also, the dado of durable material covers the portion of the wall most subject to damage and dirt. Thus, it is a wall treatment combining usefulness, economy, and beauty. It is a little more than one-quarter the height of the walls, a little lower than the top of the fireplace opening and the chair backs, and becomes the bottom of the window frames. Rectangular panels, mostly horizontal but adapted when necessary to the available area, rest on a baseboard and are topped by horizontal moldings. Wallpaper covers the middle section of the wall, which is a little more than two-thirds of the wall height. Its pattern merits study: double lines of beadlike forms suggest vertical panels; highly formalized, almost symmetrical arrangements of foliage, flowers, and garlands have a precisely ordered rhythm and yet, somewhat paradoxically, look lively and free (which is an important characteristic of 18th-century design); and the total effect is quietly unobtrusive but neither innocuous nor monotonous. The top cornice (horizontal moldings at the top of a wall) is forceful enough to stop the vertical movement of the walls and to relate the walls to the horizontal ceiling plane. The cornice becomes more than a mere transitional element because of the stately, measured rhythm of the dentils (regularly spaced rectangular blocks somewhat resembling teeth).

All openings are symmetrically located, rectangular in shape, and strongly framed to establish them as important individual units, worth looking at. The doorways are markedly tall and slender in proportion and are framed by two sets of projecting moldings. Again what might have been an excessive verticality is held in check by two devices: the line of the frame is broken at top and bottom and the moldings extended an inch or two to get the observer ready for the horizontal floor and door top; and the frame is capped by a full-bodied convex molding and projecting cornice. The doors are divided into six panels which are similar to but not dull repetitions of the dado panels (an example of developing an idea to produce variety in unity). The windows, too, are vertical holes cut in the wall, but their shape is a little more nearly square than is that of the doors. Each window has two double-hung sashes glazed with small, almost square panes of glass, but notice that the shadow pattern they cast on the floor has elongated proportions much like those of the doorways. Clearly, the windows are intended to admit some light and air, but one tends to look *at* rather than *through* them because of the grid pattern in the sash, the closely-spaced horizontal slats of the blinds, and the enclosing, guarding draperies. The silk damask draperies have conventionalized floral patterns echoing the wallpaper motifs and the curves in the chairs, mirror, and sconces. They are hung to emphasize, yet humanize, the architectural rectangularity of the room: the long vertical folds are restatements of the window shape and wallpaper pattern while the curves formed by the tie-backs give a curtsy-like gesture, and the swag-like valences relate the draperies to the clothes and manners of the people for whom the room was designed.

The fireplace dominates the room because of its central position, large size, and decorative treatment. The firebox opening is a horizontal rectangle framed with marble and then with moldings like those on the door, but reduced in size to put them in scale with the shape they outline.

It is capped by moldings almost like those above the door but again with just a little variation. The overmantel treatment, basically a rectangular panel slightly longer than high, echoes the opening below. Interest is focused on this area by the variety in the enclosing frame. It rests on or begins with scrolls to differentiate it from the bottom of the door frames, and it is surmounted by a broken pediment which forms an incomplete enclosure for the pineapple finial. Thus, the overmantel introduces three forms not found elsewhere in the architecture of the room though hinted at in the wallpaper and draperies—scrolls, the interrupted diagonals of the broken pediment, and a finial derived from a fruit. It is no wonder that we look at the fireplace unit first and longest.

What effect does this room produce? It seems formal and dignified yet gracious and hospitable, carefully reasoned but with touches of the fanciful, not austere but certainly not casual. Its complexity does not permit full appreciation at a glance because it is full of details and refinements that do not demand your attention and yet are there when you want to see them. It would hardly be proper to call these walls and fireplace, windows and doors a "background" because in large part they make the room what it is—a beautifully appropriate enclosure for the handsome, sturdy yet graceful mahogany furniture designed for gracious, upper-class 18th-century life. It is no wonder that formal 18th-century design is well liked today, but it is more often than not embarrassing to see how crudely it is imitated and how inappropriate it is for the way all but a few now live.

American Colonial Semi-Formality

From about 1750 to 1850 many modest living rooms on or near Cape Cod resembled the one shown in Fig. 11-2. Thus like the Daphne Room it is part of our cultural heritage, and the same materials are used on walls, floors, and ceiling, but it is a much less formal room. Random width planks and the braided and hooked rugs give the room an unassuming but interesting base. A slightly recessed fireplace wall is paneled in painted wood in a simple but orderly pattern. This paneling unifies the fireplace, stairway opening, and adjacent door in an effective geometric organization (fundamentally surprisingly like some of the most contemporary designs), but it visually separates them from the remainder of the room (again much as contemporary designers do when they treat one wall differently from the others). The fireplace is appropriately emphasized by the moldings around the opening, the horizontal panels, and the simple mantel shelf, so that it is quietly dominant. Wallpaper with a lively, but not aggressive, small, diagonal pattern, contrasting pleasantly with the panels, covers the other walls. On the stairway walls, however, the wallpaper is of an active curvilinear design nicely suggesting the movements one makes in climbing stairs. Too vigorous for the whole room, it is wonderfully appropriate for these walls. In this room the openings are placed where they function best. If asymmetry is indicated, as in the doors, asymmetry is followed; otherwise, as in the windows, symmetrical design is used for the sense of order it gives. Unpretending and unaffected, this room has a heartwarming, natural, livable character.

A jump of almost two centuries and across the country to California brings us to the two contemporary rooms illustrated in Figs. 11-3 and 4. These, too, are rectangular in character and rely on the age-old materials of wood, stone, plaster, and glass. But these rooms seem more open, flexible, informal, and active because almost every part of them leads to something else rather than holding attention at separated spots with ornament.

Twentieth-Century Semi-Formality

In Fig. 12-3 a massive floor-to-ceiling stone wall begins well outside the room to the left and almost *but not quite* fills the wall. It is as though this wall, actually long enough to have completely enclosed this end of the room, had been slid over so that one end is in the garden and the other corner is freed for windows. The firebox seems little more than a large cavity until one notices the projecting stone ledge at its left, the recessed wall at its right, and the three vertical stone blocks. These devices bring a three-dimensional movement and help prepare one for the spacious view. The random-ashlar masonry gives a definite horizontal movement informally interrupted by the varied sizes and shapes of the stone. This substantial horizontal wall meets the narrow floor-to-ceiling windows squarely and with no transition other than the three vertical blocks of stone to the right of the fireplace. The strongly vertical windows carry around the corner to fill most of the adjacent wall, and open that part of the room to the yard. Opposite the fireplace is a broad unadorned opening into the entrance hall, while the fourth wall is opaque except for the windows which in the photograph are letting

11-1 The Daphne Room in the Raleigh Tavern, Williamsburg, Virginia, is a handsome room for formal 18th-century dining.

11-2 This Cape Cod living room demonstrates that not all American Colonial rooms were formal.

11-3 A massive stone fireplace wall and a band of floor-to-ceiling windows enclose and open a large living room. The exterior of this home is shown in Figure 8-11. Anschen and Allen, architects.

11-4 Wood, stone, and glass make this living room forthright. Spaciousness is achieved by broad openings and continuing rhythms. Richard Neutra, architect.

sunlight into the room. The ceiling is plastered and the wood floor is covered with rush matting. This room seems serenely peaceful and relaxing because all of the forms are simple, applied ornamentation has been minimized, and each material is used in a large continuous area; it gains interest through satisfying proportions, materials used so that you can appreciate their character; and the pleasant contrast of a stone wall holding you in and a glass wall letting you out.

Twentieth-Century Informality

The second living room is a smaller room in a smaller house, but it, too, looks more spacious than it is because of the way in which floors, walls and openings, and ceiling are designed. The durable and handsome flagstone floor extends without break into the terrace and is partially covered in the non-traffic areas with a textured carpet closely related in color value to the stone. The beamed ceiling is as substantial-looking as the stone floor, and its pronounced horizontal movement makes the room seem broader and relates the ceiling to the bookcases. Plywood and stone on the walls in the fireplace corner give a feeling of warmth and protection, while the large sliding glass door makes terrace and living room one continuous space. In this room one's eyes move freely *along* uninterrupted surfaces and lines rather than *from* one spot of interest to another as in the Daphne Room. In a few places, as in the stone pier at the fireplace corner, attention is held for a while, but then is carried either around the corner to the left or back along the shelves and davenport to the terrace. The room suggests easy movement from one place to another but does not demand it. Here again asymmetrical balance gives a sense of movement and space; large areas of one material give continuity and encourage you to enjoy each material's characteristic beauty; no frames enclose and confine units; all ornament is structural, none is applied; and the walls are either opaque or transparent, rather than solid enclosures punched with holes for doors and windows.

Three-Dimensional Design in Materials

The living room in Figs. 11-5 and 6 is notable for its rhythmic movement, relation to the site, and structural ornament. It is in a hillside house built on two levels with the entrance at the upper level behind the brick wall. As one walks from the entrance door along the hall, one can

PHOTOGRAPHS BY ROGER STURTEVANT

11-5, 6 A living room which reflects the hillside on which the house stands and combines secure enclosure with expansive openness. William Hempel, architect.

survey the room as a whole over the low parapet wall and then see it from gradually changing points of view on the stairs.   The ceiling, like the hill on which the house is built and the person entering the room, has a downward movement, bringing site, room, and person into harmony. Three materials make the walls, each in large areas and each on two adjacent walls to give the feeling that the space is wrapped and enveloped rather than rigidly and statically bounded: a glass wall opens the room broadly to the view and then turns a corner to meet a wall of brick; this brick wall juts out to permit a fireplace open on two sides, turns a corner to form a substantial background for the sofa, and then meets the wall of wood; and the board wall, too, goes around a corner as it follows the hall and stairs.   Each of the enclosing surfaces makes a definite contribution: the brick walls with continuous vertical and horizontal joints provides a substantial, secure corner enlivened by the grid-like pattern of mortar and bricks; the wood walls have the easy verticality of growing trees; the gently sloping, beamed ceiling projecting well beyond the windows adds a moderately active diagonal; the window wall is as stable in its simplicity and horizontality as the field beyond; and the square rush mats joined in a diagonal pattern make a rhythmic floor.   No surface is dull or life- less but none of them competes for attention.   During the day the wall of glass is the most conspicuous element; at night with the curtains drawn the fireplace and brick wall take over.   (The draperies and their instal- lation merit comment.   Plain material was chosen because no pattern is needed; they fall in simple folds from traverse rods well concealed by the valence board, and they can be easily drawn to where they are needed.) The fireplace, raised to the height of a chair seat and open on two sides, allows maximum enjoyment of the fire.   In sum, it is three-dimensional design in materials for pleasant living.

Twentieth-Century Economy

Plywood, Plaster, and Tile.   Plywood, plaster, and tile are skillfully brought together in Fig. 11-7, which shows a view from the dining end of a living room into a patio entrance and then on into the kitchen.   Hand- somely grained plywood has been carefully matched to sheath a wall with- out noticeable joints and has been cleanly tailored around a crisp open- ing.   Painted walls in the patio entrance are not only a good foil for the dishes but give an increased sense of spaciousness through their contrast

11-7 Handsomely grained sheets of plywood are carefully joined to give the
walls a smooth precision. The contrasting plaster and tile add richness. Michael
Goodman, architect.

with the wood.   The clay-tile floor (although questionably non-resilient in a much-used kitchen) contributes color, texture, and pattern.

Wallboard in a Boys' Bedroom.   The boys' bedroom (Fig. 11-8) has space-saving double bunks well fitted into one end of a room, and port-hole windows that would delight most boys.   But our major concern in this chapter is walls, and here we can see wallboard of three types: square tiles on the ceiling, rectangular tiles on one wall, and vertical strips on

PHOTOGRAPH BY FRANK RANDT

11-8   Wallboard needs no concealing, apologetic covering when used as effectively as it is in this boys' bedroom.   Edward D. Stone, architect.

11-9   An ingenious pattern of different-sized tiles on the walls makes this much more than just another tiled bathroom. Glass blocks give light plus insulation.

11-10 Patterned glass fixed in a simple wood frame brings diffused lighting, spaciousness, and privacy to a small entrance area. Gordon Drake, architect.

the other. The varied sizes and shapes suggest motion, which makes this room seem larger than it is. All are of the same composition, are tan and brown in color, and are inexpensive; but, most important in boys' rooms, they also withstand abuse, can be refinished, and absorb noise. Little more could be asked of one wall material for this use!

Tile, Glass Blocks, and Plaster in a Bathroom. Waterproof, easily cleaned materials are desirable, almost essential, in a bathroom, and tile has been used with more than ordinary taste on the walls shown in Fig. 11-9. It is small in scale in keeping with the room size; harmonious in color value; and placed in an ingenious pattern on the walls. On the floor, where less interest is needed, tile is laid in a simple pattern. Glass blocks, too, have been used exceptionally well. They provide ample light while insulating the room against heat, cold, and would-be in-lookers. Their shape is harmonious with the tile, and they have been used in sufficient number to avoid spottiness or glare. Plaster makes an unobtrusive ceiling.

Glass in an Entrance Hall. Translucent glass makes the entrance hall illustrated in Fig. 11-10 flooded with either artificial or natural light, greatly extends the apparent space, and affords sufficient privacy in a very small house. The patterns used—Diffusex in the walls and Skytex in the ceiling—are but two of the many now available in patterned glass. Simply, handsomely, and inexpensively held in place by wood frames, these panes of glass are merely screens for partial protection. How small and cramped this entrance would have seemed with opaque walls and the typical small window or two!

It should certainly be evident now that variety in character and ma-terials is feasible in the walls of homes. In each room discussed above, the walls, by contributing their share to the rooms' personalities, became more than noncommittal backgrounds. Even if none of these rooms had a stick of furniture in it, the character of appropriate furnishings would be indicated by the walls. More important, they indicate patterns of living.

The unique function of walls is to divide space into livable units. In terms of *use,* they are primarily protective screens separating the house as a whole from the outdoors and partitioning the inside space into areas suitable for group and private living; they are also important in making outdoor space usable. But they have other functions such as insulating against heat, cold, and noise; reflecting light and absorbing sound; pro-viding space for pipes, wires, and storage; and, in typical construction, holding up the roof. In terms of *economy,* the good wall has low original cost, lasts long, requires minimum maintenance, keeps fuel bills low, and takes minimum space. Regrettably, it is next to impossible to find a wall with these five characteristics, which forces us to do some thinking and make some compromises. For example, masonry walls are durable and just about take care of themselves, but they are thick and expensive. In terms of *beauty,* walls should be pleasant and appropriate for the activi-ties they enclose. The exterior walls shape the mass of the house and are its most conspicuous feature, the interior walls shape the rooms and establish their character. Thus, walls can give our living quarters *individuality* if they genuinely express the needs and preferences of the family.

MATERIALS MAKE WALLS

Although we take walls for granted, the building of vertical walls has been compared in importance to man's learning to stand erect, and it is worth noting that early man made paintings, sculpture, and implements long before he knew how to construct a wall.

Wall Construction

The technology of wall construction is beyond the scope of this book, but a brief discussion of what walls are and how materials affect their character can help us in choosing the most appropriate walls for the several parts of our homes.

The walls simplest for us to understand and for the inexpert craftsman to build are those that are fixed, opaque, and of one material. Log cabins are examples in wood, and structures of solid stone, brick, concrete block, or poured concrete illustrate this kind of wall in masonry. These walls are the same inside, outside, and all the way through. They are rare today because they are expensive, inflexible, comparatively poor insulators, less strong than they would seem, and they provide no space for pipes, ducts, and wires.

Today most walls are compounded of different materials or of the same material used in different ways. Masonry is reinforced with metal to increase its strength and often surfaced, especially on the inside, with some covering. Wood-frame walls are now the most common type in houses because they are familiar to builders, are resiliently stable, allow space for insulation and pipes, permit varied surface treatments, and are comparatively inexpensive. They can be thought of as three-layer sandwiches (although actually they may have five or more separate layers).

1. *Structural frame* of wood studs (2 x 4's or heavier posts) from floor to roof.
2. *Exterior layers* of diagonal wood sheathing and insulation or sheets of strong insulating composition board, and then a weather-resistant surface of wood, asbestos, or metal siding, shingles, or sheets; lath and stucco; or a veneer of brick or stone.

3. *Interior layers* of lath and plaster, plywood, wallboard, or wood paneling.

Prefabricated wall panels of wood, composition board, and metal have been tried with varying degrees of success. Made in factories under efficient working conditions, they ought to be better and cheaper, but few have been completely successful on a large scale. For two decades writers of books have been saying that some day at least the walls of our houses will come ready-made from factories—but very few have to date.

Although we generally think of walls as being fixed, opaque, and supporting the roof, they no longer need have these characteristics, and the following types are rapidly coming into use:

- Thin walls or storage cabinets which are not part of the structure and can be moved as needs change.
- Transparent or translucent walls of glass or plastics.
- Movable walls (or are these doors?) which slide into pockets or fold like accordions (Fig. 12-16).
- Walls less than ceiling height to give visual privacy without tight enclosure.

Wall Materials and Surfacings

The materials from which walls are made or with which they are surfaced profoundly affect the character of our homes. The Chart of Wall Materials enables you to compare their many differences. In studying this table notice that:

- All exterior materials can be used for inside walls, a possibility highly regarded by contemporary architects and designers because it cements indoor-outdoor relationships, and equally by housewives because it reduces housework.
- Some materials usually thought of only as flooring, such as linoleum, bring to walls the same serviceability they give floors.
- A number of recently introduced materials expand the range of possibilities.

None of this need concern you if you are completely happy with plaster or wallboard painted white or buff. All of it should if you want qualities other than these have.

Wall Materials

Exterior and Interior

MATERIAL	CHARACTER	USE	FINISHES	ADVANTAGES	DISADVANTAGES
Asbestos (panels, shingles, siding). Cost: moderately low.	Noticeable textures and new colors make these interesting; may resemble wood from a distance.	Interior: occasionally where durability and easy upkeep are important. Exterior walls.	None needed, but can be painted.	Rare combination of low cost and upkeep; high resistance to fire, weather, and insects.	None except rather commonplace quality.
Brick (adobe). Cost: varies greatly from one locality to another.	Earthy solidity; handcraft irregularity; informality.	Interior around fireplace, one wall, or whole house. Exterior: usually in mild climates. Garden walls.	Stucco, special paints, or transparent waterproofing.	Unusual character, resists fire and insects.	Damaged by water and hard to keep clean unless sealed; poor insulator.
Brick (fired clay). Cost: high but less than stone.	Substantial and solid; small-scale regularity.	Interior: around fireplace, one wall or whole house. Exterior and garden walls.	None unless waterproofing is necessary; interior walls can be waxed.	Satisfying texture and pattern, durable, easily maintained; fireproof.	Poor insulator; reflects noise; little possibility of change.
Concrete. Cost: moderately high.	No decided character in typical use other than smoothness, solidity, and simplicity.	Interior: (same as exterior) in mild climates. Exterior walls.	Exterior: stuccoed, painted, or left natural. Interior: surfaced with any material.	Permanent, durable; resists almost every attack; minimal maintenance.	Poor insulator, requires expensive foundations.
Concrete blocks (light-weight aggregate). Cost: moderate.	Somewhere between brick and stone.	Interior: any room where this character is wanted. Exterior and garden walls.	Exterior waterproofing necessary; no interior finish needed but can be painted.	Moderately handsome, durable, easily maintained; fireproof; fair insulator.	Reflects noise, difficult to alter.
Glass blocks. Cost: moderately high.	Somewhat hard, brittle, bright in decided contrast to most wall materials.	Interior: partitions. Interior-exterior walls in baths, kitchens, entrances, etc.	No finish needed.	Transmits light while giving privacy, insulation; not easily broken, needs only dusting and washing, resists fire and deterioration.	Can be broken.

Material / Cost	Appearance	Use	Finish needed	Advantages / Durability	Disadvantages
Glass (patterned). Cost: moderately high.	Transmits diffused light; patterns are varied.	Interior: partial partitions between rooms. Exterior-interior: similar to fixed windows.	None.	Gives both light and some privacy.	Breakable; reflects noise.
Metal (panels, siding, shingles, and tiles). Cost: moderate.	Varies greatly depending on size, shape, and finish; often regarded as un-homelike.	Interior: limited use in kitchens, baths, but increasing in popularity. Exterior: very limited use in homes.	Aluminum needs no finish except for color; others need paint; some have baked-on enamel finish.	Resistant to weather, fire, and insects; enameled panels and aluminum take little maintenance; if painted need refinishing every few years.	Poor insulator, reflects noise.
Plaster (and stucco). Cost: moderately low.	Smooth and precise; noncommittal background foil.	Interior: any room. Exterior and garden walls.	Exterior: special weather-resistant paints. Interior: paint, paper, or fabric.	Moderately durable and easy to maintain if properly finished, suited to many easy-to-change treatments; fireproof; special types absorb sound.	Monotonous and common, cracks, chips.
Plastic (panels embedded with glass fibers). Cost: moderately high.	Translucent, textured; colorful; flat or corrugated.	Interior: partitions. Interior-exterior walls. Garden walls.	None.	Similar to patterned glass except breaks less easily, lighter in weight, can be sawed and nailed.	Not thoroughly tested for longevity.
Stone. Cost: high.	Substantial, solid; impressive; natural colors and textures.	Interior: usually around fireplace. Exterior and garden walls.	None unless waterproofing is necessary.	Beauty and individuality; durability, ease of maintenance; fireproof; ages gracefully.	Poor insulator; reflects sound; not amenable to change.
Wood. Cost: moderate.	Natural beauty and individuality of grain and color.	Interior: one wall or entire house. Exterior walls and garden fences.	Needs protective finish to seal it against water, stains, dirt.	Fairly durable, easily maintained; good insulator; adaptable to many forms; ages well inside.	Few kinds are weather-resistant unless treated; burns; attacked by termites.

Wall Materials
Interior Only

MATERIAL	CHARACTER	USE	FINISHES	ADVANTAGES	DISADVANTAGES
Cork. Cost: moderately high.	Sympathetic natural color and texture.	Interior: any room; only plastic-impregnated types suitable for baths and kitchens.	None needed but can be waxed.	Durable, easily kept, sound absorbent, good insulator.	Harmed by moisture, stains, etc., unless specially treated.
Glass (opaque tiles or panels). Cost: high.	Smooth, shiny surface; many colors.	Interior: bathroom or kitchen walls.	None.	Lasts long (unless broken), easy to clean (but spots show), unharmed by water, stains, etc.	None except noise reflection, brittle appearance and possible breakage.
Linoleum. Cost: moderate.	Smooth, mat surface; great variety of colors and patterns.	Interior: hard-use rooms.	Needs no finish but can be waxed.	Durable, easily maintained, reduces noise somewhat.	None unless you do not like its character.
Plastic (thin, rigid tiles). Cost: relatively low.	Similar to clay tile except variety is sharply limited.	Interior: kitchens and bathrooms.	No finish needed.	Easy to keep and apparently durable; simple to install; light weight.	Similar to clay tile.
Plastic (Vinyl tiles or sheets). Cost: expensive.	Similar to linoleum.	Interior: can be used where durable, resilient walls are wanted such as in play space or above kitchen counters.	None needed but can be waxed.	Similar to linoleum but more resistant to cuts and stains.	Cost.
Rubber (tiles). Cost: expensive.	Much like linoleum.	Interior: can be used where durable, resilient walls are indicated.	None needed.	Similar to linoleum but colors are brighter and clearer.	May be harmed by grease and stains.

Material	Appearance	Location	Finish	Advantages	Disadvantages
Tile (clay). Cost: moderately high.	Repeated regularity sets up pattern; great variety in size, shape, ornamentation.	Interior: kitchens, bathrooms, and around fireplace. Exterior: occasional ornament.	No finish needed.	Can have great beauty and individuality; very durable, easily maintained; resistant to water, stains, fire.	Hard and cold to touch, reflects noise, can crack or break.
Wallboard (cane and fiber). Cost: low.	Soft, porous surface; no pronounced character in typical tan or gray but available in harder, textured surfaces resembling leather, cloth, etc.	Interior: any room.	If not factory-finished, needs paint or wallpaper.	Moderately durable, good heat-cold and sound insulator.	Absorbs moisture and dirt, shows wear.
Wallboard (Gypsum or plaster). Cost: moderately low.	Looks like the heavy tan surface paper; some have imitation wood patterns.	Interior: any room.	Paint, wallpaper, or fabric.	Not easily cracked, fire-resistant, can be finished in many ways.	Visually uninteresting in itself; needs protective surface.
Wallboard (plastic laminates). Cost: high.	Smooth, shiny, hard surface; varied colors and patterns.	Interior: kitchen, bathrooms, or any hard-use wall.	None needed.	Very durable, unusually resistant to moisture, stains, dirt; cleaned with damp cloth.	Hard, glossy appearance; reflects noise.
Wallboard (pressed wood). Cost: moderate.	Smooth, mat surface; texture of wood fibers but effect is hard, unyielding; also comes with checked and leather-like patterns or with tile-smooth enameled surface.	Interior: hard-wear rooms.	Needs no finish but can be stained, waxed, painted.	Tough surface is hard to damage.	None of any importance.
Wallpaper and fabrics. Cost: moderately low.	Tremendous variety of color and pattern.	Interior: any wall or ceiling.	Usually none but can be protected with lacquer.	Inexpensive, can give decided character, some kinds very durable and easy to keep.	Must be chosen and used carefully.

11-11 Permanent wall materials can be durable and beautiful.

a. Striated plywood has deep, irregularly cut grooves that give crisp shadow lines, camouflage nail holes and joints on interior or exterior walls.

b. Grain pattern is given three-dimensional emphasis in this plywood.

c. Hard-surfaced, pressed-wood wallboard is durable and smooth but has a pleasant texture.

d. Compressed wood chips give this wallboard a rich, varied pattern.

e. Marble is as beautiful as it is expensive.

f. Antique mirror, available in many colors and patterns, lends an extra-dimensional quality of space.

g. The cork tile wall is sympathetically soft to eyes and hands, the corrugated plastic screen transmits diffused light.

U. S. PLYWOOD CORP., WEDGE-
WOOD, MASONITE CORP.,
MARBLE INSTITUTE OF
AMERICA, ABBOTT GLASS CO.

DESIGN GIVES CHARACTER

A number of specific factors combine to give walls their character. Some pertain primarily to use, others to economy, beauty, or individuality. It is important to keep in mind that walls can have any degree of any of these specific factors or any combination of them.

Degree of formality or informality

The Daphne Room is formal; the Cape Cod living room semi-formal; and the rooms in Figs. 11-4 and 15 are informal. Formality comes when a room's design makes one feel a strict, firmly established, unchanging order. Symmetrical balance and pronounced regularity are the fundamental means; but formality is increased when the forms are stable and precise, enclosed with frames; surfaces are smooth and workmanship precise; and proportions make one feel upright. Use almost never indicates symmetrically balanced walls, but they have their own kind of beauty.

Degree of enclosure or openness.

The brick fireplace corner in Fig. 11-6 is enclosing and protecting, the window wall in the same room extends the space into the view, and the translucent glass in Figs. 11-9 and 10 suggests partial enclosure. Enclosure is brought about by opaque, substantial-looking walls of materials or designs interesting enough to hold attention; by warm, dark colors and noticeable textures; by small, separated, framed doors; by windows with small panes and protective blinds or draperies; and by small-sized rooms.

Openness comes with a maximum of transparent, translucent, or apparently thin, unobtrusive walls and a minimum of walls that block view and movement; receding colors and inconspicuous textures; moderately bright illumination; and all kinds of continuity of materials, forms, and colors not only within the room but with the space in adjacent rooms and the landscape.

Degree of horizontality or verticality

The high, light, inconspicuous ceiling and the up-and-down movement of fireplace, doors, windows, and wallpaper give the Daphne Room a dominant verticality; the narrow floor-to-ceiling panes of glass held by uninterrupted, noticeable wood frames make the living-room window corner in Fig. 11-3 look tall; but the living space in Fig. 11-4 is stretched out by the dominant horizontals of the fireplace stonework, bookshelves, dark beamed ceiling, and the broad openings. Low ceilings and furniture, broad doors and windows, horizontal lines on the walls and draperies—these give horizontality, greater apparent space, and informality.

Degree of activity or passivity

Typical smoothly plastered, uniformly painted walls are passive backgrounds; the wallboard in the boys' bedroom (Fig. 11-8) is slightly activated by the pattern of joints and color variation, and the tile pattern on the bathroom walls (Fig. 11-9) sets up a lively rhythm. The walls in Figs. 11-4 and 8 are active because they are *used* for built-in furniture, those in Fig. 11-15 because they shape the space unconventionally.

Walls become active to the degree that their material, color, texture, and pattern arouse interest; that they are integrated with furnishings, especially built-ins; and that they divide space interestingly.

Largeness or smallness of scale

Of tremendous importance is the scale of the walls in relation to the size of the space, character of the furnishings, and personalities of the people. The scale of the walls is large in Figs. 11-3 and 15, moderate in Figs. 11-4 and 5, and small in the Cape Cod living room. Large scale is produced by big, bold forms and ornaments. It reduces visual space, but is impressive when appropriately furnished and peopled. Moderate- to small-scale walls make rooms seem spacious and homelike.

Degree of smoothness or roughness

Here the range is from glassy smoothness to stony roughness with countless intermediate steps provided by plaster, wallboards, tile, wood, and brick. Smoothness is often associated with formality, roughness with informality.

A dominant consistency of one kind of surface quality is desirable, but variety and contrast are usually needed. Window glass brings textural contrast to nearly every room, but few of us would want all other surfaces covered with opaque glass and mirrors (except possibly in a bathroom).

Degree of light reflection or absorption

Color value is the most important factor, white reflecting 89% of the light striking it and black only 2%, but surface texture is also important because the smoother the surface the more light is reflected. In the past when windows were small and artificial illumination poor, very light walls were frequently needed to make rooms bright.   Today, with large windows and good artificial illumination, many people find that darker, textured walls create a more sympathetic enclosure for themselves and their furnishings.   Nevertheless, light-colored walls are refreshing, increase apparent size, and make rooms easier to illuminate.

Degree of sound absorption or reflection

Smaller houses, open planning, greater freedom for children to act like children, labor-saving but noise-making devices, and the trend away from massive upholstered furniture and heavy draperies make many houses noisy unless the walls, ceiling, and/or floors are of quieting materials. Cork, soft wallboard, and acoustical tile or plaster soak up noise while brick, ordinary plaster, tile, glass, and metal send it back.   Room shape also affects sound: simple, boxy rooms are the least pleasant acoustically; those with breaks or non-parallel surfaces are generally better.

Durability and maintenance

Refresh your memory on this factor by looking again at the table of wall materials, because the amount of time and money your walls take is a great factor in the satisfaction they give.   The nature of the *material* and *use* vie for importance on this factor.   Some materials—masonry, tile, vinyl plastics—are durable and easily maintained anywhere.   Some, such as fragile but colorfast wallpapers, last long with little care on walls not getting hard use.   Others, like transparently finished, soft wood, scratch and mar quite easily but are easily taken care of.   Plaster is somewhat harder to damage, much harder to repair well.   The basic questions are: How easily is the material damaged?   How easily can it be cleaned or repaired?   What kind of use will the wall get?

Degree of heat-cold insulation

Purely in the interests of economy and comfort, this factor deserves consideration.   This is a reminder; insulation is discussed in Chapter 15.

APPLIED WALL FINISHES

When a wall surface is not completely satisfactory, different kinds of wall finishes can be applied in the interests of use, economy, beauty, and individuality.   Paint, wallpaper, and wall fabrics are the most common types.

Paint

If you have ever counted the number of coats of paint that may have to be removed to reach the original plaster or wood of an old structure, you realize how much paint has been used, how vulnerable and beneficial it is. Being the easiest of all finishes to apply, it has led many into doing their own redecorating job. Nothing so quickly and inexpensively puts life back into dreary quarters. Courage in one hand and a brush or roller in the other is all you need to bring a dingy room out of the dumps by painting the walls with lively colors. Paint finds its place in the smallest apartment and in the most elaborate mansion chiefly because it is the one finish in which you can dictate the exact color. But although color is probably its most important quality, texture and durability need consideration.

Next to color in importance is paint's ability to give a smooth, even surface to whatever it covers. It is the householder's great hide-all. Sometimes, though, smooth paint will not cover all blemishes in the wall and sometimes we do not want smoothness. Then it can be *stippled* by hitting a stiff brush against a freshly painted surface to obliterate brush marks and give a soft mat finish, or *spattered* with one or more colors to give some vibrancy and minimize spots or scratches. More pronounced textures are produced with special thick texture paints. Some of these are mixed with sand to give a *sand-finish* while others, when still wet, can be gone over with a roller covered with nubby carpet, or a sponge or whisk broom can be used to produce varied textural surfaces. All these are easy, inexpensive ways to cover plaster cracks or wallboard joints and give walls some texture.

Although it is customary to paint all wall surfaces in one room the same color and then leave them alone, variations are possible:

- Different colors can be used for different parts of walls—one color for the lower part to band the furniture together, and another (usually lighter) to bring light and space above.
- One wall can be painted a color to harmonize or contrast with the color on the other three walls, or an indentation or bay can be painted differently from the major walls.
- The trim around doors and windows, and the baseboard are sometimes painted a darker value of the same hue used on the walls, very rarely a different color.

- Stencils can be used around a window to take the place of draperies, where wall meets ceiling, or wherever else they are needed.
- Decalcomanias can be bought and applied to the wall, the big problem being to find suitable ones and then to find a good place to put them.
- Murals can be painted directly on the wall or on canvas which is then fastened to it. For these you need an artist, unless you can live with your own art.

Durability in wall paints consists of resistance to scratches and abrasion, permanence of finish, and ability to withstand cleaning. Once upon a time, and not very long ago either, it was easy to divide wall paints into two classes: the calcimines mixed with water, and the oil-based paints. Today there is far greater complexity, for the base can also be rubber, casein, and many resins which vary not only in kind but in the ways they are combined. Generalities are no longer safe guides for selecting a paint for a specific situation. Having absolved ourselves of blame for failure of a specific paint to perform perfectly, we can say the following.

- Gloss and durability usually go together. A high gloss paint almost always has a harder, denser finish which lessens permeation of soil or stains, and it can be washed or cleaned many times without harm. It is thus of great advantage in kitchens and bathrooms.
- Calcimine of the old-fashioned type (lime, pigment, and water) has lost most of its former popularity. Very cheap, easy to apply, and drying to a pleasant softness, it was once widely used. Being almost impossible to clean, it required frequent new coats which later had to be washed off.
- Casein-based wall paints also have a soft finish but they are more durable than calcimine and can be cleaned.
- Rubber-based wall paints dry quickly and with little odor, can give high or low gloss, have a rubbery resistance to cracking and scratching, and are reported to be extremely durable.
- Oil-based paints, long the standard for durability, are still with us (although the oils are different), and are still durable, washable, come with varying degrees of shine, and have a paint smell.

Paint of poor quality is a tremendous extravagance because the cost of the material is only a small fraction of the cost of the finished job.

In addition to being brushed onto a surface, paint is now frequently sprayed on (many vacuum cleaners have questionably efficient spray guns) for speed and smoothness but not for ease.   Homeowners doing their own work more frequently put it on their walls with rollers which are easy, speedy, and almost foolproof.

Wallpaper

Long known in the Orient, wallpaper has been used in Europe for about five centuries and in this country since early days.   "Poor man's tapestry" was a good name because it originally came into use in humble homes as an imitation of the expensive textiles used by the wealthy. Wallpaper's advantages are many and varied:

- Can be used on any room in the home.
- Effect can be tested in advance by borrowing large samples.
- Is available in great variety of colors, patterns, textures, and degrees of durability.
- Has the most positive character of any wall surfacing in its price class and therefore can revitalize a nondescript room.
- Makes rooms seem to shrink or swell, gain height or intimacy, become more active or quiet and more or less formal.
- Compensates for lack of outlook or fireplace as a focus of furniture arrangement when one wall is of an attention-attracting pattern.
- Minimizes by illusion or camouflage ugly proportions or architectural awkwardnesses.
- Hides disfigured walls.
- Makes rooms with little furniture seem furnished.
- Distracts attention from commonplace, miscellaneous, or ugly furniture.

Wallpaper has no inherent disadvantages.   To be sure some persons do not like the "papery" look it often gives rooms and many patterns are too ugly or too dull to bother with, but these are not faults of the material.

Now it is possible to find papers appropriate to almost any way of living, any kind of furniture, any exposure or special factor.   They range from solid colors through textured effects, small and large patterns, to mural or scenic patterns.   Most have a dull mat finish which may or may not be washable; next come the glossy, washable papers; and finally the less usual types—flock papers which with their raised, fuzzy nap look like

THOMAS STRAHAN CO., TALISMAN WALLPAPERS,
KATZENBACH & WARREN, INC., LAVERNE ORIGINALS, TROPICRAFT,
IMPERIAL PAPER AND COLOR CORP.

11-12 The diversity of paper and fabric wall coverings is only hinted at in these examples. *Top row:* Two variations on the floral theme: loose, large, and lively; and compact, small, and quiet. *Second row:* A satisfying background of well-composed fern leaves and a novelty pattern of mermaids and fish for the bathroom. *Third row:* The three-dimensional six-pointed star pattern fits with either modern or historic furniture. The textured mosaic pattern has a rich interplay of light, color, and movement. *Bottom row:* The simulated weaving pattern (left) is a soil-proof wall fabric. Grass cloth and mattings (right) bring natural textures to walls.

textiles; marbleized papers which hint at the gloss and depth of marble; and metallic papers which in addition to bringing luster help a little in insulating rooms against heat and cold.

Selecting a suitable pattern and color is not easy. Wall-length samples should be brought home, fastened up, and observed at different times of day and night. Your critical abilities will be stimulated if you bring several samples at one time. In general, wallpaper should be regarded as ornament that noticeably affects the apparent size, shape, and character of your rooms. Consider it in the light of the criteria for ornament cited in Chapter 6, making these more specific by keeping in mind that the wall and paper are flat and continuous (like fabrics) and that in most instances you will see a lot of whatever pattern you choose. Also think about the effect of the color and patterns on your rooms—and on your living!

- Plain colors look much like paint but come in a variety of textures and obscure damaged walls.
- Textural patterns are a little more active, a little more pronounced in character, and more effective in concealing minor damage than are plain colors.
- Abstract patterns—stripes, polka dots, plaids, and many others—do not go out of fashion, seem especially suitable to walls, and seldom compete with furnishings and people.
- Stylized patterns almost always seem like more appropriate wall coverings than do naturalistic patterns.
- Naturalistic patterns give somewhat the effect of hanging the same picture many times in your room, and scenic wallpapers are like mural paintings.
- Bold conspicuous patterns reduce the importance of the space, furniture, and people.
- Conspicuous, isolated motifs often make a wall look spotty.

There are no best patterns for all purposes. Appropriateness to your home and quality of design are the major criteria. First ask yourself:

- Is wallpaper the most suitable material for my walls?

If the answer is affirmative, look at many patterns and types while you think about these questions:

- How much pattern and color do my rooms need?
- Which patterns and colors are most suitable?

Then when you are about to make your decision, ask these:

- Is the wallpaper appropriate to my walls, rooms, furnishings, and family?
- Is the design good in itself?

Wall Fabrics

Fabric wall coverings are closely allied to wallpapers, both historically when wallpaper was an imitative substitute for wall hangings and nowadays when plastic-coated textiles often resemble wallpapers. Just about every textile known to man has at one time or another been used on walls. Silk damask and velvet brocade, chintz and cretonne all had their days and quite lovely days they were. Any dress, drapery, or upholstery textile (there are very few woven for walls alone) can be draped over, stretched on, or pasted to a wall. Today—if we think of fabrics untouched by plastics—we are more likely to think of such durable customers as canvas, burlap, gingham, or denim. Or we may consider grasscloth, as appropriate today as it was years ago, with its subtly textured woven grass glued to a tough paper backing of soft colors or dull metallic luster.

Most likely, though, we will think of the host of new plastic-coated, plastic-impregnated, or just plastic materials. At first they betrayed their immediate oilcloth ancestry, even to smelling like that humbly useful product, but they have spread their wings. Some are embossed with textures, while others have printed patterns, and still others combine the two. So varied are these products that, again, generalizations are risky—but they are likely to be more durable than wallpapers, resist stain and dirt far better, withstand repeated cleanings, and hide more serious wall defects, even to holding cracked plaster in place. A number of them perform equally well as upholstery, thereby opening the way for close harmony between two parts of the interior. The better grades, regrettably, are expensive.

Paint, wallpaper, and wall fabrics are indeed wonderful devices for enlivening and protecting walls. Their relatively low cost makes fairly frequent change possible and their lack of permanence makes new applications necessary. They do not have the substantial feeling of wood or stone but they compensate with their low original cost and their challenging variety.

FIREPLACES

Fireplaces and fires are *costly:* a fireplace may cost as much as a bathroom and a good log fire in many parts of the country is about as expensive as a home-cooked meal for two. Further, storing the fuel takes dry space, getting it into the firebox takes labor, and the after-fire cleanup is a matter of quite a few minutes. Most fireplaces are *used* for their primary purpose of open fires less than one per cent of the time and are likely to stand the rest of the time as soot-blackened holes in the wall. When in use, they provide heat for people and for cooking, and light and ventilation, all of a hard-to-control sort. But open fires are *beautiful,* and the fireplace even without a fire can be a permanent, substantial center of interest in a room. The tremendous appeal of open fires comes from their warm, unpredictably and constantly changing, beautifully shaped and colored flames and embers which fascinate people of all ages and produce a kind of lighting equaled only by sunrises and sunsets. Less immediately, open fires are associated with pleasurable outings, direct contact with nature, and probably deeply buried feelings about the importance of fire to man. There is nothing else that lifts the spirits on a cold, cheerless day or night like a fire, warming hands and hearts. Then, too, every fire has its own *individuality;* in fact every moment of a fire differs from every other. Thus, even though the most perfectly designed fireplace is hopelessly out-of-date in terms of use and economy, open fires will never be out-of-date in terms of human satisfaction.

Purposes of Fireplaces

Light, today, is the chief purpose of fireplaces because the illumination they provide is unique. It is restfully soft and warm enough in color to make even the most pallid person look healthy. The concentration of flickering light in one spot is almost hypnotically relaxing and draws people together like a magnet.

Heat is the second purpose. When it is cold outside, the heat from a fireplace seems well worth its cost even though it creates drafts on the floor, may throw thermostatically controlled furnaces off balance, and now is costly in fuel and labor. Heat output can be increased and con-

11-13　An informal brick barbecue fireplace near the eating corner of a kitchen. The rectangularity of the bricks is echoed in the linoleum floor, plaid pillow covers and band of wallpaper, and the tileboard above the counters.

trolled by designing the firebox to throw heat into the room; having a damper to control the draft; having a projecting hood which radiates heat; and installing a prefabricated unit which, like a small warm-air furnace, circulates heated air.

Cooking, a third purpose, is a good way to make fun out of much work. Once the chief way to cook food, today it is a way of entertaining informally and of dividing labor among host, hostess, children, and friends. If done often indoors or outside, good equipment is needed: a fire over which you have some control; adjustable grills and perhaps cranes and special oven devices; long-handled pans, forks, and spoons; a location very near the kitchen (where most of the used items are kept), special cupboards where equipment is permanently stored, or a good wheeled cart; and a floor not harmed by sparks and coals, dropped grease and food. It sounds complicated and it is unless one is well equipped, but it is enjoyable, especially for those often-difficult occasions when adults and children are part of the same party.

Ventilation is hardly a primary purpose of fireplaces but they do ventilate rooms, rather violently when there is a good fire, moderately when the fireplace is cold and the damper is open.

Continuing the *traditional symbolism of "hearth and home"* is the fifth purpose. Gathering around a fire for stories, popcorn, or whatever, unifies persons of all ages and interests, makes then feel cheerfully warm and secure.

A sixth purpose is to provide rooms with a *dominant element*. This is readily achieved by fireplaces which differ in function and often in materials from everything else. When fireplaces were the only source of heat, their dominance was unquestioned, but it was underlined by giving them important positions and ornamentation. Today, they are not essential to comfort and they have to compete with large windows and television. Accordingly, they are treated more quietly, more as part of a wall than as a keyed-up focal point, and they provide a link between "architecture" and "furnishings," a little more active than the walls, floor, or ceiling and more passively permanent than most of the furniture.

Finally, fireplaces provide busy housewives with a somewhat dangerous place to burn trash, and the hyper-active host or hostess with a harmless outlet for nervous energy.

Fireplace Design

The first thought in fireplace design ought to be directed towards getting one that permits a good fire, because one that does not draw well or sends smoke into the room is worse than useless. This, however, is a technical matter best left to experts. Safety is a second thought because sparks may fly out the chimney or into the room; logs may roll out; and children can get burned. These hazards are reduced with a fireproof roof and a chimney top that retards sparks; a screen to keep sparks out of the room; andirons or a basket to keep fuel in place; and a hearth high enough to keep babies at a safe distance. Then comes fireplace work, and this can be lessened if indoor-outdoor fuel storage is nearby, an ashpit permits outside ash removal, and the firepit is lowered a few inches to restrain the ashes.

Location. When fireplaces were the major source of heat, nearly every room had one. Today they are much more strongly associated with group living than with work or private activities (one person by a fire seems almost unbearably lonely) and therefore are usually in the living room, perhaps with others in the library, den, or play space; sometimes they are adjacent to the kitchen and dining space (Fig. 11-13) if the people like indoor barbecues; and outdoor fireplaces are usually near the living patio, terrace, or loggia, although they may purposely be at some distance to encourage inexpensive, short vacations away from the house.

Where should they be put in a room? Keep in mind that fireplaces are usually large, permanent, dominating elements; demand considerable maintenance when burning and therefore should be easily accessible; attract as many people as can get near them so that space should be allowed; are natural centers of furniture arrangement; have unique qualities of security which are markedly lessened when they are too close to windows, doors, and traffic paths; and are frequently on outside walls where they give opportunity for interesting exterior design and accessibility to an indoor-outdoor wood box. Provided these factors are carefully considered, they can be any place in the room!

The typical location is the center of the long wall, a safe, sane, and perhaps too-familiar practice. This leads to a stable, static symmetry with the visual center of interest in the center of a major wall; allows maximum visibility and enjoyment for large groups; tends to shorten the room visually; strongly suggests a symmetrical furniture arrangement; and may lead to problems if the room is long and narrow and serves as a traffic lane (which, of course, it should not do) by bringing traffic through what should be a secure spot. The center of one of the short walls is also safe and sane, but somewhat less common. Again, it is stable and static, but it makes the room seem longer and suggests one furniture group near the fireplace with a secondary group at the other end. Placing the fireplace off-center in either of these walls gives the room a less formal, more active character, and usually leads to more possibilities in furniture arrangement.

Other locations include room corners, which are informally active, emphasize the room's longest dimension, and limit furniture groups to quarter circles. Fireplaces may also be in the end of a spur wall (see Fig. 2-10) which acts as a room-divider, or they may be free-standing, open on all sides and with a hood to gather the smoke. Although unusual locations are refreshing reliefs from stereotypes, they often reduce the visual importance of the fireplace because it does not have a solid background.

Appearance. Consistency with the whole house is a primary consideration, but a fireplace also ought to have enough beauty and individuality of its own to merit its cost. Here are the major questions, much like those about walls, for you to answer:

- What degree of formality do you want?
- How active and dominant do you want the fireplace to be?
- Do you prefer predominantly vertical or horizontal lines?
- Do you want it rough or smooth?

You can have almost any combination of these qualities you want, about the only exception being that it is difficult to envision a small, rough, formal design. Suppose you wish it to be formal. Then you begin to think of regularity, precision, a fairly marked degree of smoothness, and usually symmetry and ample size. A simple rectangular hole in the center of a plaster wall modestly bordered with metal, marble, or tile is likely to seem on the formal side, but a formal fireplace can also project from the wall's center, be elaborately ornamented with symmetrical carvings and/or materials rich in themselves to become the dominant element in a room (Fig. 11-14).

Size. The size of the fireplace is determined in good part by the size of the room, the scale of the furnishings, and the kind of fires you want and can afford. A fireplace that burdens the room with its bulk or roasts the occupants with a fire in scale with its size is seldom desirable—but a fireplace is most effective when generously ample, unless there is good reason for making it subordinate. Few things make a room look more pinched than an under-sized hole in the wall which will take only little pieces of wood. It is relatively easy to increase the importance and apparent size of a fireplace by enriching it with bands of tile and a simple mantel, or integrating it with bookcases and furnishings as in Fig. 11-4, or by surrounding the opening with sizable masses of masonry (Fig. 11-5). Also a fireplace will seem larger on a small wall than it will on a big one.

Form. Fireplace openings are usually horizontal rectangles, but they can be vertical or circular; and the shape of the opening can be strengthened or minimized by surrounding detail. For example, most American Colonial fireplace openings are horizontal rectangles, but pilasters and small columns at the side plus the overmantel decoration make the total unit predominantly vertical.

As mentioned, fireplaces can be simply a hole, the least noticeable treatment. They can project from the wall, coming forward in a friendly manner a few inches or several feet; and the whole chimney-fireplace mass may stand out a foot or more either from floor to ceiling or only to the height necessary for the fireplace. Finally, they can leave the wall entirely and be a free, clear, isolated element either in a block of masonry between spaces or as a pit on the floor with a hood and pipe suspended from the ceiling. Going in the other direction, fireplaces can be recessed slightly or in an alcove deep enough for built-in seats which makes them especially cozy, comfortable, and sheltering. The bottom of the firepit may be at the floor, raised a few inches to provide a resting place for cold or wet feet, or it can be at seat height, in which case the hearth usually is extended to give sitting space. It can go down, too, from a few inches to a foot or more. Raised fires are more comfortably seen and enjoyed, become a little more a part of the room, than do those at floor level. Lowered fires, particularly if the depressed space is large enough for seating, tend to draw people into a convivial huddle and subdivide a room without partitions.

Materials. This turns our thoughts at once to masonry because it is solid and fireproof and takes a little smoke without complaint. Brick, stone, and tile are naturally suitable. Wood and most wallboards next to the fire are, of course, out of the question and so is glass, as far as the writers are concerned, but one sees from time to time fireplaces faced with opaque glass, mirrors, or glass blocks. Metal, though, is perfectly satisfactory if one wishes the shiny smoothness that is its chief beauty and guards against its potentially dangerous hotness.

Ornamentation. Enrichment of a fireplace is a logical way to emphasize an important feature and to make the fireplace interesting at all times. At one extreme are the unadorned openings that focus full attention on the fire and at the other are the fireplaces so ornate that the fire is a mere incident. Both extremes are defensible if appropriate to the owners and their room, but most of us want something in between. If the fireplace is in a large wall of brick or stone (Figs. 11-3 and 5), many people feel that the color, pattern, and texture of the materials require no further enhancement. If in a wall of plaster, wallboard, or wood, a band of durable, fireproof material is indicated to keep the edges from being knicked by logs or tools, burned or cracked by heat. Mantels, once popular as a repository for arrangements of candlesticks, vases, and other bric-a-brac, are seldom found in contemporary design because they so easily degenerate into picayune shelves out of scale and character with and detracting from the fire. The truly glorious carved stone and wood or tiled fireplaces of the past contributed enormously to the richness of interiors, but regrettably are well beyond the resources of most of us today. Thus, most contemporary fireplaces have little or no ornamentation beyond their form and materials.

11-14 A carved stone fireplace of formal character as are the chair and all of the accessories. The intricately ornamented fireplace equipment provides interest at the firebox even without a fire.

A black hole in the wall, though, is pretty grim without a fire unless relieved with good fireplace accessories such as andirons, fireplace tools, and screen. Brass has long been a favorite material because its warm color and sparkling reflections are attractive with or without a fire.

11-15   A fireplace as "built-in" as that in Figure 11-14 is "set-in."   Also, it is as vigorous as the other is refined.   Roger Lee, architect.

Black iron takes almost no upkeep but is not very attractive; the white metals look "modern" but cold.   Then, too, accessories throughout the room which "respond" to firelight greatly increase the effectiveness of a fire.   We are thinking here of one all-wood interior in which many objects of brass, copper, and glass pick up and reflect the light from the flames so that the whole room seems to glow even with a modest fire.

There is nothing timid, hesitant, or half-hearted about the living room shown in Fig. 11-15, which is an addition to a dwelling near a stone quarry. Walls, fireplace, windows, floors, and ceilings are as forcefully unified as they were in the Daphne Room—but here the similarity ends. Stone, wood, and glass are the materials, each used in large areas and each fully revealing its inherent qualities. The massive, solid masonry is rough on the vertical planes but smooth on the ledge and floor. The wood, too, is strongly and naturally handled. Heavy beams support the sloping plank ceiling, lighter beams form the indoor-outdoor trellis, and foot-wide boards and narrow battens sheath the wall at the left. Large sheets of glass unite the room with the landscape.

These materials are organized in simple, strong, continuing design. A seat-high stone wall encircles two sides of the room, forms a planting box partly inside and partly out, and then becomes the fireplace hearth. The large fireplace, a simple cavity open on two sides, is part of a wall as decisively vertical as the ledge is horizontal. At one side of the fireplace, glass opens the room *over* the planting box and *through* the trellis to the wooded hillside. Then the glass continues across the adjacent wall to open the room broadly to a dramatic view of San Francisco bay. The other walls are solidly enclosing. Thus one part of the room is as sheltering as a cave, the other as open as protection from weather permits.

In conclusion, fireplaces are a delightful extravagance; natural focal points for group living and furniture arrangement, although their position is being challenged by window walls and television; and most effective when they are clearly part of the architecture, not a decorative afterthought. Today most fireplaces are simple and sturdy much like those in 17th-century American houses and in part are greatly appreciated because so seldom used.

CHAPTER 12

Windows, Curtains, and Doors

WINDOWS AND GLASS WALLS, doorways and doors are the openings in walls that visually and physically relate one space to another. The "wind's-eye" of old was a narrow opening in a wall just large enough to let out some of the smoke from the fire and to let in a little fresh air, to help light the room, and to permit peep-hole glimpses of what was going on outside. These are the three functions ordinarily performed by windows—*ventilation, light,* and *views*—but of these three only the last is unique. Ventilation can be handled possibly better through air-conditioning, louvered and shuttered openings, exhaust fans and the like; light of any amount and quality can be produced and precisely controlled electrically at lower total cost than natural light can be brought through windows (which, all things considered, are very expensive); but only through transparent windows, doors, and walls can we see the outdoors from protected enclosures. Although most areas of glass do and will probably continue to serve us in three ways, keep in mind when thinking of their design, placement, and treatment that their unique contribution to good living is visual relationship between one part of our living space and another. Usually, but not necessarily, this is between the indoors and the outdoors.

PHOTOGRAPH BY JULIUS SHULMAN

12-1 Windows and door integrate a kitchen, a sheltered terrace, and a dining space at the side. Fixed glass above out-swinging casement windows and a translucent glass door light and ventilate the kitchen and provide the housewife with a pleasant outlook. No curtains are needed because the openings have been wisely located and protected by the roof. Fig. 12-2 shows the exterior. Alice Choate, designer.

Two handsome, contemporary organizations of windows and doors are illustrated in Figs. 12-1, 2, and 3. In both, sizable sections of the walls are made transparent by organizing windows and doors in large units to gain spaciousness and continuity. In Figs. 12-1 and 2 the spaces between the structural members are filled with windows, doors, or opaque materials as use and appearance indicated, and the framework produces an over-all, rhythmic unity. In Fig. 12-3 the structure of the house and the frames for the glass are held to a minimum in a visually exciting, but not eminently practical or economical, result.

TYPES OF WINDOWS

The major types of windows used today are illustrated in Fig. 12-4, and can first be classified as *movable* or *fixed*. The movable types can *slide* as they do in the *double-hung* and the *horizontally* sliding, or they can *swing* as they do in the *casement* and *awning* types.

Double-hung windows usually have two sashes (the frame, usually movable, in which panes of glass are set) which slide up and down. Weights

PHOTOGRAPH BY JULIUS SHULMAN

12-2   A straightforward pattern of structural posts and beams brings rhythmic unity to this outdoor-indoor area. Spaces between the posts are filled with transparent, translucent, and opaque materials or are left open for pleasant livability.

PHOTOGRAPH BY JULIUS SHULMAN

12-3 Large panes of fixed glass and equally large metal-framed glass doors merge indoor and private outdoor living space. The high clerestory windows give additional light and ventilation. Simple draperies mounted on an inconspicuous ceiling track can be pulled over the glass when needed. Bamboo roll blinds are used for the window wall at the right. Richard Neutra, architect.

or springs hold them in place at any position. Usually they are higher than wide and the sashes are the same size and shape. They can, however, have more than two sashes, sashes of different heights, or the whole window can be predominantly horizontal. Advantages include ease of weatherproofing, simplicity of hardware, ability to open at top and bottom for good ventilation, and the important but often overlooked fact that when open they do not project beyond the surface of the wall to get in the way of curtains and people inside and of people and plants outside. Disadvantages include not being able to open more than half of the area, and the cross-bar, typically in the middle of the opening, which may be visually annoying. We could, of course, have "single-hung" sashes such as the windows on automobiles, which disappear into the bottom half of the car door; but these do not fit into typical house construction.

Horizontally sliding windows are like double-hung windows except that they slide sideways, and their advantages and disadvantages are about the same. Usually, however, they are wider than high, which emphasizes the currently popular horizontality in rooms and house exteriors.

Casement windows, hinged at one side and swinging either out or in, were in common use long before the sliding type. Their major advantage is that all of the area can be opened, and if adroitly placed they catch the breeze and send it into the room. If not well placed, they keep the breeze out and a stiff wind can give the out-swinging type a beating. Other disadvantages include the following: they are usually narrow or reinforced with vertical and/or horizontal bars for the necessary strength, which break the outlook into little pieces and complicate cleaning; if casements swing in they interfere with furniture and draperies, and if they swing out over terraces or walks they are hazardous; screens and operating hardware are complicated and expensive if really efficient; weatherproofing is somewhat difficult; and open casements offer little or no protection from wind and rain.

Awning-type windows are like casements but hinged at the top (or occasionally the bottom) rather than the side. Although they are new in homes, they have been widely used in schools and factories. Disadvantages are much like those of casement windows: small panes of glass, complex hardware, and sashes that take space when open. But they have two notable advantages if they swing up and out as they usually do: they give precise control of the amount of air coming into the room and admit little if any rain. A recent development is the *jalousie,* or louver, type.

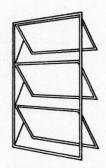

LIBBEY-OWENS-FORD GLASS CO.

12-4   Three typical window types are the double-hung sash on the left, the out-swinging casement in the center, and the awning type on the right. Turning the double-hung sash on its side gives the horizontally sliding type.

It is an awning-type window with very narrow (4 to 5 inches) strips of glass which open up and out. In appearance and action it resembles a Venetian blind. It has the advantages of the awning-type plus that of taking little space when open. Its disadvantages include relatively high cost and interference with the view brought about by the pattern of overlapping glass strips.

This brings us to *fixed glass,* something we have already seen in the large panes in Figs. 6-17 and 11-5, the smaller panes in Figs. 6-11, 12-2, and 12-3, and in translucent types in Figs. 11-9 and 10. It can be in very large single pieces and it is inexpensive to install because it needs no hardware or screens. The only disadvantage is that it provides no ventilation, but this is minor because ventilation can be handled in other ways.

Skylights and *clerestories,* not window types in the sense in which we have used that term, are windows in the ceiling (Fig. 2-2) or in a wall space between two roofs (Figs. 12-5 and 19-7). Both have advantages: good light and ventilation with no loss of privacy and no interference with furniture arrangement. Further, they can bring light and air into the center of a house, an important factor in interior design. Their only drawbacks are difficulty of cleaning and of controlling the light.

Wood and metal are the materials typically used to hold the panes of glass in windows and walls. Metal is stronger, thus making possible thinner strips, does not swell or shrink noticeably, and has a smooth, uniform texture like glass. With the exception of aluminum and stainless steel, the metals used in windows must be protected by coats of paint and, because all metals conduct heat and cold readily, moisture may condense on the inside of metal sashes in cold weather to an annoying degree. Wood shrinks, swells, and has to be given a protective finish, but it does not get cold enough to condense the moisture in the air. All things considered, metal is probably superior to wood, but a good many people choose wood because of its appearance and because it is far less expensive for windows of special sizes and shapes.

DESIGN AND LOCATION OF WINDOWS

Views and privacy, light, ventilation, heat and cold, and furniture arrangement are the major factors to be considered in designing and locating windows. Cleaning and curtaining follow closely. Interwoven with all of these is size of window units and groups, size of the panes of glass, and the whole pattern of windows and doors.

Views and Privacy

Normally, the larger windows should face the best outlook from the house, whether it be a view of distant mountains or of one's own private yard. Those necessarily facing the street or nearby neighbors should be smaller, high in the walls, or of translucent material. Many persons, though, seem to forget that glass is transparent and unthinkingly turn "picture windows" toward the street, thereby sacrificing either privacy or the windows' chief virtue with view-blocking curtains. This is a foolish waste of glass. Windows should allow those inside to look out but should not encourage neighbors or passers-by to look in. This is achieved by placing large windows toward the rear of the property or by building fences or planting a hedge.

Light

Natural light is cheerful, and for the eyes and the spirit it is almost impossible to have rooms with too much daylight. But it is very easy to get rooms that seem unpleasantly bright because strong contrasts of light and dark areas yield glare. This comes from too little rather than too much light and from having the light in the wrong place. *More light means less glare if the windows are well planned.* Until recently the windows in most houses were rectangular holes cut out of the wall and about the first thing one thought of was getting curtains, draperies, and blinds to "soften" the light. The large areas of glass in much contemporary design, however, seldom seem too bright provided the light is well balanced and spread throughout the room. A window wall opposite a wall with a strip of windows near the ceiling gives balanced, pleasant light. Here are some of the factors to keep in mind:

- Light coming from more than one direction minimizes heavy shadows and sharp contrasts and produces a feeling of being enveloped by light rather than having light shot at you.
- Light entering the top of a room illumines the ceiling and spreads

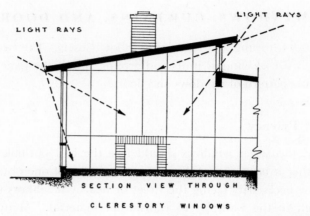

LIGHT RAYS   LIGHT RAYS

SECTION VIEW THROUGH

CLERESTORY WINDOWS

VICTOR THOMPSON

12-5 Abundant light coming through the glass wall at the right is balanced by that coming through high clerestory windows which also are efficient ventilators.

through the room more effectively than does light entering at lower levels.

- No part of a room should be more than 1½ times the ceiling height away from a wall with adequate windows.
- Overhangs projecting beyond the windows reduce the glare of the sky and mellow the light entering the room.
- Windows that reach to the floor are best when the material outside does not reflect a glaringly bright light.

No discussion of the light from windows is complete without reminding you that windows, the lightest elements in a room by day, are black at night unless they are lighted or curtained.

Ventilation

In general, the best ventilation comes when you can let the stale air out at the top of the room and let fresh air in near the floor. This system is ideal if the upper openings are protected from rain and too much wind and the lower openings deflect drafts. There are times, however, when most of us wish to feel a breeze coming through our houses from an open window or door. Rooms are most quickly ventilated if the openings are on opposite sides, least well when all ventilation is concentrated in one wall. In climates where summers are hot, it is important to concentrate ventilating windows or other devices on the side from which the prevailing breezes come.

Heat and Cold

Because window glass is a poor insulator, heat and cold are important factors in window design and placement. Double glass, by reducing fuel consumption, usually pays for itself in about three years in cold climates and also keeps houses cooler in summer. Perhaps more important is getting the glass in the proper place. Glass facing south brings in the welcome winter sun, but with a properly designed overhang excludes the summer sun because in summer the sun is high in the sky (Figs. 12-6 and 12-7). Glass facing east brings the morning sun, especially pleasant in the winter and seldom too hot in the summer. Glass on the

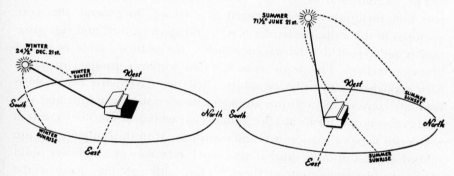

LIBBEY-OWENS-FORD GLASS CO.

12-6 Winter and summer position of sun at noon in Chicago. In winter the sun is low and stays well south of due east and west. In summer it is high and its arc is well to the north.

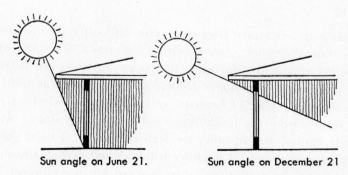

Sun angle on June 21.   Sun angle on December 21

LIBBEY-OWENS-FORD GLASS CO.

12-7 Properly designed overhanging roofs let desirable winter sun in and keep undesirable summer sun out.

west, however, brings the hot afternoon heat deep into the house. Then, because interior curtains or blinds help only a little, one is forced to rely on something outside the house such as nearby shade trees, vine-covered trellises, exterior Venetian blinds, or awnings. Glass to the north brings no heat from the sun except a very little in the summer but much cold in the winter. Thus from the point of view of heat and cold in most parts of the country, glass on the south is by far the best, followed by that on the east; glass on the north brings winter cold and that on the west brings summer heat.

Furniture Arrangement

The location and design of windows and doors determines in large part how furniture can be arranged in a room. In general, the more openings in the walls, the harder it is to arrange furniture, and this situation is aggravated if windows come below the ordinary table height of 27 to 30 inches. This leads us to say that windows grouped in bands high enough to allow placing tables, chests, or davenports below them facilitate convenient furniture arrangement—clerestory windows and sky-lights raise no problems at all. Windows reaching to the floor create a wonderful sense of spaciousness and continuity with the outdoors but are robbed of most of their value if very much furniture or any heavy, solid pieces are placed in front of them. Thus, although they increase the *visual* space they often reduce the *usable* space, as is evident in the room shown in Fig. 12-3.

Cleaning

All glass must be cleaned frequently, especially often in dusty or sooty locations, but also when glass is within the reach of small children. Windows are easiest to clean when the panes are large, can be reached without stooping or climbing a ladder, and the outside as well as the inside is easy to get at. Casements and awning-type windows can be cleaned readily from the inside, but double-hung and sliding windows are a little harder; and in order to clean both sides of fixed glass it is necessary to go outdoors. Clerestory windows and skylights bring their own special cleaning difficulties, often lessened but not eliminated with figured glass. It is well to take into account these aspects of the various types of windows before making a choice among them.

Curtaining

This problem is simplified if windows do not vary much in size, shape, and distance from floor and ceiling. It becomes most complicated when windows are diverse in size, shape, and location. For example, an isolated small high window, excellent for ventilation in a bedroom or bath, is hard to curtain so that it looks well, the generally best solution being a material that matches the wall. Narrow bands of high windows, clerestories, and skylights are so difficult to curtain that usually no attempt is made to control the light they admit, and thus they are unsuitable for rooms that need to be thoroughly darkened. Another problem-raiser is the window that follows a sloping ceiling. Then the curtain is usually hung along a horizontal bar, and the upper portion, which needs the protection of an overhanging roof, is uncovered. And there is the band of windows stretching from one side of the room to the other but leaving no wall space for the draperies when pulled back. Then you have three alternatives: no window treatment; blinds or shades that move up and down; or draperies over part of your window all the time.

Windows in Architectural Composition

So far windows have been treated in terms of what they can do to make living comfortable, and this is the first logical step, but if we stopped there the effect would be hodge-podge. Windows and doors today as in the past are one of the most important factors in architectural composition, but in no aspect of home planning has there been greater change. The availability of large sheets of glass (coupled with improved heating and cooling systems) has changed interiors from boxes with separated holes in the wall, as in Figs. 11-1 and 2, to space enclosed with large areas of transparent, translucent, and opaque materials. No longer do we seek an arbitrary, exterior symmetry (Fig. 19-1) regardless of its effect on the interior, nor do we attempt a self-conscious, asymmetrical picturesqueness. Glass is used liberally where it serves best, but it is ordered for visual pleasantness inside and out. The same tried and true aims and principles of design still operate as general guides but the resulting patterns are notably different from anything known heretofore. Contemporary trends can be summarized as follows:

■ Windows and doors designed as integral parts of the architectural shell rather than as isolated, ornamented cut-holes.

12-8 Windows in this plywood house are organized in groups and fit into the pattern of plywood panels and framing. Ventilating louvers above and below windows provide ventilation and make insect screens on windows unnecessary. John Yeon, architect.

- Windows grouped in bands, usually horizontal, and when feasible windows and doors integrated in harmonious units.
- Large areas of glass placed where they serve best, such as window walls toward the garden or view.
- Small areas of glass strategically located for balanced lighting and ventilation plus privacy.
- Large panes of glass favored.
- Limited variety of shapes, sizes, and types.
- Minimum emphasis on frames and trimmings.

Windows are costly. Glass is expensive to buy and replace, difficult to make weather-tight around the edges, must be cleaned often, is likely to run up your heating and cooling bills. If the glass is movable, screens and window hardware must be furnished, and almost all windows bring the added expense of curtains, draperies, and/or blinds. But sensibly large, well placed windows are worth what they cost.

It is not too far-fetched to think of windows as the eyes of the house, the glass like the pupil admitting light to the space in back. Our eyes are wonderfully protected and have magnificent controls only approximated in the best of windows. They are shielded by our eyebrows and eyelashes, which are directly comparable to overhanging roofs, vine-covered trellises, and awnings. They adjust automatically to different brightnesses of light by changes in the size of the pupil and by opening or closing our eyelids with their filtering lashes. Venetian blinds, roller shades, glass curtains, and draw curtains perform similar functions at windows. And when we no longer wish to see, we can close our eyes—or pull heavy draperies or blinds entirely over our windows.

WINDOW TREATMENT

It is a temptation to say that the perfectly planned window needs no treatment, but we would then ignore the great changes in outside light and heat and the varying needs of the people inside. Thus, in terms of *use* we ordinarily have curtains, draperies, blinds, or shades inside to control the privacy of the home, the amount and kind of light entering, and heat and cold. From the point of view of *economy* the less you have at your windows the more money you will have for other expenditures (or savings!). Furthermore, what you put there ought to be durable; resist the ravages of sun, moisture, and moths; and be easily maintained.

MATT KAHN

12-9 Separated windows with small panes of glass give an effect quite different from that produced by a band of glass with a minimum of bars.

Beauty comes from relating the windows appropriately to the whole room and the people using it. *Individuality,* here as elsewhere, is less a matter of being "different" than of solving *your own* problem well.

Window treatments can be divided into those inside the house and those outside. Exterior window treatments, often neglected, have the distinct advantage of being out of the way of furniture and not covering wall space inside the room. In addition to those mentioned below we should not forget overhanging roofs, trellises, trees, shrubs, and fences.

Awnings can be of the well-known rolling or folding canvas types which are available in varied designs, protect windows from sun and rain, give a pleasant, soft light inside, and can be good looking. Stationary types are made of weather-resistant aluminum, translucent plastics, and wood.

Exterior Venetian blinds made of metal perform all the functions of those used inside and in addition deflect sun heat, rain, and cold winds from windows without cutting off all air movement, but they are expensive.

Shutters are seldom used today except for securing vacation houses against marauders and windows against violent storms in some sections.

Interior window treatments (other than curtains and draperies) can be divided into those that move up and down or sideways and those that remain in one position. Those moving up and down have the distinct advantage of being completely out of the way when unwanted, but if they are hung from the top as they usually are, they cut out the best light. The major types include the following:

Fabric roller shades on rollers are inexpensive; can cover part, all, or none of the glass; reduce light, heat, and cold, and give privacy in direct relation to their thickness and degree of opaqueness; are easily cleaned or replaced; and now come in a challenging variety of plain colors, textures, and printed designs. At first glance they seem very good, and they actually are, but here are their drawbacks: when pulled down they cut the light from the top of the window first, and that is your best light; they block the breeze or whip around annoyingly if the window is opened; and they contribute little to the window's or room's beauty.

Bamboo and split-wood shades, once used only on summer porches, have come into the house and perform much like those made of fabrics (Figs. 3-3 and 12-16). They differ in that they let some air through, give some notion of what is outside, contribute a pleasant texture, and are often large enough to cover several openings. They seldom give complete privacy.

Venetian blinds, much used in Colonial days, now come in metal and plastic as well as wood. They give almost complete light control—they can direct it straight into the room, down toward the floor, or up to the ceiling—and at the same time let air through; they can be raised so that they cover none of the window and disappear completely behind a cornice or valance; they are durable but not expensive; and their horizontal lines are pleasant. They do, however, collect dust and dirt which is not easy to remove.

Shutters of the old-fashioned inside type have recently staged a minor comeback. They become a unified part of the wall (Fig. 3-4), last indefinitely, and are moderately easy to keep looking well.

The above might be called "hard" window treatments. Since none of them does much toward humanizing windows, they are often combined with curtains and draperies.

CURTAINS AND DRAPERIES

In addition to controlling privacy, light, and heat, curtains and draperies are good acoustical materials, soaking up noise in proportion to the area they cover, the thickness of the fabric, and the depth of the folds. They make rooms home-like and effectively cover the bareness of a room not completely furnished, an important point to keep in mind if you do not get all of your furniture at once. They are also useful in concealing architectural defects; small rooms look larger if curtains and draperies blend with the walls; low rooms look higher if draperies go from floor to ceiling; gloomy rooms look brighter if yellow is used near the windows; walls chopped-up with windows and jogs can be simplified and unified by generous glass curtains and draperies; and some eye-sores can be completely concealed. You can direct almost any degree of attention you want toward your windows by the fabrics you select and the way you hang them: unpatterned materials similar in color to the walls act as an inconspicuous transition between opaque walls and clear glass and encourage you to look *through the window;* moderate color contrasts and patterns make you look *toward the window;* and strongly attention-get-

12-10   A bamboo drapery partially screens a dining space, glass curtains diffuse the light and give some privacy, and draw curtains, which have a printed design in harmony with the wood walls and linoleum floor, can be drawn for complete privacy.

ting patterns and colors cause you to look *at the draperies* rather than the window.

Although curtains and draperies are usually associated with windows, people all over the world have used them as space separators. The great halls in medieval castles were often partitioned with tapestries at night to make them more suitable for sleeping, and the American Indians divided their tepees with skins or blankets. Portieres, as curtains hung across doorways are called, were extensively used to close the large openings between rooms in Victorian houses. This practice has been revived in many contemporary houses, especially to give partial separation between living and dining spaces. Sometimes the draperies used this way are heavy and opaque, but they may be moderately thin and translucent or of very thin open mesh material so that you can see indistinctly the space beyond.

A few definitions are now in order to keep us together in the following discussion.

- *Glass curtains* are of thin materials and are hung next to the glass.
- *Sash curtains* are a type of glass curtain hung on the window sash.
- *Draw curtains* are those of translucent or opaque fabrics mounted on traverse rods and traditionally come between glass curtains and draperies. Nowadays they are often used alone.
- *Draperies* are any loosely hung (not stretched) fabric. Thus, the term really includes all curtains. Generally, though, draperies are thought of as heavier than draw curtains and they can be of the type that hangs idly at the sides of windows purely for decoration.
- *Cornices* are horizontal bands from about 4 to 8 inches wide across the tops of windows to conceal the tops of curtains and draperies and the rods from which they hang and to relate the whole window treatment to the wall and ceiling.
- *Valances* are simply wide cornices and are often varied in shape.

Glass Curtains

Glass curtains soften and diffuse light, reduce glare and the sharp contrasts of dark shadows cast by furniture, temper the brittleness of glass and relate it to the rest of the room, give partial privacy, and decrease the necessity of keeping windows spotless. They make a room seem light and airy, especially when used without draperies, in which case they

12-11 A wall with two separated windows is a typical curtaining problem which can be solved in a number of ways with different effects. At the left, curtains aligned with the windows cover the wall space and produce a horizontal band. In the center, tier or cafe curtains hung from two rods can give a checkerboard effect as illustrated, but they could be slid along the rods to cover either the windows or the walls. At the right, curtains from window tops to floor make the wall and windows seem tall and narrow.

usually cover the whole window frame. They are needed most when windows are isolated, small, or poorly placed, when the outlook is un-attractive or there is constant need for some privacy. They are needed least when windows are large and grouped together, daylight is well balanced, and when the outlook is good and privacy is comfortably as-sured. Glass curtains can make, along with lamp shades, one unique visual contribution—they bring light *through* color and pattern into the room a little as stained glass does in cathedrals and did in Victorian houses. If an outlook is poor and a room needs more life, colored and patterned glass curtains present an unusual opportunity.

Materials. A great variety of simple materials have taken the place of our great-grandmothers' beautifully rich lace curtains. Any fabric that is thin and drapes well, whether produced for curtains, dresses, or other uses, is suitable *if* it hangs well and will stand sun and washing or cleaning. Among the more common materials are many open nets and laces, such as delicate *bobbinets*, square-meshed *filets* of many degrees of fineness, and sturdy *fishnets;* soft, informal *scrims;* durable, slightly wiry *marquisettes* and *theatrical gauzes;* dependable, semi-translucent *Swiss muslins* either plain or dotted; refined, sleek rayon *ninon;* crisp *organdy;* and closely woven *voiles.* Many of these are now woven from man-made fibers, such as rayon, nylon, and fiberglas. Translucent *plastic film,* waterproof and easily cleaned, is useful in bathrooms and kitchens.

Color and Pattern. Color is important because the light filtering through glass curtains takes on their color, giving the whole room that color cast, and also because they are conspicuous from the outside. Therefore, they are usually a neutral, light color slightly higher in value than the walls and for exterior harmony they are identical or very similar in all rooms. They can, however, be white for a clean, refreshing contrast, rosy pink or yellow to warm a cold room, or pale blue, green, or lavender to cool a hot one. Strong colors, though, should be used with due regard for their inside and outside effect. Although customarily plain, glass curtain fabrics are available in woven and printed designs of value for rooms that need some enrichment at the windows without adding draw curtains or draperies.

Tailoring and Hanging. Simplicity is the best guide: a neat heading that quietly fits its space and is shirred or pinch-pleated on a simple brass rod, a double hem at the bottom for weight, and a minimum width of at least twice that of the window for ample fullness.

If used with draperies, glass curtains are usually hung inside the window frame, as close to it and the glass as possible, and are long enough to clear the sill without leaving a noticeable gap. If used alone, they can be hung outside the frame, often covering two or more grouped windows with a unifying film. Then they can be dropped to cover the lower part of the frame—or to the floor. Sometimes it is desirable to hang two or more sets of glass curtains in the *cafe* or *tier* manner (see Fig. 12-11) to emphasize horizontality and/or to give privacy without

MATT KAHN

12-12 It is difficult to believe that the windows in the drawings at the left and in the center have the same size, shape, and position in the wall. Two factors account for the difference in effect: the size and shape of the panes of glass and the design of the curtains. The window at the left is an integral part of the wall composition and looks large and unified; that in the middle looks like an isolated hole in the wall, chiefly because the curtains are at variance with window and wall shape. The drawing at the right shows a window wall effectively treated with thin glass curtains and heavier draperies.

always reducing the light from the upper window. In all cases they look most sensible when allowed to hang in straight folds. If, however, one has an urge for ruffles, fancy tied-back or criss-cross arrangements, many glass curtains are suitably thin and delicate for such treatment.

Sash curtains are often stretched taut between rods on the top and bottom of a casement sash or on one of the two sashes of a double hung window. Hung in this way they look trim and architectural. They may, however, fall in loose folds. Unless used with draperies they reveal the frame of the window, which makes the opening seem smaller. Consequently they are used less frequently than in the past.

Draw Curtains

Flexible control of light, heat or cold, and privacy is the primary purpose of curtains that slide easily on traverse rods. Often, though, they are the only window treatment and then they take over all of the esthetic purposes of curtains and draperies.

Materials. Fabrics used for draw curtains need sufficient strength, durability, and flexibility to withstand being pulled back and forth and to hang in good folds when stretched out or pulled together. Thus, many thin glass-curtain materials and many heavy upholstery and suiting fabrics are good. Between these two extremes lies a challenging array in the drapery, bedding, dress, and suiting goods sections of almost any store. Coarse or fine *nets* of all sorts, provided they are strong, soften without obscuring windows. *Organdy, pongee,* and *silk gauze* are relatively smooth and rich looking. *Burlap, desert cloth, monk's cloth, Oznaburg bagging,* and *sack cloth* are thicker, rougher, and more casual. *Denim* is sturdy and durable; *Indian Head* is clean and crisp; *chambray* has a smooth, slightly silky texture; *gingham* is informal. *Glazed chintz* has a crisp, shiny surface that intensifies its colors and patterns a little like *taffeta*. *Satin* hangs in soft folds, is dressy when woven of smooth silk, informal when woven of heavier, loosely twisted threads to give a nubby texture, in which case it is known as *jaspé* or *antique satin*. *Damasks, brocades,* and *brocatelles* have woven, often formal, patterns.

To this standard list we can now add *bamboo* and *wood* textiles which are substantial and informal in character plus a selection of *plastic* materials that increases daily.

Color and Pattern. Appropriateness to the whole room is the only generalization that can be made. Draw curtains and draperies are part of the whole room but are most intimately related to the walls and windows. They are least noticeable if identical or highly similar to the wall, in which case they perform their functions without distracting from the window or from other features of the room. They become more noticeable if they repeat or echo the colors and character of other large surfaces and objects such as the floor and furniture. At times it may be advisable to use the same fabric for draw curtains and some upholstery, or one can attempt to unify a room by selecting curtains that repeat all the colors used elsewhere. They become emphatic when they are in strong contrast to the rest of the room or if their color and pattern are attention-demanding. This is usually desirable only when one wishes to distract attention from the walls, floor, and furniture and to divert it from what is outside the window.

Color, chiefly color value, is probably the most noticeable factor—very dark curtains against a light wall, or vice versa, stand out sharply. Scale and character come next—large-scale patterns or those contrasting with other surfaces become centers of interest. Color schemes for rooms are sometimes built around the colors in draw curtains or draperies as they may be around a painting. As an easy way to get a ready-made color scheme that you can study in advance, this approach has its good points. But—colors that are pleasant in draperies may not be satisfying when blown up to room size, and the draperies will be among the first items to be replaced. It is more sensible to find window treatments appropriate to your whole room than to force your room to fit the window treatment.

Although the shape and position of individual windows are less important than that of the whole wall, they too deserve consideration. For example, small windows (the kind that used to be built over bookcases flanking the fireplace) look ridiculous if the draperies are large and bold in pattern or contrasting in color, even though such effects are appropriate at other windows in the same room.

Hanging and Tailoring. Draw curtains, and draperies, too, are almost invariably most effective and useful when they hang in straight folds, which at least cover all of the window frame and begin and stop at sensible points. They should begin either slightly above the top of the frame or at the ceiling and end slightly below the bottom of the frame or just off the floor. Usually, the longer the better unless there is good

d

KNOLL ASSOCIATES, LEHMAN-CONN
JOFA, GOODALL, BRUNSCHWIG AND

12-13 Printed textiles for drap
or draw curtains come in a tre
dous range of patterns, each wit
own distinctive character. Some l
an almost architectural regularit
windows—and rooms—while other
loose and informal. Some are c
nant, others subordinate. Abstra
almost naturalistic, small to large
over-all to separate motifs—these
among the many differences. Sele
terms of what you and your
need.

a. The substantial, blocky regu
of this pattern is somewhat
niscent of wood and masonry
architectural character would
it harmonize with walls and
dows.

b. Organic forms are disciplined
semi-formal, crisp, bold yet fri
design. It is moderately sm
scale and combines whimsy
charm with a strong design qu

c. Uninhibited and sprightly, sm
scale and informal, this t
would lighten and free the
of a room without becomi
dominant force.

a   b   c

d

ese versatile, small-scale prints
simple, precise, refreshing, and
eless in character. They increase
apparent size of windows and
often associated with moderately
ull but sturdy provincial furni-
e.

rsythia" is a spirited, informal
angement of delicate branches
flowers on translucent cloth
t would bring a spring-like,
h-air quality to windows, espe-
ly in an apartment bedroom.

ghtly colored fruits stand strongly
clearly against their dark back-
und to produce a striking nov-
drapery material which makes
think of dining or kitchen win-
vs.

ge, splashy floral prints have
n so frequently used as a tonic
tired interiors that they no
ger seem as dominant as they
ly are. This unusually good
mple is an adaptation from an
French wallpaper.

e   f   g

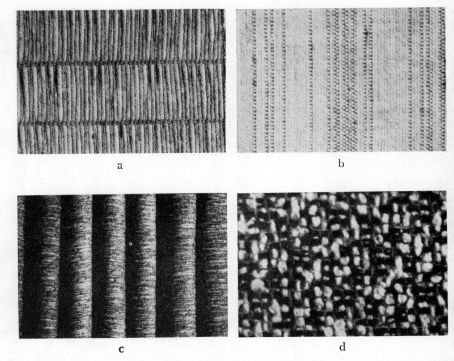

12-14 Drapery textiles can rely on weaves and fibers alone for long-term appeal.

a. Twisted cellulose fibers woven with cotton threads every 1¼ inches make an
open, informal textile which is treated with plastic against moisture and dirt.

b. Sturdy, closely-woven cotton with irregularly spaced ribs also suggests casual
living.

c. Rough-textured silk has great richness and hangs in handsome folds.

d. Tweed-like textiles bring warmth to simple, informal rooms.

reason for stopping them short. Also, the fuller the better (from 1½ to
2½ times as wide as the space they cover), but when pulled back they
should cover frame and wall, not window. French, box, or pinch pleats
take care of the fullness at the top and a generous hem at the bottom
helps make them hang well. Trimmings can be added but only with
great discretion and for real reason.

Draperies

Draperies began their life in the textiles, such as tapestries that warmed
physically and visually the cold, damp stone walls of early homes and
migrated from the walls to thrones, beds, chairs, and even tables and

pianos as well as to windows. Today they are most often found at windows, sometimes at large doorways or separating parts of a room, and occasionally as wall hangings. They differ from draw curtains only in that they are usually heavier and do not necessarily pull across the opening they guard.

Materials. The heavier end of the range of draw-curtain fabrics can be used for draperies as well as materials substantial enough for women's or men's suits or for upholstery. When thin textiles are used, they are often lined with sateen or similar materials so that they hang in straighter, more uniform folds which remain in place; exclude light, heat, and cold more effectively; and protect the more expensive material from the sun.

Color and Pattern. These are almost exactly like the colors and patterns of draw curtains, and what was said about them applies here.

Hanging and Tailoring. With one exception, all that was said about draw curtains could be said about draperies. The exception is those draperies that do not slide on a rod but are held with tie-backs (Fig. 11-1). Today, permanently tied-back draperies seem out of character with the way we live and are seldom seen outside museums or rooms furnished in authentic period styles.

Summary: Curtains and Draperies

Use

- List the exact functions you want curtains or draperies to perform at each group of windows. Put these in order of importance.
- Consider alternatives—blinds, shades, exterior controls—before committing yourself.
- Then make certain that the material selected, the way in which it is cut and sewn, and the manner of hanging bring the desired result.
- Buy the best rods you can, especially if curtains are to be pulled back and forth.

Economy

- Choose fabrics that will not deteriorate or fade in sun or strong light (or plan to line them); do not soil easily and are easy to clean; and do not stretch, shrink, or pull out of shape.
- Remember that good curtains, draperies, and fittings can cost quite a bit of money, take a fair amount of housekeeping time, and with a few exceptions are relatively short-lived.

Beauty

- *Appropriateness* to your whole house, room, and window are first considerations. Think of them in much the way you think of wallpapers and rugs.
- Select those that underline the character you seek, and that will attract just as much attention toward your windows as you wish directed there.
- Always bring home a window length sample of any material you are considering. Drape it in place. Study it by day and by night. Estimate the effect on your room of many times as much of it as the sample shows.
- Keep in mind that all the fabrics in a room belong to one family and ought to combine pleasantly. Beware of too many conflicting patterns. Coordinated groups of fabrics for windows, furniture, and walls are now available.
- *Line and shape* that emphasize and strengthen the basic lines and forms of window and room are the most generally satisfactory. Most windows are assets needing no camouflage treatment in spite of much to-do about "problem windows." Be wary of criss-crosses and diagonals, draped swags and tie-backs, because they conflict with rectangular windows and unless done with great taste and skill look fussy, pretentious, or both.
- Length should be determined by the architectural divisions of windows and walls, unless you are trying to ameliorate house-planning errors. Draperies that spill out on the floor exemplify conspicuous waste, while those that stop at arbitrary points look either droopy or bob-tailed.
- *Width* should be ample to give generous folds. Better to have sufficient inexpensive material than a skimpy amount of a better grade.
- *Tailoring* skill is almost as important as enough of the right material. Curtain rods, like plumbing pipes, ought to be as inconspicuous as possible.

Individuality

- Since curtains wear out quite quickly, they are one of the best places to express your ideas with some freedom—but they cost money and they are conspicuous.

Windows are a valuable asset. Do not rob them of their primary purposes of outlook, light, and air by treating them as though they are embarrassing necessities. Underdo rather than overdo curtains and the like. In the early days of glass, windows were treasured and exposed. Slowly but surely more and more was put over them until the Victorians frequently used up to five layers of curtains so that the glass was all but obscured. Now, as in the early days, we treasure what windows can do for our homes.

DOORS

Doorways allow us and our vision, as well as light, sounds, smells, breezes, warmth and cold to travel in or out of the house and from one room to another. Doors control these in varying degrees depending on their location, design, and material. Doors today run the full gamut from the stout, opaque door that shuts everything in or out through those filled with translucent glass or plastics to those partly of transparent glass up to sheets of glass narrowly banded with metal and, the last step, just glass with no frame at all. Further, doors can be designed so that only part of them opens: the Dutch or barn door in which the top can be opened but the bottom left closed; the highly convenient door in which adjustable louvers of wood, metal, or glass operate like a Venetian blind.

In rented quarters or in a home already built you can do much less about the doors than you can about the windows, but the following are possibilities:

- Remove unneeded doors to create greater openness.
- Refinish the doors and their frames so that they blend with the walls.
- Paint the doors in contrasting colors or decorate them so that they become dominant features.

If you are planning to buy a house, it will pay you to look carefully at the location and design of the doors. And if you are planning to build, consider very carefully how doors and openings without doors can serve you best.

Types of Doors

As with windows, doors can swing, slide, or fold.

Swinging doors, by far the most common type, like casement windows are hinged at one side. They are widely used because they are easy to

BLUE RIDGE GLASS CO. PHOTOGRAPH BY JULIUS SHULMAN

12-15 This unpretentious, inviting entrance is slightly recessed under a protecting roof. Patterned glass panels suggest without disclosing what is beyond both from outside and from within the entrance area. J. R. Davidson, designer.

operate, have simple hardware, can be made to close automatically with a spring, and can be effectively weather- and sound-proofed. Their only disadvantage is that the arc through which they swing must be left free of furniture.

Sliding doors take no otherwise usable room or wall space when opened, can disappear completely to give a great sense of openness, and can be much wider than swinging doors. They do, of course, have to go some place, and, if they vanish into a typical wall, construction becomes a little complicated. They can, however, slide in front of a wall, especially if they and the wall are glass (Fig. 12-3). Although sliding doors can be suspended entirely from overhead tracks, they usually perform better if they also slide along tracks or grooves in the floor (which are hard-to-clean dirt catchers). On the debit side, the movements required to open and close them are not as easy and simple as for swinging doors; they seldom glide as quietly, smoothly, and easily as one would wish; and there is no inexpensive way to make a sliding door in a house, especially a screen door, close itself as do the doors on automatic elevators.

Folding doors slide along tracks, usually in the ceiling, and fold like an accordion. They take little space when collapsed and ordinarily do not complicate construction. In general, they are not as soundproof as other types and sometimes have a tendency to stick, but they are excellent for those situations in which you want only occasionally to separate one space from another as in Fig. 12-16.

ARMSTRONG CORK COMPANY

12-16 Folding doors make it easy to separate a kitchen alcove from the dining space. They are equally good in other parts of the home. The window has bamboo roll blinds and coarse net curtains.

Location of Doors

Because doors and windows have so many points in common, almost everything said about locating windows applies to doors, but there are these differences: doors govern traffic paths much more than do windows; and doors are often opaque.

Views and privacy are controlled primarily by using opaque doors where there is no view and complete privacy is always needed, translucent materials where there is neither view nor the need for complete privacy, and transparent glass where you want to look out and do not mind those outside looking in. Location of doors also governs privacy. In a bedroom, for example, it is desirable to place the door so that even when open it does not bring the bed or dressing area into full view. Similarly, open doors between dining and kitchen areas should not expose the working part of the latter and entrance doors should not offer an immediate full view of the living space.

Light can come through doors as well as windows, and transparent doors are frequently combined with windows (Figs. 12-2 and 3) in which case the glass areas in both are desirably as similar in size, shape, and location as is feasible. Glass doors give a special pleasure, permitting you both to look and to go out. It is more difficult, though, to cover doors than windows with draperies or blinds because doors move and people move past them.

Ventilation can be quickly accomplished by opening doors, preferably on opposite sides of the room, during hot weather. There is nothing like opening the doors "to air out the house," but ordinary doors are not suited to gentle, controlled ventilation. It tends to be a drafty, all-or-none proposition.

Heat and cold coming through glass doors is exactly the same as that coming through windows, and the same facts apply. Opaque doors are different and although they do not provide as effective insulation as walls, they do an adequate job if they are well weather-proofed and concentrated on the side away from winter winds.

Furniture placement is controlled by the location of doors because you have to leave a traffic path between every set of doors in a room and allow space for those that swing. From this point of view, *have as few as feasible and keep the necessary ones as close together as your plan permits.*

Cleaning a glass door is like cleaning a window except that there is a greater tendency for finger marks to appear on the door and it is easier to get at both sides of a door.   Cleaning a wood door is like any other woodwork except, again, that it gets more finger marks, particularly around the knob.   Metal or plastic plates around the knobs help but are usually not very attractive in appearance.

Curtaining a glass door is always troublesome because curtains hanging on the door reduce light, look too small, and are subject to much wear and tear.   The usual procedure is to curtain windows and glass doors as one unit with one set of movable draperies, which is perfectly satisfactory until you want to go through the door when the draperies are drawn.   By far the best solution would be to put doors with glass in them where they will never need to be covered, but that is seldom easy.

Door frames and trim today are invariably reduced to a minimum for the reasons cited under windows.   Door trims do, however, serve useful purposes: namely, putting a durable, easily cleaned, and replaceable if necessary band at a part of the wall getting harder than average wear; and inexpensively masking the joining of two materials, one of the basic reasons for moldings.

Design of Doors

In historical houses the design of doors afforded architect and craftsmen opportunity to display their inventiveness and to enrich interiors. Even the crudest doors of vertical planks held together by horizontal and diagonal braces gained interest through their structure, material, and usually decorative nails and hardware.   Panel doors in which the spaces between the necessarily rather heavy and strong framework were filled with thinner wood automatically set the stage for exercises in proportion and design of moldings (Fig. 11-1).   More elaborate treatments, including carving, inlaying, and richly patterned knobs and hinges were enjoyed by designer and user alike.   In quite another tradition, Japanese craftsmen have made delicately beautiful doors of carefully joined wood as shown in Fig. 12-17.   Today, the great majority of doors are of the completely plain, flush-panel type in which plywood sheathes a strong but light core.   They are easy to clean, as beautiful as the wood or other covering used, and as noncommittal and inconspicuous as can be.   Hinges show themselves as little as possible and the knob is usually a simple ball projecting on a simple shaft from a small circular disk.   These are popu-

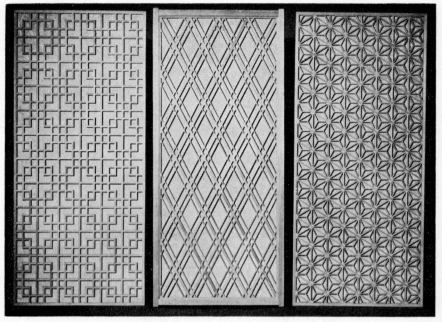

UNITED ENTERPRISES   PHOTOGRAPH BY KAMEO-KIDD

12-17   A refreshing change from the ordinary are these Japanese doors of handsome wood grillwork which can be backed with rice paper, any textile, or plastics.   They are equally effective as free-standing screens.

lar today because they are simple and undemanding and because we want to emphasize movement and continuity, and de-emphasize whatever might block our movements or interrupt the continuity of our enclosure.

Design and location of windows and doors are fundamentals in home planning.   Indeed, it is hard to overestimate their importance.   The most conspicuous and the most used parts of walls, they deserve far more thought than they often get.   Two common errors result from failing to balance all factors.   The first is putting doors and windows of diverse character wherever they seem to be needed, a practice that leads to a hodge-podge effect.   The second is insistence on certain kinds of doors and windows organized arbitrarily in what may be a visually satisfactory pattern but which does not meet utilitarian needs.   These are extremes to avoid.   The openings in our homes can be beautiful and useful—if both aims are kept firmly in mind.

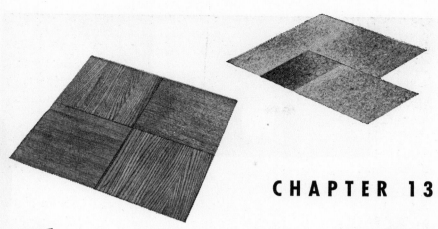

CHAPTER 13

Floors, Floor Coverings, and Ceilings

FLOORS AND CEILINGS, together with walls and windows, are the big enclosing surfaces that keep us warm, dry, and safe. Like walls, they are extensive and not easy to change. When you think about them, remember or re-read what was said about design with form, line, texture, space, light, and color. Keep in the front of your mind *appropriateness* and *relationships* in these big, permanent, stationary architectural elements. Play around to your heart's content with flower arrangements, table settings, the pictures on your walls, and even furniture arrangements. Change them daily if you wish, because that costs nothing but your time. Not so with your major background areas, where changes are troublesome and expensive.

FLOORS

Floors are usually flat, horizontal surfaces meant to be walked on, less often to be run, jumped, or danced on. They take a limited amount of wheel traffic such as vacuum cleaners, serving carts, and children's toys, and they support the weight of furniture. Furthermore, they insulate

PHOTOGRAPH BY JOHN H. LOHMAN

13-1 Ceiling, floor, and walls are happily integrated in a hall in which the ceiling and floor are, for a change, more interesting than the walls. Beams, planks, and a lighting fixture give the ceiling a positive character. Terra-cotta colored tiles complement the intricate beauty of the Oriental rugs. The thinly plastered adobe brick walls complete the handmade character. Darker paint on the lower portion eases upkeep and adds a needed horizontal line. Leslie I. Nichols, architect.

us and our possessions against the cold damp of the earth. As we all know, but sometimes forget, floors get the greatest wear and the most dirt of any part of the house. The problem of getting a good floor seems simple enough, and fundamentally it is, if we do not try to make floors do things they ought not be asked to do.

Floors in houses with basements are of two sorts. The basement floor is a concrete slab poured directly on the earthen subgrade or on a specially prepared foundation of crushed rock; it is less likely to crack if reinforced with metal rods. Floors above the basement conventionally consist of supporting floor joists, a rough floor of an inexpensive wood laid diagonally for strength, a layer of paper to retard the passage of air and moisture, and a finish flooring of hard wood. In another, less expensive method sheets of thick plywood or suitable composition board are used instead of the finish flooring, and these are covered with such hard floorings as linoleum, asphalt, and cork, or with carpets.

The growing popularity of the one-story, ground-hugging, basementless house has changed these procedures. In many of them the living floor is a concrete slab resting on a crushed rock foundation, is metal-reinforced to minimize cracking, and provides radiant heat from pipes carrying hot water, flues carrying warm air, or wires carrying electricity. Heating masonry floors has greatly lessened one of their former disadvantages—cold, tired feet for the persons walking on them. Many believe that it was the combined coldness and hardness rather than hardness alone that brought foot fatigue. Concrete slab floors reduce construction and maintenance costs and make possible a low house intimately related to outdoor areas.

What are the desirable characteristics of a good floor?

- *Durability* comes first because floors take severe punishment, chiefly from the abrasion of feet but also from the weight of furniture, especially when moved. Durable floors have a hard and tough surface sufficiently thick to prevent wearing through to another material. They do not crack, splinter, get permanently indented, disintegrate, or make noticeable the hard use they get.

- *Economy of upkeep* might also be considered of first importance because floor maintenance takes a good portion of the housekeeper's time. The easy-to-keep floor absorbs neither dry dirt nor liquids, resists stains and bleaches, takes little scratches and other blemishes without complaint, and does not call attention to the typical floor dust which appears daily, but also does not make it hard to dislodge. Maintenance is lightened if floors are smooth, non-absorbent, neutral in color intensity and moderately dark in value, have a camouflage pattern and dull surface, and if the area to be cared for is simple in shape and the floors join walls with a cove, not a right-angle crack. Rugged three-dimensional designs, bright hues and very high or low values, solid colors, and/or glossy surfaces all increase maintenance.

- *Resilience* cushions impact, thereby reducing foot fatigue, breakage of things dropped, and the inevitable noise. A little bounce or spring underfoot makes life pleasanter, less expensive, and quieter.

- *Warmth,* actual and apparent, is welcome in all but excessively hot climates, and this explains the typical rug-covered wood floors because wood and rugs are not only good insulators but look warm. There are three ways to make floors actually warm: put the heating elements in the floor, have the heat in the ceiling so that the floor will be warmed by radiation, or insulate the floor. There are also three ways of making floors look warm: warm hues, middle to dark values, and soft textures.

- *Light-reflection* is usually associated with ceilings and walls, but considerable quantities of light hit floors day and night. The more they reflect the brighter your home will be and the lower the bills for electricity. Smooth, shiny, light-colored floors reflect the most light.

- *Sound-absorption* is not the same as the sound-reduction resulting from resilience. Rough, porous materials absorb and deaden noise already made and, although ceilings and walls offer better possibilities for absorbing noise, floors can help.

- *Firmness* would need no mention were it not for the number of floors that creak when walked on, sag, or get out of plumb.

- *Appearance* brings us again to that everyman's land of likes and dislikes and to specific situations. Let us leave this matter until we have looked at the many kinds of floor coverings now available.

If you have not been conscious of the conflicts set up in the above discussion of desirable floor characteristics, then you had better read it again. For example, the floor that absorbs sound is more than likely to absorb dirt, the floor that can be mopped is often cold, the floor that is tough and durable is more than likely to be non-resilient, and the floor that gleams takes hard work to keep it that way despite new polishes and power polishers. These conflicts explain the almost universal practice of covering the permanent floor in part or completely with removable rugs. It is customary and logical to distinguish between the *hard* flooring materials which are more or less permanent and are either part of the structure or securely fastened to it and the *soft* rugs and carpets which are relatively easy to remove.

Wood, flagstone, and cork make interesting floors.

E. L. BRUCE COMPANY

13-2 Random width, wood-pegged planks are informal, accentuate one dimension of a room.

E. L. BRUCE COMPANY   PHOTOGRAPH BY HEDRICH-BLESSING

13-3 Square flooring blocks with grain in opposite directions make a sturdy, somewhat formal pattern.

THERMOPANE   LIBBEY-OWENS-FORD GLASS CO.

13-4 Flagstone laid in an unusually good random pattern makes a durable, interesting floor—for inside or out.

13-5 Cork tile in varied tans and browns has been laid to create an active floor pattern.

HARD-SURFACE FLOORING MATERIALS

Ground beaten down by use and the rock floors of caves were the first hard-surface flooring materials used by man. Stone smoothed and set in place, brick, and tile followed as man began the long process of adapting the environment to human living. Branches and leaves, rushes and sand helped make these hard, cold floors warm, dry, and resilient, and also absorbed and concealed the dirt. Wood, which came into use later, is still the most common permanent flooring in domestic buildings, although there are many other materials. The chart of Hard-Surface Flooring Materials gives the important characteristics of those frequently used or

Linoleum, rubber, asphalt, and vinyl tile do not differ from one another greatly in appearance although the patterns in each are varied.

SLOANE-BLABON

13-6 Linoleum tile with an irregular, textured stripe gives visual softness and interest and simplifies maintenance.

SLOANE-BLABON

13-7 Rubber tile in marbleized pattern gives richness and rhythm.

SLOANE-BLABON

13-8 Asphalt tile in a good camouflage pattern.

SLOANE-BLABON

13-9 Vinyl tile in a lively crystal-like pattern.

deserving to be. You will notice that some of them—clay tile, concrete, and stone—belong to masonry and have the general characteristics of those inorganic materials; asphalt tile, magnesite, rubber, and vinyl combine minerals and organic substances; and cork, linoleum, and wood are organic. In comparison with rugs and carpets, all are durable, relatively cool and non-resilient, more or less impervious to stains and unharmed by water (wood and cork must be properly sealed), easily cleaned with soap and water, and most of them are conventionally surfaced with waxes. This latter raises a problem: wax protects any surface to which it is applied and can be given a beautiful luster—but it must be applied frequently, quickly shows wear and usually water spots, and often looks and is slippery. Good on furniture and walls, wax is a questionable, time-consuming, troublesome finish for heavily used floors.

Hard flooring materials deserve a few comments of a more personal type than fit into a table. All of them except wood and possibly cork seem to some persons better suited to offices, factories, schools, and stores than to homes, where they believe their use should be confined to kitchens, bathrooms, and activity space. Asphalt tile is hard, the colors are muddy rather than subtle, and the typical marbleized pattern, while resembling stone, also looks like spilled, partially wiped-up paint; concrete is a hard, cold, unprepossessing sidewalk material (unless colored, hardened, and well-surfaced); and magnesite is used on the floors of New York subways. Linoleum is for kitchens and bathrooms, most people would say; rubber tile at first glance looks like asphalt or linoleum but a second look shows the color range to be brighter; vinyl flooring looks like linoleum but is so new that not many people have seen it; and tile, brick, and stone are hard and outdoorish looking, and they are expensive. Wood, of course, has been used for so long that everyone accepts it, but cork is only now coming into any prominence. Yet it may be that we had better take another look at those types of hard flooring, because quite a few housewives, househusbands, and housechildren, too, have, after living with them out of necessity, found that home life may be pleasanter with floors built for use.

Permanent floor coverings are often selected without careful thought: linoleum for the kitchen; tile for the bathrooms, and wood, to be covered with rugs or carpet, in the other rooms. This is a formula that has worked well enough for years. Or has it? Few would question tile for the bathroom if there is a scatter rug or two for warmth and firm footing, and

MATERIAL	SOURCE OR COMPOSITION	USE	SIZE AND SHAPE	PATTERNS
Asphalt Tile	Natural asphalt, asbestos, or mineral fibers, pigments.	The only composition flooring recommended for laying over concrete directly on ground. Especially suitable in much-used areas.	Standard is 9″ x 9″ but others available.	Tiles are plain marbleized; lay creates typical patterns.
Concrete	Cement, sand, aggregates, and water.	Can be left uncovered on any floor indoors or out; also the standard foundation for clay tile, brick, and stone; can be covered with asphalt tile, wood, cork, rugs, etc.	Usually poured in slabs but tiles are available. Sometimes marked off in rectangles by wooden or metal screeds.	Could be given patterns while s but seldom is.
Cork	Cork shavings and granules compressed in sheets and baked to allow natural resins to liquefy. Sealers and resins may be incorporated or applied to surface.	Any room in house but only special types suitable for kitchens and bathrooms.	Squares 9″ x 9″ to 18″ x 18″; also small and large rectangles; easily cut to special shapes.	Chunks of cork slightly different color give textur pattern.
Linoleum	Wood flour, ground cork, gums, linseed oil, and pigments pressed onto burlap foundation.	Floor of any room but especially kitchens, bathrooms, children's rooms, activity spaces, and the like; also suitable for tops of counters, desks, and tables. Not recommended for use over concrete laid directly on ground, unless well insulated.	Standard tiles are 9″ x 9″; in rolls 6′ to 15′ wide.	Practically unlimited; ease of inlaying permits individual desig
Magnesite	Magnesium oxide mixed with wood fibers, asbestos, cork, and sometimes marble chips.	Over concrete laid directly on ground, in any room but chiefly play and activity spaces.	Poured in continuous slab; or 9″ x 9″ tiles.	Slight texture when plain; like terrazzo if marbl chips are added.
Rubber Tile	About 25% rubber and 75% minerals and cotton fibers.	Same as linoleum.	Same as linoleum.	Same as linoleum

COLORS	DURABILITY	MAINTENANCE	COMMENTS
ll range of hues but ors are neutralized; :oming available in hter, clearer colors.	Good if not cracked by impact, dented by furniture weight, or softened by radiant heat in floor. Some types not greaseproof.	Easy—mopping and usually waxing.	Least expensive composition flooring, eight times as hard as rubber tile, noisy, and slippery when waxed.
nited range of low ensity colors, but ı be painted, waxed h colored wax, etc.	Very high.	Markedly easy if surface is hardened and not waxed.	Least expensive of all floorings since it is foundation and finish flooring all in one; but hard, noisy, cold unless radiant-heated; not very attractive in appearance.
ght to dark brown.	Not as high as linoleum but has long life if well maintained.	Difficult—wax applied rather frequently; if left unwaxed quickly becomes rather dirty-looking.	Some types now impregnated or topped with vinyl, which makes them more impervious to stains, need less waxing.
.ctically unlimited.	High in better grades; resists denting.	Moderately easy—wash and wax, do not use varnish or shellac.	Attractive, flexible, quiet, moderate in cost. No real disadvantages, except need for frequent waxing.
rk browns and reds, :k.	Very high; but not greaseproof.	Easy—minimum mopping.	Light weight, fire-resistant, but moderately hard, noisy, cracks if underflooring is not stable. Moderate cost.
limited range; often ghter and clearer n in linoleum or ıalt.	Very high; but older types not greaseproof.	Average—washing with soap and water; wax or rubber polish.	Very similar to linoleum, but twice as resilient and twice as expensive.

MATERIAL	SOURCE OR COMPOSITION	USE	SIZE AND SHAPE	PATTERNS
Stone	Slate, flagstone, marble, etc.	Chiefly entrances, outdoor paving, and near fireplaces, but can be used in any room except kitchen.	Usually not more than 2' square; rectangular or irregular.	Natural veining, shapes of stones, and patterns in which they are laid.
Tile and Brick (Clay)	Unglazed or glazed ceramic tile.	Areas getting hard wear, moisture, and dirt—entrances, hallways, bath-rooms, activity space, or any place except kitchen where effect is wanted.	Tiles are ½" to 12" square; or rectan-gular; hexagonal, etc. Standard bricks are approxi-mately 2" x 2" x 8".	Many arrange-ments of single different colors.
Vinyl	May be all vinyl, vinyl mixed with asbestos fibers, or vinyl coating on cork base.	Any surface not subject to heat and indentations.	Same as linoleum.	Plain, marbleize striated, texture etc.
Wood (Hard)	Oak, birch, beech, maple, pecan.	Any room in house except kitchen and bathroom; usually most of it is cov-ered by rugs.	Strips 1½ to 3½" wide; planks 2" to 8"; parquet blocks 9" x 9", etc.	Color and grain wood. Usually l in parallel strip also comes in blocks of varied parquetry patte

until recently linoleum was the only flooring suitable for kitchens. Every square foot of the wood floor getting hard wear is covered with rugs or carpets to protect it from wear, and beyond that as much is concealed as one's bank account allows. No one would question the desirability of soft floor coverings except in terms of cost and maintenance.

Thus for several reasons we are beginning to look for flooring ma-terials that do not necessarily have to be covered. We like the straight-forward frankness and the economy of durable, pleasant materials that need no layers added on to them and that can be used throughout the

COLORS	DURABILITY	MAINTENANCE	COMMENTS
Usually grays and tans with variation in each piece and from piece to piece.	Very high.	Easy—minimum sweeping and mopping.	Striking in appearance, permanent; but cold, fatiguing to stand or walk on if not heated, noisy, difficult to repair chips or cracks. Usually expensive, depending on type of stone, pattern, locality, etc.
Unglazed usually terra-cotta; glazed tiles in all colors.	High, but unglazed absorbs grease, stains.	Easy—soap and water; often waxed.	Striking appearance, can be used both indoors and out; but cold and fatiguing unless radiant heated; noisy. Expensive.
Wide range including light, bright, and clear.	Promises to give long service, greaseproof; cuts tend to be self-healing; but dents easily; softens over radiant heat.	Very easy. Wash and buff to restore luster. No waxing needed.	Pleasant, satiny surface maintained without waxing; flexible; but not yet the complete answer to need for attractive, durable, very easy to maintain floor covering. Expensive.
Light red, yellow, tan, brown.	High but shows wear.	Medium high; must be sealed, then usually waxed and polished.	Natural beauty, warmth, fairly permanent, moderately easy to refinish; but fairly hard, noisy, moderately difficult to keep looking well, especially in traffic areas. Moderately expensive but some variation in price according to wood, design.

home for a space-increasing harmony and unity. We look carefully at some materials that may have been discarded too hastily. Cork, for example, has about everything except marked ease of maintenance and low cost; rubber is quiet, beautiful, and durable and has now been made greaseproof; linoleum, now available in many good colors and patterns, is attractive; vinyl tile has all the advantages of linoleum except low cost and appears to be more durable and maybe easier to keep; asphalt tile is moderately satisfactory; magnesite has no faults other than lack of resilience; and even lowly concrete radiantly heated and brown in color can

13-10 Jaspé striped linoleum in two colors, laid so that the stripes are at right angles to each other, both unites and separates two related areas. Also worth noting are the bulletin board, lighting fixture, and curtains; the louvered sliding and folding doors that make it possible to separate the two rooms; and the unit stove with the oven at working height.

win one over, as it has the writers during the past few years, when small children *live* in a house.

Design and Character

From the material chosen, its size and shape, color and pattern, and the way in which it is laid, comes the visual effect. Wood can be laid in long narrow strips to accentuate one dimension of the room or in square blocks with the grain in alternating directions for equal emphasis in both dimensions (Figs. 13-2 and 3).

Size and shape of materials affect design in character. Stone can be laid in random patterns (Fig. 13-4) or with geometric regularity (Fig. 8-10). Linoleum comes in tiles which can be arranged as one wishes, or in room-width rolls. Ceramic tiles, too, come in many sizes and shapes, and all of the composition materials—cork, linoleum, etc.—can be easily cut into pieces of almost any shape and fitted together.

Color and pattern possibilities are legion. Linoleum, rubber, and vinyl range from white through yellows, greens, blues, reds, grays, and tans to black. Plain, marbleized, striated or jaspé stripes, spattered and crystal-like patterns vie with those resembling tiles and carpets. Wood can be bleached, stained, or painted. Then, too, the manner of laying offers possibilities. The squared wood floor would have been quite different had all the grain been parallel. The cork tile floor in Fig. 13-5 shows varied rectangles laid in alternating directions. In the kitchen-eating space in Fig. 13-10 linoleum yard goods of the same pattern but different colors and direction of pattern has been laid to suggest separation of the two areas. The normal traffic path is indicated by the square insets. Linoleum has also been sensibly used to line the toy cupboard which gets almost as hard use as a floor.

For the majority of us, it is important to surface our floors with a material that gives a useful and economical base for living. To be sure, beautiful floors are an esthetic asset and often individualize homes, but their expense leads most of us toward pleasantly unobtrusive floors which are subordinate to walls, furniture, and family life.

RUGS AND CARPETS

Soft floor coverings bring warmth, visual softness and texture, resilience, quiet, and a degree of friendly intimacy to floors; add color, texture, and pattern to homes; and relate the floor to upholstered furniture, curtained windows, and the clothed occupants. They can be taken off the floor to be sent to the cleaners, replaced, or carried along when you move. Much like wallpaper, rugs give rooms a "furnished" look even with little furniture; they can alter the apparent shape and size of a room; they can markedly alter its character; and they can cover up an unattractive or disfigured floor. They also cost money, time, and effort. They are unique in two important respects: first, they are the only walked-on fabrics; and second, of all the fabrics in the house, rugs are the most architectural because they literally become the floor. What does this mean? First, that they should be durable and, second, that in their design and color we might expect something of the structure we associate with building.

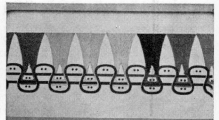

13-11 Axminster weave permits great variety of pattern because each pile tuft is individually set by machine.

13-12 Velvet weaves are usually plain. Patterns can be made by printing after weaving or, better, by printing the yarns before weaving.

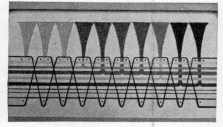

13-13 Wilton usually has a uniformly cut pile but can be woven with high and low uncut pile to give a corded effect.

13-14 Chenille gives a luxurious carpet—plain, woven colored patterns, or sculptured.

Rugs and Carpets

Machine-Made Pile Weaves

Axminster
Cut pile carpet with tufts inserted mechanically in rows and bound down, but not knotted.

Great range of colors and designs—Oriental, tone-on-tone, two-toned.

Only rug which can be rolled lengthwise only, due to stiff back construction. Back has a heavy ribbed effect.

Long-wearing if closely woven, but not as durable as Wilton.

Price and quality depend on number of tufts per square inch.

Brussels
Similar to Wilton but with uncut pile.

Chenille
Dense, close, deep pile; thick, soft, woolly back. No line of space between tufts when rug is folded.

No limit to length or shape, number of colors, character of design, thickness of pile up to one inch or more.

Luxurious; and durable because of thick back.

Most expensive machine-made weave.

Tapestry
Similar to velvet but with uncut pile. Machine-made hooked rugs made by this method.

Gives longer wear than velvet but may lack resilience and sound absorption.

Velvet
Short, dense cut-pile surface with none of the surface yarn buried deeply in the fabric.

Largest percentage of solid color broadlooms made are velvets and tapestries.

May have pile of varied heights, also twisted yarn surfaces.

Pattern made by printing design on yarn before it is woven, or by printing design on to finished fabric (cheapest method).

Durable and satisfying if closely woven of good yarn, but not for heavy-duty areas.

Least expensive pile rug.

Wilton
Short, straight-standing, cut pile with several layers of yarn imbedded in back, making it very durable.

Plain-colored or patterned (seven colors generally the limit); woven on Jacquard loom.

Worsted Wilton shows up minute detail in design, texture lustrous and velvety.

Wool Wilton has heavier, coarser pile, making it excellent for heavy-duty areas—halls, etc.

Many modern textures are Wilton, Brussels, or combinations of the two.

Extremely durable.

High quality carpet; expensive.

Rugs and Carpets (Cont.)

Machine-Made Flat Weaves

Linen
: Made of flax yarn, woven on plain or Jacquard looms.
Variety of *rough* textures and patterns.
Typical linen luster.
Reversible, fire resistant, durable.
Inexpensive.

Braided Rugs
: Fabric cut into strips, braided, stitched together; or heavy cotton yarns braided into wide and narrow strips, then stitched together with criss-cross stitch. Similar effect produced by twisting strips of fabric and stitching together with criss-cross stitch.
Multi-color effects, stripes, checks, plaids, with dyed yarns.
Usually small, round, oval, or oblong.
Inexpensive.

Fiber Rugs
: Fir or spruce woodpulp formed into long tough sheets— "Kraft fiber." Sheets cut into strips of various widths, tightly twisted into heavy yarns, woven in plain, twill, and Jacquard weaves, or variation and combination.
May be all Kraft fiber or combined with cotton, sisal, wool.
Plain, multi-color, or plaid designs, or may have stencil design on one side.
Good summer rugs or for informal rooms.
Inexpensive, short-term covering.

Rush Matting
: Tough, wire-like sea-grass woven in plain weave into rugs or squares which may be sewn together to form rug.
Natural green or straw-grass color or printed on one side by stencil or spray. Different-colored warp yarns may be introduced.
Sometimes varnished for protection. Reversible.
Good for exposed porches or terraces, and much used in modern interiors because of texture and color.
Inexpensive, short-term floor covering.

Sisal Rugs
: Sisal fiber (from leaves of plant related to hemp) woven in plain, twill, or Jacquard weave, variation or combination.
Plain color, patterned, or may have one side stenciled.
Attractive sheen.
Fairly durable for a fiber rug.
Inexpensive.

Handmade Rugs

(See Figs. 1-1, 13-1, 18, and 19, and 19-3.)

Oriental

Include a varied assortment from many countries.

Persian
: The most popular, distinguished by their expert craftsmanship, soft, harmonious colors, and intricate, small-scale, refined, and graceful designs of conventionalized foliage,

Rugs and Carpets (Cont.)

flowers, birds, and animals distributed over all of the surface.

Turkish
Vigorous designs, stronger color, and architectural as well as natural motifs.

Turkoman
Predominantly red with geometric designs, the best known coming from Bokhara.

Caucasian
Resemble Turkish but more vigorous in color and in the designs, which often look like interlocked mosaic patterns.

Chinese
Best type have the subtlety of Chinese paintings in their adaptation of natural forms beautifully spaced on plain backgrounds.

European

Aubusson
Very fine and delicate flat tapestry weave, made in varied authentic designs of the best French periods, usually in soft colors.

Savonnerie
Soft, silky, deep pile with the pile carved around each design motif to make it stand out. Designs vigorous and large-scale, colors rich and strong.

Scandinavian, Algerian, and *Spanish*
Vary widely in surface texture, color, and pattern, like rugs from many other parts of the world, but all of them have the honestly felt, simple vigor of craftsmen who design with their hearts and souls as well as with their heads and hands. They supplement the simplicity of contemporary machined furniture with an invigorating human quality.

American and **Canadian**
Hooked, braided, or woven of yarns or strips of cloth; have an appealingly rural, "native American" quality that ties our present to our past.

Indian
From our own southwest; flat weaves of great durability and a desert-like combination of strength and subtlety in their natural colors and geometric designs.

Machine-Made Rugs

The great majority of rugs used today are textiles woven by machine from organic fibers twisted into yarns; a few more than half of the common types have pile surfaces, the remainder are flat weaves. Of course, this is not the whole story of rugs, because some are made by hand; some are knitted, braided, or felted; some are formed from grasses, reeds, and rushes used pretty much as they grew—and rayon and nylon are rapidly coming into use either alone or combined with cotton or wool. Many rugs have patterns that are part of the weave, a few are printed, and a small number have patterns sewn on after weaving. Their variety makes selection a complex but fascinating problem if you want to get your money's worth over a long time. The chart on rugs and carpets, which presents the characteristics of the major types of rugs, gives some of the information needed, but if you have not fixed in mind the characteristics of different fibers as charted in Chapter 10, now is the time for review, because cotton is cotton, wool is wool, and nylon is nylon whether used for upholstery or carpets.

We have said that more than half of the types of rugs made today have a pile surface, but far more than half of the *quantity* of rugs used in homes are pile weaves. Why? Pile weaves are durable, resisting abrasion especially well; they mask a little dust and minor damage conveniently; and they are soft and resilient to touch and see. In masking dust they also make dislodging it a little hard, but a good, upright vacuum cleaner makes cleaning them child's play, at least the first ten to twenty times. Pile rugs can have the loops uncut (as in bath towels) to give a somewhat hard, brisk, pebbly surface; they can be cut (as in velvet) to give a luxurious smoothness, or cut and uncut pile can be combined to give pattern; the pile can be short or almost ankle-deep and different lengths of pile can be combined to give design, sometimes by carving or sculpting; and the pile can be densely spaced (important for durability) or rather sparse.

In view of all this, what is the place of flat weave rugs? Low cost is their primary virtue and when woven of such durable fibers as linen or Kraft they give unexpectedly good service. Their second virtue is that they expand the vocabulary of soft floor coverings by giving us warmth and resilience that look precise and tailored without even a hint of plushiness. And then there are braided and hooked rugs to give still more possibility of variety on your floors and of finding the rug best suited to specific conditions. We have become so accustomed to assuming that the one best floor treatment is wall-to-wall broadloom of a plain or slightly figured weave that it is refreshing for those who do not wish to follow this floor formula to realize that there are opportunities for greater individuality.

A few definitions are in order at this point. *Rugs* are floor coverings finished on four sides ready for use; *carpets* are finished only on the sides, vary in width from 27 inches to 18 feet, and come in almost any length you want; *broadloom* is carpeting 54 inches or more in width—the term does not describe the weave, fiber, color, pattern, or any quality other than width.

Handmade Rugs

Were it not that handmade rugs are almost always very expensive, we would give them considerable space because they are usually—but by

BIGELOW RUGS AND CARPETS

BIGELOW RUGS AND CARPETS

13-15 This rugged, looped textured, all-rayon carpet is woven of different colored yarns to give a rich but informal effect.

13-16 Casual looped pile in varying heights creates a tree-bark effect in this velvet weave.

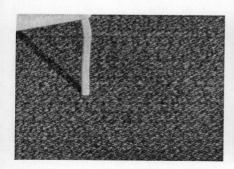

MONTGOMERY WARD

13-17 Fiber rugs come in plain colors, heather mixtures, and plaids.

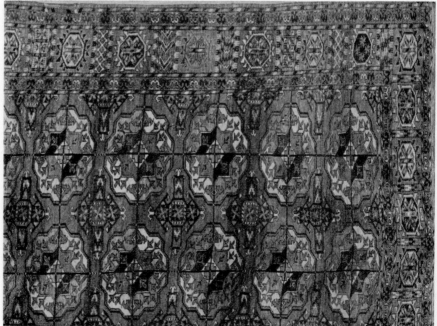

13-18a, b Oriental rugs are among the most beautiful of home furnishings. The 16th-century Persian rug has a typical delicate, curvilinear design quite different from the geometrical abstraction of the early 19th-century Tekke Turkoman rug.

no means always—very beautiful and bring individuality to a room. It should be noted that many types of Orientals are now being cheaply and coarsely imitated, substituting a confused scattering of ornament for the organized profusion of richness found in the best. Good Oriental rugs have such intrinsic beauty that they arouse a tendency to use them insensitively on the assumption that their beauty makes them "go with everything." Quite the reverse is true. Their beauty is not of a noncommittal, characterless type but has considerable power.

Full discussion of the best use of different types would take a chapter—or a book—but if you would like to use Oriental rugs, give them a chance to speak for themselves by placing them with furniture and especially other textiles that are harmonious in character, scale, and color, and which do not contend with them for supremacy. Oriental rugs can be genuinely handsome in modern homes with contemporary furniture, under which conditions they frequently reveal their special beauty more

13-19 Handwoven in Spain, this handsomely simple rug has a deep cocoa ground, coral and white stars, and is well suited to informal living.

emphatically than when they have to fight for their life with patterns everywhere else in the room.

Because of their cost, good handmade rugs are usually seen in small sizes which makes them especially appropriate for accenting one part of the floor. Thus, a conversation group in a living room can be brought together, or a quiet reading corner enriched, by an American Indian or Oriental rug—but if you try this, you will want to be sure that the rug is appropriate in design and color and that it is large enough to perform its function of unifying and emphasizing.

Size of Rugs

The days when a rug was 9 x 12 feet and what it did not cover was left bare have been over for some time, because now rugs vary from 2 x 3 feet to 12 x 18 feet and larger. Carpeting materials range from rush mats one foot square to broadloom up to 18 feet—or even 30 feet—wide. It is up to you to decide how much of your floor you want covered, but since most of us want our rooms to look spacious, here are some of the ways of getting that effect.

- Use the largest amount feasible of *one* floor covering, not merely in one room but throughout the house.
- Keep contrast between bare floors and rugs to a minimum.
- Choose colors that are low in intensity, middle in value, and cool in hue.
- Select plain colors or unobtrusive patterns.
- Get flat weaves or relatively low pile.
- Avoid—if you want your rooms to seem big—rugs with borders, emphatic central medallions, big or widely spaced patterns, and thick textures, just as you stay away from strong colors; also avoid many little rugs, and place the few small ones you use parallel to the walls and related to furniture groups.

Patterns in Rugs

We repeat: rugs are fabrics to be walked on and they belong to the architectural shell of the house. They are fabrics—but they are not draperies, tablecloths, or bedspreads. Although soft, they take hard use on a hard floor. What, then, are the potentialities and limitations for patterns? Let's see what diverse peoples have done.

American braided rugs rely on concentric bands of different colors, often with considerable variation in each band; the hooked rugs vary from abstract patterns to bold, quaintly clumsy representations of nature. American Indian rugs have bold, simple designs, rich with symbolism to the makers but to us, sensitive geometric shapes; and the colors in the better ones are wonderfully subtle tans, grays, and almost whites, combined with desert yellows, pinks, and greens. North African rugs usually have thick, coarse pile and simple, vigorous designs in the natural colors of wool. In the Near East and the Orient where rug making started and reached its greatest heights, some of the patterns are tightly structured geometric shapes, some interweave highly conventionalized naturalistic objects with geometry, and some capture the growing grace of natural forms but never in an imitative way. In Europe from the Renaissance on the variety of rug patterns makes generalization impossible other than to say that up to the 19th century all were either conventionalized or abstract and all looked as though they belonged on the floors of the rooms for which they were woven.

This pelletized glance at patterns in rugs apparently does not give us any great help, in the face of their great diversity—except that each of these groups of people made rugs to fill their own needs and that were appropriate in their architecture. The typical home today is not large, costly, or kept by servants, nor is it richly decorated with handsome materials exquisitely worked. To the degree that this generalization is true, it suggests that our rugs should be good, simple floor coverings, quietly giving us warmth and resilience underfoot and getting along without too much upkeep. Perfectly plain carpets seemed like the answer until housewives found how much time it took to keep them at their best. Since then, manufacturers have produced a multitude of patterns planned for service and beauty; undemanding, unpretentious, yet quite lively patterns as illustrated in Figs. 13-15 and 13-16. For those who wish to have more "going on" on their floor, there are such patterns as shown in Fig. 13-11 to make the room's foundation more dominant in the decorating scheme.

Let us apply our aims and principles of design specifically to patterns in rugs. A beautiful floor covering can be defined as one that fits into the whole decorating scheme, contributing its share but only occasionally taking attention away from the people, furniture, or pictures.

Form follows function indicates that the pattern ought to look as though it belonged on the floor where you walk, not on the furniture on which you sit or at the windows through which you look. You expect a floor to look strong and substantial enough to give a feeling of support, neither delicate nor brittle; but most of us also like it to look resilient, not stony hard (unless it *is* handsome stone). Motifs derived from nature (if any) should be of the "underfoot" type, preferably those associated with the ground and pleasant to step on. However, almost all objects—flowers, fruits, animals, clouds, and so forth—can be so conventionalized that they seem quite appropriate on rugs, as the Persians and Chinese have ably demonstrated.

Variety in unity is less a matter of the rug itself than of the whole room. Ordinarily we expect a high degree of unity in the floor covering (it is the base and a coordinator of the room or whole house) and we do not expect much variety of the type that makes you want to inspect it closely— it is one thing to walk up to a painting or bend slightly to look more closely at upholstery, but another to squat or kneel to enjoy a rug. Always, though, there are exceptions such as the genuinely handsome rugs treated as real events in the furnishing scheme.

Balance in the rug itself is important because, above (or below) all, the floor should be in equilibrium if we are to maintain our own comfortably, but it is equally important that the whole room be balanced and the floor is the lowest part. Does this mean that the rug should be the darkest value in the room? We might take some hints from nature: the ground is usually darker than the sky (except during storms) but usually not as dark as the trunks and foliage of trees; a sandy beach or a snow-covered field, however, is often higher in value than the sky. How do these make you feel? In general, of course, a moderately dark floor is safest although it inevitably darkens your whole room.

Rhythm of a type suggesting easy walking is appropriate in the part of the house taking movement, but checkerboards that arouse the hop-scotch instinct, swirls that practically sweep you into a Viennese waltz, or abrupt and vehement changes that suggest jitter-bugging should be used with due regard for the type of movement they suggest you execute.

Emphasis on the floor inevitably distracts from emphasis elsewhere, and emphasis on parts of the floor—rich borders, complex central medallions, or isolated spots—distracts from the floor's continuity. Another point to consider is the directional emphasis that you get with any kind of stripes, because, if these are marked, you often feel as though you should follow them rather than going where you want to. But do not forget the use of smaller rugs carefully placed to emphasize conversation groups.

These suggestions may sound as if there is no place for richly beautiful soft floor coverings in today's homes; this is not at all true. We have been talking about the whole floor in typical homes, not the spots you want raised to higher keys with lively accents or made to glow with genuinely handsome rugs. These are exceptions that submit to no generalizations.

Durability of Rugs

The wearing quality of rugs is the product of four factors: kind of fibers; density of pile and tightness of backing in a pile rug, or tightness of weave in a flat surface; resilience of floor under rug; and good care.

- Fibers vary conspicuously in the wear they will take, as was noted in the table on fibers: briefly, wool, rayon, and linen wear well, nylon wears very well, and cotton only moderately so.
- Density of pile is the most important single factor in the life of a pile-weave rug, the durability of the backing and the tightness with which the tufts are interlocked are important, but the length of pile is of little consequence. In a flat weave, tightness of yarn and weave prolong usefulness.
- The life of a rug is greatly lengthened (and it is more pleasant to walk on) if it is properly cushioned. Thus, it is good economy to have a rug pad under each rug, sponge rubber being much better in every way than felt; under small rugs, pads should always be non-skid.
- Good care is important: embedded dirt is harmful, as are many stains and spots, and moths eat wool; periodic professional cleaning is advisable, and excessive wear on one part of the rug can be lessened by turning the rug or covering the heavily used portion with a small rug that is replaceable—although this is a rather unattractive expedient.

SELECTION OF FLOOR COVERINGS

This is a double-headed problem, selecting floor coverings for beauty and durability, but it is one which must be faced and solved as though it were single. For variety, try solving it by answering the following questions.

How much and what kind of use will the floor get?

- How heavy will the traffic be?
- Will it bring mud and grit?
- Will it be concentrated in certain spots or paths or distributed throughout the space?

What is your approach to the economy of flooring materials?

- How much money do you want and can you afford to put on your floor? Now and later?
- How much time and upkeep money do you want to spend on your floors?

What are your feelings about the beauty of floors?

- How dominant do you want them to be in your total scheme?
- What do you want them to *do* for your rooms, your whole house?
- How much pattern do you want? What kind? Where?
- How similar do you want the floors in different rooms?

What is your attitude toward individualized floors?

- Do you want yours to differ noticeably from those of your friends?
- How can your floors best contribute to the character of your home?

CEILINGS

Only flies and a few other odd and assorted insects walk on ceilings, so that we can dispose at once of the traffic wear-and-tear that were among our chief problems in floors. Ceilings do not get *used* as do other parts of the house, but they have their functions: they protect us; affect illumination and acoustics; and offer unique decorating possibilities because they are the largest unobstructed single area in a furnished room. The typical ceiling is the same size and shape as the floor which it parallels, is covered with plaster, and is painted white or occasionally a pale tint of some hue. There are good reasons for this stereotype: it literally designs itself and is inexpensive to build and maintain; it gives an unobtrusive spaciousness to our smallish, rather low-ceilinged rooms; and it reflects light well. We notice ceilings little and do correspondingly little about them. Perhaps it is just as well in a busy world to have one large undecorated area in every room even if you do have to be on your back to appreciate it fully. But ceilings can have other treatments as we shall see in discussing their height, shape or direction, material, color and texture, ornamentation, and acoustical characteristics.

Height

Ceiling height is determined by resolving our needs for head room, air to breathe, and economy with our desires for pleasantly proportioned rooms in character with our living. It would seem hard to generalize in view of these varying needs and desires but there are few variations in standard practice. The Federal Housing Administration recommends a minimum of 6'6" for basements, 7'6" for first floor rooms, and 7'0" for those above, but these are certainly minimums. More humane heights would be 7'0" for basements, 8'6" for the first floor, and 8'0" for the second. Heights beyond these may well be justified in terms of their effect. There is, of course, a difference between actual and apparent heights. A ceiling will look higher if the room is made smaller, the illumination is increased, the windows and/or curtains are taken to the ceiling, the color is made white or nearly so, the texture is smooth, decoration of any sort (including lighting fixtures) is eliminated, and contrast between walls and ceilings is minimized.

There are notable differences between the effects of low and high ceilings. Low ceilings are enclosing, sheltering, intimate, and informal, and they bring people together in close social groups—a point well illustrated by a friend who decorated his room for a New Year's party by hanging a great many balloons at just about head height over a double bed in one corner of the room. The guests immediately went to that part of the room and stayed there, forsaking the relative spaciousness of the rest of the room. If, however, ceilings are too low, the effect may become cramped and stuffy. High ceilings, in contrast, seem formal and dignified as well as airy, but, if too high, they make rooms well-like and hard to heat with conventional heating systems. Do ceilings throughout the house, or the ceiling of one room have to be all the same height? No, except that it is usually simpler and cheaper to have them so. Ceiling heights varied thoughtfully in relation to the size and use of the space they cover add interest and define activity areas without separating them by walls, a point well illustrated in Figs. 2-10 and 13-21.

Shape and Direction

It is easy, inexpensive, and customary to have ceilings echo floors, a practice strengthened by the increasing use of flat roofs. It is definitely indicated in the first floor rooms of a two-story house or a one-floor, flat-roofed structure, but it contributes little to visual interest or sound control. Here are some of the more common deviations.

Coved ceilings, in which walls and ceilings meet in a curve rather than at right angles, make the space seem a little more plastic and flexible, and have a little of the spaciousness of the curved and undefined sky. They are also excellent for diffused, indirect lighting. If carried to their logical conclusion, ceilings become vaults or semi-spheres, wonderful shapes but beyond the pocketbooks of most of us.

GUMP'S

13-20 A double-pitched ceiling following the roof over a room adds interest and spaciousness.

PHOTOGRAPH BY EZRA STOLLER

13-21　This single-slope ceiling reaches a high point at the fireplace. The lowered section provides for indirect lighting, improves acoustics, and makes the sofa corner more intimate.　Carl Koch, architect.

Gabled, or double-pitched ceilings, follow the lines of the pitched roof above, and are commonly seen in barns but also in homes (Fig. 13-20). They lead the eye up and along the line where the two halves meet, giving the room direction and emphasizing the large triangle-on-rectangle end walls.

Lean-to, single-slope, or shed ceilings, like those double-pitched, echo the roof. Informal and spacious, they handle noise better than do horizontal planes and lead the eye to the highest part of the room (Fig. 13-21). Many other designs are not only possible but pleasant, as the history of architecture shows, but are infrequently used today because of cost.

Materials

Plaster is the common ceiling material because it is the only one giving a smooth, uninterrupted surface which can be left natural, painted, or even papered. Ordinary plaster reflects noise, but specially prepared acoustical plasters have remarkably quieting effects. Wallboard is much like plaster except that it leaves joints which can be concealed with tape and paint or emphasized with wood battens. Wood, either strips or sheets of plywood, is finding favor because of its beauty and home-like quality but it has the disadvantages of being expensive and reflecting little light. Then there are several acoustical materials—tiles one foot square of soft fibers with regularly spaced round holes and larger sheets of natural fibers loosely compressed and bound with cementing materials—that bring overhead texture and noise reduction.

Not all ceilings are opaque, for skylights of clear or translucent glass or plastics can bring light from the sky into a room or a terrace (Fig. 2-2). Even more than windows in a wall, skylights envelop a room and everything in it with the kind of light we are accustomed to outdoors.

Color and Texture

"Heavy, heavy hangs over your head" is usually not a pleasant sensation unless you know the weight is supported, and that is one of the reasons for which ceilings are usually high in value and fine in texture. Special effects of considerable impact, however, can be achieved with ceilings painted in strong colors or papered with appropriate (usually small-scale and undemanding) designs. Remember, though, that the color of

PHOTOGRAPHED BY DEAN STONE & HUGO STECCATI

13-22 Stairways open possibilities for coordinate floor and ceiling design. Here the ceiling meets the wood wall in a curve reflecting the curve of the lower steps, but the stone pier at the left goes its upward way without interruption. The paneled wall and the stair-rail are beautifully detailed. The rush carpet and the stonework add contrasting textures. Anschen and Allen, architects.

the ceiling, especially at night if much light is directed toward it, bathes everything below with its reflected color. A yellow ceiling, for example, would enliven yellows, oranges, or yellow-greens below it, but would make dull any blues or violets.

Ornamentation

With the exception of exposed beams (and lighting fixtures), almost no decorative treatment is found on ceilings today. The elaborate beamed and coffered, painted and carved ceilings which make the topside of many mansion and palace rooms things of great beauty are no longer built. Beams frankly exposing the structure of the roof bring a three-dimensional play of light and shade and a pleasant feeling of direction to quite a few contemporary ceilings. Lighting is another means of adding interest to the ceiling, by cove lighting which gives us forms dropped below the ceiling but echoing its planes, or by lighting fixtures either set flush in the ceiling or suspended below it. They enrich ceilings, and some thought should be given to their placement from the point of view of the pattern they create as well as their function of lighting the room.

Acoustics

More comprehensively treated in Chapter 15, acoustics are mentioned here because the ceiling is an excellent place to absorb noise: it is large, unobstructed, more or less parallel to the floors and working surfaces where most noise originates; and its freedom from wear makes possible the use of porous, non-durable, hard-to-clean, noise-absorbing materials.

In conclusion, the ceiling is the easiest part of the house to forget. If you do next to nothing to it, not one person in a hundred will know; moreover, a good plain foil is welcome whether people are conscious of it or not. On the other hand, the really interesting home makes use of every possibility, and the ceiling can certainly be numbered among these.

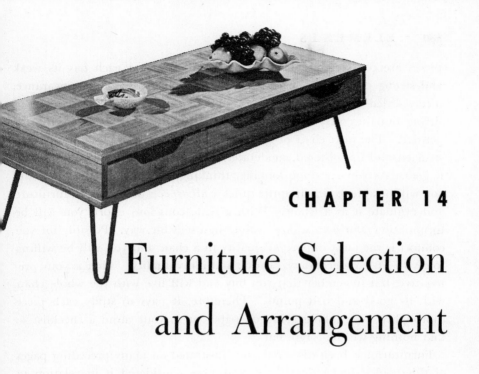

CHAPTER 14

Furniture Selection and Arrangement

A HOUSE is not a home until it has furniture. We live *inside* our enclosed space but *with* and *on* our chairs, beds, tables, and cabinets. Another way of saying this is that furniture is the transition between architecture and people. Selecting and arranging your furniture are challenging, life-long adventures for which most people are not well prepared, but preparing yourself can be easy and pleasant. Critical ability is a requisite, and this comes from experience, knowledge, and consciously sharpening your own native aptitude for seeing and evaluating differences. All of us have walked through furniture stores saying or thinking, "This is pretty." "I don't like that." "I wish I could have that." "I wouldn't give that house room." Then, when we look at the price tags, words often fail us and we leave bewildered and frustrated, knowing neither what we want nor what we can afford.

Suppose, though, that we go into a furniture store or look through a magazine or catalogue with a different attitude; we are not going to buy or want to buy, but simply to look at all the kinds of chairs or tables or cabinets available. Compare and contrast one with the others, noting carefully the ways in which each one is good. You will discover that few pieces are completely good or totally bad, but that each has its weak and strong points. Some chairs will be neat and trim in appearance, nicely scaled for the typical room, and comfortable for short periods of sitting but they may be covered with a fragile textile and may be expensive. The next chair or sofa may be very comfortable, durably constructed and upholstered, moderately priced, but big and bulbous. So it goes. As you continue looking, thinking, and comparing, gradually you will be able to size up quite quickly *all aspects* of a piece of furniture and evaluate it as a whole. With a little conscious effort, you will be formulating your own scale of values in a sensible way. Possibly for you comfort is the most important quality in a chair and you will be willing to give a little on economy, beauty, and individuality. That is your prerogative, but remember that you buy and will live with the whole chair with its good and bad points. Therefore, it pays to study each piece thoroughly, even taking along on paper or in your mind a checklist so that nothing will be forgotten.

Furniture has been discussed and illustrated on many preceding pages of this book. In Chapters 2, 3, and 4 we considered it in relation to group and private living and to keeping house; in Chapters 5, 6, and 7 we focused attention on its design quality; and in Chapters 8, 9, and 10 we thought about materials. Keeping these previous discussions in mind, we are now ready to look at furniture as the major items of home furnishings.

SELECTING FURNITURE

Our four objectives can advantageously be applied to selecting furniture just as they can to every other phase of home planning and furnishing.

Use and Economy

Whether furniture be for sitting, sleeping, eating, working, or playing, there can be no question that use and economy should come first in our thoughts. This means that the form of furniture should follow its function, in general and specifically; that furniture should give long service; and that its cost in money, time, energy, and space should not be excessive. Convenience, comfort, flexibility, space required, length of service, and cost of maintenance are the major factors.

- *Convenience* applies to all furniture but chiefly to good storage facilities and to the ease with which often-moved furniture, such as dining and pull-up chairs, can be handled. All furniture, however, is moved from time to time and should be no heavier than necessary for strength, use, and appearance; the heavier pieces could well be on casters.
- *Comfort* applies primarily to furniture on which we sit or sleep but also to the height of tables, desks, and work surfaces and to sufficient leg room under them.
- *Flexibility,* or multi-usefulness, is often overlooked, but furniture that can be used in more than one room or for more than one purpose saves money. Only a few years ago furniture was designed for one room and one use. The typical dining-room set had a table, china cabinet, and buffet suitable only for a sufficiently large separate dining room; only the chairs could possibly be used elsewhere, but no matter where placed they had a strong "dining room" character. Now many pieces are multi-purpose: tables useful for eating, working, or recreation; unit cabinets and chests suitable for any room and in many combinations; and chairs appropriate in many rooms.
- *Space required* definitely governs the ways in which you can use furniture. Small quarters make space-saving furniture logical, and here is what contemporary designers have done to make furniture earn the space it costs:

  - Eliminated protruding moldings, curved legs, and carving on case goods so that they can be fitted tightly together.
  - Brought storage units down to the floor.
  - Designed cupboards and drawers to fit their contents.
  - Used materials—metal, plywood, foam rubber—that reduce size.
  - Explored the possibilities of folding, stacking, and nesting tables, chairs, and stools.
  - Made multi-purpose pieces such as the case goods mentioned above and davenport-beds.
  - Reduced both size and scale to a minimum.

These developments have been so gradual that one scarcely notices them until one tries to move an inherited antique into a new little home.

- *Length of service* depends on physical and psychological durability. Physical durability is determined by materials, construction, and finish which are discussed below. Psychological durability is equally important: much furniture is discarded long before it is worn out because it no longer satisfies our total needs. For continued satisfaction choose furniture in which the basic proportions are good, the materials are suitable and honestly used, the size and scale are moderate to small, the design permits flexible use, and the character is satisfying to you but does not clamor for attention. Avoid revivals, for they seldom last long; and at the expense of seeming timid, do not jump for the latest novelty or fad. Good sense and moderation might be your theme.

■ *Cost of maintenance* includes cleaning, repairing, refinishing, and re-upholstering. Cleaning burdens are lightened if surfaces are smooth, non-porous to dirt and stains, dull rather than glossy, of colors and textures that camouflage a little dust and a few finger prints, and also if the pieces either go to the floor or are supported on simple legs around which a vacuum cleaner can be maneuvered; repairing is lessened by firm construction and strong materials; refinishing depends on toughness of material and the finish—painted furniture may need refinishing every two or three years, transparent finishes supplemented by wax or polish last a long time, and plastic-impregnated surfaces, aluminum, and chromium apparently never require it; and lastly, re-upholstering may be needed at periods varying from five years up to twenty or more depending on the material and the use it gets.

Beauty

Good design and appropriateness to your home are the ingredients of beauty in furniture. "Good design" means that the form, line, color, and texture express their purpose, combine variety in unity, and are balanced and rhythmic; that the whole and the parts are suitably emphasized, and the materials are well chosen and worked. "Appropriateness to the room" means that the furniture looks right in its place. Generally, this implies that each piece of furniture must be in harmony with the character of your home, of suitable size, and appropriate in scale; occasionally, though, it means choosing furniture for the sake of contrast, subtle or obvious, in order to gain interest and impact.

Individuality

Never before have so many kinds of furniture been available to so many persons. In Chapter 1 some of the differences among chairs were listed, but this list could be greatly expanded if all available types were included. From the abundant diversity, each family can select pieces suited to its individual needs. Happily, too, we have been freed from arbitrary standards which formerly restricted the possibilities of combinations and arrangements. Today we are free to have all of our furniture of one type if unity is our goal or to combine different kinds if we want variety. Thus we can express our individualities without unreasoned restraints, but do not forget that lasting individuality is more a natural consequence of a problem well solved than a self-conscious seeking to be different.

FURNITURE TYPES

Furniture can be divided according to its primary use: beds, chairs, sofas, and stools; tables, desks, and work surfaces; and storage units.

Beds

Reducing physical strain to a minimum is the purpose of beds, and this is best achieved with a flat, horizontal surface large enough to permit moving around and stretching out, and resilient enough to yield to and yet support the body in the position that feels best. Individuals vary in their ideas about sleeping comfort, but very few sleep well in a bed that sags or is too soft or too hard. About the only way to find out whether a bed is right for you is to try it and furniture stores are quite willing to let you lie on their samples, although in public places it is difficult to relax sufficiently to check bed comfort.

Most beds today have a springy foundation and a resilient mattress. The foundation is usually either an inexpensive, light-weight, moderately comfortable flat spring or the more bulky, expensive, and comfortable coil springs. Mattresses have been filled with just about everything from straw to hair—and just air. Today the least expensive and least comfortable are filled with cotton, the better grades have inner-springs covered with padding or are of foam rubber. Foam rubber has advantages: it is light weight, easy to keep clean, harbors no insects or allergy-producers, never needs to be turned, lasts just about indefinitely, and has about one-half million air cells in each cubic inch for resilience.

Even if your funds are low, buy good mattresses and springs and support them on simple wood legs or the more useful metal frames on casters. Add the useful but not essential headboards, footboards, night tables and other paraphernalia later. In small quarters or for occasional guest use, a studio couch or a davenport that opens to become a bed is a sensible economy.

Bedspreads are usually the most conspicuous part of a bed. Serviceable bedspreads do not wrinkle excessively when taken off the bed or when one naps on them. They are heavy enough to stay in place and can be laundered or cleaned easily. Pile-weave textiles, such as tufted cotton or corduroy, are good looking and sensible; firmly woven, moderately heavy cotton with patterns or prints also gives good service; chintzes and the like (usually with ruffles) can be pretty but are more to be looked at than used. Strong colors or vigorous patterns on bedspreads make the bed loom large in the room; unobtrusive colors and patterns make the room seem larger. Bedspreads, curtains and draperies, and rugs with a "family resemblance" bring unity: spread and draperies can be obviously matched or more subtly related with harmonious color, texture, or pattern.

Chairs

Logie [1] writes that sitting has become the most universal occupation of man because we work, study, relax, eat, and travel while seated. Leading such a sedentary life, we should be expert sitters, but we are not because until very recently no serious studies of sitting were made. We now know that comfort results when weight and pressure are spread and tension is eased by having:

- The height of the seat somewhat less than the length of the lower legs, so that the feet rest on the floor and the legs can be relaxed.
- The depth of the seat somewhat less than the length of the upper leg so that there is no pressure point under the knee.
- The width of the seat ample to permit some movement.

[1] Gordon Logie, *Furniture from Machines.*

14-1 The cushioned seat and back are designed to relax the body and are supported on a straightforward, sturdy frame of wood. Although comfortable, the chair is not massive and is visually lightened by the spirited upholstery.

- The seat shaped as in a Windsor chair or an Eames chair (Fig. 8-3) or resilient so that pressure is not concentrated on the small weight-bearing edge of the pelvis.
- Both seat and back tilted backward to buttress the weight.
- The angle between seat and back of 95 degrees or more.
- The chair back support the small of the sitter's back.
- The position of the seat and back adjustable for different persons (as in typists' chairs) or for different ways of relaxing (as in the old-fashioned but sensible Morris chairs).

Comfort is further increased if the chair offers a place to rest the head and relax the neck and has arms to support our arms.

Chairs are used for several purposes and their form should follow their function. The typical family needs chairs for each of the following purposes:

Relaxation and Comfort. In the group-living space and possibly in the seclusion room and bedrooms, seating that allows each member of the

WIDDICOMB FURNITURE CO.   PHOTOGRAPH BY MAYNARD PARKER

14-2 Handsome proportions, subtly shaped frame, and beautiful workmanship distinguish a comfortable chair and ottoman. Robsjohn-Gibbings, designer.

family to relax is needed. Upholstered chairs and davenports are about the only kind that adjust themselves to varying individuals and are comfortable over long periods of time because they spread one's weight over large areas. New types of springs and foam rubber have greatly decreased the space-consuming bulkiness typical of all really relaxing furniture of a few years ago and enable us to get pieces as light, trim, neat, and comfortable as those shown in Figs. 14-1 and 2. Even so, such pieces are heavy and ought to have permanent positions in the room.

Conversation and Reading. Although these activities are quite possible in the seating mentioned above, "pull-up" chairs that support us well without inducing sleep are helpful. These can have shaped seats of wood or metal, or they can be lightly upholstered, webbed, canvas covered, or, the unbeatable in terms of price, Chinese split cane chairs (Fig. 4-10). Chairs for these purposes should be easy to get hold of, light to lift, and strong enough to stand frequent moving.

Eating, Working, and Games. For these activities one needs sturdy, easily moved chairs with a relatively upright back to keep the sitter alert, a seat and back shaped or lightly padded to lessen pressure, and upholstery that resists abrasion and dirt. The most frequently used family eating place ought to have enough chairs or built-in seats always ready to seat the family, but it is sensible to have more of the same kind of chairs elsewhere to bring out for large groups. Chairs of this sort can be seen in many illustrations throughout the book and some especially worth study are shown in Figs. 14-7 and 10.

Sofas

Chesterfield, couch, settee, settle, davenport, divan, lounge or sofa— which do you call the seat for two or more people?

PASCOE

14-3 These pull-up chairs are easy to move and fit compactly together. Cane, webbing, and upholstering used on the same bent-wood frame provide varying degrees of comfort. They differ notably in scale and character but all are the same size.

Chesterfield is an overstuffed sofa with upholstered ends.

Couch is a sofa with a low back and one raised end.

Davenport is used in the United States to describe an upholstered sofa often convertible into a bed, but originally meant a small writing desk, named after its maker.

Divan is a Turkish term used for large, low couches without arms or backs which developed from piles of rugs for reclining.

Lounge is a type of couch often with one high end for reclining.

Settee is a long, light seat with a back and sometimes arms, and is often upholstered.

Settle is an all wood settee.

Sofa comes from an Arabic term and is used to describe any long upholstered seat for more than one person.

Being American, we will use davenport and sofa interchangeably to describe that piece of furniture around which the living-room arrangement

VALENTINE SEAVER

14-4   A comfortable davenport with arms and textured fabric.

KNOLL ASSOCIATES

14-5 Straightforward simplicity characterizes a sofa, coffee table, and webbed chair. The sofa consists of a wood frame, removable foam-rubber mattress, and upholstered back. Notice that the back does not meet the mattress and is covered with a different fabric.

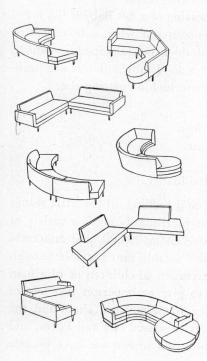

MODERN DESIGNS

14-6 Sofas in one piece or in separate units come in many sizes and shapes to meet different needs. Those in separate units offer opportunity to fit furniture to space.

usually centers. The variety is legion: straight, curved, or angled to fit your room; with or without arms but more comfortable with them; in one piece or sectional, the latter permitting different arrangements; long enough for a six-footer to stretch out on or not quite, but better if they are; heavy and massive, delicate and graceful, or light and simple but sturdy. Here are suggestions:

- No more bulk than needed for comfort and strength.
- Long enough to stretch out on.
- Low and deep enough for relaxation but high and firm enough so that you can get up under your own power.
- Arms for comfort.
- Foam rubber for comfort, long-term economy, and lightness.
- Convertible into a bed if you need extra sleeping space.
- Sectional if you like to change your arrangements and can keep the sections tightly together.
- Upholstery that combines beauty and durability.

Tables

The essence of table design is the supporting of a flat slab off the floor; this is reduced to its lowest common denominator when a home craftsman supports a piece of plywood or a flush door on four pipe legs—which, by the way, is an inexpensive way to get a good table. There are problems, however, in all table design and these include getting the:

- Necessary strength and stability.
- Supports out of the way of feet and legs.
- Right height, size, and shape for its use.
- Durable materials.
- Appropriate kind of beauty and individuality.

Tables are used for eating, games, work, and holding all the little things that collect temporarily in rooms. The typical family needs a variety of tables differing in use and therefore in size, shape, height, and materials.

Dining Tables. Sit-down meals require a table that is stable enough to be unjarred by the unpredictable movements of children or of a man carving meat; has a top large enough to give each person two feet of elbow room; is high enough to give leg room between chair and the lower surface; has supports out of the way of sitters' feet and knees; and can be extended in size. Since tablecloths and underpads have become

14-7 Chromium tube frames in an unusually graceful design, plastic table top, and plastic upholstery make this dining furniture durable and lessen housework.

rare in daily living, it pays also to look closely at the durability, ease of maintenance, and beauty of the top surface. Most dining tables are rectangular because they are harmonious with rectangular rooms, can be pushed snugly against a wall or into a corner, and are slightly less costly to make, but if you have the right space for it, a round or oval table will give a friendly group feeling with a distinct flavor of its own. Be sure to check dining chairs and tables together because often their legs interfere with each other, the heights of the two are not co-ordinated, or the space between chair and table is insufficient for the sitters' comfort.

Expanding a table can be done in many ways, but three are most commonly used. Drop-leaf tables, in use since Elizabethan days, can be quickly and easily expanded or contracted, but unless well engineered the leaves may be wobbly and their supports may interfere with leg room; even so, they are probably the best solution for today. Add-a-leaf dining tables can be expanded to large size but they cannot be changed quickly or easily and the leaves require storage space. Add-a-unit tables have one major table to which you can add units normally placed elsewhere in the house. It is a good idea except that moving tables is a nuisance and may leave other parts of the house un-tabled when you need them most.

Coffee Tables. We have come to think that no davenport is complete unless faced with a long low table on which ashtrays, books, magazines, newspapers, accessories, plants, flowers, and snacks abound. This is a modern invention somewhat taking the place of the older, higher living-room table. Most coffee tables, though, seem to have been designed only for the "long, low, open" look, because they have no storage space for the little things needed in that part of the room, they are too low to be reached comfortably from the sofa and to give foot room, and if in scale with the sofa they usually block traffic. Really functional coffee tables are about 20 inches high, have some storage space and ample room for sitters' feet, and might well be in sections. Their tops are durable and their supports strong but slender. There is no reason why coffee tables have to be rectangular, and some deviate happily from the right angle. Circles make good conversation centers and organic shapes dispel monotony.

End Tables. It might be said that the old living-room table disintegrated into many little tables, for convenience now seems to demand a table however small within easy reach of every chair. Thus one usually finds a table at each end of the davenport and probably for each group of chairs. Unlike coffee tables, these seldom interfere with feet and can provide shelves or drawers for supplementary storage. They look better if of the same height as the arms of upholstered davenports and chairs but are more convenient and less a spill-hazard if somewhat lower or higher. Often these tables are used for lamps, although a lamp table, strictly speaking, is a little higher. Nests of tables, the top one acting as an end or coffee table, simplify entertaining greatly.

Card and Game Tables. Seldom handsome, the folding card table is a wonderful gadget. Cards and other games are best at tables several inches lower than those for eating, and collapsible card tables are ideal for occasional games, bridge luncheons, or buffet suppers, and supplementary serving at festive dinners. Space permitting, a permanent card table with at least two chairs always there is a handy set of equipment for any family liking games, doing homework, or enjoying varied eating spots.

Kitchen Tables. Once banished in the drive for compact efficiency, tables in kitchens or adjacent alcoves are again found to be as useful as our grandmothers knew them to be. Since they often serve for eating and food preparation, they differ from dining tables only in having greater strength and durability. Not all of them are glaring white and

14-8 A simple desk, ample built-in storage units, a modified Windsor chair, and a couch on casters give the study in the home of Danish architect Erik Stengade unpretentious, individualized charm.

chrome; in fact some have become so friendly that few mind seeing them from the living room.

Desks. The essentials of desks are a suitable surface for writing and convenient and accessible storage for writing materials and papers, placing them midway between tables and storage units.

That every household needs at least one good writing place is obvious. How large and complex the unit and where it is placed depends on the family's habits. A desk can be a table with only one drawer, a compartment in an arrangement of unit furniture (Figs. 14-8 and 10), or a piece of furniture designed for serious desk work (Fig. 2-11). Space-saving devices include writing surfaces that fold down and out or slide in and out, but unfortunately many of these soon get wobbly. A vertical file drawer or two is the most sensible way to store all the pieces of paper related to household operation compactly, conveniently, and accessibly. The file can be part of a desk or purchased separately in units of one to four drawers.

Storage

Storage today is a major problem. Living quarters are smaller and attics, "spare" rooms, barns, sheds, and basements have all but disappeared; good furniture for storage is extremely expensive; more people have more things to put away and, for reasons not clear to the writers, apparently have less time in which to do it; and we favor the "uncluttered look" in our homes. An intelligent program is needed.

- Discard things you neither use nor like.
- Cut down on your purchases of seldom-used things, especially the bulky ones.
- Plan your active storage for:
  convenience—at or very near the place where it is used.
  visibility—as little hidden as possible.
  accessibility—frequently-used items at most convenient height, heavy ones below, and those seldom used above.
  maintenance—everyday items can be stored on open shelves, but less used ones should be in enclosed storage to lessen dusting.
- Provide as much dead storage space as feasible for seasonal or seldom-used objects of all sizes and shapes. The typical family can easily use space equivalent to a one-car garage (10' x 20'), but it is more convenient if distributed where needed most rather than concentrated in one spot.

Making these housewives' dreams come to life means three things. *First,* sufficient storage in each room of the house for the things used in that room, and as close as possible to the spot at which they are needed—phonograph records near the player, books convenient to reading chairs, and foods and utensils at the spot in the kithen where they are first used. *Second,* storage that will accommodate efficiently the objects to be stored. No one can predict exactly what he will want in each part of the house during the next five years so that it is wise to plan for as much flexibility as possible—adjustable shelves, drawers with removable dividers, and relatively small units of movable furniture that can be put together in different combinations. *Third*, keeping most of your storage space shallow so that you can see and get hold of what is there. Avoid deep drawers and deep shelves except when their contents demand depth; otherwise, what you want always seems to be under everything else in the drawer or behind everything else on the shelf.

The above plan takes us beyond what most of us call furniture and that was precisely what was intended because good storage, even more than good seating and sleeping, is part of total home design. The least that architect and builder ought to do is to provide *space* for cupboards, cabinets, chests, and for trunks, baby carriages, bicycles, outdoor furniture and the like, and it is far better if these needed facilities are built into the house.

We store things by standing them on the floor or on shelves; hanging them on walls or the backs of doors, or from the ceiling; or putting them in drawers or chests. Which of these is used depends on the use, size, shape, fragility, and value of the object, but it is provident to use to best advantage every inch of available space. The drawings in Fig. 14-11 suggest ways of organizing useful storage.

Let us now look at some of the furniture known in the trade as *case goods*.

Bookcases are the simplest because even though books come in some eighty different sizes they are all approximately the same shape. More than half of them are about 5″ x 7½″ and few exceed 7½″ x 10″. The shelves should be adjustable but seldom need to be more than 8″ to 9″ deep. Books on open shelves are good enrichments and also absorb noise, but without protection they are hard to keep clean.

Some book storage space is needed in every room in the house with the possible exception of the dining space.

A single shelf in the kitchen may hold all of your cookbooks and a few shelves in the living-room wall or under tables will hold currently used volumes. Near desks, especially if used for study, book shelves are essential. Table-height bookcases double as tables in living rooms and if sufficiently long, unify a wall. They can reach to the ceiling to become forceful elements in the decorating scheme; they can be used architecturally as frames around doors or windows, to bring to life otherwise unusable space, or as free-standing partial or complete dividers between two rooms or two parts of one room.

Chests of drawers are invariably used for clothes storage, and your criteria should be: strongly joined drawers that slide well; handles you can

DUNBAR FURNITURE MANUFACTURING CO.   PHOTOGRAPH BY FRANK WILLMING

14-9 Cases with drawers and doors, part of a coordinated line of unit furniture, are of amber mahogany and supported on turned aluminum legs. The doors are textiles, woven of molded plywood and aluminum rods, to give contrast. Notice the efficient finger slots on the drawers and also the effectively simple, large plaid wall covering.

easily grasp; shallow drawers at the top (or better, a row of small drawers) and deeper ones at the bottom; and relatively small units for flexibility. Drawers either in chests or combined with cupboards are used for table linens and silver; these should be very shallow and should have adjustable dividers.

Surprisingly, we can find no mention of the convenient drawer, which we take for granted, until 1583, and it was not widely used until the 17th century.

Cabinets with doors and with adjustable shelves and/or vertical dividers are needed in every room in the house although they are found only infrequently outside the kitchen, dining space, and bathroom.

Doors on cabinets beget the same problems as do doors between rooms.

Swinging doors work easily and allow narrow storage racks on the back, but they get in the way when open; sliding doors open only part of the cabinet at a time and give no door-back shelves; and doors that roll, like those on roll-top desks, may stick. Where space in front of the cabinet is at a premium or people move around while the doors are open, sliding doors are probably better, but in other places swinging doors are more satisfactory.

Radio, phonograph, and television cabinets are furniture for which there was no historical precedent. The early ones seemed intent on making themselves conspicuous and carried the germs which rampantly took over juke-box design. Nowadays, radios, phonographs, and television receivers often take their place as units of case goods—rather than as isolated, assertive, homely accessories—or better as part of the wall. (Figs. 2-2, 4-1, and 16-9.)

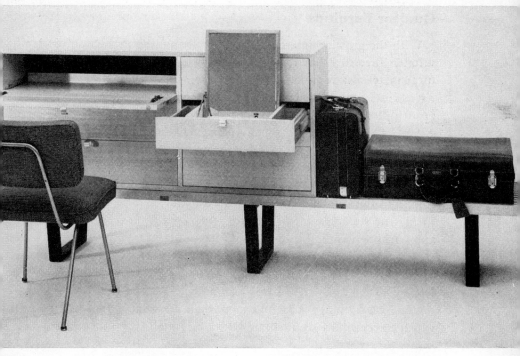

HERMAN MILLER FURNITURE CO.   PHOTOGRAPH BY DALE ROOKS

14-10 Modular unit case goods combine desk space, a compact vanity unit, storage drawers, and space for luggage or sitting. The chair could be used for many purposes. Although the photograph suggests guest-room furniture, these units would function well in a small apartment. George Nelson, designer.

Screens have a venerable history as ornaments, space dividers for privacy, and protection from draughts and the heat of roaring Medieval fires. In China, screens were known in the 2nd century, B.C., and were elaborated with carving, inlay, and painting, and also with mica or, later, glass to combine shelter and view both indoors and outdoors. Since then, screens have been made of almost every known material: sheer silk, tapestry, brocades, leather, clear or translucent glass, mirrors, bamboo poles, shutters, plastics, and curved or flat plywood. Their great advantages are that they can be moved and adjusted, a matter of great importance in open-plan houses, and that they divide space into comfortable units without shutting out what is beyond. Screens can be almost as heavy and substantial as a wall, or light and delicate; transparent, translucent, or opaque; plain or ornamented; the same on both sides or different; and they can blend or contrast with their surroundings.

Outdoor Furniture

With the growing interest in outdoor living, the problem of designing suitable furniture has received much attention. We have good structural materials: redwood, cedar, and cypress resist weather; aluminum never rusts, stays cool in the sun, and is light weight; copper weathers beautifully; and chromium-plated steel is durable. Tables present no special problems, nor do the frames of chairs and chaises. But as yet there is no truly relaxing seating that will withstand sun and rain and remain a comfortable temperature in sun or shade. The difficulty is twofold: weatherproof synthetics and plastics get unpleasantly hot and cold; and the stitching and buttons with which fabrics are fastened over springs or stuffing allow water to penetrate. The seating most nearly approaching weatherproof comfort has aluminum frames with treated canvas or synthetic webbing seats and backs (Fig. 9-9). Then come the wood or metal chairs and benches with cushions and pads that cannot be left out in the rain (Fig. 20-12). If you have these, it is advisable to have weatherproof storage space not more than a few steps from the point at which the cushions are used.

BUILT-IN FURNITURE

The first built-in furniture may have been a natural rock ledge found in a cave and used for sitting or sleeping, but from that time on until a

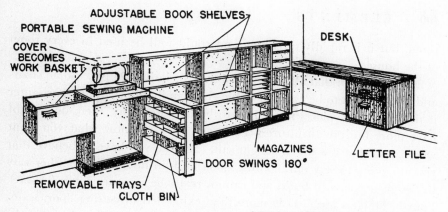

ADJUSTABLE BOOK SHELVES

PORTABLE SEWING MACHINE

DESK

COVER BECOMES WORK BASKET

MAGAZINES

LETTER FILE

DOOR SWINGS 180°

REMOVEABLE TRAYS

CLOTH BIN

DOUGLAS FIR PLYWOOD ASSOCIATION

14-11 Built-in furniture is worthwhile in any room in the house. A built-in sewing, book, and desk unit makes efficient use of space for work in a living room or bedroom. General storage, often overlooked, is well provided for in the storage wall. Nick Athens, Joseph J. and Carolyn Roberto, designers.

century or so ago furniture that is part of the architectural shell was seldom used. Even clothes closets were unknown, clothes being stored in bulky wardrobes. In the later 19th century home-designers and builders began to make more intensive use of their walls. We may no longer care for the elaborate fireplace mantels that provided display space for bric-a-brac, but we cannot help admiring the remarkably sensible dish cupboards with doors opening into both kitchen and dining room. Frank Lloyd Wright early in his career began thinking of the house as one unified whole, and built storage, seating, and tables as an integral part of the architecture. Built-in furniture, surprisingly enough, more often than not promotes flexible living. This is hard to understand until we realize that such furniture takes less space than movable pieces, thereby leaving a maximum of free space in the center of rooms to do with as you wish.

Built-in furniture saves space, eliminates dust-catching corners and crevices, gives a feeling of permanence and unity, and can break up the boxiness of rooms. At the same time it reduces the clutter brought by many isolated pieces of furniture which have an irritating tendency to get out of their best positions. You cannot, of course, move it around in the house or take it with you if you move.

The most common built-in furniture includes medicine chests, linen closets, and kitchen cabinets. In many late Victorian—and contemporary—houses, dish cupboards are part of the dining space. Built-in furniture came into the house through the kitchen, dining room, and bathroom, but it is rapidly spreading and could well be used in every room of the house.

Does this mean that all furniture should be built in? No. Some chairs and tables ought to be *easily* movable—but family life would be pleasanter if the big, heavy pieces never had to be moved. Why, then, do we not have more built-in furniture? First, you have to know what you want where, and that is a tough assignment. Second, you have to believe that you are going to stay put. Third, good built-in furniture is neither easy to design nor easy to build and cannot really be seen until it is finished. Fourth, budgets are usually more than exhausted in getting floor, walls, and roof, and the dreamed-of built-ins are among the first things to be eliminated when the bids are too high. One can always add them, so one thinks! Fifth, some contemporary furniture has almost all of the advantages, can be purchased a unit at a time, shifted until it looks and is right, and taken when you move (Figs. 4-9, 14-6, 14-9, and 16-9). But it is not as easy to maintain and seldom gives the secure permanence and architectural unity of the real thing.

MATERIALS AND CONSTRUCTION

Grandfather used to say that he could quickly estimate the quality of a man's suit by the way the buttons were sewed on, but there is no quick and easy way to size up furniture materials and construction. Much time and disappointment would be saved if clear and specific labels appeared on each piece or if the manufacturer's specifications were available for each line. Lacking such, it is up to you to look at every piece you are considering literally from every angle, get all possible information from the salesman, and try to purchase from stores that will really "stand behind" their merchandise. Furniture is no better than the materials from which it is made, the methods by which it is joined, and the ways in which it is finished. Here are some preliminary tests:

- Does the piece stand firmly on the floor and resist staunchly your efforts to make it wobble? This is particularly important in tables, especially if expandable, and in desks, and chairs.
- Do all movable parts—drawers, drop leaves, and the like—operate easily and steadily?
- Are all joints tightly and smoothly fitted together?
- Is the finish hard, smooth, and evenly applied? Is it composed of

many coats properly dried and rubbed, or one or two coats which look thick and gummy in any crevice or indentation?

Then look at the places of greatest wear.

Tops of tables, desks, counters, bookcases, cabinets, and chests. Ideally, these should resist scratching, denting, breaking, staining, and wetting. Properly finished hard woods are satisfactory if kept reasonably free from liquids; plastic laminates are remarkably durable but noisy and shiny; linoleum is quiet but the lighter colors show stains; vinyl tiles or sheets have all the advantages of linoleum (except low price) plus greater resistance to stains and cuts; vinyl cork is good to look at and touch, resilient, and stain resistant; glass is light and airy, a breakage hazard, and needs constant cleaning; and marble is rich, very heavy, noisy, and can break and stain.

Edges of tables, doors, and drawers. These are the surfaces most easily nicked and marred and all but the most durable materials show wear. Hard wood, the best glue, or metal strips (commonly used in kitchen counters) all help.

Runners of drawers. Hard wood or non-corrosive metals are needed here. Often-used, large, and heavy drawers should be suspended on rollers and tracks, but as yet these have been reserved for offices and kitchens.

Handles, knobs, and hinges. The soil that collects on and around handles and knobs is ample evidence of the use they get. Hard woods and dull metals are as yet the most serviceable, but plastics are entering the field. Hinges, a relatively minor item in the cost of furniture, ought to be of the best possible quality and securely fastened into wood hard enough to hold screws under strain.

Lower part of legs and bases. To be kicked by feet, caressed by mops and brooms, and nuzzled by vacuum cleaners is the pre-ordained fate of this part of furniture. Reduce to a minimum parts that touch the floor and then make the necessary ones simple, of medium dark wood or of metal, both with finishes that do not scratch or chip readily.

Seating surfaces, stuffing, and springs are discussed below. We now look in more detail at wood, metal, and upholstered furniture.

Wood

Wood, the standard furniture material, should be thoroughly dry and of a variety that is stable in size and shape so that there is minimum

14-12 Typical wood joints include rebated, dovetailed, mortise-and-tenon, tongue-and-groove, doweled, and butt.

shrinking, swelling, and warping. Each wood has its own qualities and the knowing craftsman may combine several kinds in one piece to take full advantage of their individualities. Structural parts should be of strong wood such as ash or birch but need not take a good finish or be beautiful unless visible. Exposed surfaces ought to wear well, be hard enough to resist scratching and denting, have a pleasant finish, and be beautiful in themselves. Mahogany, walnut, oak, maple, and birch have these qualities. Redwood, on the other hand, has a pleasant color and stands weather, but it is soft and splintery. The advantages of plywood have been stated and recently some of the hard pressed composition boards have proved their value for table tops, backs of chests, and parts of drawers.

Wood in furniture can be joined in a number of ways, of which the commonest are plain butt, doweled, mortise-and-tenon, tongue-and-groove, and dovetailed.

Rebated or rabbeted joints have a groove cut from the edge of one piece to receive the other member.

Dovetailed joints have a series of flaring tenons (or tongues) on one piece and corresponding mortises (or grooves) on the other. They are used in all good drawers.

Mortise-and-tenon joints have a mortise (a hole or cavity) in one piece of wood into which a tenon (projecting piece) cut in the end of the other fits securely. They are usually stronger than doweled joints.

Tongue-and-groove joints are much like mortise-and-tenon except that the tongue and groove extend the width of the boards.

Doweled joints have wooden pegs (or dowels) inserted into holes in the two pieces of wood to be joined.

Butt joints are the simplest and weakest and have no place in furniture unless reinforced with corner blocks.

All joints need glue, and synthetic resins are very much stronger than vegetable or casein glues. Frames of chairs, sofas, and case goods also need triangular wood or metal corner blocks tightly screwed and glued in place for reinforcing. Screws strengthen joints much more than do nails.

One can almost say, too, that furniture is no better than its finish, and it might pay you to look again at the discussion of wood finishes in Chapter 8 with your thoughts concentrated on furniture.

Metal

Used since antiquity, metal is enjoying a new popularity. Why? It is relatively inexpensive, easy to machine, strong and durable, and reduces bulk. Steel with a baked enameled finish is well known in kitchen and bathroom cabinets and more recently in outdoor chairs and tables. It comes in many colors, is easy to wash, and lasts very well indoors if not kicked or banged—outdoors on tables and chairs it needs a new coat of enamel in a few years. Steel is also much used today for legs and frames of chairs, tables, and case goods, and it is usually in the shape of round rods and tubes (Fig. 5-1) or right-angle strips (Fig. 9-7). Being strong it can be thin, and rusting quickly it needs paint. The usual black color gives many pieces a spidery look, but it could just as well be any other color. Most surface treatments on metal wear off in time; but chromium plated on steel in sufficient thickness gives lasting protection, and aluminum never rusts or deteriorates (Figs. 14-7, 9, and 10).

Metal can be joined by welding, riveting, or bolting. Welding gives smooth, strong joints, but bolts and rivets are quite satisfactory if you do not mind seeing what holds the piece together. Most metal furniture is so much stronger and more rigid than normal household use requires that construction is less a problem than with wood.

Upholstered Furniture

This term refers to all interior furnishings made with textiles, leather, and the like, but today it is used primarily to describe the stuffing and covering put on chairs and sofas to make them conform to our contours rather than forcing ours into theirs. It can be of several degrees of complexity and comfort.

1. *Fabric stretched over frame.* From ancient times up into the Renaissance, upholstery was chiefly textiles, rushes, or leather stretched over wood or metal frames and often supplemented by loose cushions. This is still widely used in chairs with cane, canvas, or webbing seats and backs for light-weight, inexpensive resilience (Fig. 14-3). In such furniture, one should look for a frame that is good looking as well as strong, upholstery that is durable and securely fastened to the frame but easily removable—beware of webbed chairs in which the webbing is glued into the frame. This makes replacement difficult.

2. *Simple padding.* The next step consists of putting a layer of cotton, moss, hair, or foam rubber over wood or webbing and then covering it with muslin and the finish fabric, in short, fastening thin cushions to the frame (Fig. 14-7). Since the 17th century, this has been the standard way of making dining and other light- to medium-weight chairs comfortable. The chief concern here is padding that lasts long. Until recently, long, curled hair was the best and most costly; but rubberized hair and foam rubber have proved most satisfactory; and down, kapok, moss, and cotton are moderately successful.

3. *Stuffing and springs.* Although it was during the reign of Louis XV (1715-1774) that springs were placed under the stuffing, not until about 1914 did the massive, over-stuffed pieces which were to come into prominence raise comfort to a new height and drop beauty to a new low. At first springs were fastened into the seat, then into the back, and then also put into the removable cushions. This complicated approach to comfort includes the following:

Frame of strong wood strongly joined, or occasionally of metal.

Webbing of jute or linen bands from 2½ to 10″ wide, woven in a simple basket weave and tacked to the frame. The best quality is firm and distinguished by red lines on each side. Sometimes wood slats are used if the springs are deep.

Springs, usually coiled, are tied to the webbing at the bottom and then securely held down and in place with strong twine. They should be close enough to prevent sagging—9 to 12 in each seat—but not so close that they rub. In cheap furniture they are widely spaced and not well tied.

Burlap comes next to cover the springs and give foundation for the padding.

JENS RISOM DESIGN   PHOTOGRAPH BY BEN SCHNALL

14-13 A strong wood frame of comfortable size and angle supplemented with foam-rubber cushions and removable fabric makes a good, economical chair.

Padding or *stuffing* comes on top of the burlap and is the same as discussed under *simple padding*. On the best furniture there may be two layers of burlap and padding. Felt padding is then placed on the back and arms to give smooth contours and protection from the frame.

Muslin covers the padding on the best chairs and sofas.

Final fabric—at last—put over all of this, is about the only thing you see.

Cushions, as a postlude, can then be placed on the seat and against the back and may be filled with any of the above-mentioned paddings, today usually supplemented by springs—or simply of foam rubber.

Getting ourselves comfortably seated is quite a job when done in this way, which is still the standard practice, but it can be enormously simplified (but not made less expensive to the consumer) by using foam rubber of sufficient thickness on a rigid base of plywood, or, more comfortably, on webbing or firm but thin springs. The last word in complexity and presumably in comfort is provided by "contour chairs" shaped to relax all muscles and equipped with built-in heating, cooling, and vibrating mechanisms!

Upholstery Fabrics

These can be just about anything you want from expensive, fragile silk brocades to long-lived, durable leather and plastics. In woven fabrics, service and appearance are determined by fiber, weave, and weight. The most durable, soil resistant fibers are wool, nylon, and some of the newer synthetics, such as saran, orlon, and velon, used alone or combined; rayon, too, gives good service; cotton, if moderately dark in color and textured, lasts longer than its price indicates; and linen is pleasant, expensive, and musses easily when used for slip covers. Silk is now a luxury. The longer the fiber and the more tightly twisted the yarn, the longer the wear. In weaves, the first thing to look for is tightness, for loosely woven textiles snag easily. Pile fabrics, such as frieze, usually retain their attractiveness much longer than flat weaves, although nubby, textured, or patterned textiles also conceal wear. Soft, silky velvets distinctly show where people have sat. Weight is a primary factor in looks and longevity.

In addition to textiles, leather has long since earned its place because of its durability, pleasant surface, good looks, and ease of maintenance. Plastics now come in good colors, dull surfaces, and textures sympathetic

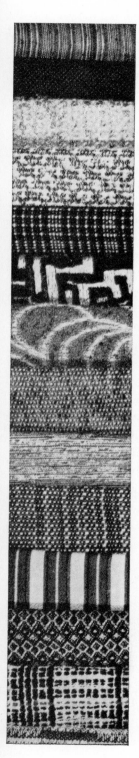

14-14 The fabric used on an upholstered chair can greatly affect the character of the piece. Both of these brocatelles are suitable for this chair but the one at the left makes it quiet and formal while the one at the right makes it much more dynamic and dominant.

14-15 Upholstering textiles range from plain weaves to vigorous patterns. Appropriateness to the furniture they cover and to the whole room is primary in selection.

to hands and eyes; and the better grades last long with minimum care. Plastics not only come in woven and non-woven sheets but also as coatings on or impregnations of familiar textiles. Some are elasticized to give a smooth, tight fit on complex shapes.

Upholstery fabrics are part of the chair or davenport to which they are fastened and they are the part with which you come into contact. Therefore, they should look comfortable to sit on, feel good to touch, resist abrasion as well as soil, and be appropriate in color and pattern to the size, shape, and character of what is underneath them.

What do we want today? For the most part, upholstery that does not knock our eyes out or make us question the advisability of sitting on it; small-scale patterns (if any); neutralized, quieting colors; and perhaps nature-like textures. But occasionally, a lively pattern that tells from a distance, such as that shown in Fig. 14-1 lifts a room or a corner to an invigorating importance. If, however, the pattern has large, readily noticed repeats, these should be carefully fitted to the forms underneath, not applied at random as though the upholsterer did not have enough material to do the job properly.

Slip covers are such a sensible way of brightening up old furniture in an easy-to-maintain way that it is too bad that they so often make furniture look like a woman in an old Mother Hubbard wrapper or like a bird cage covered for the night. They can be made of almost any medium-weight, not-easily-wrinkled fabric from chintz to corduroy and denim, and have much to recommend them if the material can be easily removed and cleaned. Too often, though, they look like ill-fitting, temporary makeshifts: the material is unsuitable; the tailoring poor; ruffles or pleats make a vain attempt to conceal various awkwardnesses; and they do not stay neatly in place. None of these defects is inherent in the idea but they are common in practice.

PLANNED BUYING

Without a plan (and by *plan* we mean something that grows and develops, not a static blueprint), getting your furniture can become as frantic and disordered as Christmas shopping often is. It can be even worse than Christmas shopping because you will be spending much more money and have to live with your purchases. Underlying all plans should be buying the essential, large pieces first, then filling in with smaller, less costly items. Over the first two years, you might want to do something like this.

| FIRST YEAR | SECOND YEAR |

Living Room

FIRST YEAR	SECOND YEAR
Sofa or studio couch	1 or 2 chairs
1 lounge and 1 pull-up chair	End tables
or	Desk
2 of either type	Draperies if needed
Coffee table	Accessories
Rug and curtains	
2 lamps	

Dining Space

FIRST YEAR	SECOND YEAR
Table	2 more chairs
4 chairs	Additional storage units if needed
Unit chest and cabinet for dishes,	Draperies if needed
linen, and silver	Accessories
Rug and curtains	

Bedroom(s)

FIRST YEAR	SECOND YEAR
Springs and mattresses on legs or	Dressing table
frames	Room-size rug
Chest of drawers for each person	Accessories
Mirror	Draperies if needed
1 chair	
Lamps	
Scatter rugs	
Curtains	

Depending on your budget and personality, it may or may not be wise to purchase in the first year one or two really good pieces to have and enjoy even if that means going without some of the things your friends have. By the third year, things start accumulating as they will continue to do the rest of your life, and it is probably just as well to put most of your furnishing money away this year and the next so that about the fifth year you can afford a few of the good things that you know you need and want.

When buying furniture, keep these points in mind:

- Take your time.
   Do not hurry or be high-pressured into spur-of-the-moment buying. At least take time to walk around the block while thinking it over, and take a day or a week on an important purchase.
- Watch your budget.
   Things you cannot afford seldom give pleasure.
- Get only what you know you need.
   Seldom is it advisable to clutter your house and exhaust your resources with things you think you might need in the future.
- Keep in mind the total harmony of your furnishings.
   Piecemeal buying leads to patchwork effects.
- Select furniture as small in size and in scale as is compatible with use. Space is too expensive and beautiful to be lost with oversized furniture.
- Buy furniture good in its own way.
   Stay clear of imitations of expensive items.
- Express yourself rather than trying to impress your friends.

ARRANGING YOUR FURNITURE

Furniture arrangement is a matter of coordinating your family, your architecture, and your furnishings.

This section is a summary coordination, purposefully bringing to your attention again some of the practices and principles stated earlier, especially in Chapter 2, *Living with Others;* Chapter 3, *Private Living;* Chapter 4, *Keeping House;* and Chapter 5, *Aims and Principles of Design.* We will begin with a discussion of furniture arrangements in living, dining, and sleeping spaces which will be followed with a chart and table of furniture shapes and sizes and a suggested procedure for studying your own problem. And we will conclude with a statement of general principles.

Living Space

The *major conversation group* is usually also the family multi-purpose group center for music, television, reading, and buffet suppers. It is the

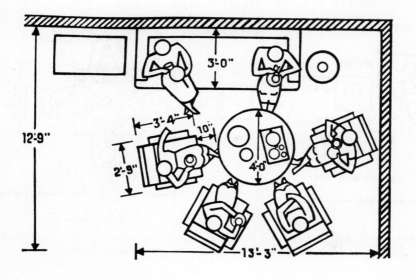

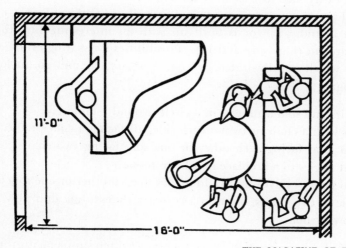

THE MAGAZINE OF BUILDING

14-16 Major conversation groups are most satisfactory when they are more or less circular in shape and when the maximum distance between the heads of the people is 8 to 10 feet. Large upholstered chairs and sofa around a center table are comfortable but space consuming. Pull-up chairs and a sofa take less space.

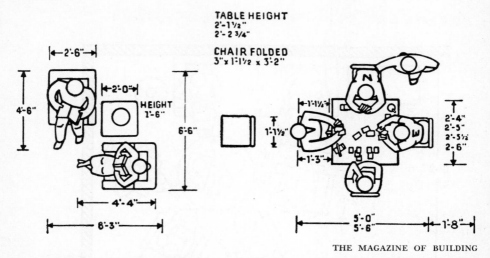

THE MAGAZINE OF BUILDING

14-17 Secondary conversation or reading groups and a table for games, snacks, or conversation are useful additions to the major furniture groups.

dominant group, should put people so that they face each other (and also can easily face television or music), and is best when stabilized in a corner (Fig. 1-6, 5-10), around a window wall or fireplace (Figs. 1-1 and 4, 2-1, and 2, and 5-15), or is built up with an interesting furniture-and-wall treatment (Figs. 5-12 and 13). Possibilities for seating arrangements, some of which are illustrated in Figs. 14-16, 17, 19, and 20, include the following:

- Chairs and sofa arranged in a circle around a table.
- Sofa with a chair or two at each side, all facing a coffee table.
- Two sofas facing each other or one sofa facing two chairs, often at right angles to a fireplace in a large room.
- Two sofas or daybeds at right angles to each other or one sofa at right angle to two chairs, often in a corner although one unit may project into the room.

A *secondary conversation* or *reading group* often supplements the major group in larger rooms. It is usually planned for two to four persons and is placed in a secondary position.

- Two chairs (and the necessary table) at right angles to each other.
- Two, three, or four chairs (or a love seat or two) facing each other over a table and usually near a window.
- Three chairs near a small round table.
- Four chairs at the sides of a game or card table.

A *desk group* in the living room is best in a quiet spot out of traffic's way. Desks are of several types and can be located in different ways.

- A separate desk and its chair can be placed flat against the wall or, more pleasantly, at right angles to the wall near a window.
- Placing an easy chair, side table, and reading lamp nearby makes it double as a reading or small conversation group.
- Combining the desk with bookcases, cabinets, sewing center, and the like (Figs. 3-3 and 14-11) conserves space and unifies a room.

Radio and phonograph equipment vary tremendously in their importance to different families.

- Small radios and record players can be put almost anywhere but are more satisfactory if integrated with other case goods.
- Records require convenient storage space and if the collection is large, a corner of the room or part of one wall can be given over to them.
- Combining equipment and record cabinets with other unit or built-in furniture makes sense.

Pianos are visually large and impressive, and need free space around them for acoustics and people.

- Upright models can be flat against the wall or at right angles to partition a room.
- Grand pianos are physically large and should not be crowded.

Dining Space

Dining tables and chairs or benches, whatever room they are placed in, can be arranged in the ways illustrated in Fig. 14-18.

- Rectangular or round table in the center of a dining room or large kitchen or at one end of the living room increases the importance of meals and simplifies serving.
- Table with one end against a wall takes less floor space and fits into the room (Fig. 2-7).
- Table and seating, especially built-in, in an eating alcove take minimum space, relate strongly to the room, and stay in place, but somewhat complicate getting in and out and also serving the meal (Figs. 2-6 and 8).

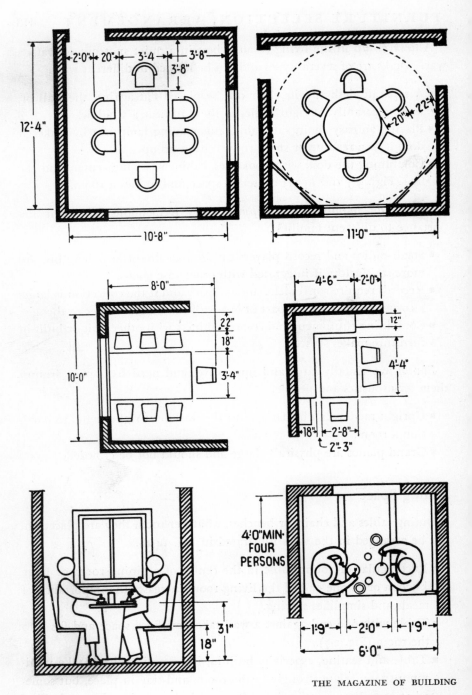

14-18 Dining tables can be in the center of the room, in alcoves or corners, or at one end. Space is saved when they are against the wall and seating is built-in, but such arrangements complicate getting in and out and serving meals.

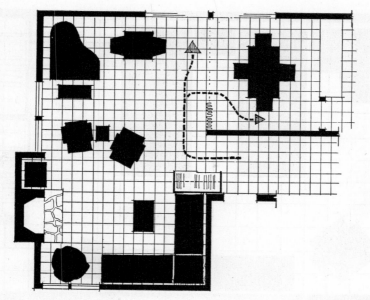

14-19 An L-shaped living-dining space well planned for group living. Two sofas and three chairs make a congenial conversation group around the fireplace and radio or television at its right, the piano and card table are appropriately located, and the dining space can be opened or closed with a curtain. The excellent circulation pattern enables people to enter the room from the entrance area and go to the conversation area, piano, card table, dining space, or terrace without going through any furniture group. Each square represents one foot.

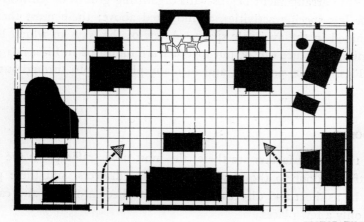

14-20 A long, narrow, symmetrical living room with two doors presents problems and potentialities. The most serious problem is that of arranging a major conversation group that is relatively free from traffic. Potentialities include zoning the ends for different activities, in this case a music center and an area for quiet reading and desk work.

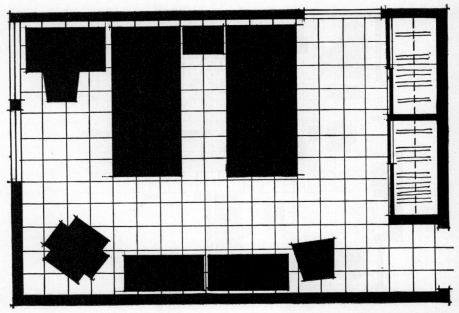

VICTOR THOMPSON

14-21 Twin beds or double beds are conventionally placed with the heads against a solid wall. In this arrangement the beds do not interfere with the frequent trips from the bedroom door to closets and chests, but they wisely segregate the desk and the comfortable chair.

Furniture arrangement begins with organizing groups of furniture for more or less specific activities, as indicated above; these must then be co-ordinated in the available space. A few of the ways in which living and dining furniture can be put together are indicated in Figs. 14-19 and 20; in Figs. 18-1, 2, 3, and 4; and in many photographs throughout this book.

Bedrooms

The two major factors are these: the most used traffic paths are from the entrance door to the closet and chest of drawers, and these paths should be as short and direct as possible; and beds are large and can be put in only a few places.

- Beds are usually placed with the heads against a solid wall and with adequate space on three sides.
- Single beds placed broadside against the wall or in a corner give more free floor space and can double as seating units.
- Double-deckers really conserve space but are hard to make.

- Chests of drawers are ideally placed next to closets which they supplement, and near windows if they have mirrors above. Two chests placed side by side or one double chest will save space as well as visually balance the bulk of the bed.
- Drawers combined with cabinets, a dressing table, and possibly a desk will also conserve space.
- A dressing table is best placed at right angles to or in front of a window so that adequate light will fall on the face of the person using the mirror. A dressing table will often fit into the space between two closets.
- A chair placed adjacent to the closet and chest of drawers will complete the dressing center.
- An easy chair, lamp, and small table placed near a window form a pleasant reading spot in a bedroom.

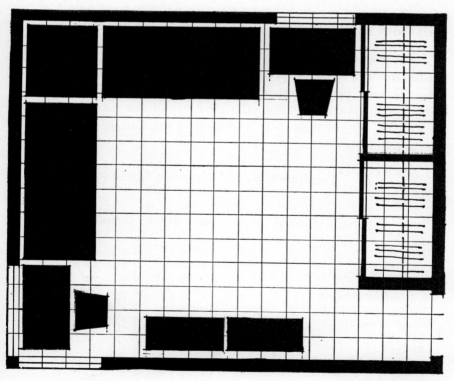

VICTOR THOMPSON

14-22 Twin beds placed broadside against the walls and in a corner make a bedroom seem larger and offer comfortable sitting space. Such an arrangement also provides nicely sequestered locations for two desks.

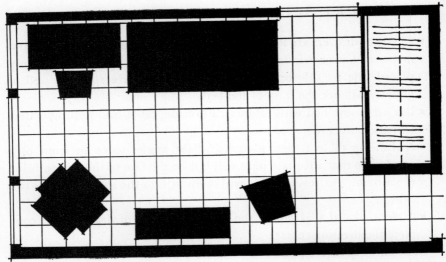

VICTOR THOMPSON

14-23 A small bedroom furnished so that it functions as an individual's retreat.

Sizes and Shapes of Furniture

Little progress can be made in arranging furniture without knowledge of the size and shape of specific pieces and also the all-important clearances between pieces of furniture or furniture and walls for foot room, circulation, and the like. Fig. 14-24 shows typical furniture pieces drawn at a scale of ¼″ equaling 1′0″. The range of sizes and shapes is indicated in the following table.

Furniture Sizes and Clearance Spaces

Living Room

	Small Depth	Width		Large Depth	Width
Sofa	2′6″	x 6′	to	3′	x 7′
Love seat	2′6″	x 4′	to	3′	x 5′
Easy chair	2′6″	x 2′4″	to	3′4″	x 2′10″
Pull-up chair	1′6″	x 1′6″	to	2′	x 2′
Coffee table, oblong	1′6″	x 3′	to	3′	x 5′
Coffee table, round	2′ diam.		to	4′ diam.	
Coffee table, square	2′	x 2′	to	4′	x 4′
End table	1′6″	x 10″	to	3′	x 1′8″
Bridge table	2′6″	x 2′6″	to	3′	x 3′
Flat top desk	1′6″	x 2′8″	to	3′	x 6′
Secretary	1′6″	x 2′8″	to	2′	x 3′6″
Upright piano	2′	x 4′9″	to	2′2″	x 5′10″
Grand piano	5′10″	x 4′10″	to	9′	x 5′2″
Bookcase	10″	x 2′6″	to	1′	x —

Furniture Sizes and Clearance Spaces (Cont.)

Clearances

Traffic path, major	4' to 6'
Traffic path, minor	1'4" to 4'
Foot room between sofa or chair and edge of coffee table top	1'
Floor space in front of chair or sofa for feet and legs	1'6" to 2'6"
Chair or bench space in front of desk or piano	3'

Dining Room

	Small Depth Width	Large Depth Width
Table, square	2'6" x 2'6"	to 5' x 5'
Table, rectangle	3' x 5'	to 4' x 8'
Table, round	2'7" diam.	to 6'4" diam.
Chairs, straight	1'4" x 1'4"	to 1'8" x 1'8"
Chairs, arm	1'10" x 1'10"	to 2' x 2'
Buffet	1'8" x 4'	to 2' x 6'
Serving table	1'6" x 3'	to 2' x 4'
China cabinet	1'6" x 3'	to 1'8" x 4'

Clearances

Space for occupied chairs	1'6" to 1'10"
Space to get into chairs	1'10" to 3'
Traffic path around table and occupied chairs for serving	1'6" to 2'

Bedroom

	Small Depth Width	Large Depth Width
Bed, twin, Hollywood	6'2" x 3'3"	to 6'8" x 3'8"
Bed, full, Hollywood	6'2" x 4'6"	to 6'8" x 5'
Bed, twin, head and footboards	6'10" x 3'3"	to 7'2" x 3'8"
Bed, full, head and footboards	6'10" x 4'6"	to 7'2" x 5'
Bed, youth	5'9" x 3'	
Crib	2' x 4'	to 2'6" x 4'6"
Night table	1'0" x 1'3"	to 2' x 2'
Dresser	1'6" x 2'6"	to 1'9" x 5'
Chest	1'4" x 2'6"	to 1'7" x 3'2"
Dressing table	1'6" x 3'4"	to 1'8" x 4'
Bench	1'3" x 1'10"	to 1'6" x 2'
Wardrobe	1'6" x 3'2"	to 1'9" x 4'
Chair, easy	2'4" x 2'4"	to 2'8" x 2'8"
Chair, pull-up	1'3" x 1'6"	to 1'6" x 1'9"
Chaise longue	2' x 4'	to 2'4" x 5'6"

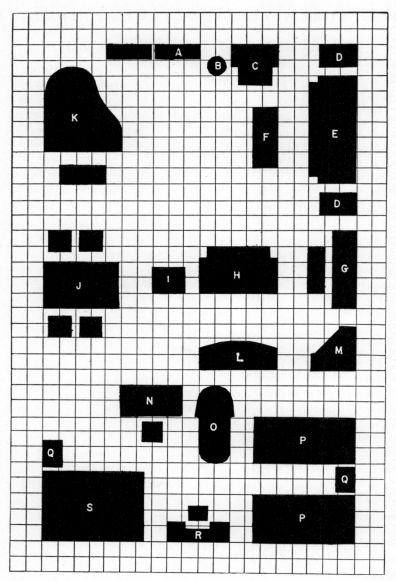

14-24 Becoming familiar with furniture shapes and sizes is an important early step in planning arrangements. Each square on this drawing represents one foot.

A. Bookcases
B. Floor lamp
C. Easy chair
D. End tables
E. Sofa
F. Coffee table
G. Spinet piano

H. Love seat
I. Television cabinet
J. Dining table and chairs
K. Grand piano
L. Sideboard
M. Corner cabinet

N. Desk and chair
O. Chaise-longue
P. Single beds
Q. Bedside table
R. Vanity dresser
S. Double bed

Furniture Sizes and Clearance Spaces (Cont.)

Clearances

Space for making bed	1'6" to 2'
Space between twin beds	1'6" to 2'4"
Space in front of chest of drawers	3'
Space for dressing	3' to 4' (in both directions)

Kitchen

	Small		Large	
	Depth	Width	Depth	Width
Range	2'	x 3'	to 2'1"	x 3'4"
Refrigerator	2'1"	x 2'6"	to 2'4"	x 2'8"
Sink	2'1"	x 3'6"	to 2'1"	x 6'6"
Automatic washer			1'10"	x 2'9"
Automatic dryer			2'1"	x 2'6"
Ironing board	3'8"	x 11"	to 4'6"	x 1'3"
Ironer	1'3"	x 2'8"	to 1'3"	x 2'10"
Cabinets, base	2'1" deep; 15, 18, 21, 24, 30" wide; 3' high			
Cabinets, wall	1'1" deep; 15, 18, 21, 24, 30" wide; 12, 18, 30" high			

Clearances

Working space in front of cabinets and counters	2' to 6'
Counter space between equipment	3' to 5'
Attachment or ventilation for some washers, dryers, stoves, etc.	3" to 5" (at back)

Bathroom

	Small		Large	
	Depth	Width	Depth	Width
Bathtubs	2'6"	x 4'	to 3'	x 5'
Lavatory	1'3"	x 1'6"	to 2'	x 2'
Toilet	2'	x 1'10"	to 2'6"	x 2'
Shower	2'6"	x 2'6"	to 3'6"	x 3'6"
Bathinette	1'9"	x 2'11"	to 2'	x 3'

Clearances

Space between front of tub and opposite wall	2'6" to 3'6"
Space in front of toilet	1'6" to 2'
Space at sides of toilet	1' to 1'6"
Space between fronts of fixtures	2' to 3'

Arranging Your Furniture on Paper

To save time, energy, and money, frustration and disappointments, it is wise to know what you want and how it will fit in your home before you start placing the furniture in your rooms. Better yet, do this before you buy your furniture.

Planning on paper is worth many times the small effort it takes. It consists of two major parts: *first,* listing your activities as discussed in Chapter 1; and *second,* making drawings of your rooms and cut-outs of your furniture as illustrated in Figs. 14-19 through 14-24 and as described below.

1. List all of the activities you want to provide for, the furnishings and equipment they will require, and then begin thinking about which of your rooms will accommodate them best.

2. Make accurate drawings of the floor plan of each room so that $\frac{1}{2}$ inch on the paper equals 1 foot in the room, or with $\frac{1}{4}$ inch representing 1 foot. Cross-section paper greatly simplifies this step. First measure the total length and breadth of the rooms, and draw the major outlines on your paper; then locate the doors, windows, fireplace, radiators or heating vents, jogs, and any built-in features.

3. Make cardboard cut-outs of your furniture, similar to those shown in Fig. 14-24 but at the same scale as the drawings of your room. Label each one.

4. Put the cut-outs on the plan, placing the large pieces first and working down in size and importance to the accessories. Move them around until you have a satisfactory arrangement. Check the livability of each group and of the whole room. Then check the paths of circulation by drawing them on your plan.

5. Review the arrangement a day or so later and make such changes as are necessary in terms of your own needs and our four general objectives as detailed in the following section.

General Principles of Furniture Arrangement

Use

■ People are more important than furniture. Arrange it for them to use and enjoy. Common sense and your own experience are the best guides. Do not subject yourself and your family to inconvenience for the sake of effect.

- Group together all the furnishings used for one activity. Locate these groups for maximum convenience and pleasure. Keep the pieces within each group as close together as is sensible.
- Separate furniture groups for different purposes by a reasonable space, by screens, draperies, or by room-dividers. Keep noisy groups as far as possible from those planned for quiet activities, to reduce interference of activities and to make each group a visual unit.
- Provide ample space for people to get in and out of the room and to travel from one group to another gracefully. Indicate as clearly as necessary where you intend traffic paths to be rather than making your friends wonder how a move can best be maneuvered.
- Keep one sizable portion of the room, usually near the center, open for such purposes as circulation, setting up a card table, and enjoyment of uncluttered space.

Economy

- Space and furniture are expensive today.
- Arrange your furniture for maximum use of your space. Align major pieces with the walls.

  Do not waste space (and bring visual confusion) with large pieces placed at angles, or with a few or many unneeded inches between pieces that ought to fit compactly together.
- Arrange the major pieces so that they seldom or never have to be moved.

  This saves time, energy, and wear and tear.
- Locate the groups, and the pieces within each group, to reduce traffic to a minimum.

  Put the most frequently used furniture group near the room's entrance. Keep the pieces used together within arm's reach of one another.
- Hold your furniture to a moderate amount.

  Do not waste your money and crowd your space by filling your room to capacity before the people get in.

Beauty

- *Beauty* comes primarily from heeding the aims and principles of design.

- *Unity* comes when your whole furniture arrangement, and the groups of which it is composed, are consistent with your furniture and your rooms.

Size up your room and furniture to see what they have in common, then emphasize their communality in your arrangement. Rectangularity is usually one of their basic consistencies: do not obscure it.

Informal furniture and rooms suggest less rigid, arbitrary arrangements than do those more formal in character.

Solid, enclosing walls are a natural background for large or heavy furniture, window walls for small or light pieces. Key up the unity of each group by noticeable consistency—large tables, lamps, and pictures related to the davenport, smaller ones to a desk.

Unify furniture and architecture by treating the wall behind, possibly the floor below, and maybe even the ceiling above furniture as an integral part of the arrangement. Select and place lighting fixtures, paintings, rugs, and other enrichment in relation to furniture.

- *Variety* is always needed to keep even the best of ideas from growing tiresome.

Some chairs are usually placed at angles for sociability and variety.

Bookcases or cabinets, sofas, or pianos at right angles to the wall subdivide the room into interesting, useful units (Figs. 2-10 and 14-25). Subordinate symmetrical arrangements intensify the basic asymmetry of informal rooms.

Furniture in different groups is seldom identical.

- *Balance* is gained by sensitive distribution of visual weights. Check by dividing your room in several ways—lines connecting the midpoints of walls or from corner to corner. Avoid having everything of interest in one part; also avoid having each part exactly equal in weight.

- *Rhythm* comes from repeated shapes, sizes, and textures, progressions and transitions from one part to another, and from forcefully continuing lines.

Echo a color, etc., dominant on one side, with a small amount elsewhere.

Look carefully at the heights of furnishings seen together. Avoid a series of ups and downs.

- *Emphasis* comes when you make a real point of one group or feature, subordinating the others in varying degrees. Fireplaces and window walls are natural centers. Distract from them only with good reason.

14-25 A remarkably pleasant, friendly, contemporary Danish room. Living and dining space are partially separated by the piano, the window locations, and the two-level ceiling. Notice the built-in cabinets near the piano and in the dining space, the decorative effectiveness of the wall map. The study in this house is shown in Figure 14-8. Eric Stengade, architect.

Dominance can be built up in any room by a judicious concentration of furniture and enrichment.

Individuality

- Your home is your own domain.
- Arrange your furniture to promote the kind of living *you* want.
- Take over ideas suggested by others that seem to be made for you—humans are as much alike as they are different.
- Pay no attention to what anyone may tell you is "correct" or fashionable.
- Change your arrangement whenever your needs change or you think of a better plan.

CHAPTER 15

Lighting, Heating, Ventilation, and Acoustics

CONTROLLING the light, heat, air movements, and sounds within an architectural shell makes that space comfortably habitable. Throughout much of history, little attention was paid to these factors in their own right. Windows were often placed with little consideration of the light, heat, and ventilation needs inside, and artificial illumination was a dim matter for all but a few until electricity came into use. The Romans planned efficiently for heating by locating their large windows on the south and by circulating warm air from central heating plants through ducts in their floors, but these practices were forgotten after Rome declined. Until recently ventilation was more a matter of chance than of planning, and the sounds of home life, pleasant and otherwise, were taken for granted. Today all of these forces can be precisely controlled, and this control determines in good part the design of contemporary residences.

Lighting will be given the lion's share of this chapter, because it is the factor you can do most about. Heating is so complicated beyond first facts and principles that a little knowledge may be more dangerous than useful; and ventilation and sound control are important but relatively

426

simple in homes. Of the four, lighting is the only one you want to notice at all in a pleasant, comfortable home.

LIGHTING

Light was discussed as a plastic element in Chapter 7 and as a factor in window design in Chapter 12. Now we consider illuminating our homes when daylight is inadequate. Illumination should serve us in several ways.

- Enable us to see quickly and easily.
- Prevent accidents, especially at such hazards as stairways.
- Protect our health by minimizing eyestrain (which can lead to general fatigue and nervousness) and by disclosing potentially harmful dirt.
- Contribute beauty and individuality to our homes.

At night, much of a room's character is determined by its illumination, as illustrated by the great differences among the living rooms of several of the writers' friends. The first is a medium-sized, squarish room in an old house made into apartments. Walls and ceilings are white and the furniture is light and airy. Illumination comes from two 150 watt bulbs hanging from ceiling cords in undecorated, light-tan Japanese lanterns— one fairly high over the dining table and the other lower over the coffee table—plus one floodlight partially concealed behind an open-shelved storage unit shielding the kitchen door. The entire room is suffused with a warm friendly glow, shadows are transparent, the lightness of the furniture is emphasized, and you feel that you can move easily in any direction you wish. The second living room is in a contemporary house with an open plan, a large window wall, ceilings and walls of moderately dark wood, and a slightly darker asphalt tile floor. Here three lamps with opaque shades closed at the top send cones of light down onto the furniture and floor in three parts of the room while walls and ceiling are hardly noticeable. Contrasts between the almost spotlighted furniture and areas of darkness are marked; shadows are heavy and the bulk of the furniture is made evident. People cluster in intimate groups and moving from one group to another becomes something of an adventure. The third room has a fairly high, white, coved ceiling illumined by concealed lighting of controllable brightness plus lamps near reading chairs, radio-phonograph, and piano. Nearly shadowless light reflected from the ceiling bathes the whole room evenly; the brighter light from the lamps is good for reading or music and also emphasizes the more important furniture groups. The fourth room is furnished with inherited 18th-century American pieces and enriched with fine Chinese ceramics in lighted cabinets and with notable paintings individually lighted. Large floor and table lamps near conversation groups serve as the basic illumination except when guests express interest in studying more closely the paintings and ceramics. Then the cabinet and painting lights are switched on and what was formerly a rich but inconspicuous background makes the whole room both glow and sparkle.

Which of these is best? That depends on what you want. The first room, done for temporary occupancy on a minimum budget, is wonderfully inspiriting and heartening but has no good local illumination for reading or sewing, and would be monotonous were it not for colorful paintings and textiles subtly placed on the walls. The second room has good local lighting for various activities and draws guests into compact groups, but the heavy contrasts between brightness and darkness may fatigue one's eyes and are almost more dramatic than the furnishings and people. The lighting in the third room, planned as part of the house and not inexpensive, gives flexible control of general and local lighting. The fourth living room has so much and many kinds of local lighting that almost any effect wanted can be achieved—and, of course, the owners have much that is worth illuminating. Each has its merits, but all things considered the third is probably more suitable for the varied activities of group living than are the other three.

In illuminating our homes, we have much to learn from theaters, aquariums, museums, stores, factories, and restaurants. Theater lighting has long exploited every trick of the trade as a vital part of the dramatic production. The house lights lower, footlights come on as curtains part, and from then on lights of all colors, brightnesses, degrees of sharpness and diffusion focus attention where wanted and contribute to the dramatic production while the audience sits in darkness. In aquariums light is concentrated on the fish while the observers have just enough light to let them see their way around, a practice sometimes followed in museums and in some stores to rivet attention on a few things. At the opposite extreme are the factories, laboratories, and offices flooded with bright illumination everywhere to step up production. Restaurants range from flood- and spot-lighted lunch rooms to caverns of apparently deep purple with a candle on each table and Gypsy music to reassure or unnerve you, according to your mood.

Types of Lighting

In terms of purpose, effect, and fixtures, there are two major types of lighting—*general* and *local*—to which a third, *play of brilliants,* is sometimes added.

General lighting, also called over-all or "ambient luminescence," illumines the room more or less uniformly as the sun illumines the earth. Its purposes and effects are to let you see all of the room in a soft, reassuring way; to increase the feeling of spaciousness by minimizing the bulkiness of furniture and heavy shadows; to reduce the harsh contrasts of local lighting; and to bring to life the design and color of the whole room. It is most often produced with ceiling fixtures or with lamps having reflector bowls and/or translucent shades which send most of the light up and down in large spots or splashes but which spread some of it around. It is more truly general when lights concealed in coves evenly illuminate the ceiling, large wall surfaces, or curtained windows, or when large areas of translucent glass or plastic in ceiling, walls, or even floors have a low luminosity.

General lighting can be either *direct*—the light shines directly on the objects one wishes illuminated—or *indirect*—the light is thrown against a surface, usually the ceiling, from which it is reflected. Generally speaking, indirect light is more pleasantly soft than is direct light for general illumination, but it is more expensive to operate and may center more attention on the reflecting surface than one wishes to have there. General lighting alone is monotonously even and is seldom bright enough in homes for work. Therefore, it is usually combined with local lighting.

Local lighting gives the kind and amount of illumination needed at particular points for special purposes—reading, dishwashing, sewing, and the like—and creates variety, rhythm, and emphasis. Direct rather than indirect, local lighting casts its rays on what you want to see. It is often combined with general lighting in the direct-indirect lamps; but if the shade is opaque and closed at the top, all of the radiant energy goes directly down to a small area. The light source may be either high or low—but for comfort should not be at eye level—and should be shielded from the eyes. Ideally the shade should be less bright than the table or desk below it because it is the table or desk at which you work, not the shade, that you want to see. Local lighting fixtures are most often movable floor or table lamps, but those permanently attached to the wall, ceiling, or major pieces of furniture are far less nuisance.

Play of brilliants is usually seen only on Christmas trees or in Fourth of July fireworks, now that crystal chandeliers and candelabra are rare, but it can be produced by many candles or by fixtures with many small bulbs. A similar effect is produced by focusing a bright light on accessories made of reflecting materials, especially if their surfaces are richly ornamented. This lighting is of value only to the spirit, but, when one enters a room with much sparkling light, its effect is instantly appreciated.

Specific Factors in Lighting

Planned lighting demands attention to such specifics as brightness, location and size of light source and direction of light, the color of light, the effects of brightness of light on different colors, and the amount of light reflected by the colors used in rooms.

Brightness of Light. How much light do we need? Probably more than most of us have in our homes, but not as much as some experts say.

Human eyes are among the most amazing creations known, and they deserve care. The eyeball is a fantastically miniature camera in which about 137,000,000 separate elements send impulses to the brain and through these impulses come over 80% of the stimuli we receive—more than four times as many as from our receptors of sound, taste, and touch combined! Unlike any camera our eyes automatically focus, turn, adjust to different brightness, and protect themselves quick as a wink. Perhaps their greatest defect is that they have no mechanism to warn us quickly when they are being strained by too little light. Experiments have shown that most people will select as the best the middle of almost any range of brightness available to them. If the range is from 10 to 30 footcandles, 20 is most likely to be chosen. When without the observer's knowledge the range is stepped up to from 30 to 100 footcandles, the middle will again be chosen. There is a great difference between 20 and 65 footcandles but over short periods our eyes do not tell us which is better.

Some writers state that man's eyes developed with natural light, that the light on the earth's surface at noon on a midsummer day is about 10,000 footcandles while in the shade of a broad tree it is about 1000 footcandles, and that some studies demonstrate that people do more work when the light is bright. All of this is true but no sane person would attempt to read or do fine work outdoors in full sunlight at noon, and in our homes we do not always want light to key us up to maximum output.

Many experts, however, agree that the following footcandles of illumination are needed for the activities listed and for general illumination of rooms.

For Activities	Footcandles
Reading—small type for prolonged periods	20-50
—casual	20-30
Sewing—fine needlework on dark goods	75-150
—prolonged average sewing	50-100
—prolonged sewing on light goods	20-50
—ordinary sewing on light goods	20-30
Writing	20-50
Card-playing	10-20
Children's study table	20-50
Kitchen work counter and sink	20-50
Make-up table or bathroom mirror	20-50
Workbench	20-100
Ironing	20-50

For General Illumination	
Entrance halls, and stairways	2-5
Living rooms	5-10
Dining rooms	5-10
Kitchens	10-20
Bedrooms	5-10
Bathrooms	5-10
Laundry	10-20
Libraries	5-10
Recreation rooms	5-10

Keep the following in mind, too, when considering quantity of light.

- Bright light is stimulating, calls forth energy, and makes us feel as though we should be up and doing. Use it in places where you want these responses called forth.
- Low levels of brightness may seem relaxing and restful, romantic, dingy and depressing, or even frightening, depending on the context.
- Moderately bright light brings no pronounced feeling other than general well-being.
- More wattage is needed in rooms of low color value than in those of light colors.

■ Balance, rhythm, and emphasis come from appropriate distribution of quantities of light.

Glare should be avoided. It comes from exposed, bright sources of light; incorrectly designed fixtures; too much light, especially from one direction; and excessive contrasts. The contrasting glare and gloom, frequently encountered in night driving and too often in homes, is an eye-fatiguing combination. For close work the working area should not be more than 5 times as bright as the darkest part of the room, and a ratio greater than 1 to 10 is undesirable any place. But it is also fatiguing, both to the muscles of the eyes and the spirits of the occupants, to have every part of a room equally bright. Moderation in quantity and contrast of light is a sensible solution.

Location and Direction. Lighting from above seems normal, accustomed as we are to the sun more or less overhead, while lighting from other places is less expected. Here are some observations:

■ Location of both the light source and the surface from which the light is reflected are important in the total effect.
■ Light high in the room seems formal, makes us think of standing up and staying on our best behavior.
■ Light sources exactly at eye level are seldom wanted.
■ Light below eye level seems friendly and draws people together. It is also useful while watching television.
■ Light from near the floor flatters people as do theater footlights, is a good safety device near steps and in halls, and is a refreshing surprise.
■ Light from a number of sources—or, well-diffused light—makes a room seem luminous rather than merely lighted, tends to spread interest throughout the room, and is comfortably undemanding.
■ Strongly directed light, such as comes from spotlights, is dramatic, emphatic, and often harsh. Our attention tends to follow its path—up, down, sideways, or diagonally, much as it does a solid form.
■ Light for working should illumine the task without shadows and should not shine in the worker's eyes.

Size of Light Source. Much depends on the size of the light source. Compare the luminous vault of the sky by day with its myriad play of brilliants at night.

■ Broad sources of light—the sky, a skylight or an illuminated ceiling, and a window-wall—give flat, glareless, uneventful light excellent for seeing, health, and safety because they minimize contrasts and shadows. Decoratively, though, they are monotonous.

- Smaller light sources that diffuse light broadly through lenses, translucent shades, or reflectors approximate this effect.
- Very small light sources, especially if bright, have high accent value, emphasize parts of rooms, and make silver and glass sparkle, but they can be visually fatiguing and unless carefully used cause spottiness.

Color of Light. We have always been timid about using colored illumination in our homes, perhaps quite rightly because it is difficult and expensive. The color of light is determined by three factors: the light source; the diffusing or reflecting shade; and the room surfaces that reflect it back to our eyes.

- White light shows colors as they are and has no pronounced emotional effect.
- Warm light flatters people, dispels the chill associated with darkness, and brightens warm color schemes but deadens blues and purples.
- Cool light makes rooms more spacious, separates objects one from another, and may make people look cadaverous.
- Warm and cool light are difficult to combine in the same room without expert assistance.

Effect of Colors on Amount of Light Reflected. No surface in the home reflects or absorbs *all* the light that hits it, but high-value colors reflect a high percentage and low-value colors reflect little. Listed below are the percentages of light reflected by some of the common colors.

Color	Percentage of Light Reflected	Color	Percentage of Light Reflected
White	89	Buff	63
Ivory	87	Pale green	59
Canary yellow	77	Shell pink	55
Cream	77	Bright sage	52
Caen stone	76	Silver gray	46
Orchid	67	Olive tan	43
Cream gray	66	Forest green	22
Ivory tan	66	Coconut brown	16
Sky blue	65	Black	2

Clearly, white gives you the most light for the money you pay the electric company and black gives you the least.

Flames, Incandescence, and Luminescence

For untold ages man depended on the flames from fireplaces, candles, or lamps to illumine homes at night. Nowadays we seldom depend on flame light except occasionally from candles and fireplaces. Both give a warm, flickering, flattering light which seems hospitable, even a little festive. Although extremely inefficient, they produce a unique effect that calls forth deep, intuitive responses. Electricity, though, is our major concern, and it is made to produce light in two ways.

Incandescent light is produced by heating any material, but usually metal, to a temperature at which it glows. Typical incandescent bulbs have a tungsten filament surrounded by a vacuum or a mixture of argon and nitrogen in a sealed glass container. There are many types for home use: sizes range from tiny $7\frac{1}{2}$ watt night lights to 300 watt bulbs; shapes can be spherical, conical, bulbous, bell-like, or cylindrical; the glass can be clear, frosted to diffuse light, blue to give a daylight effect, or orange or pink to give a warm light; and special types include those with a bowl silvered on the lower half to reflect light upward for indirect lighting, and projector, flood, or spot lights with a metallic reflecting surface to direct the light in a broad or narrow beam.

Luminescent or "cold" light is not produced by heat. Although there are many ways of producing luminescence, only one is used in homes and that is *fluorescence*. A glass tube is coated on the inside with a fluorescent powder, filled with vaporized mercury and argon, and sealed with two cathodes. The electric current activates the gas which produces invisible ultra-violet rays which in turn cause the fluorescent coating to produce visible light. Although fluorescent bulbs vary somewhat less than incandescent, there is considerable diversity for different purposes and effects. All are tubular but they may be straight or circular. Typical straight tubes range from 9 to 60 inches in length, $\frac{5}{8}$ to $2\frac{1}{8}$ inches in diameter, and 6 to 100 watts. Colors include:

- *Daylight,* emphasizing blues and greens.
- *White,* emphasizing yellows and yellow-greens.
- *Standard Cool White* and *Standard Warm White,* stressing yellows but lacking in reds.

- *Deluxe Cool White* and *Deluxe Warm White,* which have some reds.
- *Soft White,* stressing pinks and tans.
- *Gold, green, blue, pink,* and *red* of fairly pronounced hues.

This is quite a palette from which one can produce color effects.

To date, fluorescent lights have been chiefly used near bathroom or make-up mirrors, on stoves and over kitchen counters, and in light troughs. Fluorescent desk lights are also available but many persons find the flicker annoying. This, however, is greatly minimized when more than one bulb is used.

Incandescent and fluorescent bulbs each have the following desirable qualities.

Incandescent	*Fluorescent*
Fixtures and bulbs cost less.	Bulbs last about 7 times as long as do incandescent.
Light is sympathetically warm and "full" in color.	Produce about 2½ times as much light for current used.
Textures and forms are emphasized because the light comes from a relatively small source.	Light source is considerably larger, which spreads the light more and produces less glare.
Light comes the minute you push the switch.	Almost no heat is produced.
There is no flicker or hum and less likelihood of radio interference.	

LIGHTING FIXTURES

Ideal lighting fixtures give you the kind and amount of light you want (use); consume minimum electricity, are moderate in cost, are easy to clean and to get at to replace bulbs (economy); fit into your decorative scheme in a contributory way (beauty); and underline the character of your home (individuality). Inevitably they contrast with other furnishings because they are so different in purpose, but insofar as their function permits, they should be appropriate in size, scale, and character to your rooms. In one room, or better throughout the home, they should set up their own pattern of variety in unity. The greater the number of fixtures, the greater the need for similarity or repetition among them.

Fixtures come today in such variety, from those that show nothing but

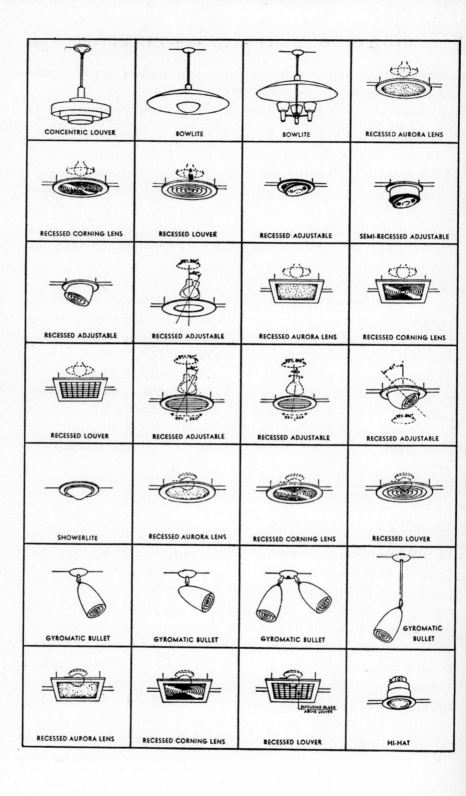

CONCENTRIC LOUVER	BOWLITE	BOWLITE	RECESSED AURORA LENS
RECESSED CORNING LENS	RECESSED LOUVER	RECESSED ADJUSTABLE	SEMI-RECESSED ADJUSTABLE
RECESSED ADJUSTABLE	RECESSED ADJUSTABLE	RECESSED AURORA LENS	RECESSED CORNING LENS
RECESSED LOUVER	RECESSED ADJUSTABLE	RECESSED ADJUSTABLE	RECESSED ADJUSTABLE
SHOWERLITE	RECESSED AURORA LENS	RECESSED CORNING LENS	RECESSED LOUVER
GYROMATIC BULLET	GYROMATIC BULLET	GYROMATIC BULLET	GYROMATIC BULLET
RECESSED AURORA LENS	RECESSED CORNING LENS	RECESSED LOUVER	HI-HAT

a coin-sized hole in the ceiling to big exclamation points, that we will merely enumerate and comment briefly on the major types. Worth noting is the fact that built-in, ceiling, wall, and portable fixtures can all give general or local, direct or indirect, light or any combination thereof.

Architectural or Built-In Fixtures

Built-in fixtures have advantages and disadvantages similar to those of built-in furniture. Their use makes it evident that lighting the home was not an after-thought, they contribute to the total unity and give effects unobtainable by other means. The large glass panels in Fig. 2-2 illustrate a trend, more common in commercial and industrial than in domestic architecture, to gain illumination from large surfaces of low brightness rather than from strongly concentrated sources. Light sources can also be part of kitchen cabinets, bookcases, and other case goods to bring local, direct lighting where needed for work or reading, or to light walls and ceiling for general, indirect room illumination.

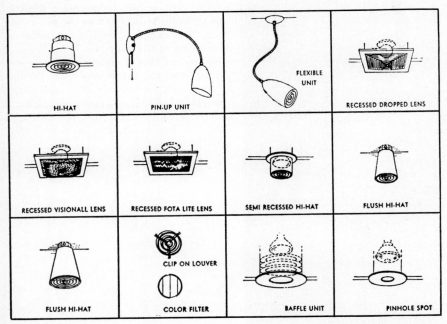

LITECRAFT MFG. CO.

15-1 Permanent lighting fixtures can hang from the ceiling, project a little, or be flush and almost unnoticeable. Some are adjustable.

LEDLIN LIGHTING CO.   PHOTOGRAPH BY
LIONEL FREEDMAN

15-2 Ceiling fixtures can be handsome
and efficient. The top fixture is a simple
opaque shade that reflects indirect light
from a bulb with a silvered bottom for
straightforward economy. The next fixture directs light from a single bulb in
many ways: bright light comes directly
down through the opening in the cone;
softer light comes through the translucent
lower part of the cone and is further diffused by the shade; and light goes to the
ceiling from the top of the cone. In the
large middle fixture, the light from three
concealed bulbs is indirectly spread over
a large area by the broad metal shade.
The two bottom fixtures are of translucent glass.

Ceiling fixtures, once banished from consideration, have staged a healthy come-back (Figs. 15-1, 2). They can be built in flush with the ceiling, and the light can be softened with louvers or diffused with lenses. Shallow glass or plastic bowls, dropped only a few inches below the ceiling, give reflected light from the ceiling and diffused light through the bowl, and can also send a large pool of strong light directly down, making them good, inexpensive, three-in-one ways to light dining tables. Other fixtures are dropped well below the ceiling with spherical glass shades to diffuse moderately bright light in all directions; with opaque metal shades with diffusing shields for direct light or with the shade acting as a reflector for concealed bulbs directly beneath—either of which can be perforated for sparkle; or with translucent shades of many shapes. Those adjustable in height give welcome flexibility and facilitate maintenance. Bullet-shaped units, mounted on ceiling or wall, can be turned for direct light on work or center of interest or for indirect light on walls or ceiling. They come in single or multiple units, solid or pierced metal or plastic shades of many colors and shapes and with or without louvers or lenses. Unless well balanced with diffused light, the lighting they produce is harsh.

Wall fixtures, with a few exceptions, closely resemble ceiling and portable lights. Some, such as the ones in Fig. 15-3b, are similar to those mounted on freestanding supports while others, as in Fig. 15-3a, are identical with ceiling fixtures. In fact, even those most distinctly belonging to the wall (Figs. 15-3c, 15-3d) are basically like those used in other locations in our homes. Like ceiling fixtures, wall units were once popular, fell from favor, and are now back. It is true that once in a while they interfere with hanging pictures and do not suggest changing furniture arrangements, unless they are of the pin-up kind, but these are small prices to pay for their convenience.

Portable Lamps

Floor and table lamps can be moved when and where you need them and they can be important decorative accessories. Thus, in spite of their disadvantages, few of us are ready to discard them entirely. Not so long ago the writers thought that all portable lamps should be as plain and inconspicuous as possible, preferably an unadorned column of wood, cylinder of ceramic, or metal pipe to hold a colorless parchment or plastic

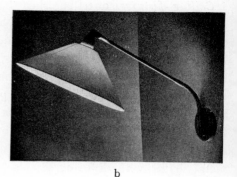

b

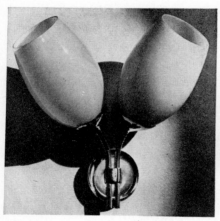

d

a

c

BUFFALO, KURT VERSEN CO., FINNISH-AMERICAN TRADING CORP., M. A. VAN ESSO, INC.

15-3 Wall fixtures are available in many types and have certain advantages over table and floor lamps.

a. Wall lamps of the adjustable, bullet-shaped types are inexpensive, undemanding, and focus direct light over relatively small areas.
b. The arm of this lamp can be adjusted to many angles while the shade swings through a 180 degree arc. The translucent parchment shade gives good direct light and some diffused illumination.
c. Beautifully shaped translucent glass bowls on a handsome brass base make this wall fixture an object of beauty.
d. Most of the light is reflected on the upper wall and ceiling but some comes down through the translucent glass circles.

shade. This was a reaction in part to the layers of chiffon and fringe absorbing the light from many floor and table lamps thirty years ago, and in greater part from the plethora today of "cute," "decorative" lamps in which beauty and function are nonexistent. Simplicity still seems generally advisable—but a genuinely handsome, decorative wall or ceiling lighting fixture or table lamp can greatly enrich a room at the same time it provides light. A beautiful piece of ceramic or glass, or of richly modeled metal, profits from light above it. On the other hand, figurines poised or huddled under a spreading shade often look like they were trying to avoid rain; miniature urns or classical columns are usually pathetically small; and a lamp base is not a sensible place for living plants, fish, or birds. Does it make sense in itself, is it beautiful in your room, and does it give the illumination needed? These are the queries.

Base and shade, different as they are in function and often in material, should be regarded as one unit because they are seen and used together. This means a fundamental agreement between the two, some qualities in common, but not necessarily exact repetition. Figs. 15-4 and 5 illustrate a few of the ways in which variety in unity can be achieved.

Color in portable lamps is important, especially in translucent shades, but also in the whole ensemble, because at night lamps are one of the most conspicuous elements in an interior. Liking warm artificial light, most of us rule out blue, green, or violet lamp shades of translucent materials although in some rooms these colors may be desirable in opaque materials. Lamp bases can be any color needed in your room and can harmonize or contrast with the shade. Strong color contrasts between the two make lamps more conspicuous and can weaken the unity between the two parts.

Shapes of lamps ought to grow from their functions: the base supports the lights and shade; the shade shields our eyes from glare, diffuses and directs the light. But materials, as discussed in Chapters 8 and 9, ought also to play a determining role. The simplest base is a cylinder with a footing large enough for stability—breadth is more important than weight in keeping the lamp upright. Then come the many vase and urn shapes into which wood, metal, clay, glass, and plastics can be shaped. If the support is of metal (Fig. 15-5c) or wood (Fig. 15-5a), it can be more slender than if of clay or glass (Figs. 15-5b and 5d). All can be plain for simplicity of effect and maintenance or ornamented for enrichment and concentrated interest; the most useful selection criteria are the aims and principles of design. Shades are usually truncated cones to spread the light downward, and these can be tall and steep for concentration or low and wide for dispersion. Shades can, of course, be rectangular or pyramidal, but rounded forms seem more congenial to light than do angular ones, and we welcome the few curves we can sensibly get in our homes.

Size of lamps is indicated by the illumination requirements together with the size of the room and its furnishings. These are the fundamental but not the only determining factors. We know that high lamps with large shades illumine large areas and are in scale with large furniture,

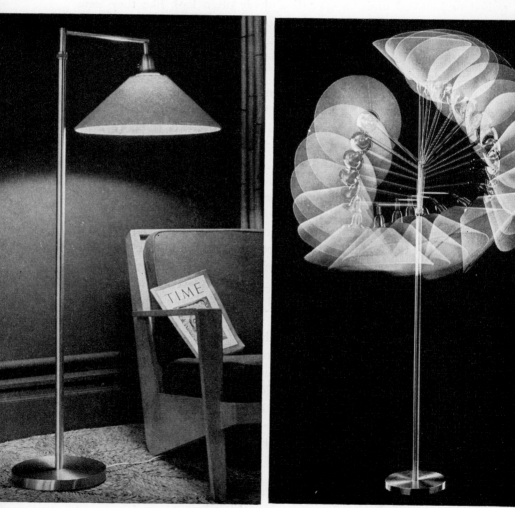

HOSMER LAMPS   PHOTOGRAPH BY CHILDRESS & HALBERSTADT

15-4 This simple floor lamp has unusual flexibility.

KURT VERSEN, PAUL HANSEN CO.   FREDERICK COOPER STUDIOS

15-5   Four table lamps of different materials and character.

a. Subtle shaping of the wood column and base and a well-proportioned plastic
shade give a lamp an unobtrusive distinction.

b. Wood base, ceramic vase, and textile shade make an unusually harmonious
unit.   All are refined in character and are delicately textured.   Notice how
the edging on the shade brings into equilibrium the predominantly vertical
lines of the textile and how well it echoes the shapes of the walnut base.

c. A vigorous, large-scale lamp unified by having shade and base of the same
burnished, metallic finish.   The turned base is greatly enhanced by the light
coming down on it.

d. Glass and light have an unusual affinity for each other.   The rich shape of
the glass is emphasized by the thin metal designs and also by the strong contrast with the simple shade and solid base.

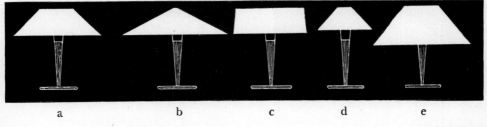

15-6 Which shade is most appropriate in size and shape for this base?

a. Shade and base are pleasantly compatible.
b. Shade is a little too broad and sloping, although the total effect is not un-pleasant.
c. Size and shape relationships are satisfactory; effect is more blocky and abrupt than in a.
d. Shade that is too small makes lamp look pin-headed.
e. Shade that is too large produces overpowering, top-heavy feeling.

and that "over-scaled" lamps can be dramatic focal points, although, unless carefully used, they seem to crowd small spaces. Further, the more lamps in a room the smaller each can be; but this should not lead us to forget that too many small lamps clutter a room.

Lighting for Activities

Planned lighting takes thought. Look at your own living quarters.

- Is there sufficient, glareless light where you need it for close work?
- Is there adequate and pleasant general illumination to reduce strong contrasts, to lighten dark shadows?
- Is there good illumination at danger points?
- Is your pattern of artificial lighting balanced and does it show to advantage what you consider important?

If you are planning your home or revising the decoration of your rooms, it might pay you to draw a plan of your rooms with their furniture arrangements. Next draw circles of appropriate size where local illumi-nation is needed. Should these circles fail to overlap or if they are con-fined to one part of the room, you will probably need either more fixtures or some general illumination. In all parts of your home except halls and stairways, general and local illumination are needed; sparkling light is cheerful in group living areas.

Entrance areas need friendly, welcoming illumination as a transition between the dark outside and the brightness of your living room, to let your guests see you and you see them in a pleasant light as an introduction to your home. Diffused, possibly indirect, light from a ceiling or wall fixture, possibly supplemented by more concentrated, sparkling light on a mirror, painting, or other object of interest makes a balanced effect.

Living rooms need general illumination from permanent fixtures and/or reflector lamps, some of which should be indirect, to bring walls, floor, ceiling, and furniture into soft visibility; flexibly controlled, direct pools of light at all places where people may read, play games, sew, or do homework; low level illumination for television; and if feasible some sparkling light. This is the room needing the greatest variety of illumination and the greatest flexibility, consequently the room where the greatest variety of lighting fixtures and the most portable lamps are found. Thus it gives opportunity to exercise your ingenuity in achieving variety in unity, balance, rhythm, and emphasis—and in finding forms that function well.

Dining rooms need illumination on the table and on the people around it, some of the light preferably directed down to make silver, glass, china, and food sparkle, but some indirectly diffused to prevent glare and unbecoming shadows. A ceiling fixture is definitely in place here, and if thoughtfully designed, like those in Figs. 15-2 and 16-9, will suffice; or it may be that you will want to supplement its effect with others casting more light on the walls. But keep in mind that the people and food are most important: minimize distracting side lights.

Kitchens need good light directed onto work counters, sink, stove, and eating table plus a fairly high level of general illumination. Ceiling fixtures are almost indispensable, plus bands of light at strategic points. The kitchen is usually the best illuminated room in the home because much thought has been given to the problem and we are likely to think in straightforward terms about this room.

Bathrooms need lights near the mirror which give shadowless illumination to a person's face—up, down, and sideways—and this is best produced by a band of light on all sides of the mirror, next by lights above and below or on each side. In addition, general illumination from a ceiling fixture is needed to light the rest of the room.

Bedrooms should be lighted for dressing, reading in bed, and such activities as desk work, sewing, reading in a chair, or anything else you do in that room. As elsewhere, this means local and over-all illumination: semi-indirect lights over the bed, reading chair, desk or work surface, and around the mirror. Direct downlight lets you see the top of things, such as your head, but unless the floor is almost white casts disheartening shadows, and therefore is inferior to light coming horizontally, especially near the mirror. You may want a free-standing lamp or two here, for they seem appropriate only in quiet activity rooms like the bedroom or living room.

Halls and stairways usually need only soft, over-all illumination—local lighting is more apt to be distracting than helpful. Halls can be adequately lighted from ceiling fixtures, more pleasantly lighted from those above eye level on the wall, or the fixtures can be almost at the floor as in theaters—the floor is about all you really want to see and it is fun for a change to have light low in the room.

Good light, needed on stairways to prevent accidents, is easily achieved if your light clearly distinguishes the treads from the risers. Ceiling fixtures sending adequate light down do this much better than those on the wall; diffused, over-all lighting is unsatisfactory; and spotty lighting is dangerous.

Exterior lighting has begun to be seriously considered, now that we are conscious of the importance of what is outside our walls. To be sure, entrance doors have long been lighted, but usually poorly. Only occasionally do entrance lights let the visitor identify the house unmistakably, appreciate the doorway, and quickly recognize the person who opens the door while letting the host see the visitor in a good light. The most common error is failing to place and illuminate the house number so that it can be seen from the street.

Terraces, patios, and gardens come into the picture at night if properly lighted. This is especially important if they are easily visible from inside the house (Figs. 12-2 and 3). Proper lighting of outdoor areas greatly increases the apparent size of the living space, makes outdoor living space more usable at night, lightens windows which if uncurtained would be inky black, and brings a little general illumination inside. The typical solution is a weatherproof, bullet-shaped fixture mounted on the house and directed down onto the terrace or out onto the garden, but more elaborate installations have spot and flood lights concealed in the garden. Those fixed to the house add surprisingly little to original or continuing costs.

Switches and Outlets

Every room in the house needs a light switch convenient to any door by which you may enter or leave it; stairs need switches at top and bottom; and halls need them at both ends. Groping around in the dark, stumbling over furniture, and possibly knocking over the lamp whose switch button eludes you are unpleasant and dangerous experiences. What is more, the switches should turn on the lights that you usually need in that room.

Outlets for lamps and appliances ought to be in every wall space three feet or more wide that is separated from other walls by doors or floor-length windows. On long walls you may need two or three outlets to lessen the tangle of cords.

There are some minor refinements in the placement of switches and outlets which make for pleasant living.

- The switch controlling a bed lamp should be within easy reaching distance, not across the room or just far enough away to make turning it off while in bed an acrobatic feat.
- Switches for outdoor lighting should be within the house.
- Some outlets are more convenient if at table height:
  near the ironing board for the electric iron.
  near the dining table for the toaster and coffee pot.
  along the back of the counter space in the kitchen for the many electric appliances used there.
  near the wash basin for an electric shaver.
  near the sewing center for the sewing machine.
  near the workshop counter for electric tools.
  in back of the electric washer and dryer.

Many people find properly protected outdoor outlets a convenience for an electric lawnmower, electric barbecue, portable lighting, or even a radio.

That lighting your home well is a challenging, complex but rewarding adventure is self-evident. It is relatively easy to get sufficient light on work surfaces to avoid eyestrain but it takes thought and usually experimentation to achieve completely satisfying illumination in the whole home. Our eyes and our spirits deserve efficient and beautiful artificial as well as natural illumination.

HEATING

Apartment dwellers can do little about heating other than adjust the controls on radiators, open and close windows, and cover windows with heavy draperies to confine some of the excessive heat or cold from outside to the space between glass and drapery. Those who rent houses and operate the heating plant themselves have somewhat greater control. Those who buy not only can but should look carefully at the provisions for heating while those who plan to build had better give serious thought to the advantages and disadvantages of the systems now available. But let us consider some primary facts first.

1. Heat is a form of energy closely related to light and often coming from the same source, as in an open fire, incandescent electric bulb, or the sun.

2. Heat is transferred from one place to another in three ways:

- *Conduction* is the transmission of heat through solid matter and is exemplified by the way in which an all-metal skillet brings heat from a stove burner out to the end of the handle. Playing an almost negligible role in artificial heating, it is of great importance in insulating our homes against extreme temperatures outside. Generally speaking, dense and uniform materials like metal and solid glass conduct heat readily, while porous materials such as wood or foam glass are poor conductors (that is, good insulators).

- *Convection* is the transference of heat by air (or other matter) in motion. We all know that warm air rises, cold air sinks, and that if any surface is heated to a moderate or high temperature convection currents carrying some of this heat are set in motion. Warm air furnaces distribute heat by convection.

- *Radiation* is easy to understand if you think of the way in which the sun heats the earth. Between the earth and the sun there is insufficient matter to carry heat by conduction or by convection: heat simply jumps from the sun to the earth, raising the temperaure of the earth's surface, but not appreciably affecting the temperature of the space between the sun and our atmosphere and having only moderate direct effect on our air. Radiant heat differs from convected in two significant ways: it has relatively little effect on air temperatures and it travels equally well in all directions. Infrared lamps and radiant, or panel, heating systems operate in this way.

3. Heat is brought from furnaces to our living space by heated air, hot water, or steam; or it can be produced on the spot by sending electricity through materials which conduct it and at the same time set up enough resistance to produce heat, as in portable electric heaters or the heating elements of an electric stove.

4. Our bodies ordinarily give off more heat than they absorb, because our surface temperatures are ordinarily higher than those of the air, walls, floors, and ceilings in our homes. Thus, the purpose of artificial heating is less a matter of transferring heat to our bodies than of making certain that we do not give up an uncomfortable amount to the cooler air and enclosing surfaces. Artificial cooling is designed to take heat away from our bodies when our environment is uncomfortably hot.

Artificial Heating Systems

Only a few years ago one could have written that there were two types of central heating: warm air, and hot water or steam, produced in a basement furnace and kept in circulation by gravity; and although seldom mentioned, their chief effect was to raise the temperature of the air which through convection currents indirectly raised the temperature of the architectural shell and the furniture, to keep people from sacrificing too much bodily heat. A major improvement came with fans or blowers attached to the furnace to force warm air into the room and cold air out, and pumps to push the steam or hot water through radiators. This meant that the furnace no longer had to be in a basement so that gravity would pull the cold air or water down; it gave better control of the circulation of heat; and it made it possible to put warm air outlets near the ceiling out of furniture's way. At about the same time, oil, gas, and electricity began to take the place of wood and coal, and thermostats were introduced to keep the temperature about where you wanted it. Then an old concept of heating large surfaces of the room to a relatively low temperature was revived in the reintroduction of radiant or panel heating.

Warm-air furnaces heat the air in a shell around the firebox and send it through ducts and vents to the rooms. Their advantages include low initial cost; simplicity of design and maintenance; quick responsiveness to the need for heat; keeping the air in motion to dispel stuffiness, maintaining a near-comfortable humidity, and keeping the air more or less free from dust; and the ease with which they can be combined with artificial cooling. The disadvantages are that it is next to impossible to keep rooms at an even temperature; furnace noises are often audible; and space for the seldom decorative, dirt-collecting, hot and cold air vents must be left more or less free of furniture.

Steam or hot water systems are essentially boilers and radiators connected by pipes. Their major advantage is relatively uniform heat rather than the sudden and constant ups and downs of warm air models. This is important—but they have disadvantages: expensive to purchase, install, and keep in good order; neither circulate nor moisten the air; cannot easily be combined with cooling; may be noisy if not operating perfectly; and in most cases necessitate radiators located under windows (although the new convectors are much less conspicuous and annoying than old-fashioned radiators).

Panel, or radiant, heating has pipes for hot water, ducts for warm air, or electrical heating elements embedded in the floor, ceiling, or walls, bringing whatever surface they are in up to a moderate temperature. The major advantage is that the occupants, and the walls, floors, and furniture, are comfortably warm while the air remains cool in contrast to the hot air and cool surfaces experienced with other types of heating. In theory and probably in actuality, this provides a healthier environment and takes less fuel. A second blessing is that all parts of a room have the same degree of comfort (no hot and cold spots). The third asset is the lack of sudden temperature changes (which is also sometimes a drawback in poorly designed installations). A fourth point in favor of radiant heating is that these systems are much cleaner than the others discussed: they have no open outlets to carry dust from ducts into a room, nor are convection currents set up which all too often deposit the dust which has settled on radiators or hot air vents on to the wall above. And finally, the complete absence of vents or radiators gives freedom of furniture arrangement.

Their disadvantages look impressive: they are expensive at first (but usually not to operate); complicated and not thoroughly understood as yet by many heating contractors; and the typical installation does not respond quickly to changes in outdoor temperatures or needs of the people inside. Two other factors are that panel heating demands good insulation (because warmed floors, walls, and ceilings readily conduct heat to the outdoors) and effective ventilation (because panel heating does little about keeping the air in motion). These are not serious drawbacks because insulation and ventilation ought to be efficient regardless of the type of heating system.

The most common type of radiant heat consists of copper or iron pipes embedded in a concrete slab to make floors wonderfully warm for babies, cold-footed oldsters, or anyone. It may take from two to four hours for the slab to warm up or cool off, but outdoor thermostats automatically anticipate the need for more heat and start it on its way long before those inside begin thinking of it; they do not, however, cool the slab quickly in case the sun suddenly streams through your south windows. A type more recently reintroduced (it was used by the Romans in their heyday and for long has been in continuous use in China and Korea) circulates warm air through hollow clay tiles in the floor, and occasionally the walls, and seems a little better because the floor can be warmed or cooled more quickly. The third type has electrical elements embedded in a concrete floor or a plaster ceiling, and where electricity is cheap this is undoubtedly the best—there is no central furnace, each room can be controlled by an individual thermostat, and the response is rapid, particularly with ceiling installations.

We have discussed so far only central heating systems, but heaters to take care of a room or two, or part of one room, are available. Warm air floor or wall furnaces are often used in mild climates, and panels of many sizes, mounted in walls, transform electrical energy into radiant heat. None of these, of course, gives the uniform comfort of a good central system, but they are economical, useful in rooms not regularly used, and give quick heat when you want it, as you well may in the bathroom on a cold morning.

Solar Heating

As mentioned in Chapter 12, well-oriented windows can reduce heating bills, and well oriented for this purpose almost invariably means big windows on the south, small on the north. In a Minneapolis house with glass concentrated toward the south, on one sunny winter Sunday the temperature outside hovered around zero, directly inside the south window wall it was nearly 100, while the rest of the house stayed at 70 with no help from the furnace until the sun set. Over the years, this saves money. To be sure, the house was insulated.

Many of the intricacies of solar heating have yet to be worked out. Ventilation and adjustable, insulating window treatments are important since we have no thermostats capable of turning off the sun when a south-facing room becomes too hot. And this may happen unless enough air is circulating through the house to carry off some of that 100° heat concentrated inside a window wall to other parts of the house.

15-7 Double-glazed windows pay big dividends in extreme climates. The moisture condensation on the windows at the right comes from warm air hitting cold glass. The other window with two panes of glass keeps the cold out, the warmth in, and the window free of moisture.

Insulation

Good insulation pays for itself in a relatively short time not only in comfort but in heating and/or cooling bills. Windows, roofs, and the cracks around windows and doors deserve first attention in most parts of the country, followed very closely by walls and floors. Double-glazed windows are a sensible economy in cold climates, and the type in which two pieces of glass less than an inch apart are sealed into one frame frees one from the nuisance of "storm windows." Roofs and walls absorb much heat in summer, and together with floors lose much in winter unless something is done to retard the heat transmission. Most insulating materials—from sawdust to spun glass—are porous, and it is the air imprisoned in small spaces that makes them effective. Another type is a thin coating of metal mounted on heavy paper, the metal reflecting the heat. All of these can be put in roofs, walls, and floors. The inevitable cracks around windows and doors, through which wind loves to blow and whistle, can be quite thoroughly sealed with weatherstripping.

In planning your heating, your first thought should be getting the major rooms and large windows properly oriented, then choosing your type of equipment, and then considering your needs for insulation. This sounds a little like you could plan it yourself, which you cannot do unless you are an architect well versed in the problems of heating, because the whole matter is complex and full of pitfalls for the uninformed. Try to understand the fundamentals but leave the details to experts you can trust.

Some of the details you can concern yourself with, however, are the ones connected with the color and furnishings of rooms as they affect the amount of heat needed for comfort. The effects of color on the psychological warmth or coolness of a room has been treated in Chapter 7, but we remind you here that color can, by looking warm, make us feel warm. The amount of furniture and the textures of the materials in a room influence us in much the same way. Near the extremes, a crowded room looks warm, a sparsely furnished room cool; smooth, textureless materials seem cold, fuzzy ones hot; an open wooden chair looks cooler, actually is cooler, than an overstuffed lounge chair upholstered in wool frieze. Draperies, rugs, and screens are useful heat-retaining devices, draperies to insulate against night coldness transmitted through window glass, rugs to insulate a cold floor, and screens to shut off drafts in otherwise comfortable rooms.

VENTILATION

Good ventilation should get the hot stale air out of the top of the room, bring fresh air in, keep the air in gentle motion, and accomplish all of this without drafts around the feet, on the back of the neck, and other vulnerable parts of our anatomy. The ventilating devices at our disposal are operating windows and doors, ventilating grills, exhaust fans, warm-air furnaces (especially those with blowers), and the gravitation of warm air up and cool air down.

The hot high air can be removed effectively by an exhaust fan in the ceiling, usually regarded as essential over the kitchen stove but seldom used elsewhere because of its noise; by non-mechanical ventilators through the roof, often used in factories and on ships but seldom in houses; by windows or ventilating grills in the walls at or very near the ceiling; or by forced-draft warm-air furnaces which pull the air down. Unless you have one or more of these, a layer of practically motionless air is likely to stick near the ceiling. If the stale air is taken out of the room, fresher air is bound to come in. Usually it is brought in through doors and windows, but in many new houses ventilators in the wall relieve windows and doors of this added responsibility (Fig. 12-8). They are often placed below fixed panes of glass, but they can be panels located at any place between the floor or ceiling or reaching from one to the other. Such ventilators usually have horizontal louvers on the outside to ward off rain, then a fixed screen to keep out insects, and on the inside sliding or hinged panels to control the amount of air admitted. Their good points are numerous: being unobtrusive they permit much greater flexibility of size, shape, and location than do highly conspicuous windows; combining privacy with fresh air, they can be placed where windows are not suitable; and having permanently fixed screens which do not dull the outlook, they minimize the nuisance of insect barriers at windows. Their one obvious disadvantage is that they may make additional precious wall space unsuitable for furniture placement. Air can be kept in motion by operating windows or ventilators in at least two walls, preferably opposite each other, of a room; by the many kinds of fans, built-in or portable; and by the heretofore-mentioned air currents set up by different temperatures.

Of all our rooms, kitchens need the best ventilation and usually get it with exhaust fans. Bathrooms come next but almost never have what is needed, except in those windowless hotel cubicles where ventilation is provided by mechanical systems. Windows or grilles that are high in the wall and can be opened just a little or a lot, or a controllable ventilator in the ceiling, would serve far better than the typical bathroom windows, which when opened cause the occupant to forsake privacy and probably suffer the consequences of a cold draft. Dining rooms and living rooms need good ventilation, too, but, since they are usually fairly large and well-windowed, the need for special devices is less acute. Bedrooms, though, require a brand of thought they seldom get, for here one really needs fresh air without drafts while too far from consciousness to fuss with adjustments during the night. Again high windows or ventilators on two walls, supplemented of course by low windows and/or doors for a good breeze when you want it, are the solutions.

Form and color have a psychological effect on ventilation needs just as they do on every other aspect of our behavior. Warm, dark colors and heavy forms make it seem a little harder to find fresh air than do cool, light colors and small-scale, slender furniture. Thus, the problem is not only to get adequate ventilation but to furnish rooms so that they seem ventilated.

ACOUSTICS

Noise, noise, noise! Radios, vacuum cleaners, washers, dishwashers, exhaust fans—and children—all bring noises unknown in the house a generation or two ago. Yes, there were always children, but remember when they were "to be seen but not heard"? Contemporary psychology has made it clear that repressing the natural, noisy activities of small or large children may be harmful, and any sensitive adult cannot help thinking that the little ones are only carefree children once. Coupled with an actual increase of noise are three factors that make it more noticeable: houses have fewer and smaller rooms; open planning has reduced the number of floor-to-ceiling partitions and even those that do arrest vision are often not as soundproof as those thick, expensive walls of the good old days; and furnishings are not as bulky and noise absorbing as they used to be.

Sound is much like light. It travels in straight lines until it hits something that reflects or absorbs it; and like light it is reflected by hard smooth surfaces and absorbed by those that are rough and porous. Unlike light, sound can carry through opaque materials.

A first principle of acoustics in homes is to keep the noisy spots together and isolate them well from the quiet areas. Fortunately, in application this principle usually fits nicely with other desirable outcomes. Thus, for reasons of use as well as acoustics, it is logical to have the kitchen, laundry, garage, shop, and indoor and outdoor play space as near together as possible; and to have a progression through the semi-noisy dining and living space to the quiet bedrooms, study, and seclusion room. The spot where this applies least well is the bathroom, which is noisy but should be near the bedrooms. To take care of this and other situations we need three more principles.

The second principle is reducing noises at their source. Prevention is inevitably superior to cure, and this certainly applies to the many household noises that start with two hard objects coming together. In the kitchen, one of the noisiest parts of the house, this principle indicates the use of resilient materials on as many as possible of the surfaces against which pans, dishes, and leather-heeled shoes are likely to bang. Counters covered with linoleum or vinyl cause less noise than do those surfaced with stainless steel, clay tile, or laminated plastics. Similarly, floors of linoleum, vinyl, or rubber are quieter than are those of concrete, clay tile, or asphalt tile. The kitchen has been singled out, but this principle applies in every room.

The third principle is absorbing noises already made. This can be accomplished by using sound-absorbing materials and sound-diffusing forms. Let us think for a minute of the poorest materials and shapes—a precisely rectangular empty room with walls, floor, and ceiling of smooth glass or metal; the acoustics of such a room would not be helped much if a few pieces of rectangular, smooth metal furniture were placed parallel to the walls. Every surface would make a noise if hit, and this noise would be reflected to the opposite parallel surface and continue to bounce back and forth until the energy was spent. At the opposite extreme would be a room in which at least two of the walls are not parallel to each other and the ceiling is not parallel to the floor; the walls are broken with a projecting or recessed fireplace and storage cabinets and the plane of the ceiling is interrupted by beams; the walls and floor are surfaced with cork, the ceiling with a porous, soft-surfaced material; and the room is furnished with a thick rug, upholstered sofa and chairs, many books in open cases, large plants on floor or tables, and windows well shielded with draperies. In brief, sound-absorbing materials are soft and porous; sound-diffusing shapes are almost anything other than uninterrupted, smooth, parallel planes.

Fourth, use sound barriers to keep noise out of quiet areas. Closets retard the passage of sound between bedrooms and bathrooms, halls, or other bedrooms. Bookcases, storage walls, and thick fireplace walls can be used advantageously to retard the passage of sound in group living space.

Lighting, heating, ventilating, and acoustics make our homes physically comfortable or not, depending on how they are controlled. With the notable exception of lighting, they have little to do with beauty or individuality but they have much to do with human happiness. For the first time in history we now have at our command the knowledge and technics needed to control these four factors precisely. Planning them should be fundamental in planning and furnishing a home, but all too often their effect on our lives is slighted. Progress, however, is being made and although we may be impatient, we should not fail to appreciate the accomplishments made in the past few decades.

CHAPTER 16

Setting the Table

SETTING YOUR TABLE can be a daily, actually thrice daily, adventure in decorating, although far too many of us overlook the opportunities in the haste to get the table set and cleared quickly. Because it is the one place where you can change colors and accessories three times a day, it is a good place to exercise your decorating sense and to satisfy your need for variety.

Why do we "set tables"? In order to eat together with comfort and pleasure. Comfort means good chairs and tables well arranged in sufficient space; suitable light and ventilation; a minimum of noise; and appropriate tableware and table coverings. Pleasure comes from one's companions, the food, and the spirit, beauty, and individuality with which the table is set. Frequently in discussions of table settings, emphasis is put on the "setting" as though, like a painting, it were an end in itself; on "company" meals which are a small percentage of the total; or on so much elaboration that those responsible are too busy and tired to enjoy the fruits of their efforts. It is the day-to-day, regular meals that are most important in family life. Lunch-counter or cafeteria efficiency is not the primary goal, but neither is striving to go beyond one's resources of time, energy, space, equipment, and money.

Eating can be varied as was discussed in Chapter 2. What kind of meals do you enjoy most thoroughly and most often? Your answer to

16-1   Eating should be a pleasure.

this question should be your chief guide in selecting your tableware and planning your table settings. Take advantage of the experience of others but do not try to imitate them.

TABLE SETTINGS

Books on etiquette divide table settings into *formal* and *informal* categories. With the first we need have no concern because it is appropriate only for those few who can afford—and who like—a staff of servants to serve a five-course menu with the finest of tableware.

An Informal Dinner Table

The setting shown in Fig. 16-2 is about as close as most families can come to formality, but it is correctly described as informal. The tablecloth and napkins of rich, deep-red linen set the keynote, unify the setting, and show to full advantage the dishes, silver, and glass. Symmetrical balance permeates this basically simple arrangement in which a variety of shapes and patterns are harmoniously combined. The silver is a beautiful example of *variety in unity* and *form follows function*. The cigarette holder is plain as befits its subordinate role. Salt and pepper shakers have no ornamentation but are handsomely shaped. Bread and

16-2 A handsome dinner table which is consistent although the pieces do not "match." This is a good example of proper place settings.

butter plates and the efficiently covered vegetable dishes have a gadroon border similar but not identical to that on the ashtrays. Knives, forks, and spoons have richly modeled, curved ornamentation faintly echoed in the rims of the plates. And this progression from simple to complex appropriately reaches its climax in the candlesticks. The decoration on the plates emphasizes their shape, adds interesting small-scale intricacy to the table, and harmonizes in color with the cloth and flowers. The glassware is as sturdily shaped as the vegetable dishes, but its deeply cut pattern gives sparkle. Chrysanthemums in a low silver bowl bring the color harmony to its strongest intensity but are low enough to allow sociability across the table.

What kind of menu and room does this table suggest? Melon cup, consommé Julienne, lemon chicken casserole, brown rice and green peas, endive salad, vanilla ice cream with brandied cherries, cookies, and coffee would be appropriate for a setting of this degree of formality and elaborateness. One would expect the room and furnishings to be rather rich and formal, the guests to wear semi-formal clothes. This table would indeed be inappropriate for spaghetti and meat balls, a highly informal home, and guests in sport clothes.

It is a table setting which would draw your attention when you entered the room in which it was placed and which would reward closer study when you were seated at the table. Everything is harmonious. Each piece will perform its function well, is good to look at, is in keeping with the other elements, and has been thoughtfully placed. It should be a good dinner!

An Informal Luncheon Table

Luncheon served on the table shown in Fig. 16-3 would be delightfully informal, refreshing, and appetizing. The table could be set in a window-walled dining area, on a brick patio near a huge oak tree, on an open terrace high above city streets—or it could bring an airy, outdoor atmosphere to even the most drab of city dining spaces. The beautiful grain of the table shows between the mats, and this "nature" motif is emphasized by the branch angling down the middle of the table and by the leaf-shaped napkin holders. Mats are pale green piqué and napkins are the same hue but lower in value. The white china, the silver, and the clear glassware are beautifully proportioned forms needing no enrichment. Green-white grapes and fire-red geraniums make the centerpiece a real center. At this table, one would expect food that is refreshing, well-seasoned, and selected for color as well as flavor, and one would expect light-hearted conversation, for certainly this is the character of the setting.

An Outdoor Luncheon Table

An informal mood for the luncheon table shown in Fig. 16-4 is set by the indoor-outdoor furniture of black iron, cane, redwood, and patterned

LORD & TAYLOR   PHOTOGRAPH BY RICHARD AVERILL SMITH

16-3   The informality of nature is the "idea" of this informal luncheon table.
Dishes, glassware, and silver are plain; only the napkin holders are ornamented.

glass. Textures play a dominant role. The cane of the chairs is repeated, at much more delicate scale, in the reed fruit basket and in the
cane-patterned, plastic-handled cutlery. Corded mats, patterned glass,
and wood grain fill out the theme. The sturdy, squarish earthenware
dishes hold their own with what is around them. The soup bowls have
practical heat-retaining covers, but the square tumblers might be awkward to drink from. This is a simple, modern setting. Without being
rustic, it is at home outdoors but could equally well be used indoors, thus
fulfilling one of today's needs—being adaptable without losing character.
This is a table that belongs to the outdoors or to a simple, open, contemporary dining space. The meal should be equally simple, easy to
prepare, serve, and eat. Guests might well be in sports attire.

GLADDING, MCBEAN & CO.

16-4 Ribbed plastic mats, undecorated square earthenware, and plastic-handled
knives, forks, and spoons make these place settings appropriate to the centerpiece, furniture, and the outdoor setting.

B. J. BROCK & CO.

16-5   A buffet table which is efficiently arranged and effectively set.   The harvest
decoration of the dishes is carried out in the centerpiece.

A Buffet Table

The table shown in Fig. 16-5 is for an informal buffet with appropriate
tableware arranged in a logical order.   Against a plain dark brown background, white dishes decorated with harvest designs and colors have
been placed.   The harvest theme has been reiterated in the centerpiece—
squash, cabbage, corn, onions, beans, and a few autumn flowers overflow
a plain silver bowl from which arise candles repeating the color of the
cloth.   Are a silver bowl and candelabra out of place?   Strictly speaking,
they are—but these are simple and of the same material as the knives and
forks.   Sometimes a moderate incongruity of this kind relieves the tedium
of perfect harmony.   Certainly the large wooden salt and pepper shakers
are fitting, as are the hammered silver cigarette cups, the iron trivet under

the coffee pot, and the bamboo-handled salad servers. The flat silverware is of a fairly plain and pleasing pattern that would be suitable on almost any table.

The tableware has been placed in proper sequence. A diner will pick up his plate; advance to the meat platter, tossed salad bowl, and hot potato salad bowl; pick up his silver and napkin to be clutched by the hand with the filled dinner plate while the other hand gets a mug of coffee. Let us hope he will quickly find a place to sit with a convenient and clear small table nearby.

The table setting as a whole is a pleasing sight, besides being functionally efficient. It presents a well-balanced picture, the large bowls and tall shakers on the left balancing the tall coffee pot and many small tumblers on the right; the pile of plates and the platter, countered by the silverware and napkins, make a solid center grouping around the dominant tall candles and slightly diagonal centerpiece. The centerpiece is further emphasized by the two diagonal lines of ashtrays pointed toward it. The height of the centerpiece might be overpowering at a sit-down meal, but it is excellent for a buffet table to be seen and appreciated from across the room and when standing nearby. The guests might be coming from a football game and they would welcome hearty food, a crisp salad, plenty of coffee that is strong and hot, and a full-bodied dessert such as hot apple pie and cheese. It is a good buffet table appropriately informal in character with appropriate dishes efficiently arranged.

PLANNING TABLE SETTINGS

These four examples only hint at the challenging possibilities of setting attractive tables. Only one characteristic is common to all good settings: *an appropriate idea consistently carried out.*

Ideas are legion. Many are firmly rooted in our cultural traditions. Christmas bells, a Valentine heart, cherries and an ax, an Irish Shamrock, Easter bunnies and eggs, the pumpkins and corn of the autumn season—are these too obvious to start with? Not in the least, for they are familiar but inspiring points of departure for seasonal tables. Many are the times, though, when the day, the season, the guests, or the meal suggest nothing specific. Then one looks around the house, especially in the cupboards; in the yard, fields, woods, or beaches; in the stores; and in the magazines for something to give meals new life.

Appropriateness stands above all other considerations because the good meal (and the table setting is only part of this) is suited to

- You, your family, and your guests.
- Your cooking and dining space, equipment, and furniture.
- The food to be served.
- The occasion.

Appropriateness, too, means the kind of meal that can be prepared, served, and eaten with enjoyment, not strain. It does not mean a stultifying conformity to any single factor. How dull, for example, to suppose that a festive Christmas dinner with a white damask tablecloth, inherited china, and silver candelabra is inappropriate in a contemporary house! To be sure we would not expect many meals of this kind in such a setting, but the fact that they are exceptional makes them stimulating.

Consistency implies that you carry your idea far enough so that the setting has some degree of unity. It means that you would think twice before putting heavy earthenware dishes on fine damask or sheer linen or a formal centerpiece of symmetrically arranged roses on an informal buffet table. It means that your idea or theme is emphasized to the limits of your equipment.

Setting the table is an adventure in three-dimensional design. It is a miniature version of planning a house or selecting and arranging the furnishings of a room and differs from these chiefly in its more limited purpose and temporary nature. A few specifics are worth remembering.

- Table settings should look well from a distance (especially buffets) and should stand well the close study they unavoidably receive at a sit-down meal.
- Dishes, glassware, and silverware are the more or less permanent, hard, durable, bulky, and usually costly parts of table setting. They are the basic, not the expendable or infrequently used objects, and in a home their variety is limited. Those with pronounced color or decoration sharply limit the table-setting possibilities.
- Table coverings, being less expensive and more easily stored than dishes, glass, and silver, can be much more varied. Tablecloths provide the largest area of color or pattern.
- Accessories, including flowers, permit the greatest freedom of all and thus become the chief means to varied settings.

Centerpieces should be:

- Simple, for they are the center of the whole setting, not a separate picture.
- Harmonious with the rest of the setting and the occasion.
- Self-contained and separated from the place settings, but integrated within themselves.
- Proportioned to the size of the table and the room.
- Attractive from all sides if people sit or walk around them.
- Low enough to permit across-the-table conviviality.

In addition to table settings, think of the other ways of varying meals. Food, of course, is the first, but location of the meal follows closely. Move the dining table out of the room's center over to the window, serve breakfast or supper on a card table in front of the fireplace, plan a buffet meal for your own family, or take a picnic out to your terrace or yard.

SELECTING TABLEWARE

Purposely, table settings have been discussed before the selection of table equipment because your ware should be selected with due consideration to its use and appearance on the table.

But before you can actually set your table you must choose dinnerware, silverware, glassware, and linens. Most brides-to-be start with a silver pattern and then choose their dinnerware. Glassware is likely to be a gift, and linens are usually a combination of the hope chest's contents, a few gifts, and perhaps some heirlooms. It is a little unnerving, is it not, this accumulation of tableware with which to create table settings, probably in a succession of unknown rooms? Yet it does express you, your relatives, and your friends, and it is they who will use it.

Ideally, tableware should be harmonious with the room in which it is used, but how can that be done when all but a few persons get their tableware long before their permanent dining furniture and space? Do you select or design them to harmonize with your dishes? Certainly not, except under unusual circumstances. How, then, should you select your tableware? A sensible procedure is to keep use, economy, beauty, and individuality firmly in mind, perhaps weighting beauty and individuality somewhat more heavily than in choosing a chair or bed. You get the table equipment that makes you feel your best, that makes you feel that meals are going to be fun. You think in terms of:

- Yourself and your family—their personalities and way of living, color and pattern preferences.
- Your home as a whole, but especially your dining, cooking, and storage spaces and their furnishings.
- Your economy—the amount of time and energy you wish and are able to expend on your food and table equipment, on preparing and serving meals, and on cleaning up.
- Your meals—the kinds of foods and the kinds of meals you and your family most enjoy.
- Your friends—their likes and dislikes, what makes them happy meal guests.

Because all of this centers in you and your family, it should automatically result in tablewares that are harmonious with one another. Often, though, extraneous factors—something your friend has just bought, a well-advertised novelty or fad, a sale, or spur-of-the-moment buying— make one forget the whole picture. Before each decision, one should ask: Is this really exactly what I want for a long, long time? Will it fit in with my other pieces?

Selecting Your Dishes

Dinnerware is the most conspicuous element of your permanent table equipment, and therefore establishes the character of your table settings more than does your silver or glass. Although usually of ceramics, dinnerware comes in plastic, glass, and metal, all of which have been discussed in Chapter 9.

Use

- The primary purpose of dinnerware is to hold food.
- Dinnerware is handled a great deal; resistance to chipping and breaking is important.
- Shape and size are significant.
  Cups should have finger-fitting handles, rims that fit lips, and be of suitable capacity.
  Plates with a shallow bowl for food and rims that permit easy grasping and provide a resting place for knife and fork are more functional than are the rimless type.

INTERNATIONAL MOLDED PLASTICS, LIBBEY GLASS CO., FRASER'S

16-6 These dishes, glasses, and stainless steel ware are all moderately priced, durable, and easy to care for. Their beauty comes from form and material and none of them needs ornament. The three used together would make a happy trio, and any of them would make a good foil for ornamented tableware. Glass: Freda Diamond, designer. Stainless steel; G. Ponti, designer.

Economy

- Durability of body, glaze, shape, and ornamentation have to be balanced against original cost.
  Vitreous wares of compact shape, hard glaze, and durable ornamentation are usually long-term economies.
- Storage space for dinnerware is expensive; think twice before buying unneeded pieces.
- Dishes doubling as cooking and serving containers save money, time, space, and assure *hot* food.
- Open stock patterns produced by dependable manufacturers make replacements and additions relatively painless.
- A small set of durable, everyday dishes is usually an economy.

Beauty

- Dinnerware comes in an intriguing variety, opening the path to many colors and patterns that will be yours *for a long time.*
- Ornamentation, if any, should be appropriate (see Chapter 6).
- Dinnerware is seldom seen in isolation.

Individuality

- Dishes can be formal and elegant, simple and modern, or as informal and colorful as a peasant costume.
- Choose those that you think will make you feel your best *over the years.*

Selecting Your Glassware

Dinnerware and glassware are so similar in materials and use that almost everything said about dishes applies to glassware. There are, however, a few specific points worth emphasizing.

- Colored glassware enlivens a table—but the color cannot be changed for different occasions and it alters, sometimes unattractively, the color of the liquid.
- Glassware with raised or lowered ornamentation sparkles nicely but is noticeably hard to wash and polish well.
- Stemware has a buoyant, bubble-like quality genuinely expressive of the nature of the material and gives a "lift" to the table—but it, too, is hard to wash, is very easily broken, and takes much storage space.

rooms and furniture rather than allowing a lot of little things to clutter your living.

- Supplement the big accessories with a few moderate- to small-sized ones for variety so that everything is not the same size.
- Study the design of your arrangements as a painter studies the composition of a still-life painting.
  Informality is not the same as carelessness.
- Change your accessories with your own need for variety, the seasons, holidays, and special celebrations.
  Your arrangements need not be frozen once and for all.
- Maintain your accessories carefully.
  Dust, grime, and tarnish dim their beauty.
- Plan good storage space for those objects not always used.
- Consider breakage hazards if you move often or have small children.
- Weed out your collection from time to time.
  Do not hang on to something you do not need or like unless you have a capacious attic and never expect to move.
- Have courage to try something different, to express your individuality.
  Avoid choosing accessories that look as though they came as a collection from a mail-order catalogue.

As you read the following sections on *location, selection, number, background,* and *arrangement,* it should become increasingly clear that enrichment cannot be thought of apart from walls and furniture if you want to avoid the "gift shop look."

Location

There are two logical types of locations for enrichment: first, those places where people normally look; and second, those places where you want them to look with interest and pleasure.

People normally tend to look more or less straight ahead and slightly down; through arches, doorways, or wherever distance invites exploration and stretching the eyes; and at anything that is large, different, or well illumined. Thus, it is sensible to consider enrichment opposite the entrance door, somewhere near the first view of the living room, at the end of a hall, more or less opposite seating for conversation and eating, on the wall opposite a bed, and in the space above a desk. Outdoors,

17-1 Individualized accessories over the fireplace, supplemented by books, lamps, and fireplace fittings, make the fireplace wall of a gentleman's study a focus of attention. Their rich, formal character is consonant with that of the whole room.

one thinks of enriching the major views from inside the house or the terrace as well as the ends or turning points of garden walks.

The enrichment in each of these locations should be of suitable size, scale, and character; of suitable *carrying power,* by which we mean that it can be easily seen and understood at the distance from which it is commonly seen; and of appropriate *holding power,* by which we mean the amount of time necessary to enjoy and appreciate it fully. For example, a person entering your front door will probably be fairly close to the entrance area enrichment, so that you can select something best seen at short range, but since this is not the place you want your guest to linger, what he sees need not be so complex or profound that it holds his attention for very long. A good table or chest of drawers with some flowers, plants, and/or decorative sculpture below a mirror is a possibility if space permits; but if the space is small, it is wise to confine the enrichment to the wall—a distinctive lighting fixture, a mirror, an uncomplicated painting or print, or a worthy textile are among the possibilities.

The first view into the living room is another matter, for the opposite wall or window is some distance away, and as you sit in the room you will have ample opportunity to look at it from closer range. In many modern houses, this first view carries the eyes through the room directly out into the yard, which then becomes the place for interesting planting; walls, pools, or fences; decorative urns or sculpture; or a pleasant distant view. In other houses, the fireplace wall is the first thing seen, and it may or may not need more than the architect has given in its basic design and materials. If the fireplace is small and simple, the wall above may have a painting or textile, large and strong enough to balance the opening below and to make itself understood as you enter the room—and also with sufficient holding power to remain interesting over long periods. In still other quarters, the initial view may end in a blank wall which in most cases will have a group of furniture and accessories—sofa, end tables, lamps, and perhaps a painting; a piano, radio-phonograph, or bookcases and cabinets; or a fine secretary and some chairs. Whatever your specific situation, remember that as you enter the living room, something of interest ought to greet the eyes.

We have written as though it *had* to be on the opposite wall, but of course this is by no means a rule or law. Your major point of interest may be on another wall which is seen only after you are in the room. Or it could be exceptionally beautiful rugs.

PHOTOGRAPH BY JULIUS SHULMAN

17-2 A utilitarian floor-to-ceiling mirror enhances a room by reflecting a fine view and the handsomely patterned wood. For many, no further enrichment is needed. Richard Neutra, architect.

There are a few spots in most homes where you have to entice attention, chief among which are uninteresting corners and small wall spaces that must be used. The writers have found in their own efforts to arrange furniture in group living space for both large and small gatherings that one of the most difficult problems is to suggest, not vocally but visually, that a few people might be happier in a separate small furniture group rather than all overcrowding the major seating arrangement. Often this can be accomplished by reinforcing comfortable furniture with congenial illumination; prints, paintings, textiles, or sculpture on the wall; and interesting objects (plus something to nibble on) on the table. Then, what was formerly an unnoticed, unused corner becomes pleasantly used space, chiefly of course through the right kind of furniture but also to a surprising degree through genuinely interesting accessories.

Selection

Accessories should count in your life, count in your rooms, and perform their utilitarian duties if they are of the useful sort.

Counting in your life and *counting in your room* can be quite different matters. The first means that you have personal feelings toward them, such as humans have toward family heirlooms or things they grow up with; gifts from a dear friend; something purchased or found on an enjoyable trip, or discovered at a rummage sale; and those things made by yourself or someone close. Some would say that these are not at all what *your room needs,* but they are things *you want.* Too many such objects, esthetically unrelated, can make a room visually cluttered and too intimate for group use, but if used with some discretion they are a prime source of individuality.

Counting in your room means that quite aside from sentiment and associations, the objects contribute to your basic idea. Usually, accessories build up the general character as harmony strengthens melody in music. Unity should come to mind first and never be totally forgotten. But accessories are one of the most appropriate sources of surprise, contrast, and variety in your home. How far should you go? Far enough to create interest, but not so far that the difference is more shocking than pleasant.

If your quarters are non-committal, you need only consider your furnishings; and if your furnishings are nondescript, accessories with impact, decisiveness, and individuality are needed. This suggests a few important accessories with strong personalities: a large Oriental metal tray, colorful Mexican baskets, an India print covering a studio couch, Japanese lanterns, a tall blue glass vase handmade in a southern state, a sizeable ceramic bowl made by a local potter, grandmother's soup tureen or her patchwork quilt—almost anything that adds a new strong note. These objects are suggested because they compensate for the over-mechanized, impersonal character prevalent today.

You may, of course, take up habitation in quarters of decisive character—a fine old Colonial or a profusely decorated Victorian house, or one that suggests English or Spanish parentage. Then your problem is different. The first impulse would be to search for objects from that period, but, good ones being hard to come by, the logical alternative is to think carefully about the scale and character of your rooms and get appropriate accessories, regardless of period. Or you may be one of the lucky persons who finds himself in a contemporary house, simple yet with character, which provides a congenial setting for a wide variety of enrichment, contemporary or historic, mass-produced or hand-crafted. Such homes open wide the doors for individualized accessories.

Some of the most common types of accessories deserve special mention either because their use suggests limitations or their character demands special considerations.

Bowls and vases of ceramics, glass, metal, plastics, or wood may work full time, part time, or not at all. If they are workers, check their efficiency: make certain that a bowl used for snacks is easy to pass; and that a vase for flowers holds enough water, is stable, and has a flat bottom for the flower holder.

Candleholders ought to hold candles firmly upright and catch the inevitable drip. If for the dining table, they should be either low or high to keep the light away from eye level; if they are to be left out but seldom used, they should be worth looking at repeatedly.

Clocks exist primarily to tell us the time of day quickly and with minimum danger of inaccuracy. There is no reason for them to be homely, but there is no reason for them to be slowly moving puzzles either.

Mirrors have the paradoxical qualities of allying themselves with what is opposite them by reflection and of disassociating themselves from their immediate background because of their striking dissimilarity to most wall surfaces. Mirrors are conspicuously bright and brittle. They increase spaciousness and add sparkle to a room. In entrances they provide a first or last opportunity to check one's appearance. In living and dining rooms they are primarily decorative and can cover one wall to create an illusion of space, fill the space between windows to simulate a window-wall, or be hung much like paintings over davenports, fireplaces, or

17-3 Books on adjustable wall shelves and two reproductions of Mayan sculpture complement trim, sculptural furniture.

furniture groups. In halls they are useful to gain apparent width or to lighten a dark end. Since mirrors contrast strongly with typical walls, it is especially important that they compensate by being appropriate in size and shape. Many mirrors now are hung without frames, and are usually most effective when they at least *look* as though they were part of the wall. They can be further integrated with their environment by putting shiny accessories near them to carry their glitter into the room.

Natural objects, such as driftwood, dried branches of unusual structure, rocks, and shells are in harmony with the trend toward "naturalism" in our homes. Such objects have much to recommend them: little or no expense, natural beauty, and individuality because no two pieces are identical.

Number of Accessories

The Victorian loved gewgaws, gimcracks, and whimwham and loaded their homes with what now seems like a random clutter of things against patterned backgrounds. The Japanese like a very few beautiful objects, meticulously arranged against quiet backgrounds. Should we laugh at the foolish bad taste of the Victorians? No! Their selection and arrangement may not have been very sensitive and discreet but what they did was wholehearted and individualized, and their houses had sufficient space and shelves to hold what they enjoyed. Today, however, there is a strong trend toward fewer and bigger accessories, sensible because it lightens housework and makes smaller homes seem more spacious. If a few accessories are going to do the whole job, they have to be worth the attention they attempt to hold, interesting in themselves, and effectively arranged.

No one can tell you how many accessories your home should have, and if you and your family enjoy having many of them around, do not be afraid to do so. Keep in mind, though, you will want fewer accessories if those that you have are large or important; if your rooms are small; your walls, floors, draperies, and/or upholstery are patterned; your furniture is ornamented; the views from your windows are interesting; growing plants indoors or arranging flowers are among your hobbies; or if you have small children and housekeeping fatigues you.

Backgrounds

The effectiveness of any accessory or group can be increased or decreased markedly by the appropriateness of its setting. Should contrast or harmony be emphasized? A simple white vase would hardly be noticeable against a white wall, moderately noticeable against gray, and stand out sharply from black. This raises two more questions. How much attention do you want to attract at that spot? How beautiful is the vase? The advice generally given is to have a contrasting background

17-4 Accessories profit from congenial comparisons and a suitable setting. Simple furniture of Chinese inspiration, a Chinese statue and bowl, a contemporary painting, and a large cut-leaf philodendron make a congenial family. Notice that the painting is hung low enough to join its forces with those of the statue and chest. Maurice Sands, decorator.

to "show up"—or "off"—the accessory, and if that is what you want, by all means employ contrast. But this is not the only way. The large, significant accessories ought to proclaim their presence by being put in important positions, given a background against which they can be readily seen, and built up with smaller objects. At the other extreme some accessories ought to take their places unobtrusively, being nothing more than a little murmur in a harmonious setting. Then you will avoid the extremes of having *all* of the accessories jump at you or *all* of them melt into their setting.

PLANTS

Plants in a home are inexpensive, last much longer than cut flowers, and with reasonable care get bigger. A refreshing contact with growing nature, they provide needed variety of form and color, especially in simple interiors, and give the gardener an indoor hobby.

Fashions change. The Victorians favored large, somber but durable palms or rubber plants, Boston ferns weeping over the sides of tall stands, and maybe a fancy-leaved begonia or two. The "modernistically" inclined person of the 1930's found the spiky, brazenly yellow striped sansevieria (sometimes called "Mother-in-Law's Tongue") suitably hard, sharp, and unyielding. Today we have come to accept philodendrons and their relatives (Fig. 17-4), especially the cut-leaf varieties, as favorites. And we have undergone one other change—plants are likely to be regarded as part of the whole furnishing scheme.

Each type of plant has its own requirements of light, heat, water, drainage, humidity, and soil for best growth. Almost none like a dark, hot, poorly ventilated room, but even in such unfavorable conditions some philodendrons, rubber plants, and sansevierias will survive. It may take a little experimenting to find out which ones are best for your conditions, but this is inexpensive if you buy small sizes.

- For hot sunny windows, try *cactus* and other *succulents,* or the almost indestructible sansevieria.
- For moderately cool east or north windows, try *begonias* which range from those growing only a few inches tall to some several feet high; *African violets* with colors from deep violet to white; *coleus* with their gay foliage of reds, yellows, greens, and whites; *ivy,* either plain or variegated, which can be trained around a window or up a wall; and all of the *philodendron* family.
- For parts of rooms not near windows, foliage plants such as *philodendrons, rubber trees, ferns,* and a variety of other plants becoming widely available at florists and variety stores are likely to succeed.

The containers in which plants are kept have much to do with their health and attractiveness. The importance of drainage suggests that you think three times before putting any plant in a dish or jardiniere with no outlet for excess water, because very few plants like constantly wet feet. Beyond that, you usually want something that, while attractive in itself, does not compete too strongly with what it holds. The usual materials are ceramics and metal. Ceramics can be had in any color, but those of "natural" colors seem logical with one exception: greens are difficult because almost never do they look "right" with the greens of growing plants. Metal—brass, copper, or aluminum—is durable and provides a lively accent.

Treat plants as you would any other accessory, selecting and placing them where they will be real ornaments. Big, bold plants are good for major effects, and at the opposite extreme, small, interestingly foliaged plants are suitable for dish gardens and small containers. Vary the size. On a coffee or end table, or in a small window, a few very small plants bring a nice feeling of small scale; on a larger table or cabinet, plants a foot or two high may be needed; and on the floor or a low stand, plants from three to six feet high really make their presence felt. And within the limits of unity, vary the kinds used. Plants, like everything else, seem most at home when several of one kind are grouped or distributed in a pleasant pattern; but if you are going to rely on plants as a significant source of embellishment, add a few different ones to awaken them all.

ARRANGING FLOWERS

Raised almost to the level of a fine art by the Japanese and assiduously practiced by many in this country, flower arrangement runs the gamut from stuffing some blossoms into a vase to a fascinating hobby, even a profession. You can go about solving it just as you do any other home-furnishing problem:

- Decide what effect you want.
- Obtain suitable flowers, foliage, containers, holders, and ornaments.
- Arrange these, in terms of the aims and principles of design, so that what you had in mind is made clear.

The conventional stumbling blocks are two: getting the materials you want and making them stay where you want them to. Usually, one does not have unlimited choice of materials, and then it becomes a matter of studying what you have so that its character or personality can be emphasized—letting the effect grow out of the material.

Types of Arrangements

Suppose, for example, that you have the florist's dozen of roses, carnations, or narcissuses. One type of flower, all stems the same length: plenty of unity, but no variety. The simplest solution is to take a moderately tall vase, preferably with a flaring top and somewhat constricted neck (to hold them in place), and stand the flowers in it, spreading them a little but having them all about the same height. This gives a spot of color, interesting only to the degree that the flowers themselves are interesting. The next step might be putting a typical flower holder in a low circular bowl, shortening some of the stems and producing a hemispherical mound. It would be symmetrical and orderly, good from all sides, suitable for a centerpiece—but a little obvious.

If, however, you choose as your container a low, rectangular, dark-colored dish, you bring welcome contrast of shape, height, and color. Then,

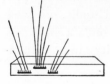

17-5 A rhythmic, asymmetric arrangement of daffodils displays the flowers to good advantage in a strongly contrasting low container. Laura Lee Burroughs, designer.

17-6 Sunflowers are large and vigorous, characteristics well exploited in this arrangement. Laura Lee Burroughs, designer.

using three holders—and saving one flower for some other place—you can arrange the flowers in three groups: a dominant, tall, central group of five (almost but not quite half); a secondary group of three, not quite as tall as the major one but clearly related to it; and a shorter group of three a little further from the center (the teeter-totter principle of balance) and at a little greater angle. This has been done with the daffodils shown in Fig. 17-5. This arrangement gives a lively feeling of rhythmic radiation from the base, the asymmetrical balance common in nature with gradually increasing weight toward the bottom. Unity is established by using only one kind of flower, variety by the different heights, angles, placement, and number of blooms in each group. If you had only five or six flowers, the central group alone would be pleasant.

COCA-COLA CO.

17-7 A formal arrangement of Lady Washington geraniums takes full advantage of their compact, symmetrical clusters. Two figurines, striped wallpaper, and a circular mirror complete the design. Laura Lee Burroughs, designer.

17-8 A decorated Oriental ceramic dish on a wood base
holds a graceful arrangement of four Oriental poppies and
two sprays of bush honeysuckle which echoes the feeling
of the painting on the wall. Laura Lee Burroughs, designer.

The sunflowers in Fig. 17-6 form a bold downward curve. The shape of the curve resembles that of the sides of the container, but in direction the two are contrasting. Notice that the big curve is stabilized by the concentration of six flowers standing upright in the center from which the three flowers on either side reach out. The effect is heavy and solid (as both the flowers and container suggest) and in harmony with the abundance and informality of summer and autumn.

The above arrangements are informal and asymmetrical, but the pelargoniums (commonly known as Lady Washington geraniums) in Fig. 17-7 have been symmetrically and primly massed in the center of an old iron stove top and flanked by their own leaves. The major direction is vertical, in contrast to the container but in harmony with the French porcelain figures; but the opposition has been softened by letting the flowers break the strongest line of the container.

The fourth arrangement (Fig. 17-8) hints at the Oriental approach of carefully selecting a few flowers and then placing them with all the subtle sensitivity to design one possesses. Asymmetric but far from casual, this arrangement fits its container and is strongly related to the painting that completes the composition.

Character and Basic Movement

A simple classification of basic movements and character can be made as follows.

Character
- Formal: symmetrical and precise.
- Semi-formal: more or less symmetrical in outline but not in details of arrangement.
- Informal: asymmetrical and free.

Basic Movement
- Vertical to slightly spreading.
- Outward spreading.
- Horizontal.
- Downward.

How does one decide? By considering the effect wanted and taking inventory of the materials available.

Usually, one thinks of a character in harmony with the home. The precise, orderly symmetry of very formal rooms suggests formal arrangements just as an informal home suggests those that are more casual. Sometimes, though, you may want variety and relief: the solid stability of a symmetrical arrangement at some points in an informal home and a spirited freedom from rigid symmetry in formal interiors. For a tall narrow space behind a console table, a vertical arrangement comes to mind—but a low spreading one might be more stimulating.

Types of Flowers

The floral materials at your command play a dominant role in your decisions because each plant has its own character and habit of growth and—as with every other material in the home—flowers are most effective when their personalities are emphasized. For example, zinnias and marigolds are usually precisely symmetrical mound shapes on stiff upright to slightly spreading stems, but lilacs and forsythia tend to arch unpredictably. Peonies are big, forget-me-nots and violets are small. Baby's-breath is filmy, while phlox is compact. Flowers will co-operate up to a point, but nothing is to be gained by pushing them beyond it.

Containers

Flower arrangements ought to be in containers appropriate to their setting in your home and to their contents, but do not push repetition too far. In the illustrations discussed above, the black dish contrasted strongly with the daffodils while the copper jug harmonized with the sunflowers: both were effective. Usually, the container is subordinate to its content, and simple glass or ceramic bowls or vases will happily hold varied flowers. Sometimes, though, a distinctive urn, cornucopia, or vase is almost as important as what it holds—in fact, there is no law saying that it cannot be more important—but common sense and the principle of dominance tell us that they should not be exactly equal. If you enjoy arranging flowers, you will appreciate varied containers because it is stimulating to have a vase just right in size, shape, color, and texture for its contents. Then, too, you will need a number of stem holders to hold flowers upright in low dishes and in position in tall vases.

No one of them will serve all purposes, and none that the writers have ever seen is really useless.

Dry Arrangements

Perhaps these should be divided into the "semi-dry" arrangements of fruits and vegetables that last from a few days to several months and the "bone dry" combinations of everlasting flowers, seedpods, bare branches, leaves, and driftwood that have indeterminate longevity. They cost little or nothing, last long, and take no care other than the somewhat tedious job of removing dust. The principles are exactly the same as those from which interesting arrangements of fresh flowers develop.

These points are worth keeping in mind.

- Start with an idea or develop one as you go along, and hew to the line. Never treat flowers as a disorganized blur of form and color.
- Build your arrangement to fit the space it occupies. Avoid blocking vision at a dinner table with a high mound of chrysanthemums.
- Let the character of your flowers and leaves show for themselves. Do not force an iris to do something which comes naturally to a rose.
- Begin with your largest flowers or leaves and work down to the small est rather than trying to deal with all sizes and degrees of importance at the same time.
- Remember that variety in unity, balance, rhythm, and emphasis are important. Many persons assume that flowers are so beautiful in themselves that design in their arrangement is unimportant.
- Select a suitable container.
- Give them physical stability, because broken vases, spilled water, and crushed flowers make a mess.
- Give your arrangements adequate light and a pleasant background. Neither dim their beauty nor make them look as though they were on exhibition.
- Realize that flower arrangements are your very best, least costly means of experimenting with individual design. Do not be frightened by rules.

17-9   A few dry palm leaves, a shallow bowl, and some pebbles—plus imagination and skill—make a strikingly decorative effect.   Jack Daniels, designer.

PAINTINGS

How do paintings differ from the patterns on textiles or wallpaper? Should they be selected and used in about the same ways?

Paintings are re-creations of experience, purified, intensified, and ordered. Painters aim to awaken and arouse, sharpen and deepen your way of seeing, enlarge your experience and understanding, and show you that life is more than a complex of mundane, materialistic concerns. Designers, too, hold these aims but not to the same degree of intensity, for their major problem is to enrich and enliven the forms and surfaces of utilitarian objects. In comparison with textile or wallpaper designs, paintings are more richly complex and intense in every way—far greater variety of form and color, more intricate handling of space and texture, and a more profound penetration of important human concerns. Paintings are not made to be repeated many times on a large surface or primarily to fit into their setting, if they are worthy of being called paintings.

This is only part of the story because paintings and decorative designs do have characteristics in common. Both are produced for man's needs, have expressive qualities, are two dimensional, are compounded of the plastic elements, and heed the aims and principles of design. Many painters are also designers and many designers are painters. Some work is midway between painting and design, about as effective used once with a frame around it as repeated many times in a drapery; but in such instances, neither use is fully effective—the work is too thin to stand by itself and too rich to be repeated.

The answer to our second question should now be clear. Paintings and patterns should not be selected and used in the same ways because there are important differences between them. This is no place for a complete discussion of appreciation of painting, but we will hit hard and fast a few basic points about subject-matter, content, medium, and style, and then proceed to color, frames, mats and glass, and location.

Subject-matter is the "matter presented for consideration," the objects the painting represents. Typical categories include landscapes, seascapes, and cityscapes; still lifes and flowers; and people and animals. It is *what* the painter paints. Some contemporary painting is abstract or nonobjective (Fig. 17-4); it bears no more specific relationship to the visual world than a symphony by Beethoven or Prokofieff imitates the sounds of everyday existence. This work has no subject-matter—but it has content.

Content is the idea, message, feeling, or mood expressed. Paintings can express healthy optimism, delicacy, reserve, joy, tragedy, or any other human reaction. In a sense, it is *why* the painter paints, what he emphasizes in his subject-matter and what he draws out of himself. The same general subject-matter can have markedly different content—seascapes can be peaceful and serene, exhilarating, ominous, or tragic.

Medium refers to the materials used in the painting, and the typical media are water color and oil. Water colors are done on paper with pigments made fluid in water, and the characteristic effect is fluid, transparent, and spontaneous, although they can be heavy and opaque or slowly and carefully worked. Oils are done with pigments in oil, usually on canvas. One tends to think of oil paintings as heavier, more solid and opaque, and painted over a longer period of time than are water colors, but oil paint can be used almost as thinly as can water color and the painting can be dashed off about as quickly.

Style is the distinctive or characteristic manner in which works of art are conceived and executed. The word is used to describe the characteristics of a period such as the Renaissance or Rococo, of a period and country such as the Italian Baroque, of a movement such as Impressionism or Cubism, and of the individuality that a painter such as Michelangelo or Van Gogh brings to his work.

Selecting Paintings

Are there any valid guides for selecting pictures for your home on the basis of subject-matter, content, medium, or style? The answer is generally negative because paintings that you are going to see on your walls ought to be those you like.

On *subject-matter,* it is nonsense to say that landscapes or flower pieces are nice for the living room, still lifes with fruit and vegetables for the dining space, and dreamy interiors for the bedroom! Paintings, if they are worth the wall they cover, are too important in themselves—and to you—to be put into categories of subjects suitable for certain rooms. It would be equally silly to say that all paintings must have subject-matter, because quite a few people enjoy abstractions. If, however, your family has a special interest in boating and swimming, by all means have pictures that arouse such associations; if they are bird lovers, collect pictures of birds and hang them in any or every room of the house. If they do not want to be tied down to specific associations, let them stretch their imaginations on abstractions.

On *content,* about the same can be said. Probably you will not want something lugubrious in your kitchen, but it does not follow that all have to be gay and light-hearted. Select the paintings that make you feel good. If it is calm serenity you want, choose a painting that communicates such a mood to you; or if it is stimulation and exhilaration you need, you will find many paintings with that content. Probably you will want varied content in your different pictures so that you can look at what you want at different times. Try to stay clear, though, of the innocuous, shallow, superficial sort of pictures commonly found on the walls of hotel bedrooms and most in evidence in the usual picture shops.

On *medium,* too, there is little to say other than that water colors are typically less heavy than oils and if it is lightness and sparkle you seek, look first at them.

Style should not concern you very much. To be sure there is a deep, often almost-hidden consistency among all works of art from one period, and in an 18th-century house with 18th-century furniture, paintings from the 18th century would be most strictly appropriate just as contemporary paintings fit into contemporary interiors. We live today, however, and assume rightly or wrongly that all art history is our heritage, and there should be no insistence on paintings that *match* furniture. If your tastes are conventional, choose a conventional painting by someone living or a reproduction of something everyone has long since assured you it is safe to admire. If your tastes are not stereotyped, find a good lively modern, a primitive, or something by a less-known historic master.

Without a few words of caution, this may lead you too far. It is not fair to you, your friends, or a painting to hang any painting so that its effectiveness is minimized. The rich, wonderful work of Rembrandt is also dark and somber, and hanging a reproduction of his work on a stark white wall in a room furnished with light modern furniture would make it little more than a black-brown spot, oppressively heavy and hard to see—but we are anticipating sections to follow.

Color is near the heart of painting, and yet choosing a painting primarily because the colors are good in your room is on the level of buying books because you like the color of the bindings. To be sure the colors in some paintings may perk up your whole room with a more exciting, inventive combination of colors than you would have dared put together in walls and furniture; but it is satisfying to have these colors bear some relationship to their surroundings. Regard color, along with all the other attributes, as one important factor in your enjoyment of the paintings on your walls. Make certain that paintings neither clash with their surroundings nor are made to look weak by them.

Size is important, and there is a tendency to hang paintings too small for the wall space and furniture with which they ought to be in scale. This is especially true of paintings hung over fireplaces or sofas, for even in the average living room the space above furniture can profit from a painting that holds its own in the space around it and with the furniture below (Figs. 17-4, 10, and 11). The character of paintings, almost as much as their physical dimensions, determines apparent size and visual weight. Thus, a misty painting in pale colors seems "lighter" and smaller than one with solid forms clearly defined in bright colors. In special situations, such as a small room with average size furniture, a painting in scale with the furniture may crowd the room. Then several smaller pictures, closely spaced, may give the needed interest (Fig. 5-13).

Frames, Mats, and Glass

Frames visually enclose a painting and thereby contribute to its importance and effectiveness; form a transition between the free, intense expressiveness of the painting and the more quiet architectural background; and they safeguard the painting's edges, may hold protective glass, and make it easier to move and hang. Although frames are transitions between pictures and walls, their first duty is to enhance the picture, their second to relate it to the background. Generally, this means that the frame should either echo the size, scale, character, and color of what it encloses—or simply be an unobtrusive band. Occasionally, rather marked contrast can accentuate the qualities of the painting, but it is hard to think of a situation in which the frame should compete with or dominate its contents.

There are two schools of thought on relationship between frame and wall. The "setting off" approach is illustrated by the wide, heavily carved and gilded frames of the past, or by any frame that comes forward at the edges to interrupt the continuity of wall and painting flatness. The "keeping in place" school favors frames that are small to moderate in width, simple in design, harmonious in color with their background, and either flat or stepped back toward the wall. Today frames are usually rather narrow, simple, and neutral in color.

Mats and glass are the typical accompaniments of water colors and prints. Mats serve to enlarge these usually small pictures and to surround them with a rest space as a foil, especially important if the picture is delicate, full of diverse objects or shapes, if the movement is strong or the background is competitive. In color, mats are usually white, pale gray, or buff paper with a slight texture, because these harmonize with typical walls, concentrate attention on the picture, and harmonize different pictures. For special effects mats can be of silver, gold, dark color, or black, and they can be of textiles, cork, patterned paper, or metal. While these can be markedly effective if well done, the effect may seem affected rather than appropriate after the novelty has worn thin.

In size, mats vary with fashions; with the size, character, and quality of the picture; with the frame; and with the location. Generous mats are fashionable now to extend and emphasize what is matted. Large mats are also indicated for large pictures, those strong in character, and sometimes for those of exceptional quality. Heavy frames lessen the need for generous mats while large or important locations increase it. To correct optical illusions and give satisfactory up-and-down balance, the width of the top, sides, and bottom of mats are usually different but not so varied that the observer is acutely conscious of the variations. On horizontal compositions, the top is narrowest, the bottom widest, and the sides in between; on vertical compositions, the bottom is still widest but the sides are often slightly wider than the top. For an 18″ x 24″ horizontal water color of moderate strength and a narrow frame, the top margin could be from 3½″ to 4½″, the side margins ½″ wider, and the bottom about 1″ to 1½″ more than the top.

Glass is a necessary evil for those pictures that cannot be protected by varnish. It gives protection from surface dirt and abrasion and it also seems to intensify and deepen the colors, but it invariably produces annoying reflections. Mats and glass usually go together on water colors, graphic prints, pastels, and photographs; oil paintings seldom have either.

Hanging Pictures

Location of paintings is determined by available wall space, furniture arrangement, the need for enrichment, and, last but not least, proper illumination. Taken purely as enrichment, pictures help mightily in relating furniture to walls, and it is normal to hang them "over something"—davenports, groups of chairs, chests of drawers, desks, tables,

17-10 A Chinese painting, symmetrically placed as are the lamps, dominates a furniture group.

grand pianos and so forth. Keeping them low does three things: lets you see them comfortably; relates them clearly to the furniture; and emphasizes the room's horizontality. Centering them over a piece or group gives a static, stable symmetry, while having them off-center creates more movement (Figs. 17-10 and 11). From time to time, though, it is refreshing to have a painting without the ubiquitous furniture underneath it, to let it stand for what it is worth on an otherwise blank wall.

Good light is important, the best being north daylight coming through a skylight. Few of us can have that, nor do we want special fixtures mounted museum-fashion on the frames. We can, however, make certain that sufficient light falls on the picture to make appreciation comfortable and easy.

"Carrying power" and "holding power," already mentioned, are even more important in selecting locations for paintings than for accessories. A painting over a davenport is likely to be seen by people in the adjacent chairs from a few feet away and for long periods of time. Select one that is most enjoyable at that distance and worth study.

In locating and hanging pictures:

- Choose spots where enrichment is needed and the illumination is good.
- Keep pictures below the eye level of a standing person.
- Select paintings of appropriate size and strength for each location.
- Group small pictures closely together to avoid spottiness.
- Relate each painting to nearby furniture and the wall around it.
- Have the bottoms of pictures in one room the same distance from the floor; or, as a second choice, line up the tops.
- Hang the pictures flat against the wall with no wires or hooks showing.

Reproductions and Originals

No reproduction gives the full impact of the original because it never has the full range and brilliance of color or the real textural qualities. Sometimes the color bears little relation to the original and often the reproductions are at reduced size. It begins to sound as though repro-

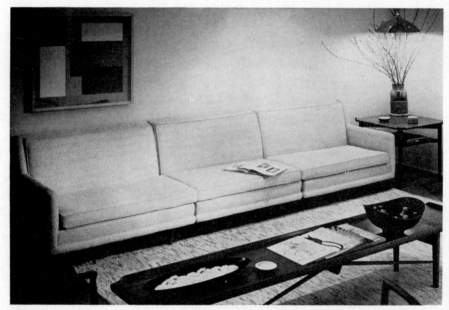

BAKER FURNITURE CO.   PHOTOGRAPH BY DALE ROOKS

17-11 Hanging a painting over one end of a sectional sofa stretches the space, brings a feeling of movement.

ductions should be avoided, but this is true only of those of poor quality. A few reproductions of water colors can hardly be distinguished from the originals, and remarkably good prints of oil paintings are available at museums and print shops for little money. Here is one of the few cases where quality and cost are only slightly related, because a good print of a significant painting costs little if any more than a print of something inconsequential. Thus, reproductions are well worth your consideration.

On the other hand, it is deeply satisfying to have original paintings, prints, or sculpture. One of the all-too-few one-of-a-kind items in your home, an original work of art has a quality that cannot be completely reproduced and which brings you much closer to the artist. Selecting an original is akin to creating one; and, when purchased, it is yours alone. Others may admire it, but they cannot own a duplicate. Not incidentally, original paintings can often be purchased for the price of a comfortable chair, and those of considerable quality may cost less than a television set.

GRAPHIC PRINTS

Etchings, drypoints, lithographs, woodcuts and linoleum cuts, and silk-screen prints are quantity-produced originals because a number of "originals" can be printed from each plate and sold at moderate cost.

Etchings are made by scratching through a waxy coating on a copper or zinc plate, then eating out (or "etching") the exposed metal with acid. Typical etchings somewhat resemble small, delicate, pen-and-ink drawings, but contemporary print makers have experimented with many effects of texture and mass far beyond the potentialities of an ink-dipped pen.

Drypoints are made by scratching directly into the surface of a copper plate with a sharp point and, except to the expert, are almost indistinguishable from etchings.

Lithographs are made by drawing with a greasy crayon or ink on a block of special stone or a sheet of metal. They are noted for their rich blacks and silvery grays.

Woodcuts and linoleum cuts are made by cutting blocks of wood or pieces of linoleum, a process well known to everyone. Often these are in color, an art raised high by the Japanese.

Silk-screen prints are made with a stencil of textile through which thick ink is forced. This medium is particularly well suited to broad, simple masses of different colors, although textures and detail are well within the range of possibilities.

Graphic prints differ from paintings in several ways important to the home decorator—smaller in size, more delicate and with less carrying power, and a good proportion of them in black and white only. Thus, the typical print is not a dominant element and is best placed where one sees it from a short distance, such as above a desk or along a hall—but not along a stairway where esthetic pleasure can often interfere with physical safety. Also, prints enjoy each other's company and are at their best in groups. One etching is likely to seem lonesome and insignificant whereas a group of three or more assumes importance. Prints are usually enclosed with comfortably large mats, glass, and simple narrow frames of black or natural wood. Those of different size and shape can be brought into harmony by frames identical in molding and size, the necessary adjustments being made in the mats.

SCULPTURE

Sculpture, which brings into three dimensions the intensity and expressiveness of painting, is a badly neglected area of enrichment in homes. Whereas almost every home has a few pictures on the wall, very few homes have any effective sculpture. Let us look at the possibilities.

Figurines, very small sculptures of people or animals, abound in gift and variety stores, and the better ones are useful as adjuncts for flower arrangements or as variety in groups of accessories, as can be seen in Fig. 17-7. The typical ones, however, are sirupy sweet and smooth, pastel-colored, and of very limited interest; but from time to time those with character are available. Figurines lend themselves well to occasional use—they are inexpensive, easy to store, and add a lot of interest when brought out after a rest in a cupboard.

Sculpture of larger size and real interest was until recently hard to come by, but now a number of museums and commercial agencies have made available good reproductions of top-quality work. Thus, from museums and art shops one can purchase replicas of serene Egyptian cats, spirited Greek horses, richly modeled Renaissance figures, forceful African and Mayan statues, and the work of contemporaries. Most reproductions of sculpture are cast in plaster or special plastics and finished to resemble the original, but in a few cases they are cast in metal or

a   b

17-12   Reproductions of worth-while sculpture are available.

a. A vigorous Italian wall plaque of Saint George and the Dragon.
b. A serene Chinese Bodhisattva.

very convincing artificial stone, or machine-carved in wood. As with
paintings, reproductions of sculpture are not the equal of originals, but
they can be satisfactory substitutes.

Where can such objects be used in a home? In much the same places
that you would put a good vase, flower arrangement, or plant—on a fireplace mantel, in an open section of a high bookcase or storage wall, on
a low bookcase or cabinet, or on any suitable table. Sculpture is used
in these ways in Figs. 17-3 and 4.

Wall sculpture relieves the flatness of walls and is out of the way. This
is important, but it is certainly damning it with faint praise! It deserves
much better treatment. The plain, uninterrupted expanses of walls in
most of today's houses not only cry out for some contrast to emphasize
their simple continuity but offer a markedly effective background for
three-dimensional richness. Masks come to mind first because they are

17-13 A powerful swirl and amazing interplay of forms make a piece of drift-wood worthy of a good setting in a home.

ready-made for walls, and some of those made not for walls but for children at Halloween or the celebrations enjoyed by Central Americans and Chinese make walls lively.   Another source is the spirited masks made by children in the elementary schools and, while they may not be the kind you want to look at for a decade, they are certainly worth at least a few months.

Enrichment is important.   Give it due thought.   But we return to our introduction—enrichment is not confined to smallish, movable accessories.   It can also be integral with the walls, floor, ceiling, and furnishings.   And a useful object, such as a coffee table, can be enriched with inlaid wood or marble or with paint to the point of becoming almost as important as a painting.

PART FIVE

The Whole House

CHAPTER 18

Plan

OF ALL FACETS of home planning and furnishing, the plan is probably the most important. It indicates the location of walls and openings; the location, size, and shape of space for living; and the ways in which furnishings can be arranged. In large part the plan determines the living patterns of the family and it also establishes the basic character of the structure. Thus architects invariably begin their designing with much study of the plan as a whole.

Good plans, however, do not always guarantee that each room will be of maximum beauty and efficiency or that the exterior will be handsome and appropriate to its total environment, because in the complexities of planning a home conflicts arise. For example, most experts agree that kitchens with U-shaped work areas are most satisfactory, but this shape cannot always be fitted in with other needs and desires; then one takes the best shape that fits. Similarly, placing windows wherever the interior needs indicate seldom leads to orderly exteriors. A home should be more than the sum of its parts, just as a family is more than the sum of its individual members, and in both the parts have to make some adjustments to the whole. It is a matter of give and take, of weighing all factors and assigning them their relative importance, of co-ordinating the components into an integrated total. Too often houses are not unified: plans look as though one room had been added to another;

furnishings do not seem at home in the rooms; and there is little consistency of plan, exterior, interior, and landscape design.

In this chapter we will concentrate on the whole plan; but, especially in the discussion of the first house, we will notice the relationships of plan to furnishings and exterior design, because they belong together.

FOUR PRIZE-WINNING SMALL HOUSES

The houses illustrated in Figs. 18-1 to 4 deserve more than ordinary study because they were judged the best of 2727 designs submitted in a competition recently conducted by the National Association of Home Builders and the *Magazine of Building*. The competition program stated that the house should meet the requirements of a typical family and of a typical builder. This meant that the floor area should not exceed 1000 square feet, chiefly because this would cost from $11,000 to $12,000 rather than because it is all the space a typical family needs; that there should be three bedrooms because the mythical typical family consists of 3.2 persons; that the construction should be of a type readily understandable to builders and economical to construct; that it should be suitable for typical subdivisions, fit on a lot 60 by 100 feet, and appeal to prospective purchasers. The degree to which these objectives were achieved is indicated by the fact that within four weeks after the prize winners had been announced, 22 builders from coast to coast were negotiating with the designers for the privilege of building from their plans.

The First-Prize Winner

Let us look at the house designed by Bruce Walker in the light of what was said in Chapters 2, 3, and 4 about the requirements for group, private, and work activities, and also in the light of what was said in the succeeding chapters about design and color, materials, and the major elements of homes.

Living with Others. Four closely related areas give space for group living in Walker's plan: indoors, the all-purpose space and a conversation alcove; outdoors, the terrace and screened porch. Moderately quiet, small-group *conversation* or *reading* is well provided for in the quiet end of the living space. It is an alcove about 8'0" x 11'0", a good size and shape for from two to five persons, which has a sofa and end tables against a solid wall, storage built in under the windows, two easy chairs, and a

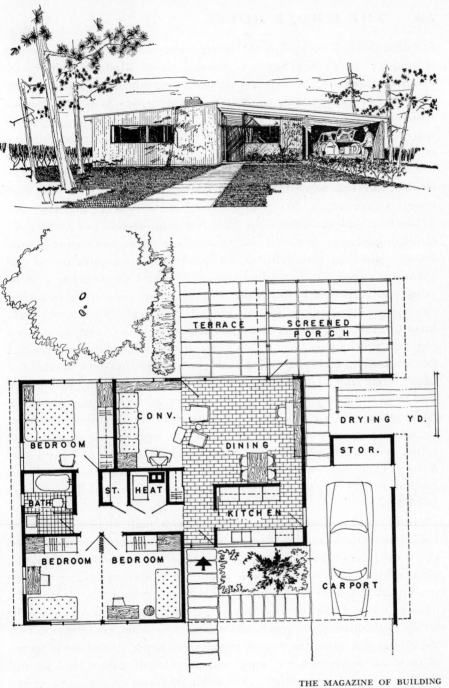

TERRACE | SCREENED PORCH

DRYING YD.

BEDROOM

CONV.

DINING

STOR.

ST. HEAT

BATH

KITCHEN

BEDROOM | BEDROOM

CARPORT

18-1   An efficient, beautiful plan based on deep understanding of contemporary needs. The exterior is a logical outgrowth of the plan and the interior design. Bruce Walker, architect.

fireplace (backed up against the heater room so that only one chimney is needed). South light comes in from a row of windows high enough above the floor to give usable wall space beneath and a feeling of enclosure, but low enough so that a seated person can see outdoors. Although no walls separate the conversation area from the all-purpose space, it is segregated by being a dead-end alcove narrower than the rest of the room, by windows that are higher than those overlooking the terrace, by the difference in floor treatment, and by the ceiling which changes direction along the line demarking the two areas. It is a moderately secure retreat that gives a feeling of permanence and enclosure without becoming a cooped-up little box, and also it can become the stabilizing element of a much larger furniture group when more persons want to join their personalities. Although the conversation area is only a few steps from the front door, the terrace, and the kitchen, it maintains its identity even in plan alone, but this separateness could be further emphasized by wise furnishings. This is the logical place for the "best" furniture in the house: comfortable, handsome chairs and sofa; a soft rug, and worthy enrichment such as paintings, wall sculpture, or a rich fabric above the sofa; metal plaques, plates, or molds near the fireplace; interesting lamps on the table and/or on the wall for reading light and decoration; a large vase or two, flower arrangements, and plants. Although in a house this small it is wise to relate all colors, this is the logical place to use somewhat warmer hues, stronger intensities, and lower values (to emphasize its enclosure) and to indulge in a few lively contrasts. There are also other natural conversation centers: the dining table at or after meals; the terrace and screened porch; and the children's bedrooms.

Music could find a good center in either or both of two locations: a radio-phonograph could be housed in the cabinets between the sofa and chair; or the wall directly opposite the sofa could accommodate a radio, phonograph, and television—or a piano. The sloping ceiling and the complex shape of the whole space would improve acoustics. *Games* of a quiet sort would most likely center at the dining table or on a card table set up in the all-purpose space, while more active ones could spread over the all-purpose space and extend to the terrace, porch, and lawn, for all of these are interconnected, open and uncluttered, and should be surfaced with durable materials. Yes, even the lawn ought to be of the tough, public park type rather than of fragile grass! *Eating* would normally and most conveniently take place at the table permanently set up for four near the kitchen where there is adequate space for serving and also for extending the table for celebrations. For variety, it would be easy to move the table over to the windows; a television supper might be enjoyed in the conversation area or in chairs grouped around the screen; outdoor meals could be eaten on either terrace or screened porch; and all of these could be combined for a large buffet dinner in clement weather.

What materials does the all-purpose space suggest? Clues come from observing that it is the largest, most open and flexible, and most heavily used part of the house. The designer has indicated a tile floor, which unifies it with entrance and kitchen, and these three areas could be surfaced with any durable, easy-to-maintain material such as linoleum, asphalt, vinyl, cork, or rubber—but not wood or carpet. The walls, too, should withstand use. Wood comes to the writers' minds first, although a hard-surfaced wallboard or washable wallpaper or fabric might be used; it does not seem like the place for smoothly painted plaster which quickly shows hard use. There is only one fixed piece of furniture, a large built-in unit which, in addition to providing for storage of miscellaneous articles used here, could incorporate a desk and a radio-phonograph and television. Beyond that, the furniture should be durable, easy-to-move, and light in design and color if the room's openness is to be preserved.

The group-living space has been given the most desirable orientation, which is south and toward the back of the lot where privacy and control of outlook are most easily achieved.

Small children's activities would center in the two bedrooms which can be united by pushing back the folding wall to give a good amount of free space, but they would also be enjoyed in the all-purpose space, terrace, porch, yard, or even in the carport (if safety precautions were taken). This would give the variety that their little souls crave, and yet all are convenient to, some easily visible from, the kitchen.

In summary, four types of group-living space—conversation, all-purpose, screened porch, and open terrace—have been skillfully integrated to give both usable and visual space much beyond that found in typical houses of this size, and they have been sensibly and sensitively related to space for work and private living.

Private Living. Bedrooms and bathrooms are nicely segregated in a unit away from the noisy, group areas with a sound barrier of coat closet, heater room, linen storage, and bedroom closets. Although not large, each of the bedrooms has a good place for the bed, adequate space for dressing, and sufficiently large clothes storage units (beside the door as they should be). Each of the bedrooms gets light and air from two sides through windows that in size and height strike a compromise between the desire for privacy and the desire to look outside. They are high enough above the floor so that furniture can be placed beneath them and some privacy gained yet low enough to give an outlook. Curtains, draperies, or blinds will, of course, be needed as flexible controls. The bathroom is exceptionally well located and planned. While not much larger than the minimum, it is subdivided into one unit with the basin and another with the tub and toilet which greatly increases its efficiency, and it has sufficient storage space for bathroom supplies at point of first use.

This plan offers a mighty good solution to the problem of getting space adequate in size, suitable in shape, and effectively zoned in terms of use. But this is only the beginning.

Housework and Maintenance. With one exception, this phase of home life has been well considered. The complicated tasks of *getting meals* and *laundering* have been simplified by a kitchen measuring 7′6″ x 11′0″. The kitchen is small enough to save steps but is not unduly cramped, and it is strategically located near the dining table, carport, and front door; it is not far from the screened porch, and in direct line of vision with the bathroom, where small children often need supervision and help. The plan is of the "opposite walls" type, putting work centers close together and not in this case inviting much through traffic because there are easy alternative routes. The washer is as near the drying yard as is feasible. *Straightening up* and *cleaning* are lightened by having some basic furniture built into each room: storage and table units in the conversation space; storage, desk and/or music in the all-purpose space; and chests of drawers in each bedroom. There is also at least one good, permanent place for such big furniture as sofa, dining table, beds, and desks. A walk-in linen storage cupboard is convenient to bedrooms and bath, and its size and central location make it the logical place to store housecleaning gear, for which space is also available in the kitchen corner near the carport. Cleaning and maintenance would be expedited by having bedroom and bathroom walls and floors smooth, durable, neutral in color, and with some texture.

The one moderately serious weakness is that there is little space to put all the stuff the househusband needs—lawnmower, garden tools, fertilizer and insecticides; painting equipment; carpentry tools; and odds and ends—to keep house and yard in shape. Nor is there adequate place for baby carriage and bicycles, skis and sleds, trunks and suitcases, and outdoor furniture in winter. True enough, there is a storage compartment well located at the end of the garage, but it would not begin to hold all that a typical family has. This lack of sufficient, convenient, and accessible space to put bulky and/or seasonal items produces a frustrating clutter and a wearisome, continuing urge to put things away when there is no place to put them. Unfortunately, this criticism can be made of almost 99% of the inexpensive, basement-less, attic-less houses of today, and could be inexpensively remedied by trebling the general storage area.

Circulation. This plan is a model of "short, straight, desirable routes from here to there." The carport is beside the kitchen door and only a few steps from the front door, an ideal arrangement possible only when these two outside doors are near each other; near the service yard; and convenient to the porch. This saves many steps through the house. From the front door, paths spread like the fingers of a hand to give direct routes to the kitchen, coat closet, multi-purpose space, conversation area, heater room and linen storage, any of the bedrooms, and the bathroom—without going through any other room. Yet the area devoted only to halls is small. The paths from front door to terrace or porch are also direct and cause minimum interference with furniture arrangement.

Orientation. Relating the house to its environment, especially putting the sun, wind, and outlook in the right place, has been simplified by designing this house for the ideally oriented lot with the street to the north. This allows facing the important rooms toward the south overlooking the private backyard where outdoor living is best. The kitchen faces north, good for the house's hottest room, and each of the bedrooms has windows on two sides, giving welcome cross ventilation and light. The plan could be adapted to lots with the street to the south, east, or west, but as it stands is suitable for none of these. This is not an adverse criticism. No house plan yet developed is equally good facing any point of the compass, a factor regrettably overlooked by many tract builders. Planned for a typical flat city lot, the house has been pushed toward the street as far as most city ordinances permit with two gains: shortening the driveway and having the private backyard as large as possible.

But how does it stand up in terms of design for beauty? Do the forms fulfill their functions, is there variety in unity, balance, continuity, and emphasis?   Are form, line, texture, space, color, and light pleasantly organized?

The preceding analysis has shown how the parts of the plan have been designed and integrated for use, but function, as we use the term, includes more than the utilitarian. Inside and outside, the design of this house promises comfortable living. The carefully studied but unpretentious plan sets the stage for informal living while the handsome, friendly exterior gives a feeling of shelter and relationship to the site. It would not jostle its neighbors. Although the design takes good advantage of new developments, notably in the windows, it is decidedly domestic in character and would never be mistaken for anything other than what it is—a medium small house for a typical American family living in the middle of the 20th century. In brief, its *form follows its function.*

Can a house plan be beautiful? It not only can but should be! Bruce Walker's plan is strictly rectangular in whole and in part with a number of interlocking L-shapes that establish a strong, all-pervading *unity.* There are three major L's—the whole enclosed area, the group-living and work space, and the zone of private living. Notice that private and group areas interlock with the conversation space, a nice refinement because it is the quietest part of the group-living zone. The L-shaped motif can also be seen in the layout of the functionally related multi-purpose space, terrace, and porch; in the furniture arrangement in the conversation alcove; and in the walk from carport to front door. *Variety* comes because none of the rectangles or L's are identical: each varies from the others in size and shape but all grow from the central idea.

The plan has a pleasant asymmetrical *balance,* for the visual weight of the slightly smaller but more solid-looking projecting bedroom wing on the left is compensated for by the greater spread and interest of the wing on the right. The front entrance is almost exactly in the center of the composition although it appears to be much less formally placed. The major *emphasis* in the plan is found in the amount of space given to group living, logical in terms of both use and effect. *Rhythm* is achieved by the consistent rectangles and L-shapes and especially by the way major lines continue through the house. A strong central axis begins at the corner of the projecting bedroom, is carried through the plan by the floor treatment, and emerges at the rear in the edge of the terrace.

Here is an important point in integrated architecture: not only is this line dominant in plan but it parallels the high point of the roof seen from outside and the ceiling seen inside. This is an example of three-dimensional design. Many other lines contribute their share to continuity: the front line of the bedroom wing is carried through by roof and paving to the far edge of the carport; the kitchen counters toward the street align perfectly with the front bedroom closets; the carport kitchen door is in a straight line with the opposite door in the kitchen, the opening into the bedroom hall, and the door to the bath; the south wall of the house continues in the wall shielding the screened porch from the drying yard; and the outer edge of porch and terrace is one line. One might ask if this is "T-square and triangle" design, rigidly and coldly geometrical. We think not at all in this case. Many lines do not carry through; but the major lines, carrying strongly through the plan, give satisfying order, clarity, and discipline too seldom found in house plans.

Now let us start erecting the enclosing walls and roof, as the builder would after laying the foundations, and see what happens. Do they give desirable privacy and protection as well as light, air, and views where wanted? What is the effect as a whole and of the parts?

From the street, the house presents a low informal composition, thoroughly satisfying at first glance and quite remarkable as its subtleties are investigated. The predominantly horizontal lines of the whole mass, the bands of windows, and the gently sloping roof relate it to the ground, but the absence of overhanging eaves (little needed on the north), the narrow siding used vertically, and the opening in the roof near the entrance area give an upward movement to balance the strong horizontality. Had it not been for such devices, the house might have looked squatty and pushed into the ground rather than standing on and rising from it. The street side is not flat, like the side of a barn, but has a sense of movement inviting one into the outside entrance area, which is set back ten feet from the front of the bedroom wing; this movement is repeated by the carport, the back of which recedes another ten feet. These setbacks give a play of light, shade, and shadow, a three-dimensional architectural quality of space, time, and movement. And they divide the composition into three units varied in size and treatment to express the interior divisions; but the simple roof lines bind them together.

Applying a ruler to the drawing shows that the almost exactly centered door acts as a fulcrum for the two asymmetrical wings ingeniously balanced. The bedroom wing at the left, almost as wide as the other two combined (although its simplicity makes it seem smaller) is a straightforward composition of vertical wood and an off-center band of windows which holds its own by its clarity, strength, and forward position. One looks at it, understands it quickly, and then looks where the designer intended him to, at the front door. The central unit dominates the whole because it is centrally placed, relatively complex in design, and includes the entrance door.

A beautifully organized series of form-space relationships are experienced as one starts into the house. Walking toward the protectingly opaque door, one comes into the hospitable shelter of the semi-enclosed outdoor entrance area as the first transitional step between outdoor and indoor scale. The width is the same as that of the multi-purpose space, and the roof introduces one to the height and slope of the ceiling inside, but a hole above the planting bed gives a last glimpse of the sky and brings light and air into the kitchen, entrance hall, and bedroom windows. The small but not cramped entrance hall is the second transitional step, and while in it one could hardly fail to notice the way in which the lines of the floor and the high point of the ceiling, carried through from outside, lead naturally into the group living space. Pausing while being relieved of coat and hat, one would almost automatically look toward the largest expanse of glass in the house. This is the most emphatic part of the interior, and it is not a confining center of interest such as the typical fireplace but an invitation to explore beyond. Fortunately, this is made possible physically by the two doors leading outside. This space is not large, but the knowledge that it is a section of a continuing pattern, the glass reaching to the sloping ceiling, the potential of outdoor living, and then the contrast of the small secure conversation alcove all give it a big feeling. The large window goes to the ceiling but not to the floor. Had this been done, the visual space would have been further increased, but the usable space somewhat decreased because you cannot put furniture as close to a wall of glass as to one of unbreakable material. The windows in the alcove are at the same height as those in the kitchen and bedrooms.

Why was a sloping roof chosen in preference to a flat one? As a matter of fact, the designer submitted an alternate version with a flat roof and, consequently, horizontal ceilings of uniform height. It does not, however, appear as lively or satisfying as does the sloping roof and ceiling which swells up in the center in a buoyant way. The sloping roof introduces the only diagonals in the house and the rhythmic building up and down gives variety, emphasis, and movement. From the exterior it fits in with commonly held ideas of what a roof should look like, and from the inside it gives a refreshing change from all parallel surfaces.

What kind of furniture and what colors? To us, the house calls for simple, natural, unpretentious, but sensitively designed furniture. We have seen that the house is not as unpremeditated and casual as it seems at first glance, and it deserves something better than crude boxes, stereotyped forms, or tricky furniture. Such pieces as those illustrated in Figs. 1-2 and 6, 2-3, 3-3, 4-1 and 10, 11-5, 14-3, 4, and 6 would take their place happily. In a house this small, usefulness and beauty would be increased if most of the pieces were small in size and scale and harmonious in color although they certainly do not have to be identically matched; and if they were not individually "eye-catching" pieces, so that the whole would be seen before the parts.

Because the house inside and out is designed to blend with nature, it would be sensible to have natural colors and textures dominate. Grays, tans, browns, or mixtures of earthy colors for the large floor areas, sparked in a few places by more intense hues; the same colors plus muted blues, greens, yellows, and oranges (not all of these in the same place in equal amounts, of course) could be used for upholstery, bedspreads, towels, draperies and on some of the walls if you wanted them there; and then a few accents of jewel-toned scarlet, cerise, magenta, violet, or a strong acid green. The exterior wood could be given a natural finish or stained lightly with gray or brown. You could, of course, paint the exterior white, yellow, or red, and you could make the interior dazzling with clear strong hues or Spartan-pure with black and white—but we doubt if you, your family, and your friends would like such treatment very long. Certainly these would go against the grain of the idea from which the house grew.

The Second-Prize Winner

The design illustrated in Fig. 18-2 differs from the first in several significant ways, but before discussing them let us read part of what the architect, Ralph Rapson, had to say.

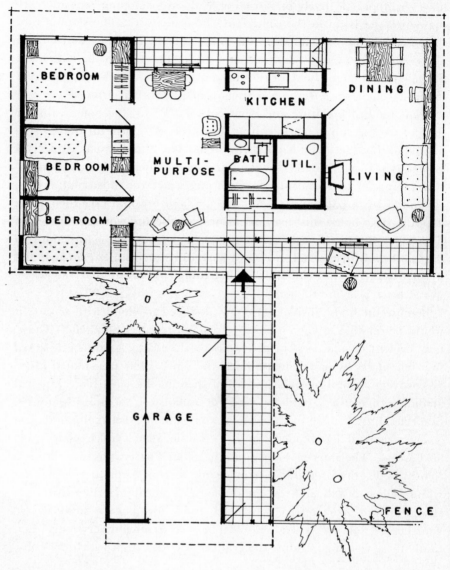

BEDROOM

BEDROOM

BEDROOM

KITCHEN

DINING

MULTI-
PURPOSE

BATH

UTIL.

LIVING

GARAGE

FENCE

18-2 A plan distinguished by a compact, economical utility core and two separated spaces for group living. Ralph Rapson, architect.

The design of this small house for a warm climate was predicated on three basic concepts: 1) that "close" living, necessitated by a house of this size, makes it mandatory that the active living be separated from the passive, with the "heart" of the living—the kitchen—in direct control-contact with each; 2) that all major plan elements have through-ventilation; and 3) that these elements be enclosed in a basically simple shape for ease and economy of construction.

The plan evolved from these basic factors provides two distinct though closely interlocking areas. One is a multi-purpose area for active living: for children and adult rumpus and play; for sewing, ironing and clothes drying on bad days; where the family might take most of their meals and which the mother would not need to worry about keeping spick and span, since guests would normally be entertained in the second area—the space for the more conventional type of living. The utility core, of which the food center is part, is placed between these elements for ease of access and direct control of both.

This has led to a plan divided into four front-to-back zones: going from right to left, we find a quiet living-dining zone 12'3" wide, an entrance and utility zone 10'8" wide, a multi-purpose space of the same width, and then a line of bedrooms exactly as wide as the living-dining space at the other side of the house. This seems like an orderly, rational division of space in a small house for a climate where through-breeze is sought and cold is not serious.

Let us study this plan by concentrating attention on the ways in which it differs from Walker's design.

1. *Group living quarters are sharply divided into two separate units.* As Rapson has pointed out, this separation has notable advantages—but it also raises difficulties. Both areas are long, narrow rectangles, and these proportions are accentuated by the concentration of windows at the ends; the two cannot be combined for large groups; and the duplication of group-living space in a house this small makes everything a little too small.

2. *Kitchen, bath, and utilities form a compact central core.* This has two advantages: the kitchen is in direct contact-control of both living spaces and the rear yard; and the expensive, noisy utilities are brought together to reduce installation costs and facilitate adequate soundproof-

ing. Sensible as this sounds, it is heavily offset in this plan by three serious disadvantages. *First,* this opaque central block closes the center of the house and robs it of its potential spaciousness. *Second,* the theoretically private, quiet, and related bedrooms and bath all open publicly off the multi-purpose space, and the only paths from bedrooms to the bath are diagonally across this highly active space with glass walls at both ends. *Third,* the kitchen and garage are inconveniently far apart; are so located that there is no possibility of having a service yard adjacent to both; and there is no direct, convenient entrance into the kitchen.

3. *The house is set well back from the street.* The lot for which this house was designed is on the north side of the street; and, as is common practice on lots of this orientation, setting the house toward the rear of the lot gives adequate space for an outdoor-living area with a southern exposure. Unfortunately in this case, however, the only entrance from the street to the house goes through the enclosed yard which thus is forced to combine the functions of guest and family entrance, service entrance, and questionably private outdoor-living space.

4. *The garage is designed as a separate unit and placed in front of the house.* This, too, was determined by the lot's orientation. Placing the garage forward shields both house and outdoor-living space and shortens the driveway, while designing it as a separate, loosely connected append- age extends the house pleasantly and informally. *But* this complete separation increases building costs, because the garage requires four in- dependent walls and a distinctly separated roof and, as mentioned above, lengthens the many package-laden trips from garage to kitchen.

5. *There is ample storage space for bulky items in the garage and some free space in the utility room.* Although neither of these locations is of maximum convenience, the space would be most welcome.

6. *Circulation paths are chiefly through rooms.* Only about 30 square feet in the entry are allotted *solely* to traffic whereas Walker's plan has around 75 square feet in the entry and bedroom hall. At first glance, this appears to be a worth-while saving of 45 square feet, but it makes many paths through rooms, interferes with the best furniture arrangement, and, as mentioned above, precludes the highly desirable close relationship among and segregation of private-living quarters.

7. *Orientation has been very well handled for a house to be duplicated on many sites in a mild climate.* The duplication of large glass areas at both ends of the group living space means that the house would be

equally satisfactory if it faced north or south, and with some attention to protection from afternoon sun it could face either east or west.

The design is clean-cut, rational, and possibly a trifle rigid with its predominant narrow rectangles of the plan. The four front-to-back zones, related in widths, give the house an easily appreciated order growing from an idea, quite in contrast to the many house plans that seem to be merely an accumulation of rooms. They give an orderly rhythm and variety, but they do not develop a satisfying emphasis and unity. This organization seems like a self-conscious effort to divide family life into four rigid slices instead of encouraging the plan to grow from family patterns.

Our analysis has purposely emphasized the weaknesses of this house, which is superior to most houses being built today, in order to stimulate your critical ability, to get you to look at the parts by themselves and in relation to the whole. In case we have gone too far let us remind you of these good points:

- Two separated living and eating spaces.
- Economical concentration of utilities.
- Abundant light and ventilation.
- Good use of the typically-wasted front yard.
- Basic logic, order, and adaptability of the plan.

What furnishings and colors does this plan suggest? One could be safe in suggesting the currently popular muted, natural colors and the real or simulated textures which would soften the forms and relate them to the yard. But the plan's clean-cut, precise, rational order might well be emphasized so that the house would affirm its man-made character and assert its independence of nature as houses around the Mediterranean always have and as our Colonial houses certainly did. Light-weight, "functional" metal furniture with plastic upholstery would be harmonious with the spirit of the plan. Pronounced, contrasting colors could emphasize the planes and space. The floor could be of tile red or a deep, bright blue; the smooth walls could be of clear, contrasting colors; the upholstery of stimulating acid colors; and the urgently needed draperies might be white. Thus, as the writers see it, this house would differ from the first-prize winner as strikingly in colors and furnishings as it differs in plan.

The Third-Prize Winner

Wallace Steele's design, Fig. 18-3, was done with the midwest in mind, a section which he knows well from many years spent in Minneapolis and St. Paul. His plan is an uninterrupted rectangle with the "front" entrance in the middle of the west side. The door opens into an entrance area 5 x 7 feet, which in turn has a 5-foot opening into the living room, giving a view through large windows, a door into a generous coat and general storage closet, and a door into the kitchen. Space flows around this solid block, strongly to the right through the living room, activity space, and into the open kitchen, subordinately through the kitchen door to the left. Were this the major entrance used by the family it would bring an undesirable amount of traffic through the living room or kitchen, but this is not the case because the door in the play space is far more convenient for the many ins-and-outs of children, mother, and even father.

The 11'2" x 18'3" living room and study has a south wall of glass and joins forces with the dine-work-play space, a 15'9" x 9'3" area, which opens into the kitchen over an eating counter and through a doorway. Thus the ample living room gains greatly in apparent space through its glass wall and wide openings into entrance and multi-purpose space— but in giving over one long wall to glass and all but four feet of the opposite wall to openings, furniture arrangement is made difficult. As compensation, this open L-arrangement makes it possible to use these two rooms as one or to separate them with screens or curtains, a flexibility not found in either of the plans described above. The 9'0" x 9'0" kitchen has the work centers organized in an L-shape, but with the eating counter it becomes almost a U-plan. The only through-traffic path is a short one and comes desirably between the food and laundry centers.

Bedrooms and bathroom are neatly fitted into a compact, segregated rectangle. The 9'3" x 16'4" master bedroom is of good shape and size (notice how well the furniture takes its place) while the children's rooms are small but adequate and well planned. The bathroom is a typical minimum installation.

The house plan leads naturally to the three basic divisions of a yard— entrance, outdoor living, and service-play—each of which is segregated from the others but integrally related with the interior. The major criticism of this plan is the lack of architectural and functional relationship between garage and house, a matter of no small importance in a Minnesota winter and one that could have been remedied easily by bring-

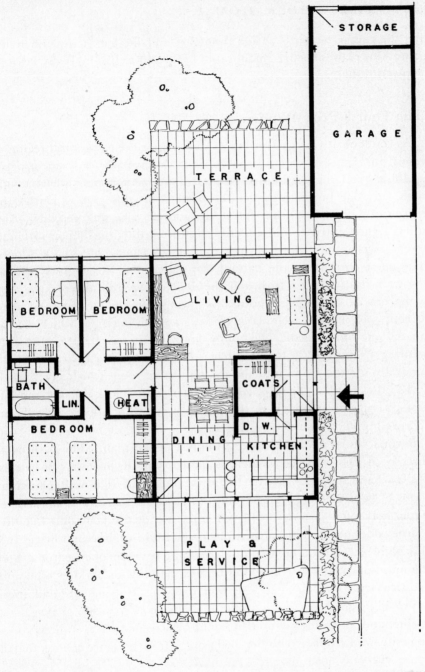

STORAGE

GARAGE

TERRACE

LIVING

BEDROOM BEDROOM

BATH

LIN.

HEAT

COATS

D. W.

BEDROOM

DINING

KITCHEN

PLAY &
SERVICE

18-3 In this plan, the group-living space is L-shaped and can be used as one
unit or readily divided by curtains, screens, or folding doors into two well separated rooms. Wallace S. Steele, architect.

ing the garage forward.　Aside from that and the hard-to-furnish living space, this plan is good, economical to build and to live in, really flexible, and not dull.

The Fourth-Prize Winner

As you look at George Matsumoto's design for the east-central region as shown in Fig. 18-4, you will realize what variety architects can bring to a problem seemingly as limited as was this one.　Another simple rectangle with only one break to shelter the front door, this plan organizes the space quite differently from any of the above.　Like the preceding plan, it has a guest entrance and a family entrance, subtly but importantly different in character from the old concept of "front" and "back" doors. The guest entrance is the natural, convenient one for visitors because the walk leads straight to it and the door opens into an entrance area with coat closet (often forgotten or inconveniently located) and then directly into the very well-planned living and dining areas which can be used as one—or divided.　The family, knowing its way about and usually wanting to go directly to the kitchen or private-living quarters, would naturally use the doors into the multi-purpose room which gives access to all other rooms.　The 9'0" x 8'0" kitchen is the ideal U-shape and has a step-saving pass-through to the dining room which opens broadly on to a well-protected outdoor eating area.

Surprises turn up as we look at the rest of the plan.　The bathroom, directly in line with the kitchen, is placed logically in terms of getting the mechanical aspects of the house together, but is it well placed in terms of family needs?　All factors considered, the answer is affirmative. True, it is some 14 unsecluded feet from two of the bedrooms but this journey does not seem quite as exposed as it did in the second house and this plan makes possible a sliding partition between one bedroom and the multi-purpose space, a flexibility most helpful for children's play in bad weather.　The multi-purpose room truly merits its name: in addition to providing good space away from the living room for work, play, games, sewing, and an eating counter, it could be screened off as a guest room or easily walled off as another bedroom.　It is hard to believe that a house with only 996 square feet can have:

- 3 bedrooms, each 9 x 12 feet
- multi-purpose room, 12 x 12 feet

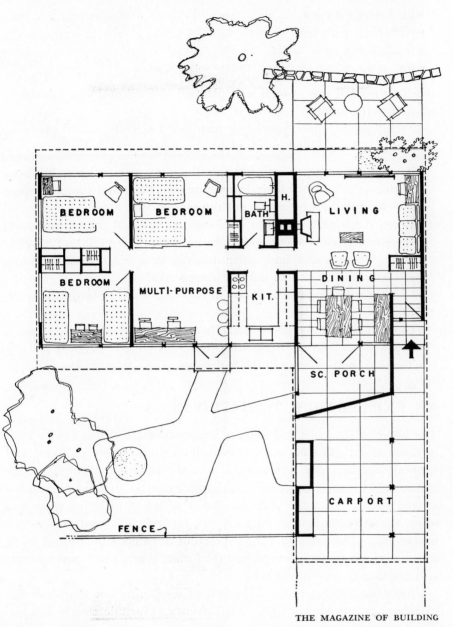

BEDROOM

BEDROOM

BATH

H.

LIVING

BEDROOM

MULTI-PURPOSE

KIT.

DINING

SC. PORCH

FENCE

CARPORT

18-4 An ample living-dining room can be divided by screens. In addition there is a useful multi-purpose room. Notice how well the plan lends itself to good furniture arrangements. George Matsumoto, architect.

- kitchen, 9 x 8 feet
- bathroom, 9 x 5 feet
- living room, 12 x 16 feet
- dining room, 9 x 12 feet

and have each of these rooms well planned in itself and well located in relation to the others.

The following points, previously mentioned as being sound planning practices, are exemplified in this plan.

- Though the living room is not a dead end room, circulation has been routed so as to avoid logical furniture groupings and comes between the living and dining areas, not through either.
- When the window walls at each end of the social zone are opened, there is a space of about 40 feet for entertaining.
- Dining space is adequate, expansible, can be screened from the living room, and is next to an outdoor eating area.
- Cross ventilation is an actuality in two bedrooms, a possibility in the third.
- Closets are near the doors of the bedrooms.
- Linen closet is in the bathroom.
- There is counter space in the bathroom.

AN EXPANDABLE, H-SHAPED PLAN

The house in Figs. 18-5 and 18-6 has been planned so that it can be built in three stages. The *basic house* provides a studio room for living and sleeping, dining space between this and the full-sized kitchen, a large bathroom with two wash basins, and ample closets. It is an economical square, 20′ on each side. *Addition No. 1* adds a large living room and foyer, heater room, storage, and carport, bringing the total area to 706 square feet. *Addition No. 2* is composed of three bedrooms which bring the total square footage to 1376, and the former studio room now becomes a dining and multi-purpose room.

Unlike the compact plans of the four prize-winning houses, this design stretches out into an H-shape. The advantages include clearly differentiated zones for different activities, much outside wall for large windows, a partially enclosed front yard and a protected rear terrace, and interesting variety in plan, interiors, and exteriors. In comparison with compact plans, this and other spreading plans have two disadvantages: they require larger lots and are more expensive to build and heat. Many persons, however, feel that their charm and the manner in which they relate themselves to the site make the additional costs worth while.

THREE TWO-STORY HOUSES

Two-story houses have certain advantages over those on one floor in that they are somewhat cheaper to build and heat and can be placed on smaller lots or leave more of the lot uncovered. Also, the bedrooms are usually placed together but away from the rest of the house at a height that gives greater privacy, more summer breeze, and often a pleasanter outlook. They have been falling from favor, however, because going up and down stairs is fatiguing and the cause of many home accidents; designing an exterior that avoids clumsy, high boxiness is a feat, especially when the house is small; and wanting to live close to the ground has come to be a national urge.

A Three-Bedroom House

The plan illustrated in Fig. 18-7, designed by Jameson and Harrison for a family in Peoria, Illinois, follows quite closely a plan type evolved in Colonial days. The main door is placed in the center of a symmetrical composition and leads into a small entrance area with a coat closet and stairway; an archway to the right leads to the living room while one to the left leads to the dining room. (In many plans of this type the hall goes through the house, opening on to a terrace or garden at the rear and making the open stairway an emphatic design feature.) The living room is as symmetrical as is feasible: the fireplace is centered in one long wall; a door and window are equidistant from the ends of the wall opposite; and a window pierces the middle of each end wall.

All of this suggests a type and arrangement of furniture more formal than we find comfortable today, but we have come to accept, rightly or wrongly, a marked difference between furniture and architecture in such rooms. This living room is better planned than most of this sort: there is adequate wall space for furniture and the only through-traffic path is at one end. The separated dining room is of good size and proportion, as is the kitchen, which is conveniently adjacent to an outside door, a lavatory, and the basement stairway. Upstairs, access to three bedrooms

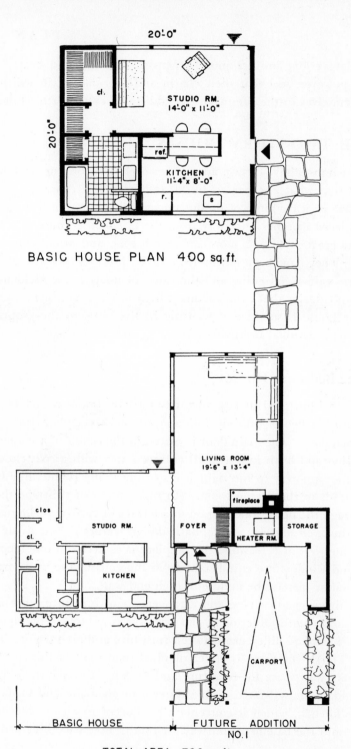

20'-0"

cl.

STUDIO RM.
14'-0" x 11'-0"

20'-0"

ref.

KITCHEN
11'-4" x 8'-0"

r.

s

BASIC HOUSE PLAN 400 sq. ft.

clos

cl.

cl.

STUDIO RM.

B

KITCHEN

FOYER

LIVING ROOM
19'-6" x 13'-4"

fireplace

STORAGE

HEATER RM.

CARPORT

BASIC HOUSE

FUTURE ADDITION
NO. 1

TOTAL AREA 706 sq. ft.

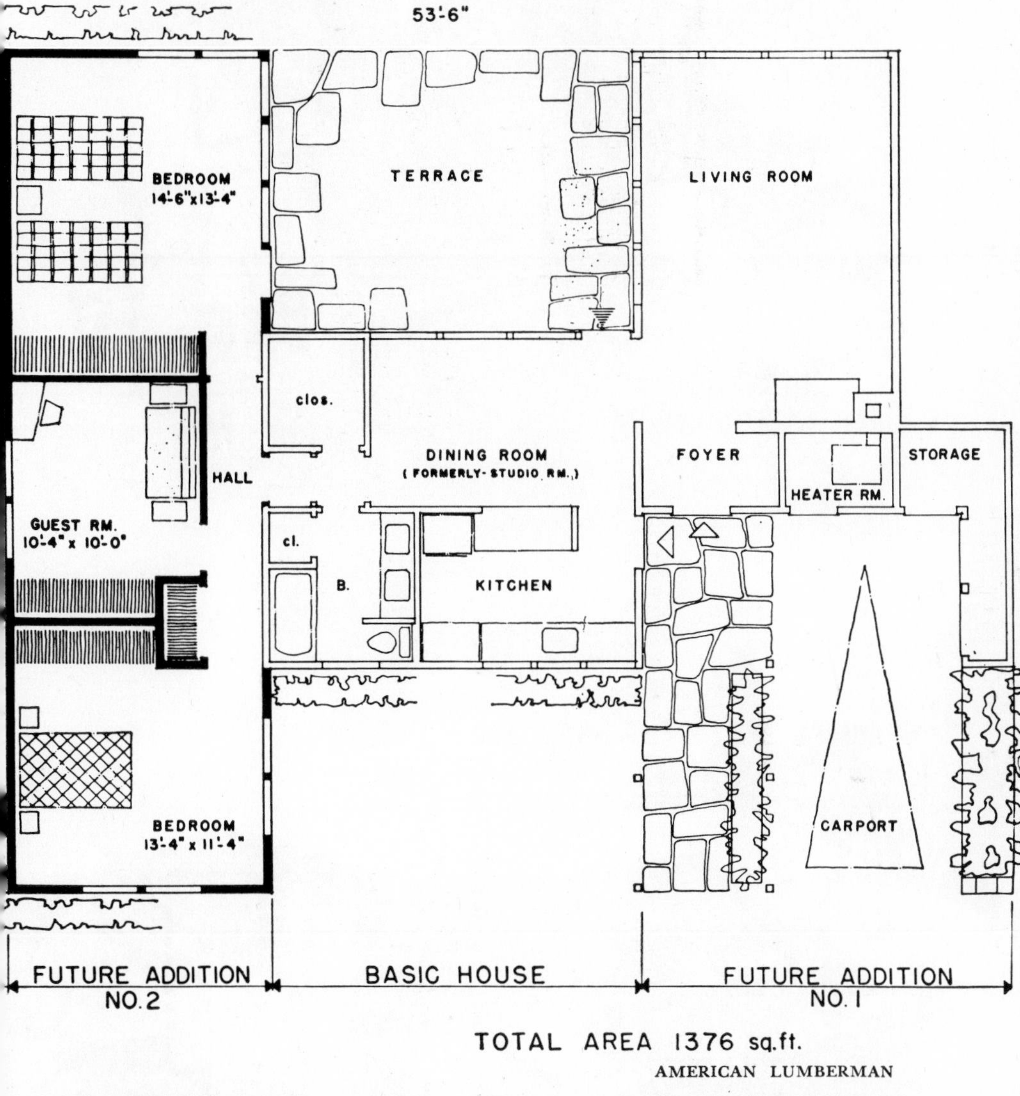

53'-6"

BEDROOM
14'-6"x13'-4"

TERRACE

LIVING ROOM

clos.

DINING ROOM
(FORMERLY- STUDIO RM.)

FOYER

STORAGE

HEATER RM.

HALL

GUEST RM.
10'-4" x 10'-0"

cl.

B.

KITCHEN

BEDROOM
13'-4" x 11'-4"

CARPORT

FUTURE ADDITION
NO. 2

BASIC HOUSE

FUTURE ADDITION
NO. 1

TOTAL AREA 1376 sq.ft.

AMERICAN LUMBERMAN

18-5 A house planned for expansion. *Opposite, top:* Comparable to a two-room apartment, the basic plan is small but comfortable. *Bottom:* The first additional wing consists of a large living room, carport, and heater room and storage. *Above:* The second additional wing concentrates three bedrooms in a secluded wing and gives the house a ranch-type character. Samuel Paul, architect.

open with its large view windows. The remainder of this floor is divided into a kitchen with a good place for eating on one side, and a room suitable for a maid, guest, or seclusion on the other. The second floor is separated into two units—two bedrooms and a bath for children, and a parents' suite of bedroom, bath, and study. All these rooms are generous in size and have bands of windows facing two exposures. The basement which comes above grade toward the lake has a large recreation room and porch, bath, laundry, and heater room. The floor area of this house is almost four times that of the four prize plans, but good use is made of all this space.

Basements give each of these houses another floor. In the first house, the basement has been divided into a laundry-heater room, a work room, and recreation space with small windows bringing a little light and air. The basement of the second house (not shown on the plans) is similarly treated. Because the third house is built into a hillside, half of the basement is entirely above grade and has been planned as a pleasant recrea-

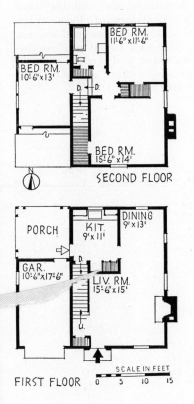

SECOND FLOOR

FIRST FLOOR

SCALE IN FEET
0   5   10   15

THE MAGAZINE OF BUILDING

18-8 An asymmetrical room arrangement, a combined living-dining room, and an attached garage show contemporary trends toward greater flexibility, openness, and usefulness. Raymond D. Goller, architect.

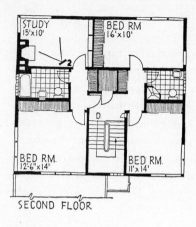

SECOND FLOOR

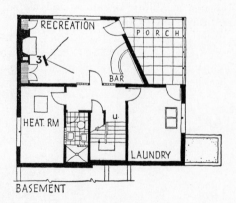

FIRST FLOOR

SCALE IN FEET
0   5   10   15

THE MAGAZINE OF BUILDING

18-9 A multiple-story, hillside house with a straightforward, livable plan. All of the rooms are of good size and shape, have well placed windows, are logically zoned, and open possibilities for sensible furniture groups. Beatty and Strang, architects.

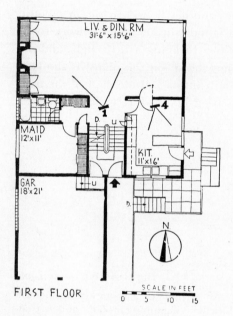

BASEMENT

tion room and porch. Although not popular today, basements have their good points:

- Add relatively inexpensive space without increasing the perimeter of the house or the amount of land covered.
- Completely segregate utilities from living areas (much more important when furnaces were fired with wood or coal than nowadays).
- May reduce cold and dampness from the earth.

Their disadvantages include the following:

- The space is usually unpleasant and uncomfortable.
- Stairs are a hazard and increase labor.
- The first floor of a house with a basement is usually set well above grade, making it difficult to relate the house to outdoor areas.
- Their cost, although low, is not negligible.

SELECTING A HOUSE PLAN

Getting a house with the plan right for you is an exciting prospect, and this section will deal with some of the specific aspects to look for.

Except for purposes of analytical study, the plan should never be thought of as independent of, or separate from, the whole house—but in the following paragraphs we will purposely focus on the plan.

Is the total amount of enclosed space, plus the usable outdoor space, suited to your needs?

Most of us think that we want as much space as possible until we see a spacious old house for sale or for rent. Then we begin wondering about cleaning, maintaining, and heating it, and how we and our furniture would fit into rooms planned for another way of life. This leads to the conclusion that the amount of space is by no means the only consideration even though there is no complete substitute for adequate square footage. Living cramped by having too many persons in too-few square feet is probably worse than living in an inconvenient, hard-to-maintain, but big house—but not as bad as living in a house bigger than you can afford. Let us hope that you do not undergo any extreme! Factors to consider are family size, ages, personalities and way of living, and finances.

- The home as a whole should give each person a minimum of 200 square feet; 250 are much better; and 300 or more give comfortable living.
- The larger the family the less square footage each person needs (or, at least, is likely to get).
- Families heterogeneous in ages and interests as well as those which are gregarious and extroverted usually need more space per person than those who are homogeneous and quieter.
- Finances—annual income and accumulated reserves to pay for original and continuing costs—are a major determinant of house size.
- Usable space is increased by good zoning, convenient relationships among rooms, minimum traffic through rooms, rooms that permit good furniture arrangement, and livable outdoor areas.
- Apparent space can be increased by large, grouped windows; generous openings between rooms; and strong relationship to outdoor areas— as well as the other space-giving devices discussed in Chapter 6.

Is the space appropriately organized for your needs?

Although the actual square footage is the most important single factor, its efficiency and effect depend on the way it is divided.

- The proportion of the space allotted to group, private, and work activities depends on the size, habits, and finances of the family as well as the size of the house. In the four prize-winners, the square footages (which can quickly be translated into percentages by dropping the last zero) allotted to group, work, and private activities are approximately as follows.

	Group	Work	Private	Total
First	370	100	530	1,000
Second	550	100	350	1,000
Third	430	90	480	1,000
Fourth	460	90	450	1,000

The space devoted to kitchen and utilities shows little variation because equipment is standardized and in small houses few people want to use any more of their precious space here than is necessary. But notice the great variation in space allotted for group and private living in the first two plans. In the first, bedrooms and bath are larger and open off their own completely private hall, which therefore must be regarded as part of that zone, while in the second these rooms have been reduced to a minimum and circulation among them is through definitely group space. The first is better suited to individuals who like privacy, the second to a family that wants to share all.

■ Divisions within the group space are the next consideration. The first plan has a minimum of divisions, the second has two rigidly separated areas, the third rather distinctly separates quiet living from eating and noisy play but without a fixed wall, and the fourth has two separated rooms, one of which can be divided into two parts by a folding screen. Which would meet your needs best?

■ Divisions within the work space in a small house are usually at a minimum, consisting of nothing more than separating the heater from the combined kitchen-laundry. In larger houses some segregation of cooking and laundry is desirable.

■ Divisions of the private space vary considerably even in houses of the same total size, chiefly in the number of bedrooms and bathrooms but also in the degree of privacy given these rooms by a bedroom hall, by movable partitions between bedrooms or between them and activity space, and by the inclusion or exclusion of a room for private hobbies or solitude.

■ The way in which space is divided—or undivided—marks the chief difference between today's and yesterday's architecture. We can neither afford, nor do we usually want, rooms for each activity, sealed off from others, but find happiness in homes with as few permanent, opaque walls as is compatible with the diversity of home activities. L-shaped rooms, folding or sliding doors or screens, and such room-dividers as curtains, draperies, or free-standing storage units less than ceiling height are widely used.

Are the rooms of suitable size?

All that was said about the total size of the house applies to room size because in general—but not always—house size is the chief determinant of room size. Below are some typical square footages of various types of rooms.

	Entrance Area	Living Space	Dining Space	Dining Alcove
SMALL	25-30	150-200	100-130	25-40
MEDIUM	35-40	220-280	150-180	50-70
LARGE	45-	300-	200-	80-

	Kitchen	Bedrooms	Bathrooms	Heater Room
SMALL	50-80	80-130	33-35	12-15
MEDIUM	100-140	140-190	40-45	18-25
LARGE	160-	200-	50-	30-

In thinking about these sizes, keep the following in mind:

- Actual square footage of floor area is probably the most important factor but shape, location and size of openings, relationship to other rooms, relationship to outdoor areas, and wall, floor, and ceiling treatment greatly affect usable and apparent space.
- The size and composition of the family greatly affects room size.
- Four persons can be compacted into a dining alcove of 20 square feet but six persons need almost 60 for any degree of comfort and ease of serving.
- Twin beds, which occupy 40 square feet, can seldom be squeezed into a bedroom of less than 130 square feet although in Matsumoto's plan (Fig. 18-4) they are fitted into 108 square feet.

Are the rooms of useful, pleasant shape?

Generalizing about room shapes is hazardous because their use, size, and total design qualify everything said below.

- Squares are seldom the best possible shape today except when they measure less than 12 feet on each side and are used for dining, particularly with a round table. Otherwise, they are hard to furnish advantageously.
- Rectangles are the normal shapes and work best when their proportions range from around 1 to 1.2 (approximately 10′ x 12′, 12′ x 15′, or 16′ x 20′) up to 1 to 1.7 (approximately 5′ x 8′, 10′ x 15′, or 12′ x 18′). If more nearly square than the first set of proportions, rooms lose their rectangularity without gaining the stability of the square and thus seem indecisive. If their proportions closely approach 1 to 2 as do the living and activity rooms in Fig. 18-2, rooms become corridor-like unless clearly differentiated by furniture into two areas (which, of course, may be a good idea if that is what you want and your furniture is suitable).
- L-shapes are happy solutions for definitely dual-purpose rooms, such as living rooms with a quiet alcove for conversation or dining and

kitchens with a semi-separated laundry. Although seldom done, bed-rooms in which either the beds, a desk and chair, or closets and dress-ing equipment are put in their own nooks are remarkably pleasant.

- Rectangles with one diagonal wall seem to open a room and give it movement, especially in group-living space, but they run up building costs and are not easy to furnish.
- All the other wonderful shapes—pentagons, hexagons, and octagons; circles, ellipses, and free curves; and non-rigid combinations of straight lines—bring variety and excitement as well as markedly increased cost and the possibility that they may be neither useful nor beautiful.

Will the rooms take your furniture gracefully and efficiently?

Beginning the actual drawing of house plans with furniture arrange-ments and then placing walls, windows, and doors where they ought to come is more sensible than the customary procedure of designing a house and then checking to see if the furniture will fit.

- First consideration is sufficient floor area for your furniture and your movements.
- Second comes sufficient unbroken wall space for beds, davenports, and large case goods.
- Third is the problem of getting the furniture into satisfactory groups, sequestered from but not hampering necessary circulation.

The means to this end, discussed above and below, are having rooms of good size and shape sensibly related to each other, grouping doors and windows coming below furniture height together, and planning circula-tion *among* and *in* rooms.

Is the space effectively zoned?

Cities are zoned by designating certain areas for each kind of use, such as industry; and homes benefit from similar planning. In both, the prin-ciples are the same, but home zoning is much the simpler.

- The minimum essential is segregating the quiet from the noisy areas. A good quick way to check a plan is to color the noisy areas with red, the quiet with green, and then check the sense that the pattern makes. (Circulation paths and areas might well be colored with yellow.)
- It is desirable to have well-defined zones for group activities, private living, and work, and these zones should extend to the landscape development.

■ The typical two-story house with second floor bedrooms is, almost automatically, at least fairly well zoned.

■ The most typical zoning errors in one-story houses are likely to be in indoor-outdoor relationships—separating the kitchen from the garage, thereby precluding a single convenient service yard; and turning the living room toward the street, in which case it is not easy to unite it with a protected terrace or lawn.

■ Circulation paths logically come between zones, not through them.

Is the circulation satisfactory?

Short, desirable routes from here to there simplify housekeeping and make home life pleasant. The tough part of the problem is achieving this goal without excessive hall area. Strangely enough, little serious thought was given to good circulation, even in palaces, until the 18th century, and many builders still forget that traffic through rooms greatly lessens their usable space.

■ The routes from the garage to the "front" and "back" doors should be short and offer protection in bad weather. Locating these two doors near each other simplifies this as well as concentrating indoor traffic to and from the kitchen.

■ Ideally, you should be able to get from outdoors to any room in the house and inside from each room to any other without going through another room except a multi-purpose room and possibly the dining space.

■ Keeping doors as close together as feasible and near the corners of rooms is a fundamental principle because it not only shortens traffic paths but promotes good furniture arrangement. This applies to the "front" and "back" entrances and the doors in each room including those on closets.

■ Living rooms should not invite through traffic as they do in the currently popular "ranch house plans" with the living room stretching as the only link between the kitchen at one end and bedrooms and bath at the other.

■ Some important differences between the newer and older approaches to planning include:

Incorporating the garage as part of the house (Figs. 18-1 and 5); more outside doors, especially from group-living space, but also from bedrooms, to terraces; making the "back" door into a "family" entrance to a multi-purpose space instead of smack into the kitchen

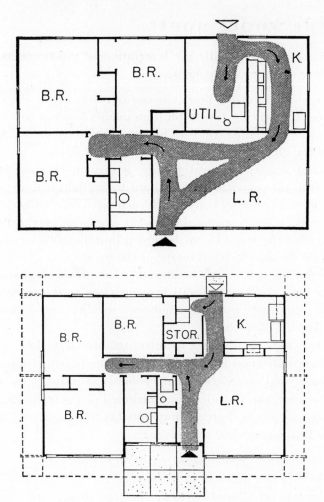

18-10 Time, energy, space, and wear on floors can be saved with an efficient circulation pattern. Above is the plan used for some years by a manufacturer of prefabricated houses. Below is the improvement made by architect Henry Hill. The exterior designed with the lower plan is shown in Figure 19-5.

(Figs. 18-3 and 4); having a guest entrance area even in small houses (Figs. 18-1, 2, 3, 4, 5, and 7); widening what would formerly have been a narrow hall into a usable activity area (Fig. 2-4) or at least lining it with storage space.

Is the shape of the plan sensible?

The shape of the plan affects construction, maintenance, and heating costs; the exposures of rooms; the size and shape of the necessary land;

the landscape plan, especially the integration of indoor-outdoor living; and the basic character of the house.

- Simple, compact shapes lower the cost of construction, exterior maintenance, and heating; can be built on smaller lots and still leave some expanse of yard; and give small houses a simplicity and unity in keeping with their size and pleasant with their neighbors.

    Squares are seldom used because a disproportionate amount of space is in the center where it is hard to get light and air—except in medium size, two-story houses with each room on a corner.

    Rectangles are economical, pleasant (the plan of the Parthenon, often called the world's most beautiful building, is a rectangle), and minimize the major disadvantage of the square.

    L-shapes are more costly because they have two more corners and a greater length of exterior wall in proportion to the space enclosed, but they give more space for windows, provide a semi-enclosed patio, and take hold of the lot.

- More elaborate shapes are expensive, require larger lots, and unless firmly controlled may lead to haphazard, complicated results; *but* they can give several exposures in many rooms, can relate harmoniously to the landscape, can provide varied sheltered places for outdoor living, and can have a high degree of individuality in themselves and in relation to their owners and to their site.

Is—or can—the plan be effectively oriented on the site?

Orientation is best defined as relation to the environment, and this includes the sun, wind, and outlook; the size, shape, and slope of the lot and its relation to the street; and existing trees, rocks, water, and so forth.   In house design, orientation affects the directions in which the different rooms face, the location of windows and ventilators, and the location of the house on the lot.   Here are some points to remember.

- The sun brings heat, light, and cheer chiefly from the south.
- Summer breezes are likely to come from the west and winter winds from the north, but there is much variation from region to region and even from lot to lot.
- Outlooks follow no pattern—except that on typical city lots the best outlook is into your own private yard.
- Most city lots are about 60' by 100', flat, have no notable view and only occasionally a tree or two, and face all points of the compass.

There is general agreement *for typical situations* on the following.

- Group-living space should take advantage of the best outlook, have the privacy needed for living behind the house's largest windows as well as for the related outdoor areas, and get winter sun. A southern exposure is generally best if it does not sacrifice privacy and pleasant outlook.
- The kitchen deserves a good outlook because much time is spent there; ample daylight, preferably with morning sun; and some privacy. Northeast is a desirable exposure.
- Private-living quarters deserve privacy, as their name suggests. South is the preferred exposure—but usually there is little choice.
- Bathrooms should be placed where they are most convenient, for privacy can be assured by high windows and there is no pressing need for sun or outlook.
- Utility rooms can be anywhere because they demand no windows.
- Garages need only be convenient to the street and house.

Location of the house on the lot varies because much depends on the size and shape of lot and house, location of the street, any natural features and community restrictions. For typical situations, though, the following is good practice.

- A maximum of usable private yard and a minimum of driveway usually come when the long dimension of the house parallels the street and the house is as near the street as feasible.
- One usable side yard can be had on an ample lot by placing the house nearer one side than the other.
- On lots facing south, the house is often pushed toward the back and some of the front yard made private (Fig. 18-2).

It is clear that no single house plan will fit every lot nor is a standardized location on all lots sensible.

Does the house lend itself to desirable or necessary change?

It is next to impossible to predict what the future will bring, but knowing that life and change are synonymous strongly suggests planning for flexibility.

- Family patterns change as children are born, develop, and leave the nest, an observation well heeded in expandable houses. The newborn infant must sleep near his parents and for several years be easily supervised; the child in elementary school is beginning to assert the independence that flowers in adolescence, and after completing high school is more than likely to live at home only during vacations.

■ Limited finances coupled with inability to predict family size often make it desirable to begin with a small house carefully planned for possible additions.

■ Business opportunities, health, or the desire for change often make it necessary to sell or rent one's home.

■ All of these indicate the advisability of:

Selecting a plan that fits, or can easily be adapted to, the needs of others, possibly at the expense of some highly individualized desires.

Making certain that future additions are economically possible unless your house is of medium or large size in the beginning.

Keeping to a minimum hard-to-move interior partitions by substituting, wherever feasible, movable storage walls, sliding or folding doors, and the like.

This may sound as if you should select a plan for others or for another way of living rather than for your own present pattern, and it does have a good bit of this quality. But it is directly comparable to insurance, which is a safeguard against what you neither want nor expect.

Is the plan beautiful?

Once the house is built, the plan is never seen as a whole—but it is certainly felt as one lives with it. Beautiful buildings do not develop from awkward plans no matter how well walls, ceilings, and roofs are designed. A plan without variety in unity, balance, rhythm, and emphasis has no more to commend it than does a fireplace or piece of furniture lacking these qualities. Study a plan with the aims and principles of design in mind quite as carefully as you would the pattern in a textile or the composition of a painting—perhaps more carefully, because the plan may well outlast fabric and picture.

CHAPTER 19

Exterior Design

AS IN THE PRECEDING CHAPTER, we will concentrate on one phase of the total home, exterior design in this instance, while remembering that the outsides of houses are expressions of their occupants' ideals and ways of living, of the plan from which they should grow, of the environment in which they stand as well as the suitability of the materials and the visual pleasantness as a whole. Exterior design includes making the house attractive from the street, but it is a great deal more than that.

TWO NEW ENGLAND HOUSES

We can profitably begin with a study of two houses built in the New England states, each of which admirably fulfills its intended functions.

An 18th-Century House

Some two hundred years ago, the house shown in Fig. 19-1 was contemporary. Now known as the Ropes Memorial, it is carefully preserved as a document of 18th-century homes in Salem, Massachusetts. It is what we think of as New England Colonial domestic architecture. By no means, though, did all of the houses look just like this one, for then as now there was diversity.

19-1 The Ropes Memorial in Salem, Massachusetts, exemplifies the formality of 18th-century New England exterior design. When built, it was "modern."

The exterior mass is simple and rectangular, pleasantly proportioned and moderately horizontal in shape. The doorway, centrally located and enriched with Ionic columns and cornice, is the dominant feature of the front, and leads into a central hall. Nine identical windows with small rectangular panes in double-hung sashes march across the façade in two ranks to give a steady, rhythmic beat. Although the windows are higher than they are wide and only about half as wide as the wall spaces between each pair, the once-utilitarian shutters stretch them out to suggest two horizontal bands. A cornice above the second floor windows makes a graceful transition between horizontal wall and sloping roof and also strongly reinforces the horizontality of the wood siding and the window pattern. Three dormer windows, each under a small roof echoing the lines of the whole roof, project to let light and air into the third story. A simple balustrade, suggesting a "captain's walk," obscures the roof's peak. Two substantial brick chimneys extend well above the roof and give clues as to the locations of the fireplaces. The beautifully detailed wood fence carries the spirit of the house out to the sidewalk and separates the front lawn from the street.

This is a satisfyingly beautiful house expressing an ordered, graceful, unhurried life. Although formal and impressive, it is neither pretentious nor rigid. The house stands frankly as a man-made addition to the landscape in somewhat assertive contrast to its setting, as does all Classical architecture. It belongs to the great movement known as the Renaissance, the rebirth of the Classic ideals of symmetry, moderation, and order. We have much to learn from houses like these, but we can no longer take refuge, honestly and happily, behind the façades of other men's architecture.

A Contemporary New England House

The house built by architect Joseph Stein for his family is not many miles from the Ropes Memorial, but it is separated from it by two centuries which have brought drastic changes in American home life. This

PHOTOGRAPH BY HANS VAN NES

19-2 Architect Joseph Stein's own home in Connecticut illustrates contemporary informality and simplicity based on a strong sense of order.

PHOTOGRAPH BY HANS VAN NES

19-3 The interior of Stein's home has the same character and some of the same materials as the exterior. Unboxlike, it is a good example of the manner in which contemporary architects handle walls and ceilings to make them more than a mere background.

is a small home for a man, his wife, and their small daughter, who live informally and without servants. Although it takes full advantage of new developments in materials, construction, and equipment, it flaunts none of these in our faces. The exterior (Fig. 19-2) illustrates many current trends.

The lot on which this house stands measures about 100 feet on each side and slopes down toward the street at the west as well as slightly toward the south, where it faces a city-maintained park and nursery. The house is elevated on an exposed foundation of local fieldstone masonry, a traditional practice in rural New England where snow may be deep, and this masonry is repeated in the low terrace wall and in the retaining wall at the left. This helps tie the house to its land.

The informally balanced south façade looks low and long because of its proportions and the dominant horizontal lines. Its two unequal units are developed differently but harmoniously. One would guess at once that the shorter unit at the left holds the living room because of its larger windows, door opening onto the terrace, and the trellis shading the terrace, all of which make it the dominant part. One would quickly surmise that the longer unit at the right is composed of two smaller, less important rooms, which in this case are the kitchen and one bedroom. This unit is simply treated as two horizontal bands almost exactly equal in height but not repetitious because the lower band is of uninterrupted vertical boards while the upper band is rhythmically divided into two unequal sections, each subdivided into three areas of glass.

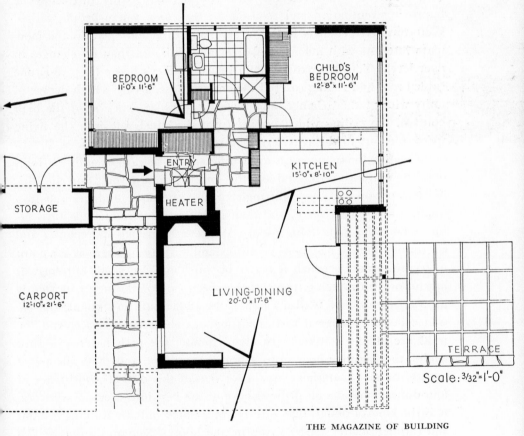

THE MAGAZINE OF BUILDING

19-4 Efficiency, pleasantness, and clear relation to interior and exterior design are among the many excellences of the plan of Stein's home.

The roof is an unusually important factor in this design, combining as it does flat and gabled sections. The flat section establishes a plane that carries *all around and into* the house. This plane, coming at the top of *all* windows and doors, is the roof over kitchen, bedrooms, and carport, the trellis over the terrace, and the overhang above the west windows; and on the inside, it is the ceiling height of entrance, kitchen, and bedrooms as well as the top line of the boarding on the living-room wall (Fig. 19-3). This unifying plane would have been merely a flat roof and ceiling had it not been interpenetrated by the gable. Inside and outside, the double-pitched roof expresses the importance of the major room. It adds variety and emphasis to the exterior and is in harmony with traditional New England roof shapes, but it is even more important in the interior where it contributes considerable spatial interest while improving ventilation and acoustics in the room where people gather. Well-considered changes in ceiling level and direction open up and modulate interiors with much less danger and nuisance than do changes in floor level. You will recall that in Bruce Walker's house (Fig. 18-1) one gabled roof and ceiling covered the entire house, giving a high degree of unity with gradual change, and that the entrance area was at the high point of the ceiling which carried from the street side into the living space and out to the rear terrace through the large window wall. In Stein's house the treatment is quite different. The carport and the trellis over the entrance walk establish the lowest ceiling level. Entering this house a person makes a right-angle turn at the door, finds himself in a small, low-ceilinged space, and then makes another right-angle turn before seeing the high living room. Walker's house has more unity and continuity, Stein's has more variation and surprise. There is no point in trying to decide which is better because both are good, but there is much point in noticing that each has been carried through consistently in every detail. In Walker's house, the traffic path is straight, the entrance flooring material carries throughout the activity space, and the walls are of one material. In Stein's house, the path has two abrupt angles, the flagstone floor stops at the living room, and the walls are of two contrasting materials. Again we repeat, this over-all consistency of four-dimensional design is the essence of the best in contemporary work. It is the kind of design that is fully appreciated only by walking around and through, better yet by living in, the house. Seldom do one or two photographs do it justice.

"Articulation" is a theme favored by contemporary designers. In dictionary phrases, it means "expressed or formulated clearly, systematically, or distinctly." In architecture, it means making the parts clear, clean, and distinct; and there is no slurring or mumbling in Stein's house or in the façade of the Ropes Memorial. Not only do the roof-ceiling planes tell their story, but so do the walls. For example, in Stein's house the cinder block end-walls of the kitchen-bedroom wing stand as vertical planes, resting on but distinct from the foundation and supporting their share of the roof. Their independence is further asserted by the way in which they project a few inches beyond the wall between them: this wall of wood and glass is recessed so that it resembles a screen (or a plane) filling the space between its masonry ends, above the masonry band, and below the slightly projecting roof. If we now look at the wall screening the living room from the terrace, we find that it is almost abruptly distinguished from the kitchen-bedroom wing by its set-back position, its large windows, the trellis, and its upward continuity with the gable. Looked at by itself, nothing could be clearer than its three large sections of fixed glass, the doorway, and the horizontal band of wood. It, too, gains freedom from the foundation by coming forward far enough to make a deep shadow.

In contemporary exteriors, articulation goes beyond a clean enunciation of planes into the realm of having the planes express what stands behind, below, or above them—the exterior tells you a good bit about the plan and the interior. This is not true of most buildings in the Classical tradition. The exterior of the Ropes Memorial, for example, tells you where the entrance hall is and how many floors the building has, both of which are almost unavoidable, but gives no hint of the size or function of the rooms behind the walls and windows. One can be reasonably sure that there is one room at each side of the entrance but their length and use are not indicated because window-size and location were determined by an arbitrary desire for a symmetrical composition of identical windows. In contrast to this treatment of a façade as a unifying but unrevealing mask, often at the expense of interior needs, Stein has placed big windows in the big room, smaller windows in the smaller rooms. This is primarily a matter of utility and economy—the large living room needs more light, less privacy, and can afford to sacrifice a little more wall space to glass than can the kitchen and bedroom—but it also raises the living room to a higher pitch and it gives the satisfaction of frank exterior expression of the interior.

Had the designer stopped with merely putting windows of the right size in the right place for good interiors, he would have committed the folly that makes a fair number of contemporary exteriors unappealing with their spotty, awkward disunity. In architecture as in speech, clear enunciation is not enough. The parts must be organized in an intellectually and emotionally satisfying whole. Repetition and progression are time-tested means to which contemporary architects have added a renewed emphasis on lines, forms, spaces, colors, and textures that carry through to a logically satisfying, or, better, an exhilarating, conclusion. Stein's house would have been much less pleasant had the trellis been higher or lower than the two sections of flat roof it joins or had some of the windows in the kitchen-bedroom wing not lined up with their partners. There is one noticeable lack of alignment in the longer dining-space window at the left of the door. Why is this longer? Three reasons suggest themselves. First, it is pleasant to eat near a window from which you can really see the outdoors; second, this section of the room would have been darker than the southwest corner (notice the large west windows in the plan and exterior); and third, this break in the strong continuity found everywhere else is a welcome variation and makes that corner a slightly dominant "stopping place" to rest the eyes from the sweeping movements of the rest of the house.

The modern predilection for simplicity and continuity might seem as arbitrary as the Classical preference for measured rhythms and symmetry, and perhaps it is. Often, certainly, lines and forms are carried well beyond utilitarian needs, and windows form bands from one wall to another even though it may be hard to defend the need for every pane of glass. But utility and economy are not the only goals of home planning! In defense of contemporary trends, one can say that some kind of over-all design or discipline is always necessary to satisfy our need for order; that present-day design devices keep our shrinking homes from looking embarrassingly small and boxy without indulging in falsifications; and that these devices (even though they have become almost a formula) permit more flexibility and adaptation to individual problems than do those of the Classical tradition. Asymmetrical equilibrium is more flexible than its counterpart, and even though an effort is made to align tops and bottoms of groups of windows, this practice allows more sensitive adaptation to special needs than does the adoption of one size and shape and insistence on identical spacing regardless of other, often much more important, considerations.

One will search in vain for any applied exterior ornamentation in this house or in 99 per cent of contemporary work. There are many reasons, among the more important of which are the high cost of ornament, the long-continued reaction to the abundantly decorated Victorian houses, the failure to date of architects in general to produce suitable ornament, and what seems to be a positive preference for simplicity. Instead of applied enrichment, the contemporary architect makes his basic forms interesting and exploits the potentialities of his materials.

We have looked at the ways in which Stein has organized his forms, and it is now time to study the materials. There are five exterior materials. *Stone*, irregularly cut and only partially smoothed, has been used where a sense of weight and relationship to such fundamentals as the ground and fire make it suitable—foundations, retaining walls, entrance walk and floor of entrance area, and fireplace. Much loved for its feeling of permanence and its variety of color, texture, and shape, the stone work here is not a few spotty patches but a minor theme carrying through the design. *Cinder blocks*, also masonry but much lighter in physical and visual weight, better insulation, more regular in shape, and less expensive than stone, form the north-south walls of the bedroom-kitchen wing. They are not carried around corners because then these walls would have lost the feeling of planes. *Naturally finished cedar boards* fill the exterior areas between masonry and glass as well as sheathing some of the interior walls and ceiling. *Painted wood* has been used in all slender, elongated forms—trim around doors and windows, trellis, and edges of roof—for variety and contrast, but also because these shapes are effective when smooth and precise. *Glass*, the smoothest and most precise of the five materials, fills more than half of the south walls and were it not for the fact that its transparency makes it inconspicuous it would have been the dominant material. In looking at this house, one is not conscious of five different materials because each has been used logically and consistently in simple areas; has been repeated or continued to produce a unified, rhythmic whole; and the areas exemplify dominance and subordination. Two other materials play an important role in the interior. *Plaster*, smooth and light colored like the painted exterior wood, surfaces some of the walls, and *cork*, dark in color and textured, covers the floor. With satisfying materials defining interesting forms, there is little need for additional ornament.

So much for the exterior, the emphasis of this chapter, but in the total picture less important than the interior or the plan.

The combined living-dining room, measuring 17′6″ by 20′0″ (or 350 square feet), is unusually pleasant. With its secure enclosure on the north side, it can afford even in New England considerable openness toward the south. Cork covers the concrete, radiantly heated floor slab and provides a quiet background for the lively rug. Cedar boarding, similar to the exterior, sheaths the walls to window and door-tops (the flat roof-plane), then plaster fills the less regular spaces to the ceiling and around the fireplace, and the wood appears again on the ceiling. This change of materials in a logical but somewhat unexpected way lightens and enlivens the interior, draws attention to the fireplace, and cleanly delineates the ceiling as two sloping planes in much the same way that contemporary painters use color and texture to define form and space.

The plan (Fig. 19-4) is simple, straightforward, and well considered. All rooms are economically related to the entry and immediately accessible from it. The only path *through* a room is from the entry to the terrace, and this is an arc between the spaces allocated to living and to dining. If there has to be such a path, and there usually does have to be one of exactly this sort, it logically comes between furniture grouped for different functions. Although almost regular and square, the living room gains greatly in spaciousness and informality through the deviations from rigid regularity. Even though no furniture is shown in the plan, the room shape and the fenestration suggest three types of activities: on the north side, secure enclosure near the fireplace and a quiet corner for the desk and bookcases near the window; the well lighted southwest section is for more active, open living; and the southeast corner within arm's reach of the kitchen and a few steps from the terrace is for dining. The kitchen is one unit of the group-living space, a practice often followed in New England houses of the 17th century. This informal arrangement makes meal-getting, as well as eating, a family affair and part of the fun when company comes. Should a rare occasion make desirable the separation of the kitchen, a folding screen could be used. Bedrooms and bath are of good size and shape, well segregated from the living-with-others space (although one could wish that the bathroom door were not quite so visible from the living room). Between the kitchen and child's bedroom is a fixed plane of glass, planned to allow Mrs. Stein to watch their baby daughter without stopping her work. Actually, according to the architect, it is the baby who seems to be supervising the kitchen activities—but at a safe distance.

The chief reason for selecting this house for discussion is that the *plan, interior, and exterior are expressions of a unified idea;* but there are other reasons, such as the intelligent use of large windows in a fairly extreme climate, the adroit use of varied materials, the sensitive relation of house to site, and the sympathetic adaptation of mid-20th-century ideas to a section of the United States rich in architectural tradition.

SMALL HOUSES

Making the exterior of a small house home-like and pleasant is a tough problem because all costs have to be kept to a minimum, an economically simple plan brings no basic shape interest, the much-desired large windows tend to be out of scale with a small structure, and often the design will be reproduced hundreds of times.

What can the architect do to make a minimum dwelling look like a pleasant home?

- Keep the total design simple and unpretentious, "quiet" rather than "noisy," so that it will take and keep its place on a street with many other houses—and yet have some character of its own.
- Proportion the basic mass pleasantly.
- Organize the openings and wall areas in a good pattern.
- Employ some of many devices that increase apparent size.
- Select suitable exterior materials.

The First Small House

When Henry Hill was retained by one of the country's largest house prefabricators to design a dwelling with only 864 square feet and three bedrooms, he produced the handsome design shown in Fig. 19-5. The mass is long and low, a character underlined by the bands of windows, the uninterrupted areas of horizontal wood siding, and the low double-pitched roof with 3'2" overhangs on all sides. It is broken only by the slightly recessed entrance for additional shelter and a note of emphasis. The street façade is composed of three equal units. Why equal? First because such divisions are indicated by the plan (Fig. 18-10), and second because this equality steadies the whole composition, an important factor when the treatment of each division has to be different for functional reasons. The central section has an off-center door balanced by a high window in the bathroom; the living room has a strip of windows from

19-5 Architect Henry Hill's design for a mass-produced small house is evidence that prefabricated houses need not be unattractive or commonplace.

table height to the ceiling; and the bedroom has an equally long window band but at the same height as the bathroom window and for the same reason. A low, substantial, centered chimney looks as though it belongs to the house. The end wall shows the same trend toward symmetry as does the front. Two small windows were needed for ventilation and light but privacy was important. Two little separated peepholes would have been nothing but picayune spots. The architect solved this problem by making them units of a well-designed vertical panel. Although small, mass-produced, and economical, it is a house that could proudly be called home.

The Second Small House

When you look at the photograph of Hill's own weekend house in Carmel, California (Fig. 19-6), you are justified in wondering what is exterior, what is interior, and what is garden because all of these are essentially one. The living-room floor is divided from the terrace only by posts supporting the roof and by floor-to-ceiling panes of glass, the ceiling goes over this glass wall (as the floor goes under it) to become overhead shelter for the terrace, and the wood wall begins as enclosure for the living room but continues as an outdoor screen secluding both indoor and outdoor living space from passersby.

About the same size as his prefab, Hill's vacation house is as individualized as his design for mass-production is standardized. The problems are totally different. Carmel is an informal, resort-like community in which effort has been made to preserve the charm of wooded, rocky land sloping down to the Pacific. Mr. Hill's lot slopes toward the ocean two blocks away and affords a view of a distant point but at the risk of losing privacy. No conventional plan and exterior would have combined enjoyment of the view from inside and outside with privacy on this site. Important facets of this ingenious solution include placing the house on

PHOTOGRAPH BY ROGER STURTEVANT

19-6 Henry Hill's own vacation house in Carmel, California, is a highly individualized design for a very special site.

the high land at the rear, turning it at the best angle, using opaque walls where needed and glass walls wherever feasible, and treating the land-scaping as part of the whole design.   Native Carmel stone is used for the fireplace wall and the floor in front of it; wood is used for the post and beam structural system, the ceiling, most of the house walls and garden fences, and raised planting beds; and concrete is used for most of the interior floors as well as for the outside terrace paving, steps, and major retaining walls.   To call it charming and delightful belies the strong underlying logic, but it does have these characteristics which are never out of place in a home.   No one, though, would want to see this house reproduced by the hundreds because it is a highly individualized house for a very special location.   Although not expensive, it is far from mini-mum in cost.   Although convenient for the Hill family on weekends, it would not be functional for family living day in and out.   But when one has an unusual site and sufficient time, money, and inclination to do something out of the ordinary, this is an example of what can be achieved. Hill's two houses are equally good *if judged in terms of all the conditions for which they were designed.*

MEDIUM-SIZE HOUSES

When the architect has from 1500 to 3000 square feet to enclose, many of the design problems that make the small house so difficult are simpli-fied.   In this size range, he has sufficient space to give the typical family enough rooms of adequate size connected by a good circulation system. He usually does not have to pinch pennies quite as hard on materials and equipment, and when he comes to the design of the exterior, the size of the house gives him a head start.   One of the early issues to settle, however, is whether to put all living space on one floor or divide it into two or more levels.

An Informal House in California

Currently, the one-story house is the favored alternative, and the house designed for the Smith family (Figs. 19-7 and 8) suggests free, informal, inside-outside living close to the ground.   Although built in Stockton, California, on a large handsomely-wooded site, this house is not nearly as specialized and localized as it might seem at first.   The ranch-house traditions which this house carries forward are century-old in California,

19-7   The Albert M. Smith home in Stockton, California, is simple and unpretentious, in harmony with its site and with century-old California building traditions, and yet thoroughly contemporary.   Wurster, Bernardi, and Emmons, architects.

and they are similar to the traditions of people all over the country who build with wood and without concern for "styles." *Indigenous* and *vernacular* are the words that come to mind.

A unifying flat roof establishes a horizontal plane carrying around and into the house, but both interior and exterior show that it is not a simple flat-top. Two clerestories extend the length of the house to bring light and three-dimensional interest inside without sacrificing usable wall space. Both face east and have roofs at a 30-degree angle which extend well beyond the glare-resistant glass. Without them, the interiors would have been dark and characterless, the exterior squat and boxy. On three sides the flat roof extends to give living porches for almost all weathers, because owners and architects realized that the uncovered terrace commonly built today is no substitute for the good old-fashioned veranda. On the east (Fig. 19-7) the porch, 15 feet wide, extends the length of the house and is useful on cool but sunny mornings or hot afternoons. On the north it narrows to 10 feet because sun is no problem there.   On the west (Fig. 19-8) it varies from 8 feet to 15 feet in width, the wider part giving space for outdoor dining protected on three sides, roofed, and

PHOTOGRAPH BY ROGER STURTEVANT

19-8 The enclosed garden of the Smith home demonstrates how exterior design can be integrated with landscape design to make outdoor living pleasant.

adjacent to the kitchen and indoor dining space. A trellis 15 feet wide and covered with deciduous vines carries the sense of partial enclosure into a walled, paved garden. Remember this faces west where winter sun is pleasant, summer sun is hot. Here the simple devices of enough roof to keep furniture out of the rain, a trellis that lets winter sun in but keeps summer sun out, a low wall that gives privacy and wind protection, and solid pavement that dries quickly and takes no maintenance make outdoor living a civilized commodity. It is a topnotch example of really thinking through what it takes to get the family happily outdoors. And it is exterior design at its most vital point—space for living.

All walls inside and out are of California incense cedar laid vertically, and ceilings are of slightly rough redwood to give color and texture variation. To preserve the warm beauty of the woods and to simplify maintenance, exteriors are protected with a clear preservative, interiors with colorless wax. Predictions are always risky—but the writers forecast that the un-self-conscious straightforwardness of this whole design will not look outdated as long as people want homes for informal family living. Nothing is forced or affected, no faddish falderals intrude. In fact, one is hardly conscious of "design" in the academic sense because the emphasis is on what happens to the people. Yet all parts bespeak their origin in a strong, underlying order. The organization is natural rather than artificial chiefly because the forms follow their function earnestly. Unity is gained through the big consistent shapes and harmonious materials, variety through variations in size and the natural variations in the wood. The means used to establish balance merge imperceptibly with the easy yet dynamic rhythms of continuing lines and regular spacing of windows, posts, and boards. Emphasis comes chiefly through size and location of features, such as the fireplace, porches, and clerestories, which bring one's attention to rest without riveting it on spots. That none of this is conspicuous or arbitrary is a matter of skill, not inattention to design quality.

A Tract House in Virginia

The house illustrated in Figs. 19-9 and 10 was constructed as one unit in a tract in Pine Spring, Virginia, nine miles from the center of Washington, D. C.

How would you describe it? To the writers it looks refreshingly clean, crisp, and contemporary—but not antiseptic; alive with spirit, conviction, and sensitivity; open and expanding without resembling a goldfish bowl or bird cage; handsomely related to its attractive site in rolling, wooded country; and like a home for warm and friendly, but also efficient, family life today. It has a hovering lightness reminiscent of a tent or a vacation shelter, yet it looks permanent and substantial. Let us compare and contrast it with some of the other houses illustrated above. As in Walker's house (Fig. 18-1), a very low-pitched, gabled roof with the ridge at right angles to the road is the major integrating element and contributes greatly to its home-like character. It is less rugged, stalwart, and blocky than Stein's house (Fig. 19-2); it is more graceful and fluent. Here is architecture developed from a unifying idea and detailed with a sure and sensitive hand. It has enjoyed ready acceptance by the buying public.

Part of its acceptance comes from the pleasant site, the large lots of one-half acre or more, the skillful fitting of the house to the natural lay of the land, and the placing of the large glass areas away from the road and nearby neighbors. But the design of the house, inside and out, more than lives up to the site. As seen from the road, the composition is ingratiatingly quiet and informal. The fully enclosed part of this dwelling is an economical unbroken rectangle half the width of the whole composition. The exact center of the façade is at the left edge of the entrance door which aligns vertically with the roof's peak. A simple, secure brick wall fills almost half of the front and acts as a substantial foil for the trimly designed section of wood and glass. Although it measures less than one-quarter of the total breadth, its weightiness, texture, and contrasting color balance and stabilize the remainder. The doorway is unassuming yet dominant because of its central position, light color, and the varied shapes of the glass. A detail worth noting is the lighting fixture which sends light down onto the house number and outside entrance area at the same time that it illumines the reflecting overhang above. Opening from the dining area through a large panel of fixed glass and a sliding door (Fig. 19-10), the breezeway would become pleasant outdoor living space if visually screened from the road (and its livability would be greatly enhanced if it were also screened against insects).

LURIA BROTHERS   PHOTOGRAPH BY ROBERT C. LAUTMAN

19-9 A "tract" house of unusually sensitive design, this medium-sized house in Pine Spring, Virginia, is refreshingly clean and crisp. Keyes, Smith, Satterlee, and Lethbridge, architects.

19-10   This photograph of the dining space in the Pinc Springs home shows why contemporary architects regard interior and exterior design as one problem. Much would be lost if there were a sharp break between the two.

Throughout the house, the window design is efficient and handsome. The entrance hall gets good light from the panels beside and above the door, and the kitchen gets cross lighting from the triangular pane on the front and the sliding windows facing the carport. As mentioned, the dining area receives abundant light from its floor-to-ceiling glass panels, and directly opposite are four similar sheets of glass visually extending the living room on to the terrace. Each of the bedrooms has one wall-height window with a ventilating sash at the bottom to bring cool air in and one at the top to let hot air out; the two large bedrooms also have windows like those in the kitchen. Thus, except on the street side, there are but two window sizes and shapes (for unity), and the variety of the shapes on the front is introduced exactly where it is most welcome.

The Pine Spring house has a simple, unpretentious character; sensitively proportioned masses; an orderly pattern of windows and doors; exterior materials that are suitable; and the appearance of being larger than it is.

A LARGE HOUSE

Many of the most perplexing difficulties in exterior design are minimized when the house is large. Usually the site is ample in size, often distinctive in character; cost is of minor importance; and the large forms and spaces are impressive in their size alone. Freed from such mundane concerns as trying to save a few dollars or making a little box look like an attractive home, the architects are limited only by their inventiveness and skill. Sometimes, of course, the clients can be a limitation, but in the house (Fig. 19-11) discussed below the clients were open-minded, informed, and sensitive.

Richard Neutra, in describing the house he designed for the desert, writes as follows:

> Early evening brings profound peace. The soft blues and purples of the mountain landscape form a dramatic backdrop for the precise, weightless, transparent forms of the mysteriously glowing phantom of a house.

The desert near Palm Springs, California, is arid, rolling country with mountains nearby. It is a big, strong, simple landscape marked by abrupt contrasts. The typical day is dazzling bright and sunny and the cool night comes suddenly with a minimum of transitional twilight. It would

19-11   This large house in the desert near Palm Springs, California, is as calm and serene as its setting.   Richard Neutra, architect.

be senseless to try to design a house in competition with this strong grandeur or to attempt to harmonize air-conditioned, glass-walled rooms with this setting.   On what basis, then, did the architect work?   By getting down to essentials, which in this instance are bigness, simplicity, and strength.   The house shares these basic qualities with its setting, but in almost every detail it contrasts strikingly.   Forms and spaces are continuing and uninhibiting in both, but in the house they are regular and precise.   The spaciousness of the site almost literally flows into and through the interiors, but in so doing it is transformed into a man-made rectangularity.   The result is a home beautifully related to its site without in any sense repeating the forms around it.

CONTEMPORARY EXTERIOR DESIGN

Growing out of a new way of living, a new technology of building, a host of new materials, and a tremendous increase in construction costs, contemporary exterior design expectedly differs from that of the past. No single aspect sharply differentiates it from all past work, except the use of very large sheets of glass and slender steel supports, because all of its other characteristics can be found in earlier work. Flat roofs, for example, have been used from time immemorial in warm, dry climates; long bands of windows (with very small panes of glass, to be sure) occurred in England as early as the 15th century; starkly simple, unadorned masses were common in our own southwest; and Greek and Roman houses integrated indoor and outdoor living effectively. As a whole, however, contemporary houses are unlike anything in history. Although individual interpretations differ greatly in specifics, the majority of the best examples have these characteristics:

- The character is unpretentious and informal, aims to *express* the way its occupants live rather than to *impress* guests.
- The structure is integrated with site and landscaping to promote easy, private outdoor living. Usually this means that the most important and interesting part of the house does *not* face the street.
- Exterior and interior are harmoniously related through large openings and glass areas, repetition of shapes and materials, and forms that carry the eyes strongly from one to the other.
- Interest and variety come from frank revelation of basic space and form, of structural members, and of the nature of the materials used. There is a minimum of applied decoration, but fortuitous and factitious ornament are stressed.
- Strongly horizontal forms and bands of windows relate the house to the ground, suggest comfort and rest, and make the house appear large.
- Unity predominates over variety, consistency over differences, perhaps to compensate for the complex diversity of contemporary life.
- Balance is asymmetric because it more flexibly satisfies functional requirements, increases apparent size, and has an active energy typical of our time.
- Rhythms are easy and fast-moving with only a few interruptions or pauses, and they carry continuously around and through the composition.
- Emphasis is spread over the whole rather than being densely concentrated in spots.
- Simplicity is a goal, the unnecessary is eliminated.

JUDGING EXTERIOR DESIGN

Architectural exteriors can somewhat superficially be compared to the epidermis covering our bodies, and this is a good beginning because we all know that beauty is more than skin deep. To be sure, an epidermis can be a beautiful, soft, wonderfully colored membrane, but the underlying bones and muscles give it shape and character and are of deeper importance than the surface texture and color. Skin treatments can enhance attractiveness, but they can never develop lasting beauty. So it is with a house. Exteriors have the primary utilitarian function of sheltering the occupants and their possessions, but they rise above the utilitarian when they are honest and handsome expressions of the living space they enclose. It is not merely a matter of turning a pretty face toward the street, or, as someone has said, of having a Queen Anne front and a Mary Ann back. It is reaching for a whole exterior that is useful, economical, beautiful, and individual. Again, we resort to a series of questions as the best way of stimulating you to think through the various aspects of exterior design, hoping that as you answer these questions for yourself you will not only become clearer on what you want your house to look like, but also will develop critical appreciation of houses you have no thought of living in.

Does the character of the exterior express your way of living?

The Ropes Memorial has the disciplined order of the 18th century, and Stein's house has a disciplined, semi-brusque freedom and ease. The prefabricated house is economical, handsomely domestic, and designed for general appeal; Hill's own vacation house is marked by spirited individuality, inventiveness, and surprise. The Smiths' home expresses friendly, informal family living, and the Pine Spring house has an almost elegant naturalism. The house on the desert is precisely beautiful, serenely quiet and simple.

Which of these suits you best? Perhaps none quite hits the nail on the head. Then it becomes your pleasurable task to begin defining your personality and needs.

Is the exterior consonant with the plan?

Ideally, all parts of the house develop out of the controlling, unifying concept that determines the over-all character, and the architect works on all phases as nearly simultaneously as one mind and two hands permit. He can, however, concentrate on only one thing at a time, and the usual first concerns are plan and interior space. Once these have taken preliminary shape he studies the exterior more intensively. Often this brings alteration of room shapes and sizes and some shifting of windows and doors in a process of take and give to produce the best possible total design.

Once the family's needs are analyzed and a preliminary plan drawn, the exterior design is indicated, although not rigidly prescribed. Thus, a symmetrical plan (very rare these days) suggests a symmetrical exterior. Less obviously, a highly formalized but asymmetric plan calls for a more regular exterior than does a wandering, ranch-house layout. Certainly we would not expect an up-to-the-minute plan to be misrepresented by an exterior straight out of the history books. How much latitude is there? Many large-scale builders give identical floor plans varying outside expressions so that the owners can quickly spot their house in the row. Different materials, or the same material in different colors; variation in roof shape, in window details, in the treatment of the entrance; possibly a different location of the carport—all of these are possibilities. Remember, though, that the plan establishes the building's outline, the position and width of all openings, and, if the plan has any personality, more than a hint of the character of the whole. It is hard to believe that the same plan is equally suitable for a precisely tailored exterior with smooth white stucco walls, a flat roof, and metal-framed windows with large panes, as well as for walls of rough naturally finished redwood or cedar, a pitched and shingled roof, and wood-framed windows with smaller panes. This could only be forgivable if the two-dimensional plan were so completely innocuous that it mattered little what happened when it became three-dimensional space and form.

Is the exterior suited to its environment?

Environment is physical and cultural, general and specific. Let us start with climate, for the shell is what divides the humanly controlled environment inside from nature's weather outside. Average and extreme temperatures control to some degree the use of glass. In almost any climate, glass toward the south earns its cost and keep, but in regions of severe winters little glass is wanted on the north; in desert climates, where not only the sun but the air is very hot, large glass areas do not contribute to comfort. The desirability of overhanging roofs, too, is related to the prevailing weather. In bright, sunny climates they reduce glare, and in places where it rains in hot weather they help the occupants get rain-free ventilation. But in climates where gray days are common, broad overhangs may darken interiors depressingly.   Geography, too, deserves consideration.   On the flat plains of our middle-western states, strongly vertical masses with steeply pitched roofs seem less suitable than forms more harmonious with the landscape.   On the treeless deserts, masonry seems more at home than does wood.   White stucco and red tile come into their own in bright sunlight, but may look naked as a plucked chicken in a dark pine grove.   It is indeed satisfying to see a house belonging to its site, whether it be an igloo near the Arctic, a grass hut in Africa, an Indian pueblo in New Mexico, or a contemporary house anywhere that shows that owner and architect considered the environment before starting to build.

Culture, traditions, and nearby neighbors cannot be ignored.   Today, few persons build a house with no neighbors in sight or in a place completely without building traditions.   It would be paralyzing to fall complacently in line with what had been designed for another age, but paying no attention to the architectural environment produces a hodgepodge; uncontrolled individuality not only shatters communal feeling but usually lessens the attractiveness of each individual expression.   Suiting a house to its environment is not a matter on which one can proclaim specific devices without being unnecessarily rigid, perhaps arbitrary.   It is rather a sensitive recognition of and responding to what was there first.

Are the materials suitable?

Sticks and stones, glass, metal, and composition materials, their strengths and weaknesses, and the forms for which they are most appropriate have been treated in Chapters 8 and 9.   Here it is only necessary to say that materials are tremendously important in exterior design, and that they should be chosen in reference to use, economy, beauty, and individuality.

Is it visually pleasant?

Our aims and principles of design are the best guides to beauty, and in the analyses of individual houses in this chapter they have been specifically considered in relation to exterior design.   When you look at any exterior, answer these questions.

- Does the form as a whole and does each part follow the function?
- Is there a unifying idea which sets the character and is this character vitalized by variety?
- Is there a satisfying equilibrium of forces and weights?
- Do the whole and the parts have a rhythmic continuity?
- Are the whole and the parts emphasized in proportion to their importance?

CHAPTER 20

Landscape

"WHAT SHALL I do with it?" might well be the question that the man in Fig. 20-1 is asking himself about his backyard, and it is a common question among home-owners. Most of the conditions he has to cope with are typical—a two-story house of undistinguished character, a narrow city lot with neighbors nearby, a backyard 40 by 50 feet, and a garage inconveniently located far from the kitchen and the street. Less typical are the living room, which overlooks the backyard and which is on a level with it, and the door which gives easy access to the yard. Atypical, too, is the slope of the ground up from the house, which both raises problems and opens up design possibilities. As the yard stands, there is little protection from sun and wind, no privacy from neighbors, and no place that suggests sitting down to enjoy life. The miscellaneous tangle of plants, the indecisively shaped lawn, the inadequate paving and the picayune steppingstones add up to just about nothing—except possibilities. As you can well imagine, this potentially valuable living space was little used or enjoyed. Alternative courses of action in order of increasing desirability would have been to leave it as it was, to keep trying to improve it without having a specific goal, to consult worth-while books on landscape design (such as those in the list of references) and formulate a plan of one's own, or to employ a landscape architect. There can be no question that the last alternative will bring a desirable solution more quickly than the others—but a good many persons can with a little study produce satisfactory plans.

Figs. 20-2, 3, and 4 show what landscape architects Osmundson and Staley did to help the owners get more living out of their lot. They accomplished the following:

Organized the space into "outdoor rooms."

Much as the architect plans rooms inside the house, the landscape architect designs the land around the house. In this plan, there are three different areas. A *service yard* near the kitchen provides space, courteously screened from the neighbors, for drying clothes and the like; a *patio* carries the living room outdoors; and a *lawn area* at the rear becomes a quiet retreat according to the plan, but it could have been a children's play space or a gardener's hobby area. Although each of these areas is differentiated from the others, they are not completely separated—"open planning" was developed in landscape design long before architects took it over.

Made the ground surface usable.

Attractive as sloping ground is in large expanses, it is not suitable for intensive human use. With none too much outdoor space at their disposal, the designers wisely made each area level. Further, they paved the most-used parts, because that is where we need hard, dry footing for ourselves and our furniture. Paving is easy to maintain, can be used almost immediately after a shower, warms up quickly even in winter if exposed to the sun, and carries the feeling and function of interior floors outdoors. Its only disadvantages are its initial expense and the hard, hot glare that comes when its surface is too smooth and bright and there is insufficient shade. In this patio, the raised planting beds, trees, and pergola overcome glare with their shadows, and the concrete has been separated into squares to give visual interest and a pleasant un-sidewalk-like quality, as well as to minimize cracking. For those who want a livable yard in any part of the country, the importance of adequate, well-placed paved areas cannot be overestimated.

Provided protection from wind, sun, and neighbors.

A *fence* of thin redwood stakes around the rear of the property was a first step in increasing privacy and reducing wind. Such a fence takes much less ground space and ever so much less care than would equally effective planting, while serving as another transition between house and garden. The small scale of the narrow stakes increases the apparent size

20-1 Before it was landscaped, this backyard was an uninviting parcel of ground.

PHOTOGRAPH BY THEODORE OSMUNDSON

20-2 Paving, a trellis, walls, plants, and furniture that are all parts of a unified design transformed the yard into useful and pleasant living space. Osmundson and Staley, landscape architects.

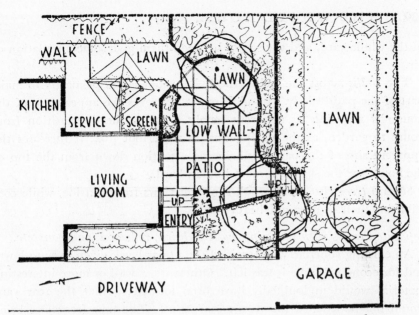

20-3 The plan shows how the area was organized into three outdoor rooms: a patio, a secluded lawn, and a service yard.

PHOTOGRAPH BY THEODORE OSMUNDSON

20-4 The free-curve brick wall makes the patio seem much larger and far more interesting.

of the whole yard, and the spaces between them give some circulation of air.

The *trellis* across the end of the living room serves primarily to make part of the patio shady. In addition, it improves the appearance of the house by reducing its apparent height. An overhead transition from house to garden, as the paving was an underfoot link, it increases the apparent size of the patio by bringing attention down from the top of the house—or the sky—to a more human level.

Several *trees* also break wind, sun, and views from outside, while contributing their own unique beauty.

Separated levels with retaining walls of brick, redwood, and concrete.

An existing concrete wall retained the upper level, given over to lawn, and for economy's sake it was left. Otherwise, a wall of more interesting material would undoubtedly have been located so that the rear yard would not be divided into two equal strips. The new free-curve brick wall which supports an intermediate level flower-bed brings welcome contrasts of shape, texture, and color. In other places, the walls are of redwood planks. Low walls such as these have numerous points of excellence. In comparison with sloping banks, they save space and up-keep-time and unify house and garden by bringing architectural forms and plants into intimate rleationships. All year they state the garden's design in clear-cut terms and create three-dimensional patterns of materials, light, and shadow. Flowers are raised to a level where they are easily appreciated, weeded, and cultivated. Finally, the low walls provide good short-term sitting space for outdoor parties. Their only drawback is their moderately high first cost. In this garden, the sloping land made walls almost necessary; but even on a flat site, raised beds do much to make outdoor space livable and attractive.

Gave the whole yard a coherent, sensible design.

Rectangles, diagonals, and curves have each been used where their character makes them appropriate. The service yard has a logical, interesting rectangularity in keeping with its use. Interest is sensibly concentrated in the patio, for this is the most important unit. The free-curve wall and the diagonals make the patio seem larger, inviting one to explore its shape, and they partake of the lively freedom characteristic of plants. As a quiet foil for the diversity in the patio, the rear lawn is an unembellished rectangle, echoing the right angles of the service area.

THREE SMALL GARDENS

To demonstrate some of the ways in which average city lots can be landscaped, Douglas Baylis produced the designs illustrated in Figs. 20-5 through 20-9. They differ from one another in the kinds of outdoor living provided for and in the character of the total design. One does not get at all the same feeling from the curvilinear patterns in the first garden that one gets from the rectangularity of the second, and such differences as these ought to express the personalities of the owners, because they will certainly affect their living patterns.

Garden Number 1

Curves dominate the first plan, giving it a big over-all unity. Sweeping around from the front of the house to the back of the development, they suggest an easy, pleasant, visual and physical movement. Here the continuing change, the growing, expanding quality of curves, are harmonious with the nature of trees and shrubs and with the normal eye and foot movements of man when he is not forced to walk in straight lines and turn sharp corners. Notice that the curves are neither rigidly geometrical, nor are they nervous wiggles. They came, as the sketches show, from creative, free thinking, but this thinking was guided by the size and shape of the lot, the location of the house, and the needs and preferences of the people using it.

Placing the house well toward the front of the lot gives maximum space for private outdoor living at the rear, and placing it crosswise on the lot opens the broadside of the house toward the garden. Economically, the garage is located near the street to minimize the area of driveway (driveways are expensive and wasteful of land), and it is usefully near the kitchen door and the service yard and moderately close to the front door. This leaves a relatively small front yard which has been secluded with a fence and planting, in contrast to the large unshielded front lawns formerly in vogue. Today, with smaller lots and houses, there is real need to make as much of our land livable as we can. If, as in this house, large windows face the street, one gains privacy either by an outdoor screen or light-excluding curtains. Outdoor screens have many advantages.

An ample living and dining terrace leads people conveniently out into the back yard. Noteworthy is the way in which the terrace is joined with the service area, but ingeniously screened from it. What might have been

20-5 Models of gardens are excellent ways to visualize the design before investing money and work. Notice the unifying curves which are the basis of this design. Douglas Baylis, landscape architect.

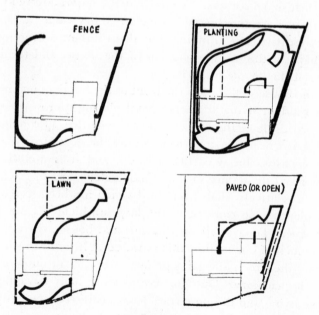

20-6 These sketches show the basic shapes of fence, planting, lawn, and paving. Together they demonstrate variety in unity.

two small, separated areas are combined to give a real sense of expansiveness, and the parents of four boys cannot help thinking that this whole terrace would be good for children's play.   Beyond the terrace a lawn performs its usual multiple functions of being useful to walk, sit, or lie on in good weather and of being pleasing to the eyes.   It is a quiet foreground for the bed of flowers, which in turn is greatly enhanced by a background of fence and planting.   Trees are sensitively placed to give shade where wanted, adding the high forms gardens need and making a pleasant pattern in themselves.   A path invites one to stroll around and enjoy the yard from varying angles.   This is of especial importance because the outdoors is seldom fully enjoyed from a fixed position.

Concentrating our attention on the curves, we might first notice that the fence at the left starts at the driveway close to the house, swings back

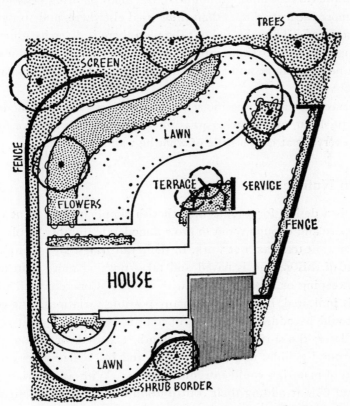

"SUNSET IDEAS FOR LANDSCAPING YOUR HOME"

20-7   Strong and simple, the plan makes the most of a medium-sized lot.

to open up the front lawn, becomes straight along the property line, again becomes a curve, and finally terminates in a screen planting area. It gives privacy without boxed-in confinement.   The path echoes the shapes of both fence and lawns.   It starts at the front entrance, parallels the fence for a while, and then goes beyond, in a curve reminiscent of the front lawn, to join the terrace.   The flower-bed is intentionally a shape of no great interest so that it will not compete with its contents.   It follows without exactly paralleling the path.   Then comes the lawn with its own shape, which is a development of and variation from the flower-bed.   It is, of course, broader than the flower-bed and because of its flatness would seem even wider than it is; it narrows slightly near its middle and then expands at the far end.   The terrace carries this progression to its final step, for it, too, has the same basic character as lawn and flower-bed, but the curve is more pronounced, the small planting beds subdivide it into more intricate shapes than those used elsewhere, and straight lines are introduced.   Thus throughout the plan there is diversity growing out of a single idea, a rhythmic progression of shapes, an intensification of interest near the house and a gradual simplification as the boundaries are approached.

In terms of areas for specific activities, this is a garden of moderation. Pavement, lawn, and growing-areas for flowers and shrubs are balanced to give everyone at least a little of what he wants.

Garden Number 2

This is a design for people who cherish simplicity but want outdoor living space and enough room to grow a moderate number of plants, and who also want to relax, not work, in their yard (Figs. 20-8 and 9). Sixty per cent of this garden is paved and takes nothing more than an occasional sweeping or washing down with a hose.   Concrete with wood dividers is indicated, but there are many possible variations: one or more colors could be added while the concrete is being laid, or it could be stained later; the surface could be smooth, textured, or expose the surface of round pebbles used as aggregate; and brick, flagstone, or a combination of materials could introduce variety.   With appropriate shrubs, trees, and flowers adding their contribution to that of well-designed garden furniture and an interesting fence, this garden would by no means be cold and forbidding.   People, though, not singly but in groups, would

20-8 Planned for a family who wish to enjoy outdoor leisure with a minimum of garden work, this garden has 60 per cent of its area in paving. The rear half could, however, easily be made into a children's play yard or a gardener's growing area. Douglas Baylis, landscape architect.

FLOWERS

SHRUBS

RAISED EDGES

FRUIT TREES

PAVING

FLOWERS

20-9 Although the plan looks rigidly rectangular, the planting softens the hard lines.

be the real elements of interest here because the garden is clearly designed for their sake, not for the sake of plants.

The garden plan is clear, simple, and straightforward—but it is not dull. Far more in the model than in the plan, one notices the shape interest (to say nothing of the wind protection) provided by the fences jutting out at right angles from the property lines. That it looks like a city garden is more an indication of our tendency to think in terms of stereotypes than that it would be unsuitable for less-urban areas. Plants inevitably soften and modulate lines which in garden plans appear to be harsh, and in this garden there are 2000 square feet given over to them. Should one yearn for a verdant lawn, and be willing to water, mow, fertilize, and weed it, any or all of the rear section could be so treated. Or the garden hobbyist could make the back half into a green-thumber's growing area.

The discussions of the above landscape designs lay before us some of the possibilities in moderate-sized lots and also some of the practices and principles by which they can be realized. Before getting into more specific details of landscape design, however, we ought to think about the fundamental matters of selecting the community and selecting the lot.

SELECTING THE COMMUNITY

One seldom has completely free choice to live in the part of the country one likes best, but there is a wide range of spots in each city from which to select. If one wishes to be in the center of city life, a hotel, an apartment, or a city house on a small lot are the answers. At the other extreme is the farm. In between are a wide range of possibilities, each with its complex of advantages and disadvantages.

In the long run, the community is more important than the individual lot, and the first searching should be directed toward finding a section of the town in which you feel at home. This means finding a group of families with approximately the same socio-economic status and interests as your own, for these make the best neighbors. Notice that *unity* is the root of *community*, and a genuine community is homogeneous, not motley. It is likely to have a high percentage of well-maintained, owner-occupied houses in which live families about like yours. A desirable community has good schools, churches, a community center and parks, well-planned shopping facilities, fire and police protection, and public transportation. Nuisances to avoid include traffic thoroughfares or railroads through the community, as well as noisy, unattractive, fume-producing industries. Light industry—quiet, clean, and attractive—can be an asset because it provides employment nearby.

The community plan, the size of the blocks and the street layout, are of far greater significance than most persons realize. It is well worth looking for a community with large blocks, possibly with parks and/or schools in the middle, and with residential streets planned only for local traffic, because such a plan offers better living than the typical small block, gridiron layout with its many wasteful, dangerous, and noisy streets and traffic intersections.

SELECTING THE LOT

With the community selected, the next step is locating a lot that has most of the advantages important to you. So many and, often, conflicting factors crowd together that one almost never finds the perfect lot. Keep your eyes open for the following characteristics:

- *Convenience:* near, preferably within easy walking distance, to such needed facilities and services as schools, churches, and shopping—but not adjacent to them because of noise and traffic. Distance from the wage-earner's work is important, too.
- *Traffic:* a quiet street, preferably dead-end to minimize traffic. Corner lots, in general, are the least desirable although often the most expensive.
- *Elevation:* a lot that is neither at the bottom of a valley nor on the top of a hill. Hilltops usually afford fine views, but they are windy, cold, and often expensive to build on. Low lots are likely to be poorly drained, damp, cold spots in winter and hot pockets in summer, and to many persons always seem depressing.
- *Size:* the right size for your family and your house is the only dependable generalization. Try to get the amount of land you want and can afford. Small to moderate lots, from 50 to 75 by 100 feet, bring you close to your neighbors and usually to needed facilities; cost less to buy, develop, and maintain; and if sensibly developed often give more usable outdoor living space than a large lot you cannot afford to make livable. Larger lots give the luxury of space, seclusion, and opportunity for larger and more varied outdoor areas—but they are either expensive, remote from necessary facilities, or both. Lot size is closely related to size and type of house. A ten-

room house requires a larger lot than a five-room house, and a sprawl-ing, one-story house takes more space than a compact two-story design.

- *Shape:* a rectangle with the narrow side toward the street is the norm. Lots of other shapes are more individualized and likely to lead to a more personalized house and garden.
- *Orientation:* with the street toward the north, the house can be opened on the south overlooking the private area. Other orientations take more ingenious planning to combine the advantages of privacy and sun.
- *Slope:* flat parcels of land are the easiest to develop—and the least in-teresting. Changes in levels bring interest and individuality at a price. On sloping land, it is generally desirable to put the house on the higher part.
- *Natural features:* even one good tree is a tremendous asset and sev-eral well-placed trees expedite landscaping. Outcroppings of rock, streams, and lakes are about equally prized by lot-buyers and lot-sellers.

Selecting your location for living is a matter of balancing *all factors in order of their desirability to you.* One or more acres of beautifully-wooded rolling land in a section where other properties are equally large gives the spaciousness and inconvenience of country living. A small house on a small lot, or an apartment, can be most economical in terms of your time.

PLANNING THE LANDSCAPE

Developing the yard is so much like all other aspects of planning and furnishing a home that practically everything said in the preceding sec-tions of this book can be applied to this phase of home planning. Here, too, we are concerned with modifying or controlling the environment for our physical and spiritual needs. Use, economy, beauty, and individual-ity stand as the objectives, and an effective procedure is to analyze spe-cifically your activities and your preferences, learn the ways and means of getting what you want, consider your resources, and remind yourself con-tinually of what you are trying to achieve.

Perhaps the commonest errors made by non-professionals in designing their landscapes come about because they assume that the plants growing in the garden are more important than the people using it. This leads to the further assumption that whereas the house and its furnishings are clearly man-made and "artificial," the garden should be as naturalistic as possible. Were such a philosophy to be carried into architecture, we would still live in caves or at least build houses of logs with the bark left on or of stones left in nature's shapes. Our furniture, too, might still be stones, logs, and limbs as shaped by nature. But we have long since given up such discomforts.

Plan your landscape to promote the kind of living you want. Select the most appropriate land you can get and then modify it as necessary. Keep constantly in mind that landscape design is essentially a matter of strengthening the relationship between you and your land. Keep that relationship simple, strong, sensible, and satisfying. The crucial question is: What do you want out of the land not covered by the house? Possibilities include:

- A pleasant setting for your house that relates the building to the ground.
- Attractive "garden pictures" to enjoy from your windows or terrace.
- Space for outdoor relaxation and eating.
- Place for active outdoor games, perhaps with emphasis on children's activities.
- Room for the garden enthusiast to grow flowers, fruit, or vegetables.

If your plot is small, it will be difficult to realize them all, and then you must select those deemed most vital. Even on a city lot, however, it is surprising how much can be achieved with thoughtful planning. Before getting carried away with dreams two questions deserve answers. How much time and/or money do you want to put into the original development? How much time and/or money do you want to put into maintenance? Just as the house is a matter of brooms, dustcloths, and washing machines as well as of color schemes, so a landscape is a matter of lawn mowers, spades, and hose as well as of flowers. Do not be a slave to either.

Of only slightly less importance than planning for use is deciding on and sticking to a general design character. Curves gave the garden in Fig. 20-7 a satisfying unity, and sensibly related rectangles hold the garden in Figs. 20-8 and 9 together. Common sense suggests hewing steadfastly to a single idea—unless a garden is large enough to integrate more variety and contrast or unless the designer has uncommon skill in reconciling differences.

Materials of Landscape Design

After you have analyzed your needs and preferences, the next step in developing your land is learning something about the nature of the materials or elements with which the landscape is designed. These include: ground surfacings; enclosing fences, walls, and hedges; overhead protection; plants; water; and man-made enrichment.

Ground Surfacings. Like floor coverings, ground surfacings can be divided into hard and soft, but lawns are about the only soft surfacing that can be walked on very much. So common are lawns as the standard ground surfacing in temperate climates that it is a surprise to find that they are rare in warmer, drier places like Italy and Spain. And they are equally uncommon in the Orient, not for climatic reasons but apparently because they have no special appeal for the Orientals. Their popularity with us is based on the low cost of getting them started, the moderate cost of upkeep, their effectiveness as a transition between architecture and higher growing plants, and their pleasantness to look at or to walk, play, or lie on. They make an excellent quiet foil, a foreground for more emphatic elements. Physically, as well as visually, they cool a garden in summer. Their often-overlooked limitations include their unusability in wet weather, the conspicuous wear and tear that comes with concentrated use, and the insistently continuous need to keep them watered, mowed, and fed, free from weeds, bugs, and diseases, and trimmed around the edges. There are a number of other soft ground surfacings, such as ivy, wild strawberry, and trailing junipers, which, while not durable for walking on, cover raw earth and require much less upkeep than a lawn.

Hard ground surfacings, being inorganic, change little through the years and give maximum use with minimum upkeep. More than any other single factor they make a garden livable.

■ *Stone.* In some Italian gardens, polished marble, laid in beautiful bold patterns, gives a pavement of exceptional richness, while cobblestones laid at random suffice in many Spanish patios. These are extremes in terms of formality, cost, and luxury. In this country and in England flagstone is frequently used for its durability and handsome variations of color and texture. It can be laid in orderly rectangular patterns (Fig. 8-10) or in informal random shapes (Fig. 8-11). Although there is no choice between these two except in terms of individual situations, flagstone is best when the individual slabs are not jagged or pointedly irregular and when they are laid in relatively large areas of strong, simple shape with the surface quite smooth and level.

- *Brick.* As effective in old-fashioned gardens as in the most contemporary, brick is sympathetic in color and texture, combining as it does qualities of earth and man. The units, pleasantly small in scale, can be laid in many patterns, and the texture and color reduce glare, heat, visual hardness, and monotony (Fig. 20-11).
- *Concrete.* Although not a material that wins the heart, concrete is widely used today because it is durable, not costly, will readily fill any straight or curved shape, and can be colored and textured (Fig. 20-4).
- *Tar and Gravel.* Certainly not beautiful, black-top or macadam as used on roads is unobtrusively satisfactory and inexpensive. With interest supplied elsewhere, it takes its place as a neutral, grayish floor.
- *Gravel.* Crushed gravel, spread, watered, and rolled, is the least expensive of the hard surfaces. It gives dry, quite firm footing and good color-texture variations harmonious with plants. That it tends to scatter and permits weed growth are not too important disadvantages.

Fences, walls, and hedges. Although fences seem un-American to many persons, an old New England saying sagely has it that good fences make good neighbors. These elements, comparable to the walls of a room, give privacy, lessen wind, provide a suitable background for plants, make the design of the landscape readily apparent, and harmonize house and garden. Unlike hedges or other screen plantings, fences and walls take almost no space or care and give immediate effect.

Their variety is legion, for they can be high or low; straight, angled or curved; have open spaces or be solid; be made from translucent, transparent, or opaque materials; emphasize horizontals or verticals, or balance both; be refined or rugged; and be painted or left natural. In addition to wood, the most usual material, stone, brick, concrete blocks, corrugated metal or plastic, plastic-impregnated screen, or even glass can be used. Space limitations preclude detailed discussions of the different types (see list of reference books), but the fence design and material should be appropriate to the house and the rest of the garden. Thus, a rough redwood fence fits easily with a redwood ranch house, and it would be in lively contrast to a smooth stucco dwelling. It would, however, be entirely out of character with a refined, formal Colonial house and garden. Although fences are usually similar in spirit to the house, they often are somewhat more rugged in character and less precise in design, partly for economy and partly to tie in with planting.

Hedges of one variety of plant, either clipped or allowed to grow freely, or of several pleasantly related varieties of shrubs, provide good green enclosures if you have adequate space and are patient enough to wait some years for their full effect. A high degree of unity comes if only one variety of shrub is used, variety comes with many—but the latter is seldom satisfying unless the varieties are limited to not more than five, with at least three (better more) plants of each kind massed together, and careful thought given to the whole silhouette as well as to the relationships of growth habit, leaf size and color, and flowers and fruit. Hedges well below eye level are useful in suggesting divisions between parts of the landscape design without reducing the sense of spaciousness.

Overhead Protection. The sky is a magnificent, but undependable, ceiling. From it we get light and heat (often too much of both) on most days, and in cool, clear weather it takes much of the heat from the earth's surface. Among the several functions of overhead protections, the most important is that of tempering the climate. Not only do they lessen light, heat, cold, and winds, but, if waterproof, protect us, our furniture, and our play equipment from rain and snow. A second function is to give us the "not altogether unenclosed" sense of protection and security that comes with having something between us and the sky. The third function, and an important one it is, is to bring at least part of the above-head landscape down to human scale. Some friends of the writers recently found that putting a wood sunshade over an ample terrace caused the terrace to look much larger because one no longer judged it in relation to the vastness of the sky.

Encompassing almost as much variety as fences, overhead protections can be completely weatherproof and lightproof roofs, as in the Smith house (Figs. 19-7 and 8), or they can be of plastic or glass. Canvas fastened to a wood or metal framework admits some light but offers protection from sun and rain. Light and colorful in appearance, it is relatively short-lived and often whips annoyingly in the wind. Fixed sunshades of wood, much like a Venetian blind used horizontally, can be so designed that heat and glare are reduced while air circulates and one gets glimpses of the sky. Pergolas and trellises (Figs. 8-2 and 20-2) with vines bring architecture and nature together in an especially satisfying way, but the protection they offer is limited. Nature's great overhead protectors,

20-10 Plants differ greatly in character, as exemplified by the loosely growing, fern-like leaved centaurea and the low, compact, woolly leaved "lamb's tongues." Light-weight concrete blocks in the walk and raised planting beds accent by their hard rigidity the softer informality of the plants. Kathryn Imlay Stedman, landscape architect.

trees, are for most of us the primary ones, and these will be discussed in the following section.

Plants. Plants are the distinctive elements that most sharply differentiate landscape design from architecture. They vary markedly from one part of the country to another and therefore exert strong regional influences. It is quite possible to develop a landscape with them alone— no pavement, no fences, no sheltering roofs—and such a landscape can be very beautiful in some seasons and thoroughly enjoyable on the best of days and nights, but with very rare exceptions it will fall far short of being a really livable garden.

It is a gross understatement to say that the variety of plants is fantastic. Each one has its own definite habit of growth (height, width, shape, kind of branching); its own growing needs (kind of soil, amount of water, amount of shade and sun, and temperature range); and its special type of leaves, flowers, and fruits. Probably in no other field of art does the designer have as much variation in materials from which to select. Even within one genus and one species there are as many individual differences as in homo sapiens. And like man, they are always changing noticeably.

Plants can be divided into types in terms of their growth habits and place in the landscape.

- *Ground covers* are spreading plants, usually under one foot in height, which cover the ground without obscuring the outlook. Trailing junipers, Vinca, ivy, and many kinds of succulents are examples, as are lawn grasses. Used appropriately, these are extremely useful as a low, permanent, generally unobtrusive foreground or growth under trees or shrubs.

- *Shrubs,* defined as low- to moderate-height woody plants with several stems, overlap ground covers at one extreme (some grow less than a foot) and trees at the other (some get to be 20 or 30 feet high). Many volumes have been written on their differences, and more could be written on the way they could be used in the landscape. For example, there are junipers with low-arched, wide-spreading branches, densely clothed with short, blue-green needles the year around. Their almost unnoticeable flowers and fruits and their retention of leaves with almost no change in color make them almost as constant in appearance 365 days a year as is a brick wall. Spiraea, in contrast, sends its many stems up from the ground to arch over in a vase shape.   In spring tender green leaves come out and then for a short period are all but hidden with a great burst of white flowers; and through the summer the shrub is a graceful green mound.   Rhododendrons retain their handsome, big, leathery leaves the year around, and produce their massive heads of flowers in late spring.   These three, out of the yet-uncounted varieties of shrubs throughout the world, merely hint at some of the possibilities and limitations. Shrubs serve us as low to moderately high permanent planting useful for visual screens, windbreaks, backgrounds for lawns and flowers, accents, or specimens, and often for their flowers, as in roses or lilacs. But a short, or even a long, burst of bloom should not make us overlook the appearance of shrubs all year, for this in the total landscape deserves consideration at least equal to that given to flowers.

■ *Trees*—high-growing, single-stemmed, woody plants—are the biggest elements in the garden and deserve the respect that large size invariably demands.   Here, too, there is diversity.   Think for a moment of the difference between a slender, small-leaved, deciduous birch tree with its delicate white bark, and a stately pine tree with its strong trunk and branches always clothed with dark green needles.   Or compare the American elm's graceful vase shape with the forthright vigor of a sturdy oak.   Choosing the tree or trees that will be most useful, economical, beautiful, and of the individual character most desired in your landscape is quite a game!   The right tree in the right spot can make a garden; but in the wrong places even right trees can be irritating.   Tempering the amount of light, heat, and wind on your property and controlling the outlooks and the inlooks are important contributions of trees, but they are also the tall accents, the last step in the progression from the lawn or terrace to the sky and as such are often focal points toward which the garden builds up.   Their large, strong masses give stability amongst the multitudinous small shapes, and they are handsome at all seasons, with or without leaves.   Some of them have showy flowers, edible or decorative fruits, and bright autumn colors.   It is hard to imagine a garden without trees!

■ *Flowers*, somewhat comparable to the enriching accessories of interiors, come on all types of plants—ground covers, trees, shrubs, as well as herbaceous (non-woody) annuals and perennials.   Although it is customary to think of flowers as handsome spots of color near the ground that take quite a bit of time, many a tree and shrub, in addition to providing shade or enclosure, has worth-while flowers to make it a genuine dual-purpose object, economical of time and space. It is impossible to set down any rules governing the use of flowers in the garden. Think of them as jewels, if you wish, which should alert you immediately to their need for a setting and a background. Flowers show to best advantage when seen against shrubbery, or a fence; are most effective in large masses of the same kind and color; and, obvious but often forgotten, low flowers should be in front of taller growing varieties. From there on we apply what we have already learned. Thus, the purpose should indicate the varieties of flowers chosen (form follows function). If you want bold displays of seasonal color that make a real splash in your landscape, choose such herbaceous materials as marigolds, zinnias, petunias, geraniums; such shrubs as lilacs, floribunda roses, or azaleas; and such trees as flowering cherry, crab apple, plum, or peach. Lilies of the valley and violets, quiet little shade lovers, never compel you to look at them, but reward both eyes and nose if you give them a chance. Which do you want? Both, probably. But then remember to put the lilies of the valley or the violets in a secluded part of the garden where they will not have to compete with attention-demanding elements. While geraniums are somewhat formal, low-growing plants with flowers similar and close to their foliage, cannas are usually conspicuously tall, stiff, attention-demanding plants with flowers held erectly above their emphatically large leaves. Put the cannas where you want an exclamation point and the geraniums wherever you want flowers that are about equally good at a considerable distance or close at hand. Naturally, too, you will want variety in unity, but keep firmly in mind that a riot of colors in flowers is only slightly better than a riot any place else. Balance, continuity, and emphasis follow hard on the heels of *form follows function* and *variety in unity* as the best guides for selecting and organizing flowers in the landscape.

■ *Fruits,* ornamental, edible, or both, bring almost as much enrichment as do flowers, and happily, most plants with conspicuous fruits also have showy flowers. All of the common fruit trees are highly decorative when in bloom, and those with larger fruits such as apples are almost as gay when the fruits are ripe. In warmer sections oranges and lemons have flowers, fruit, or both many months of the year. Many shrubs—barberry, Cotoneaster, and firethorn, to name but a few—add color to the fall and winter landscape and provide food for birds. Trees and shrubs which have decorative fruits or berries are thus a decided landscape asset, but a word of caution should be given. Avoid planting those with squashy fruits or hard pits near terraces, much-used walks, or lawns.

Water.   Water adds so much to the landscape that one wonders why it is not used more often. Quiet pools with or without water lilies are refreshingly cool and reflect the sky or plants above them in ever-changing patterns. Moving water, be it in fountains or babbling brooks, is hard to beat. Two factors limit the more widespread use of water. First, it is more than likely to be expensive; and second, pools of any depth are a hazard for small children and have an almost irresistible attraction for certain breeds of dogs.

Man-made enrichment.   Of almost exactly the kind used in houses, but of course larger in scale and more durable, man-made enrichment is a handsome way of getting permanent interest in the landscape. Sculpture, be it a marble statue or a metal horse from an old merry-go-round, is a sturdy note of emphasis, and mobiles provide constantly changing patterns. Some artists have created paintings for outdoor use, others have covered sections of wood fences with pieces of interesting scrap wood to make pictures much like non-objective painting. Flower pots and urns, usually the bigger the better, bring interest to a terrace and accents to the flower border.

Units of the Home Landscape

As a house is zoned into units for group living, private living, and work, and these zones are then subdivided into rooms, the home landscape is zoned into *foreground, private living space,* and *service space,* each of which can be organized and subdivided as space and needs indicate. *Growing space* may or may not be a separate zone.

Foreground, usually the land between the house and the street, gives the house a setting and establishes landscape relationships with the community.

- Appropriateness to the size and character of the lot, the house, and the community, and some degree of harmony with all of these are desirable. This need not mean unthinking duplication of what everyone else has done.
- The foreground may open the house boldly to the street with the

20-11 Brick walks divide a foreground garden into rectangular planting beds reminiscent of Colonial gardens and in character with the house.

typical expanse of shrub-bordered lawn, exposed entrance walk, foundation planting, and trees to frame the house—or it may seclude the house (Fig. 20-5).

- The foreground should be relatively simple and un-emphatic unless you wish passersby to stop and stare.
- The foreground area, unless secluded, is of almost no use to those living in the house and therefore tends to be smaller than it was some years ago.

Living space is the most important unit of the landscape (unless special interests dictate otherwise) and therefore is usually the largest.

- Privacy from street and neighbors is essential, suggesting a location at the rear of property.

- Typically, the living space commands the best outlook, even if that is only a distant view or one's own garden, but in some situations this may not be desirable. If, for example, the best view is in the direction from which hard winds come or toward the hot, afternoon, summer sun, another location may be preferable.
- It is most usable when closely related to living, dining, and cooking space.
- Livability is increased by protection from strong or cold winds, from uncomfortably hot sun, from rain and snow. Variety is needed so that at least part of it is livable on hot noons or afternoons, cool evenings, and windy or drizzly days.
- Firm pavement and suitable furniture are essentials.
- Outdoor living space should be made pleasant to look at in all seasons with appropriate planting, arbors, fences, and the like.
- Play space for children is best when readily accessible from children's rooms, easily supervised from the kitchen, and partially segregated and visually screened from adult living space so that adult standards of neatness need not be enforced. It should be as large as feasible and offer maximum protection from inclement weather.

Service space, suitably located and designed, can relieve the house, foreground, and outdoor living areas of needless clutter, for it is here that one dries or airs the clothes, keeps the trash cans, and puts temporarily an untidy miscellany of things.

- The best location is near kitchen and garage, play space, and the gardener's plot.
- It ought to be adequately screened from foreground, living space, and neighbors, and at least partially from the kitchen, because its use keeps it from being a beauty spot.
- Size depends on size of lot and what it is used for—but generally speaking it is too small.
- A dry, firm, easy-to-keep ground surface is essential, some protection from rain or snow almost necessary.

Growing space for vegetables, fruits, and cut-flowers.

- Ideal for the dirt gardener is a separated plot where the total visual effect is of minor consequence, planting is in straight rows for ease of cultivation and irrigation, soil and drainage are good; where there is full sun but protection from wind; and where there is convenience to the garage or a garden shed for storage of tools, fertilizers, insecticides, etc.

■ On small lots or when gardening interests are not strong, the growing area can be combined with the living space—but then its everyday appearance becomes of much more importance.

Foundation Planting. This planting often marks the beginning and too frequently the end of planning the yard. It consists of planting close to the house, which conceals the foundation and ties the house to its setting as a transition from architecture to nature. The stereotype approach is to put some rather high shrubs at the house corners, accent shrubs at either side of the door, and lower shrubs in between. Sometimes the edge of the planting beds parallels the house, more often it bulges noticeably at the corners, less so near the entrance. Quite new in the history of landscape design, foundation planting as generally practiced today came into being with romantic notions of trying to make the house appear to be growing from, or nestling in, its setting, and it has been widely employed to remedy the appearance of awkwardly tall houses, especially when part of their height is an unattractive, exposed foundation of a material differing from that of the remainder of the walls. Many houses benefit from this treatment, but more often than not it is overdone and done poorly. In the first few years, with the typical treatment, the house may seem to be settling into a garnish of mixed greens which as the years go by seriously threatens to engulf it. Then one is deprived of the pleasurable certainty of knowing where and how the house meets its site and usually of needed light from windows.

In thinking about foundation planting, here are some questions to answer.

■ Does the house really need any foundation planting? Why?
■ What purposes will it serve?
■ What plants are most appropriate?
■ Are they of suitable character?
■ At maturity, will they be of appropriate size?
■ Will they be attractive the year round?
■ Will they add to or distract from the house?
■ Are they so placed that they enhance the architecture—or if necessary, obscure an architectural mistake?

Alternatives to foundation planting include the following.

- Paved terraces for group living, children's play, and service.
- Gravel, brick, or other material which covers the ground and is not exactly a walk or a terrace but can be used as either, or simply regarded as a simple area of easy maintenance.
- Low-growing ground covers.
- Lawns which do not stop short of the house.

These can be combined in many ways. Thus, across the front of a house one could plant a wide band of ground cover from which a few shrubs arise but do not crowd up against the house. Similarly, shrubs or small trees can be put in planting beds in an expanse of brick, gravel, flagstone, or concrete, or they can be grown in large tubs or pots. Notice in the Smith house (Figs. 19-7 and 8) how the planting is kept away from most of the house to make the closest space usable and to let one see that the house really stands on the ground. There is no reason why a house has to be encircled with miscellaneous nursery stock; in fact there are good reasons for not doing so because foundation planting often complicates maintenance, making it difficult to wash windows from the outside, or to paint the exterior. It may be desirable for specific reasons, or simply for variety, to keep planting away from most of the house walls but then to bring it close along one side or in a few places. Do what is best for your family, your land, and your house.

Today when many houses are one story, without a basement, and are carefully related to the site by the architect, almost no foundation planting is needed. When space is limited, it is sensible to keep the planting away from the house and at the boundaries. At strategic points—near the entrance, against a wall with few or no windows, possibly at one or two corners—a few choice plants may be very welcome, all the more if their beauty is not obscured in a mass.

Making the Plan

If you are starting from scratch:

1. Select the most appropriate land you can get.
2. Design the house and landscape together.

If you already have your lot, or if your house is built:

1. Make a carefully measured plan at a scale of one inch to 8 or 10 feet of your property, showing property lines, house, garage, walks

and driveways, existing trees and shrubs, and anything else of a permanent or desirable nature.   A 50-foot tape, cross-section paper, a drawing board, a ruler, pencils and erasers are the tools.

2. List the activities you want to enjoy outdoors, putting them in approximate order of importance to you.

3. Read some pertinent books, look through the many magazines that have articles on home landscapes, and visit every garden you can. Keep a scrapbook in which you paste pictures and jot down ideas.

4. List the ways and means of achieving your goals.

5. Then attach the plan of your property on a drawing board, provide yourself with an adequate supply of sufficiently large tracing paper— and start to design.   This is easier than you think.

First, rough in the major units with a very soft pencil, concerning yourself at this point only with their location.   Try several locations for each (preferably on separate sheets of tracing paper) and then review them critically.

Second, begin to refine the shapes, thinking of two things at once: the best shape for each part and the unity of the whole design.   Remember that a basic design idea (curves, or right angles, or diagonals, or what you wish), repeated and varied, brings consistency, that carrying lines through from one unit to the others helps total unity.

Third, start thinking about details—the kind of enclosure, the type of ground surfacing, the location and kind of trees, and the type of planting desired.   In all of these details, as well as in the earlier stages of planning, keep reminding yourself of what you want to do in the landscape and how you want it to look.

Fourth, check it carefully as a whole and in every detail to make certain that it provides well for all desired outdoor living and that it has the spirit most congenial to you.

Fifth, set up a five-year development plan (unless you can call in a landscape contractor and have it all done at once, in which case you might better have called in a landscape architect to take over the whole job).   It seems sensible to get the ground surfacing nearest your house and the absolutely necessary enclosure taken care of first; next get your major trees planted; lawns and permanent background planting also have quite high priority.   You can wait, though, for expensive but highly desirable plants, the fences and overhead protection you want but can live without, and the en-

20-12 An unusually handsome, livable integration of outdoor and indoor living space. House and garden are literally one in use, character, and materials. Gordon Drake, designer.

richment you would like; and you can wait awhile to develop that part of your land farthest from your center of living.

DIFFERENCES BETWEEN HOUSE AND LANDSCAPE DESIGN

One's potential space for living extends to the boundaries of one's property, and the landscape ought to be an integral component of the total development. No longer do we draw hard and fast lines between house and garden, because they are more nearly alike than different. Nevertheless, they are not identical and as a conclusion to this chapter it is worth commenting on some of the differences.

Gardens are used less intensively than are houses. In part this is because the outdoors is generally less usable than the enclosed interior space, but in good part it is because of the way in which landscapes are planned. The amount of living a garden provides is directly proportional to its similarity to architecture. For example, a porch or patio, roofed, paved, and enclosed on two or three sides, is far more usable than an open lawn.

Landscapes are larger in extent than are houses and, therefore, should be larger in scale. The house seldom covers more than one-fifth of the property, making the landscape area four or more times as great as the square footage of the building. Further, the infinitely high sky, not an 8- or 10-foot ceiling, is the top of the landscape. Thus the major landscape features must be decisively strong and comparatively large in scale or the development will look trivial.

Growing plants are the distinctive landscape materials. Plants are growing organisms with decisive but changing personalities. They are not static, machine-shaped objects. Sometimes they are at their best when allowed to grow naturally. Usually, though, they need some degree of modification to adapt them to our needs. Many plants submit as willingly to shaping and pruning as our own hair does to cutting.

Landscapes change more than do buildings. We discussed in Chapter 5 the always-changing balance of interiors. Far greater change is normal in the landscape where most of the forms are constantly growing, changing color, and undergoing great modifications with the different seasons. Having far less precise control over our gardens than over our interiors, it is wise to state our basic idea, to establish our plan with unmistakable clarity and vigor. This is achieved primarily through a compelling unity, but also through balance, rhythm, and emphasis that are never obscured.

Landscape design is the modification of the land around our houses for our use and pleasure. For many years it was among the least sensibly handled phases of home design. Had the contemporary movement made no other contribution than making us aware of how valuable our yards can become, it would have earned its place in increasing human happiness.

CHAPTER 21

Costs and Budgets

DISCUSSIONS of costs and budgets are difficult and risky. Costs often vary from one part of the country to another, from one town to its neighbor, and from store to store in the same community. They go up and down with national and regional economic conditions and with new developments in each field. And they vary greatly on objects used for the same purpose, as for example on dining chairs, which can be had for as little as six dollars each and for as much as a hundred dollars or more.

The writers believe, however, that far too little emphasis is placed on costs, that unrealistic ideas are built up which are often followed by disillusionments, and that it is necessary to become conscious of prices.

There is only one way to be certain of the prices of furnishings when you are ready to buy—

■ *Visit your local stores, read the advertisements in your newspapers and in home magazines, and spend some time with mail-order catalogues.*

And there is only one way to get a budget suited to you—

■ *Study your own situation, your needs and preferences, in terms of your income.*

Having given full warning, we plunge into the important matter of costs.

HOUSE AND LOT

How much does a house and lot cost?

We can start to answer this question by looking at the current selling prices of some 1000 square foot, three-bedroom, one-story houses similar to the four prize-winning houses discussed in Chapter 18. Samples taken from Massachusetts, Ohio, Minnesota, Nebraska, Mississippi, Texas, and California show that the range is from approximately $9000 to $18,000 with a median of around $12,000 for house and land when they are units in a development tract. This means that enclosed space on an average lot ranges from $9.00 to $18.00 per square foot.

Many factors account for the differences. Among the more important are the section of the country; the location in the community; the size of the lot; the type and quality of the house; the kind and amount of mechanical equipment, especially heating but also plumbing, lighting, and kitchen and laundry equipment; and the inclusion or exclusion of such items as garages, basements, steel kitchen cabinets, tiled bathrooms, and landscaping.

Notice that these are "builders' houses," constructed at one time in fairly large numbers.

Costs of one-of-a-kind houses are higher. For these, the cost of construction varies from an occasional low of $10.00 per square foot to a high of $20.00 or more—and these figures, unlike those above *do not include the cost of land, architect's fees,* or any *landscaping.*

Land costs vary quite as much as do those for buildings. There is a great difference between the value of improved and unimproved land. Farm land may sell for not-too-many hundred dollars an acre, but very seldom is a 60′ x 100′ lot, conveniently located, with paved streets and sidewalk, water, electricity, gas, and sewer, sold for less than $1000. Lot value is directly proportional to the desirability of the location, and choice sites may be several times the price of those too near industrial plants, railroads, airports, or on traffic thoroughfares, or too far from needed facilities.

LANDSCAPING

Range of costs for landscape development is great, much greater than for house and land. In many sections of the country, a lawn costs only the few dollars needed for seed; a few trees moved in from the woods, and divisions of shrubs given by friends, complete the project. Expenditure of money, but not of time, is negligible. Thus, landscape costs for the small-home project often are not even considered.

If, though, one develops a livable garden with a paved terrace, enclosing fences, suitable furniture, and the most appropriate plants (rather than any that can be got free), costs can mount rapidly.

A few average figures will give a little more insight into garden costs.

GROUND SURFACINGS	*Per Square Foot*
Lawn	1¢ to 30¢ (depending on soil, whether or not a sprinkling system is installed, and amount of work done by owners)
Asphalt paving	20¢ to 30¢
Concrete paving	25¢ to 60¢
Brick on concrete	$1.00 to $1.25 (about the price of a medium-priced rug)

ENCLOSURE	*Per Running Foot*
Fence (wire)	$1.00 and up
Fence (wood)	$1.00 to $4.00 and up (depending on quality of wood, type of fence, and owner or hired labor)
Hedge	25¢ to $1.00
Wall (masonry)	$4.00 to $10.00

SHRUBS AND TREES	*Per Plant*
Shrubs	75¢ to $10.00 (depending on variety and size)
Trees	$1.00 to $250.00 (depending chiefly on size)

Several hundred to a thousand dollars or more can easily—and wisely in terms of use and beauty—be invested in landscaping a 60′ x 100′ lot.

COSTS OF FURNISHINGS

As with landscaping, the range in the cost of furnishings is more impressive and realistic than would be any average figure. Here are a few approximate figures. *In many instances the top prices could be multiplied several times over* to take you into the very high-quality range, and a good sale may put the cost below the lower figures.

Price tags on home furnishings are controlled by many factors: materials; type and quality of manufacture; excellence, and more especially individuality, of design; and supply and demand. Here are some examples. Silk is invariably more expensive than cotton, silver than stainless steel; handmade objects or those of complex shape often cost more than simple, mass-produced items; good design quality need not necessarily raise the price of home furnishings but it often does; marked individuality almost always costs more; and anything in high demand and short supply is likely to cost more than do those objects for which the supply is sufficient to satisfy the need. Durable home furnishings are likely to cost more than those with a shorter life, but the price is by no means a sure guide. We have stated before that wool upholstery is usually more durable and expensive than cotton, but a very expensive silk damask would probably not withstand as much hard usage as would a firm, heavy cotton. When shopping, give thought to what percentage of your money is being spent for the several factors that determine costs of furnishings.

WALL SURFACINGS (materials *only*)	*Per Square Yard*	
Grass cloth	$3.50 to $4.50	
Paint	.06 to .15	
Plastic wallcoverings	.50 to 5.00	
Wallpaper	.25 to 1.00	

FLOOR COVERINGS: HARD	*Per Square Foot*	
Asphalt tile	$.25 to $ .45	
Cork	.75 to 1.00	
Linoleum	.40 to .55	
Rubber tile	.75 to 1.00	
Vinyl	.90 to 1.00	

FLOOR COVERINGS: SOFT	*Per Square Yard*	*9' x 12' Rug*
Flat Weaves		
Flat weave (cotton)	$ 3.00 to $ 5.00	$ 36.00 to $ 60.00
Flat weave (fiber, often combined with cotton, nylon, rayon)	1.00 to 5.00	12.00 to 60.00
Flat weave (linen)	7.00 to 12.50	90.00 to 150.00
Matting (rush)	2.50 to 5.00	32.00 to 60.00

Floor Coverings: Soft	Per Square Yard	9' x 12' Rug
Pile Weaves		
Broadlooms (variety of weaves)		
Cotton	$ 6.00 to $10.00	$ 72.00 to $120.00
Nylon	35.00 up	420.00 up
Rayon	8.00 to 15.00	96.00 to 180.00
Wool	8.00 to 20.00	96.00 to 240.00

Although there is some relation between weave and price, it is too variable to permit specific comments. Usually Axminster weaves are among the least expensive, velvets and Wiltons are higher, and chenille is at the top of the machine-woven floor coverings.

Rug Cushions or Pads	9' x 12' Rug
Hair and jute	$10.00 to $15.00
Rubber	20.00 to 25.00

Window Treatments

Glass Curtains (panels 40"-44" wide, 72" long)

	Per Panel
Celanese (ninon)	approximately $1.75
Cotton (marquisette)	approximately 1.50
Fiberglas (marquisette)	approximately 3.50
Nylon (marquisette)	approximately 2.75
Orlon (marquisette)	approximately 3.50

Draw Curtains and Draperies

Prices vary tremendously with different fibers and weaves, distinctiveness of design, quality of tailoring, lining (if any), etc.

Draperies are usually sold in pairs, each panel being from 23" to 82" wide at the top after pleating. Typical size for single window is a pair of 27" pleated-width panels which are 84" long.

	Pair of Panels 27" x 84"
Cotton pebble crepe (unlined)	$12.00 to $20.00
Cotton pebble crepe (lined)	18.00 to 30.00
Celanese faille	6.00 to 10.00
Plastic	1.00 to 4.00

Linen, silk, the newer synthetics, and wool are considerably more expensive, as are unusual weaves and prints. Considerable savings are effected by making draperies at home. Drapery fabrics vary in width, but 48″ is the norm. Price per yard ranges from $.30 for plastic sheeting, $1.50 and up for cottons, to $10.00 or much more for luxurious fabrics.

Venetian Blinds

Although seldom listed in this way, Venetian blinds range from around $4.00 to $8.00 per square yard.

Roller Window Shades

From $.75 to $2.00 per square yard.

Woven Bamboo, Reed, and Wood

From $1.50 to $3.00 per square yard of window area covered.

FURNITURE

Beds

Springs and Mattresses

Foam-rubber mattress & box springs	$ 99.50 to $150.00
Innerspring mattress & box springs	60.00 to 150.00

Frames, Headboards, and Footboards

6 wooden legs	$ 3.50 to $ 8.00
Metal frame on casters	7.00 to 12.00
Headboards & footboards	11.00 to 150.00

Chairs

Upholstered, springs and/or foam-rubber pull-up for conversation	$ 30.00 to $200.00
Split cane or reed	5.00 to 15.00
Webbed	15.00 to 40.00
Padded	13.00 to 75.00
Utility—dining, games, work	6.00 to 30.00

Sofas

Studio couches	$ 50.00 to $160.00
Sofas	100.00 to 400.00

Desks

	$ 23.00 to $200.00

FURNITURE

Tables

Dining	$ 40.00 to $200.00
Coffee and end	8.00 to 75.00

Storage

Bookcases (small units)	$ 10.00 to $ 50.00
Chests of drawers	40.00 to 150.00
Cabinets (for dishes, etc.)	30.00 to 150.00

Outdoor Furniture

Redwood table and benches for 6	$ 18.00 to $ 50.00
Folding chairs with slung canvas seats	5.00 to 10.00
Suntan cots or chaises with mattresses	20.00 to 50.00

LIGHTING FIXTURES

Floor lamps	$ 10.00 to $ 50.00
Table lamps	7.00 to 45.00

UPHOLSTERY FABRICS

Cotton slipcover materials (usually 36″ wide and equally suitable for draperies) are from $1.00 to $3.00 per yard.

Heavier materials (usually 54″ wide) range from $2.00 and up for cottons to $8.00 and more for wool and long-wearing synthetics.

Plastic upholstery (also 54″ wide) can be had for as little as $1.30 per yard and goes on up to $5.00 or more.

TABLE SETTINGS

Dinnerware	*Five-Piece Place Setting*
Bone China	$ 7.00 to $20.00
Plastic	1.50 to 5.00
Porcelain	13.00 to 30.00
Semi-porcelain	7.00 to 10.00
Stoneware	4.00 to 10.00

Glassware	*Per Piece*
Tumblers, goblets, etc.	$ .10 to $ 3.00

TABLE SETTINGS

	Five- or Six-Piece Place Settings
Silverware	
Dirylite	$13.50 to $15.00
Silver plate	8.00 to 16.00
	(26 piece sets may be bought for as little as $5.00)
Stainless steel	1.50 to 17.50
Sterling silver	22.50 to 65.00

TABLE COVERINGS

Place Mats	Per Mat
Bamboo, grass, rush, etc.	$ .15 to $ .75
Cotton	.50 to 1.50
Linen	1.00 to 3.00
Plastic	.30 to .75

Table Cloths	54″ x 54″
Cotton or rayon	$ 1.50 to $ 6.00
Linen	3.00 to 10.00
Plastic	1.50 to 6.00

Dinner Cloths	72″ x 90″
Lace	$ 7.00 to $25.00
Linen	10.00 to 25.00
Rayon damask	10.00 to 25.00
Cotton (printed or solid colors)	5.00 to 12.00

Accessories

Handsome rocks and driftwood cost nothing if you seek them out. Beyond these, the tremendous diversity of kinds of accessories, to say nothing of the range within each type, makes it impossible to state any prices other than that accessories can be had for as little as ten cents and for as much as hundreds of dollars.

PAINTINGS

Originals	$15.00 and up
Reproductions	1.00 to $15.00

GRAPHIC PRINTS

Originals $ 5.00 and up

SCULPTURE

Originals $25.00 and up
Reproductions   5.00 to $75.00

This survey gives some of the raw data with which you can begin to think about planning your expenditures in a considered, budget-wise manner. If it has done no more than make you aware of price differences, it will have served a purpose. We hope, though, that it will have started you thinking about cost relationships of one item to another. Now we turn to budgets.

BUDGETS

Budgeting is the art and science of planning one's expenditures so that both ends meet with some left for savings. It is probably more a matter of emotions than of intellect, for it is remarkably easy to lay out a budget with a cool head but remarkably difficult to adhere to it when the heart warms toward an extravagance. Our concern is with wise planning for the expenses entailed by shelter and furnishings.

More than in any other part of this book there is need for caution in applying the material in this section of the book. These are the cautions.

- *No ready-made budget will fit all families.*
- *No rule of thumb or suggested proportional expenditures can be applied to all situations.*
- *Each family has to decide, after thorough consideration of all factors, what percentage of its income will be used for the many items in a family budget.*

Take them, then, for what they are—generalizations that work in typical cases. Do not assume that you should try to follow them if special circumstances indicate other ways of managing your money.

Budgeting for Your Shelter

How much of your weekly or annual income can you afford to spend for rent or your own home? What are the advantages of renting and of buying?

Proportions of Income. The answer to the first question depends on the amount, regularity, and dependability of your income; and on the size, ages, interests, and ideas of your family. If one's income is large, regular, and dependable, and there is ample provision for emergencies, more of it *could* be used for shelter than would be advisable on a small, irregular income. Similarly, shelter costs can be increased if the family is small, the children have become financially independent, or the family prefers spending money on its home to other ways of enjoying its income.

However, typical families find it wise to spend approximately 20 per cent of their income on rent. If, however, the rent includes heat, electricity, gas, and water, the percentage may go up to 25 per cent; and if other services are included, as they frequently are in apartment hotels, the percentage may be further increased.

On purchases, a long-held rule of thumb is that the total cost of a house one buys should not exceed from 1½ to 2½ times one's annual income. In general, this is a good rule, but it is safer to limit the cost to not more than twice the income. In addition to all of the factors mentioned above as affecting the percentage a family can put into housing costs, two others are important in purchases. First is the amount of savings the family has accumulated for a down payment, because the larger the down payment, the less one pays for interest on the mortgage, and also the monthly payments are smaller or the mortgage runs for a shorter term. The second factor is the resources one can call on in case of an emergency, chief of which are insurance and savings not invested in the house.

Although most of us want the best homes possible for our families, caution should be exerted to avoid becoming "house poor," no matter whether the poverty comes from payments on a purchase or payments of rent.

Owning versus Renting. Each has its special advantages, and although today there is a strong national urge toward owning one's own home, it may not be the most advisable way of getting shelter for you.

The financial advantages of owning are

- Savings of several thousand dollars on a $10,000 house may accrue over a 25-year period.
- Interest paid on the mortgage and taxes paid on the house are deductible from taxable income.
- Owning one's home is a reasonably safe investment.

- Monthly payments remain stable with no fluctuation such as may occur with rents. (This is advantageous during times of prosperity, may well be disadvantageous in depressions.)
- There is great incentive to save for one's home.
- Savings can be made by doing some or much of the maintenance whereas in renting one invariably pays the landlord (through rent) for having it done.

The monetary advantages of renting are

- It costs up to $2000 more the first year to buy a $10,000 house than it does to rent one (because of down payment, fees for title-search and lawyers, etc.).
- There are no long-term commitments to hinder one from moving to a better situation.
- Renting gives one an opportunity to check the desirability of a community before investing his money in a home.
- There are no unpredictable repair or replacement expenses.

Digressing from money matters for a sentence or two, home-ownership has such compelling advantages as the satisfaction that comes from a permanent home with its uninterrupted social life for the whole family and schooling for children. It makes a family feel as though it belonged to the community rather than as though it were merely temporarily roosting there.

Budgeting for Landscape Development

Some part of the total cost of a house ought to be reserved for the development of the yard, but (as explained in the section on costs) this is an extremely variable figure. A landscape as completely developed as is the typical house can easily come to a total of 10 to 20 per cent of the cost of the house, but most families spend only a fraction of this. To cite an example, for a 1000-square-foot house on a 60' x 100' lot costing $10,000, $1500 (15 per cent of $10,000) would be an average figure for thorough development of the 5000 square feet not covered by the house. Here, again, it is up to each family to decide for what necessities and pleasures they wish to spend their money. The cost of a garden should not be forgotten—but you may, wisely or otherwise, decide to reserve a very small amount for it.

Budgeting for Furnishings

In normal situations, these are general guides:

- Furnishings usually cost about one-half of one year's income or one-fourth of the value of the house.
- It is desirable to have one-fourth of the total furnishings budget in cash to furnish the first apartment.
- Replacements for furnishings per year average around 3 to 4 per cent of the annual income over a period of time but usually show conspicuous fluctuation from year to year. As income increases this percentage often increases.

There is some advantage in concentrating replacement expenditures in certain years so that a sizable project is carried out at one time with a resulting unity as, for example, waiting until it is possible to do a thorough job on the living room or getting rugs for most or all of the house.

Many factors determine the percentage of income available or needed for replacing furnishings.

- Family size.
- Stage of family cycle—usually there is less money available for this purpose from the time children arrive until they become independent than there is before or after.
- Amount and kind of entertaining.
- Durability of original furnishings.
- The kind of use and care given the furnishings.
- Amount of labor undertaken by family—repairing, refinishing, remodeling furniture; making draperies or slip covers; etc.

In general, furniture budgets tend to be divided as follows:

Living room	30 to 40%
Dining space	15 to 20%
Master bedroom	15 to 20%
Child's bedroom	10 to 15%
Child's bedroom or guest room	10 to 15%

The amount available for each room is likely to be apportioned as follows:

Furniture	60 to 70%
Floor covering	10 to 20%
Window treatment	5 to 10%
Accessories (including lamps)	2 to 7%

These percentages are based on a completely furnished home which usually is achieved only after some years of marriage. More often than not in the beginning, spending will be concentrated on a few good pieces of furniture for the living room and master bedroom, with the other rooms and planned-for rugs and draperies coming later. Then, of course, these figures do not hold.

Countless factors can alter these proportions:

- The money available for each room is in part determined by the number of rooms to be furnished.
- Good hard-surfaced flooring (asphalt, cork, or vinyl tile) minimizes the need for rugs.
- A separate dining room usually costs more to furnish than does dining space in the living room.
- One or two rooms unusually large or small in relation to the others make a difference.
- Even a few pieces of inherited, cast-off, or bargain furniture affect the expenditures for the rooms in which they are used.

Costs and budgets are of the utmost importance in home planning and furnishing because the way in which a family handles its money is one of the primary sources of security or of frustration and worry. It is risky to give specific advice to others, but we can urge that you plan your expenditures at least as wisely as you plan your color schemes or furniture arrangements.

Concluding this book with a chapter on costs and budgets may seem to give finances an emphasis greater than they deserve. They are neither the beginning nor the end of home planning and furnishing, but constant factors in the process. They are seldom exhilarating, but they should not be depressing: they are simply ever-present problems that must be faced and solved. Remember, too, that money is only one factor in the economy of the home, and that economy takes its place along with use, beauty, and individuality as one of the goals of getting and keeping a good home.

Planning your home is an important challenge, for its shell, furnishings, and surroundings shape your living.

Questions
and Activities

QUESTIONS AND ACTIVITIES

Chapter 1. GETTING STARTED

1. Make a careful analysis of your own living room or bedroom in terms of use, economy, beauty, and individuality. List inexpensive ways of improving it.
2. The four objectives express the writers' point of view. Evaluate them critically on the basis of your own experience and personality. Has any factor of great importance to you been omitted? Does the order in which they are listed seem logical to you?
3. To what other aspects of living could you apply these four objectives or your own set of aims and ideals?
4. Are our efforts to save time and energy in our homes justifiable? Why?
5. Why do relatively few homes today have marked individuality?
6. Select any two rooms illustrated in this book and discuss in detail the specific features that contribute to their general character.
7. Visit local furniture stores, or study catalogs and magazines, and make a detailed description (including the price) of different types of dining tables, easy chairs, and floor lamps.
8. List the changes that have been made in your own or your family's living room during the past five or ten years.
9. Loosen your imagination and describe with words, photographs, or drawings exactly the kind of home you would like to have. Then, in a more sober mood, evaluate it in terms of everyday living.
10. Draw the plan of an existing room with its furniture and make elevation drawings of one or more of its walls.
11. Begin a scrapbook in which you not only paste pictures of rooms you like but write your comments on why you like them. Reserve part of this book for ideas of any sort that you want to remember in the future.

Chapter 2. LIVING WITH OTHERS

1. What were the chief group activities of your parents? How do yours differ?
2. Would you rather have one large living space or smaller, separated rooms? Why?
3. Under what conditions do you now eat your meals? What are the good and bad points? Could the conditions be improved inexpensively?
4. From your point of view, what are the advantages and disadvantages of eating in the kitchen? Outdoors?
5. What are the advantages and disadvantages of putting a piano in the dining space? In a sufficiently large bedroom?
6. Discuss the possible effects of television on home life.
7. List the possible places for a television set in your own or your parents' home. What are the advantages and disadvantages of each?
8. Compare and contrast any two living rooms illustrated in this book from the point of view of individuality.
9. Think of the most satisfactory living room you have ever seen and then state clearly the factors on which its success depends. Do the same for the least satisfactory living room you know.
10. Look through books and magazines until you find the plan of a group living space that you like; then trace or copy it.
11. Plan the furnishings for an all-purpose room in which every piece of furniture has more than one use, e.g. storage end tables, etc.
12. Make simple cardboard models of living spaces with different shapes and characters.

Chapter 3. PRIVATE LIVING

1. What is your reaction to a scientifically planned cubicle for sleeping?
2. What are the advantages and disadvantages of two children sharing one bedroom?
3. Try rearranging the furniture in your own bedroom so that it will be a more satisfying room.

4. Look critically at the color scheme in your bedroom. How could you improve it at small cost? What would you do if you could start from scratch?

5. Look through this book and select two bedrooms. List the probable effects on the occupants of these rooms and their furnishings.

6. Find some photographs of well-designed bedroom furniture and put them in your scrapbook.

7. List the excellences and weaknesses of the bathroom you now use.

8. Look through some magazines or visit a plumbing shop and list the colors in which bathroom fixtures are now available. Collect samples of the colors. Why are most bathroom fixtures white?

9. What improvements have been made in the design of bathtubs in the past few decades? What improvements could still be made?

10. Design a small hobby room for yourself with efficient built-in furniture and equipment. How large would the room be? In what part of the house would you put it?

11. How important is solitude to you? How do you achieve it in your present quarters?

12. Describe the kind of seclusion space you would like.

Chapter 4.   HOUSE KEEPING

1. Keep a record for a week or two of the time spent on housekeeping. List the ways in which you could lessen that time and the ways in which you would spend the time saved.

2. What in your home takes the greatest amount of housekeeping time? Is it necessary—or worth while?

3. Rearrange some or all of the furniture in your present living quarters to simplify keeping it clean and orderly. Visit drapery and upholstery shops and look for fabrics that hold up well with minimum cost.

4. If you were going to add to or replace some of your furnishings, what degree of importance would you give to ease of maintenance? Why?

5. Make a list of new products that simplify home maintenance, such as long-lasting starches, silicone compounds for furniture and kitchen pans, and closet and cabinet accessories.

6. Find a house plan that would minimize housework. List the general and specific factors.

7. Visit some electric appliance stores and study the different kinds of stoves, refrigerators, washers, dryers, and ironers now available. Compare any two of them in terms of use, economy, beauty, and individuality.

8. Describe the general character of the kitchen you would like to have. Be specific about its size and shape, location in the house, pieces of equipment, wall and floor materials, and color scheme.

9. Why have all-white kitchens fallen from favor? What are their good points?

10. If you had to choose between an automatic dishwasher and a television set, which would you choose? Why?

11. Plan a laundry-garden room in detail, including the appliances you would like, the planned storage, cleaning equipment, and space for growing and arranging flowers.

12. In the home of your dreams, how much time would *you* spend on maintaining the landscape?

Chapter 5.   DESIGN: AIMS AND PRINCIPLES

1. Look around the room you are in, select any object, and list the ways in which the form *does* and *does not* follow the object's functions.

2. List the ways and means of achieving unity in the Port Royal Parlor (Fig. 1-1). Are they sufficiently strong and clear to keep the variety in bounds?

3. Search through some magazines or books for the most chaotic room you can find. What factors are responsible?

4. List the examples of symmetrical, asymmetrical, and radial balance in the planning and furnishings of your own room. Was the most appropriate type of balance used in the whole room and each part?

5. Make some quick drawings of slow and fast, angular and curved, simple and complex rhythmic lines.

6. What kinds of rhythms would you like to emphasize in your home?

7. Is balance more important than rhythm? Why?

8. List in order of dominance and subordination all of the objects in

the room illustrated in Fig. 5-14. Why might there be some difference of opinion on the exact order?

9. Do you like strong centers of interest in objects or rooms which contrast emphatically with their surroundings? Justify your position.

10. Take careful measurements of a piece of furniture and then try to find the arithmetical basis for the proportions.

11. Select a natural object and analyze its design.

12. Why are designs done by rule and regulation seldom interesting?

Chapter 6. FORM, LINE, TEXTURE, AND SPACE

1. Cut out from pieces of colored paper at least ten different angular forms. List the expressive qualities of each one.

2. Draw as many kinds of curved lines and forms as you can and suggest appropriate uses for each one.

3. Choose any room illustrated in this book and list the forms that are primarily rectangular, angular but not rectangular, and curved.

4. Do you prefer straight or curved lines. Why?

5. How many rooms have you seen recently that were not rectangular? What were your reactions to them? Which pieces of furniture most frequently deviate from rectangularity?

6. If you could add some curved forms to your living quarters, how and where would you add them?

7. Cut from old magazines or catalogs five pictures of chairs, sofas, or chests of drawers that differ markedly in scale. Arrange these in order from large to small.

8. Collect scraps of all kinds of materials used in homes. Arrange them in a texture scale from smooth to rough or in a design that demonstrates variety in unity, balance, rhythm, and emphasis.

9. Put the same vase against backgrounds that are different in texture and pattern. Note carefully in what ways the effects vary.

10. Do you prefer ornamented or plain surfaces? For what reasons?

11. With cut paper or paint make two designs, one of which emphasizes two-dimensional flatness and the other three-dimensional form and space. What applications do these have to home design?

12. Cut from a magazine a photograph of the façade of a house you like and discuss it in terms of form, line, texture, and space.

Chapter 7.   LIGHT AND COLOR

1. Investigate the relationships between light and color by getting a large white box (or painting a carton white). Direct a spotlight or flashlight toward one side of the box; describe the color of the lighted and the unlighted sides. Place the box near a surface of any high-intensity color and notice the reflected color. Hang a piece of sheer curtain material of some pale color between the light source and the box and observe the effect.

2. Become acquainted with the effect of light on form with the white box mentioned above.

   Look at it in an evenly lighted room.

   Take it into a darkened room and with spotlights or flashlights light it only from the top; from a corner; from two sides; and from the top and two sides.

   In each case notice the shadows as well as the effect on the box.

3. Make a value and an intensity scale, similar to those in Fig. 7-1, with colored paper, scraps of textiles, paint, or chalk.

4. Make complementary, split-complementary, triad, and analogous color schemes, using blue in each. For what parts of the home are each of these appropriate?

5. Make three triad color schemes using the same hues, but vary the intensity and value as follows: full intensity and normal value; full intensity and high value; two-thirds neutral and dark value. For what situations would each be appropriate?

6. Look up the synonyms for the terms *hue, value,* and *intensity.*

7. List the *characteristics* of the color scheme you would like for your bedroom. Then describe three *specific color schemes* having these characteristics.

8. Select a painting and analyze the use of color.

9. Explore the effects of textures on color by covering with the same paint materials differing in texture such as smooth paper or wood, sandpaper, burlap, and corrugated cardboard.

10. Study the effects of light on color by placing six large (at least 2 feet square) samples of the same color on the floor, ceiling, and walls of a room. Describe the differences in hue, value, and intensity. What application does this have to interior design?

Chapter 11. WALLS AND FIREPLACES

1. Analyze the design and surface materials of the walls of two rooms in terms of use, economy, beauty, and individuality. How could they be improved?
2. Make a study of Oriental influences on American wall-covering designs and materials.
3. Design a wallpaper suitable for a child's bedroom.
4. Make measured drawings of the walls of your room. Then experiment with ways in which their proportions or character could be improved without structural alterations.
5. Collect samples of as many wall-surfacing materials as you can. Select the three you like best and the three you like least. Explain your preferences.
6. List all of the factors to be considered in hanging a painting over a fireplace.
7. Design an outdoor fireplace for a family who like to cook and eat outdoors.
8. Describe several situations in which it would be advisable to have the walls and fireplace more dominant than the furnishings.
9. What are the possible pitfalls in using more than one color or material on the walls of a room?
10. What kinds of walls make the best backgrounds for paintings?
11. Conduct experiments demonstrating the ways in which the apparent proportions and size of a wall can be changed by making five drawings of the same wall. Draw vertical lines on the first, horizontal on the second, diagonal on the third, large patterns on the fourth, and small patterns on the fifth.
12. Why has the kind of wall paneling that subdivides walls into sections fallen from favor?

Chapter 12. WINDOWS, CURTAINS, AND DOORS

1. Measure the area of opaque walls and windows in a room and compute the percentage of each. Is this proportion satisfactory?

2. Visit some new houses and tabulate the number of double-hung, horizontally sliding, in-opening casement, out-opening casement, and awning-type windows used in them. Do any of them have clerestories or skylights?

3. Look through some recent issues of home magazines and tabulate the types of windows advertised in them.

4. Describe the windows in the living room of the home you would like to build in terms of use, economy, beauty, and individuality.

5. Make a study of the most efficient methods of cleaning windows.

6. Look through the curtain and drapery departments of three local stores. Make notes on the characters, colors, and patterns of the fabrics they feature.

7. Investigate the kinds of curtain and drapery rods available today.

8. Write a report on the history of curtains and draperies.

9. What are the cardinal principles of door location?

10. Why do we pay more attention to the design and location of windows today than our grandparents did?

11. Which textile fibers would you select for curtains in a sunny play-room?

12. How would you evaluate the relative importance of fibers and weaves in the durability of draperies?

Chapter 13. FLOORS, FLOOR COVERINGS, AND CEILINGS

1. Describe the characteristics of the flooring material you would like in your kitchen. Choose the three of those available today that most closely approximate your ideals and comment on each.

2. Plan the color scheme of a room in which it is desirable to have the floor higher in value than is the ceiling.

3. List all of the reasons you can think of for the popularity of wall-to-wall carpeting.

4. Get some small samples of rug materials and study with a magnifying glass the way in which they are fabricated.

5. Write a report on Oriental, American Indian, or hooked rugs and their use in American homes.

6. Write for literature on the kinds of floor coverings with which you are least familiar.

7. Plan the floor coverings for a moderate cost, three-bedroom contemporary home. Comment on the ways in which your plan differs from the floor treatment in your parents' home.

8. Choose any statement in this chapter with which you are in disagreement and defend your case.

9. Do you feel that illusionary or simulated textures in floor coverings violate the non-imitation principle?

10. What are the ways in which floor treatments can make interior space seem greater?

11. Do you agree with the typical practice of having ceilings noncommittal and unobtrusive?

12. Why have floor coverings with patterns of foliage and flowers enjoyed so much popularity?

Chapter 14. FURNITURE SELECTION AND ARRANGEMENT

1. What are your favorite furniture woods? Why do you like them?

2. What are your reactions to carved ornament on furniture?

3. How well do you like the plastic upholstery on furniture in your local stores?

4. What three pieces of furniture do you consider to be the most important?

5. Check the comparative comfort of ten chairs. What are the characteristics of those that are most comfortable?

6. Design the kind of desk you would like.

7. Analyze the unit furniture illustrated in Fig. 4-9 in terms of the aims and principles of design.

8. Compare the tables in Figs. 5-2 and 14-7 on the basis of our four objectives of home planning and furnishing.

9. Study the construction of a table, chair, and chest of drawers in your room. What kinds of joints are used? What are the materials and how are they finished?

10. Make a study of the use of plywood and laminated wood in contemporary furniture.

11. Plan the furniture arrangement for a living room that would be suitable for both large and small groups.

12. Furniture arrangement is usually regarded as a problem of fitting furniture into existing rooms. Reverse this procedure by beginning to plan your ideal bedroom with the furniture arrangement and then placing the walls, windows, and doors where they function best.

Chapter 15.   LIGHTING, HEATING, VENTILATION, AND ACOUSTICS

1. How many kinds of lighting fixtures are used in your living quarters? Which are the most and least effective?

2. What are your reactions to lighting fixtures based on designs for candles or oil lamps? To lamp bases with containers for plants?

3. How could the ventilation of your bedroom be improved?

4. How is the building in which you live heated? What are the ways in which it is insulated against heat and cold? Is it well planned in terms of the climate?

5. Write a report on lighting fixtures used in 18th-century American homes.

6. List all the reasons you can think of for using candles today. Where and when are they most effective?

7. Design a table lamp with a wood base.

8. Plan the lighting for a kitchen and for a living room.

9. Compare the effects of daylight, incandescent, and fluorescent light on textiles of different colors and textures.

10. List all the factors one should consider in planning and furnishing a home that takes full advantage of the sun's heat.

11. Collect photographs of lighting fixtures designed for general and local illumination and for play of brilliants.

12. Should the lighting fixtures used at night bring light from the same directions as from the windows during the day?

Chapter 16. SETTING THE TABLE

1. List all of the ways in which a table set for a football supper might appropriately differ from one set for an Easter breakfast.
2. How have contemporary socio-economic conditions affected table settings?
3. What color and pattern of dinnerware would be most appropriate for your home? What factors did you consider in making this decision?
4. Plan the color scheme and decorations for a child's birthday table.
5. What role should the foods served play in the colors chosen for a table setting?
6. Count the number of patterns of glassware available in one of your local home furnishing stores. Which do you prefer? Why?
7. Find out what patterns in true porcelain dinnerware are available in your stores. How does the design of porcelain dinnerware differ from that of stoneware?
8. Do you agree that formal, old dinnerware such as Haviland can be used in informal, modern homes? What would be the effect?
9. Investigate the price range of table linens in your stores.
10. What color do you think is least appropriate for the dominant note in a table setting? Why?
11. Survey the variety stores to see how many low-cost objects you can find that are appropriate for table decorations.
12. Make a study of historic French dinnerware.

Chapter 17. ENRICHMENT

1. It is often said that well-designed furniture and accessories from any period can be used together. Do you agree with this statement?
2. What are your ideas on selecting paintings for a home?
3. Can you defend the point of view that everything in the home should have a utilitarian purpose?
4. What are the advantages and disadvantages of permanently placed and movable enrichment?

5. Make a list of the non-utilitarian accessories in your home. Are they worth-while additions?

6. Collect some accessories suitable for a mantel or the top of a bookcase and experiment with the different ways in which they can be arranged.

7. Visit three gift or accessory shops and report on the kinds of objects available there.

8. Write a report on one of your favorite painters or sculptors. How could his originals or reproductions of them be used in homes?

9. Make three floral arrangements, each of which expresses one of the following ideas: gaiety, sobriety, humor, surprise, austerity, opulence.

10. Get acquainted with house plants by visiting florists, greenhouses, and variety stores. Learn the names and characteristics of ten varieties.

11. How would you enrich the walls of a room in which Oriental rugs were featured?

12. Make a mobile from some inexpensive holiday decorations available in ten-cent stores.

Chapter 18. PLAN

1. Would you place all of the bedrooms in a moderate-sized house together or separate them? What are your reasons?

2. Look through books or magazines for a house plan that you think is excellent. Make a tracing of it and list your reasons for selecting it.

3. Find a house plan that you think has notable shortcomings and draw an improved version.

4. List the differences between the house plans illustrated in Figs. 18-1 and 18-7.

5. Visit some older homes in your community and analyze their plans.

6. Which is more important—the plan of a house or its location in the community?

7. What factors would influence your putting the kitchen near the center of a home or locating it in a less central position?

8. How large would you like to have your living room? What shape?

9. Design a house for easy housekeeping.

10. What are the advantages and disadvantages of hillside locations? How do they affect house planning?
11. List all of the plan devices for making the space in small homes seem greater.
12. Will the two-story house come back into favor? Defend your answer.

Chapter 19. EXTERIOR DESIGN

1. Under what circumstances might one regard the exterior design of a house as more important than the plan?
2. Why do some persons dislike contemporary exterior design even though they like contemporary plans or furniture?
3. Comment on a house described as "having 18th-century charm and 20th-century convenience."
4. Why is white a favored color for house exteriors?
5. What are the typical objections to flat roofs? Are they justified?
6. Why are roofs usually darker in color than are the exterior walls?
7. What effects do large areas of glass have on exterior design?
8. What are your major criticisms of the exterior design of the building in which you now live? Why was it designed this way?
9. Analyze the exterior design of the oldest house in your community. What factors led to its design? How does it differ from newer houses?
10. List the exterior surfacing materials used in the houses in one block of your community. Which are most popular? Why?
11. What exterior materials require the least maintenance? Which have the highest original cost?
12. Draw some pictures of the kind of house that would make you happy.

Chapter 20. LANDSCAPE

1. What trees and shrubs native to your region might be used in home landscapes? What are their desirable features?
2. List the names of ten non-native shrubs and ten non-native trees that are dependable in your section of the country. How could each be used effectively in the landscape?

3. Which trees and shrubs in your locality have the showiest flowers? What is their appearance when they are not in bloom?

4. Investigate the kinds of garden fences and walls in your neighborhood. Which seem most appropriate to their environment?

5. Why do curved shapes seem especially appropriate in landscape design? What are the functions of straight lines in gardens?

6. Design a piece of outdoor furniture that could be made in a home workshop.

7. Find a photograph of the front of a house and plan the foundation planting. Sketch several different ideas on tracing paper laid over the photograph.

8. Plan a terrace or outdoor-living room that will give maximum livability in your area. What devices would you use to temper the weather?

9. Make a study of the gardens of the Italian Renaissance. What are their similarities and dissimilarities to contemporary designs?

10. What is the best home landscape you have ever seen? What makes it good?

11. In what ways do trees provide better overhead protection than do roofs? What are their limitations?

12. Make a model of a backyard garden for a home in your community.

Chapter 21. COSTS AND BUDGETS

1. What are the selling prices of new three-bedroom houses in your community? What factors account for the differences?

2. What are the rents on new three-bedroom houses? What percentages of the probable total costs are the yearly rentals?

3. What are the least and most expensive dining tables and chairs in your local stores? What factors account for the differences?

4. Would you rather own or rent your living quarters? How many of your friends agree with your choice? What are their reasons?

5. List the heirlooms or hand-me-downs you now have or expect to have in your home. Compute the probable savings and plan how they can be used to best advantage—if silverware, describe the other tableware that would enhance its beauty; if a broken-down sofa, describe the repairs and upholstering or slipcovers needed to make it usable.

6. Plan the complete furnishings for a living room and compute the total cost on the basis of prices in your community.

7. Notice the advertisements for home-furnishing sales in newspapers. By how many dollars and what percentages do the regular and sales prices differ?

8. Plan the "company" dinnerware you would like to have. Compute its cost. Does it seem like a justifiable expenditure?

9. How many of the furnishings in your living quarters were not worth their cost? Why were they selected?

10. On what single piece of home furnishings would you be willing to spend the largest sum of money? Is this in accord with your friends' ideas?

11. On what items in your home furnishings would you be most willing to economize? How do you account for your answer?

12. List the characteristics of the furniture that you believe would give you the longest satisfaction. Investigate the price range for this kind of furniture.

SUGGESTED REFERENCES

General

Art Today: Faulkner, Ziegfeld, and Hill. (Holt, 1949.)
An introduction to the fine and applied arts.
Elements of Interior Design and Decoration: Sherrill Whiton. (Lippincott, 1951.)
Thorough, detailed discussion from professional decorator's point of view; careful treatment of history.
Encyclopaedia Britannica.
Articles on architecture, ceramics, glass, interior decoration, landscape, metal, weaving, wood, etc.
Encyclopedia of Furniture: Joseph Aronson. (Crown Publishers, 1938.)
A necessity for anyone interested in historic furniture; fully illustrated.
Guide to Easier Living: Mary and Russel Wright. (Simon and Schuster, 1951.)
Briskly written and illustrated account of how to furnish and manage your home efficiently.
Managing Your Money: J. K. Lasser and Sylvia Porter. (Holt, 1953.)
Sensible, understandable discussion of the important factors in money management.

History

American Interior Design: Meyric R. Rogers. (Norton, 1947.)
The most comprehensive book on our historic interiors and their furnishings.

Architecture Through the Ages: Talbot Hamlin. (Putnam, 1940.)
Remarkably readable treatment of the development of architecture in relation to social conditions.

Art and Life in America: Oliver W. Larkin. (Rinehart, 1949.)
By far the best single book on American art with considerable discussion of homes.

History of Architecture: Banister Fletcher. (Scribner, 1921.)
The standard history of architecture, full of photographs, sketches, and facts.

Homes of America: Ernest Pickering. (Crowell, 1951.)
Readable, well illustrated account of the development of our houses.

Story of Architecture in America: Richard Tallmadge. (Norton, 1936.)
A clear description of the development of architecture in America.

What Is Modern Architecture?: Margaret Miller. (Museum of Modern Art, 1942.)
Brief and excellent statement of the various considerations that have shaped modern architecture, illustrated with well chosen examples.

House Planning

The American House Today: Katherine Ford and Thomas Creighton. (Reinhold, 1951.)
Well illustrated survey of contemporary homes.

Building or Buying a House: B. K. Johnstone and Associates. (Whittlesey House, 1945.)
A realistic guide to wise investment in houses.

82 Distinctive Houses. (Dodge, 1953.)
Photographs, plans, and discussions of a wide range of houses.

Homes: T. H. Creighton, et al. (Reinhold, 1947.)
Good photographs and plans.

Homes for Western Living. (Lane, 1952.)
Although oriented toward the West Coast, this book offers suggestions for homes in many other parts of the country.

The House and You: Catharine and Harold Sleeper. (Wiley, 1948.)
Sensible, factual book on home planning.

How to Plan Your Fireplace. (Lane, 1952.)
Offers many out-of-the-ordinary ideas.

In the Nature of Materials: Henry-Russell Hitchcock. (Duell, Sloan and Pearce, 1942.)

A comprehensive, well illustrated discussion of Frank Lloyd Wright's architecture.

Living Spaces: George Nelson. (Whitney, 1952.)

Handsomely illustrated book of contemporary group living spaces.

Plan Your Home to Suit Yourself: Tyler Stewart Rogers. (Scribner, 1950.)

Probably the most useful book on the specifics of house planning.

Practical Houses for Contemporary Living: Jean and Don Graf. (Dodge, 1953.)

Illustrated case-histories of forty houses that meet their owners' needs.

So You Want to Build a House: Elizabeth Mock. (Museum of Modern Art, 1946.)

Intelligent and entertaining discussion of factors to consider in planning contemporary homes.

Tomorrow's House: George Nelson and Henry Wright. (Simon and Schuster, 1945.)

An exciting presentation of present and future possibilities in house design.

Western Ranch Houses. (Lane, 1946.)

Historic and contemporary ranch houses illustrated and described.

Landscape

How to Build Fences and Gates. (Lane, 1952.)

Practical and inspiring.

How to Build Outdoor Fireplaces. (Lane, 1952.)

Good guide for the ambitious home craftsman.

How to Build Outdoor Furniture. (Lane, 1952.)

New and old designs and specific instructions for making your own garden furniture.

Landscape for Living: Garrett Eckbo. (Duell, Sloan, and Pearce, 1950.)

Exceptionally penetrating study of landscape design.

Landscaping Your Home. (Lane, 1950.)

Remarkably helpful to the person planning his own landscape.

Patio Book. (Lane, 1952.)

Both design and construction are treated in this excellent discussion of patios.

Walls, Walks, Patio Floors. (Lane, 1952.)

Detailed presentation of these major items in the landscape.

Furniture

Chairs: George Nelson. (Whitney, 1953.)

Beautiful photographs of and discerning comments on contemporary chairs.

Furniture from Machines: Gordon Logie.   (Allen & Unwin, 1947.)
Survey of the technology of industrially produced furniture.

How to Build Modern Furniture, 2 vols.: Mario Dal Fabbro.   (Dodge, 1951.)
Of considerable interest to the home craftsman.

Ideas for Bookcases and Bookshelves.   (Lane, 1952.)
Useful and stimulating illustrated discussion of this kind of furniture.

Modern Furnishings for the Home: William J. Hennessey.   (Reinhold, 1952.)
Brings together photographs showing the range of contemporary home furnishings.

Fabrics

America's Fabrics: Zelma Bendure and Gladys Pfeiffer.   (Macmillan, 1947.)
Thorough, authoritative presentation of fabrics, fibers, and processes.

Know Your Fabrics: Lucy D. Taylor.   (Wiley, 1951.)
A discussion of historic and contemporary textiles in relation to home furnishing.

Textile Fabrics and Their Selection: Isabel Wingate.   (Prentice-Hall, 1935.)
A consideration of textiles from the customer's viewpoint.

Lighting

Lighting and Lamp Design: Warren E. Cox.   (Crown Publishers, 1952.)
Non-technical consideration of effective home lighting.

Residential Lighting: Myrtle Fahsbender.   (Van Nostrand, 1947.)
A book for those who wish to study at least a little of the technology of lighting the home.

Color and Design

A Dictionary of Color: A. Maerz and M. Rea Paul.   (McGraw-Hill, 1950.)
Authoritative and comprehensive; samples of 8,064 different colors with accepted names.

Anatomy for Interior Designers: Francis de N. Schroeder.   (Whitney, 1951.)
Refreshingly written and illustrated book on relations of human size and shape to space and equipment.

Art and Industry: Herbert Read.   (Harcourt, Brace, 1935.)
Exceedingly penetrating book on design and materials in useful objects.

Art of Color and Design: Maitland Graves.   (McGraw-Hill, 1951.)
General introduction to design.

Composition: A. W. Dow.   (Doubleday, Doran, 1928.)
For a long time the standard book on the subject and still worth reading.

Design: Sybil Emerson.   (International Textbook Company, 1953.)
  Stimulating presentation of new approaches to design.
Language of Vision: Gyorgy Kepes.   (Theobald, 1944.)
  A stimulating account of visual elements and their psychological effect.
Story of Color: Faber Birren.   (Crimson Press, 1941.)
  Concerns color in relation to the history of man.
Vision in Motion: S. Moholy-Nagy.   (Theobald, 1947.)
  The best statement of the philosophy and science growing out of the
  Bauhaus Institute.

Periodicals

American Fabrics	*House and Home*
American Home	*House Beautiful*
Architectural Digest	*Interiors*
Architectural Record	*Interior Design*
Arts and Architecture	*Living for Young Homemakers*
Better Homes and Gardens	*Progressive Architecture*
Domus	*Sunset*
House and Garden	

Index

INDEX

Italicized page numbers refer to illustrations.

1920